You're going to succeed with your plans.

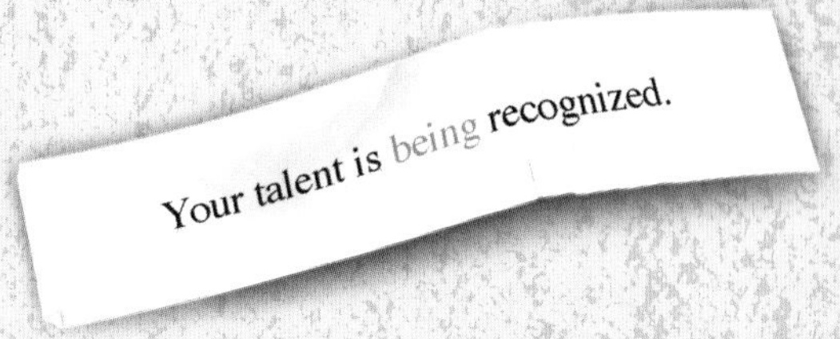
Your talent is being recognized.

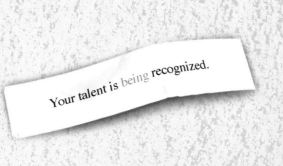

A fool is watched by a wise man.

MIND MGMT

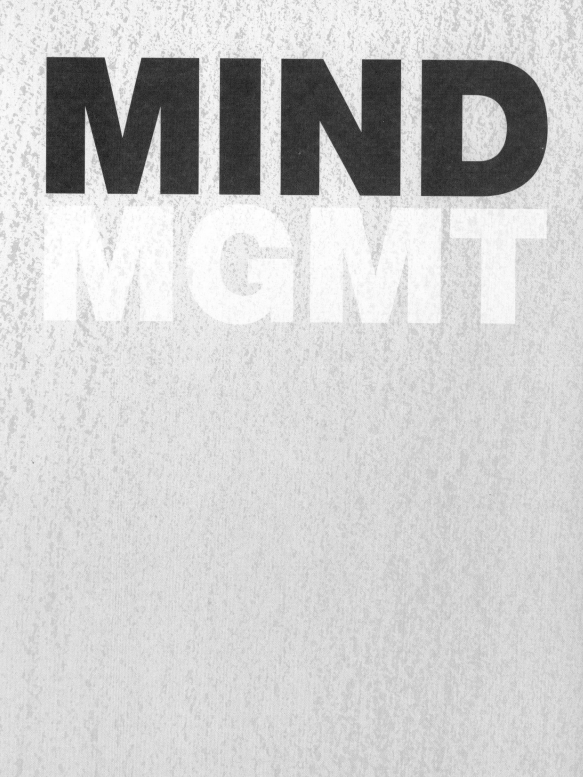

MIND MGMT

VOLUME TWO: THE FUTURIST

CREATED, WRITTEN,
AND ILLUSTRATED BY

MATT KINDT

FOREWORD BY
SCOTT SNYDER

DARK HORSE BOOKS

PRESIDENT AND PUBLISHER
MIKE RICHARDSON

DIGITAL PRODUCTION
CLAY JANES

DESIGN
ADAM GRANO
with MATT KINDT

ASSISTANT EDITOR
IAN TUCKER

EDITOR
BRENDAN WRIGHT

Special thanks to Sharlene and Ella Kindt.

MIND MGMT VOLUME 2: THE FUTURIST

This volume collects issues #7–#12 of the Dark Horse comic-book series *MIND MGMT*, along with a story from *Dark Horse Presents* #19 and comic strips from io9.com.

Published by Dark Horse Books
A division of Dark Horse Comics, Inc.
10956 SE Main Street
Milwaukie, OR 97222

DarkHorse.com

To find a comics shop in your area, call the Comic Shop Locator Service toll-free at (888) 266-4226.
International Licensing: (503) 905-2377

First edition: October 2013

Library of Congress Cataloging-in-Publication Data

Kindt, Matt.
  Mind MGMT. Volume two, The futurist / created, written, and illustrated by Matt Kindt ; foreword by
                Scott Snyder. -- First edition.
      pages cm
   ISBN 978-1-61655-198-8
 1. Women journalists—Comic books, strips, etc. 2. Spy stories. 3. Graphic novels. I. Snyder, Scott.
                 II. Title. III. Title: Futurist.
   PN6727.K54M57 2013
   741.5'973—dc23
                                2013016181

10 9 8 7 6 5 4 3 2 1
Printed in China

Neil Hankerson, Executive Vice President | Tom Weddle, Chief Financial Officer | Randy Stradley, Vice President of Publishing | Michael Martens, Vice President of Book Trade Sales | Anita Nelson, Vice President of Business Affairs | Scott Allie, Editor in Chief | Matt Parkinson, Vice President of Marketing | David Scroggy, Vice President of Product Development | Dale LaFountain, Vice President of Information Technology | Darlene Vogel, Senior Director of Print, Design, and Production | Ken Lizzi, General Counsel | Davey Estrada, Editorial Director | Chris Warner, Senior Books Editor | Diana Schutz, Executive Editor | Cary Grazzini, Director of Print and Development | Lia Ribacchi, Art Director | Cara Niece, Director of Scheduling | Tim Wiesch, Director of International Licensing | Mark Bernardi, Director of Digital Publishing

FOREWORD

After reading *MIND MGMT*, I'm just going to come right out and say it: Matt Kindt scares me. Yes, we're colleagues. Yes, we're friends, but that's the plain truth of it. He terrifies me.

This is true for a number of reasons. First, he scares me with the sheer amount of talent displayed in this second volume of *MIND MGMT*. Now, as a fan of Matt's work, I'd been looking forward to the release of *MIND MGMT* for a while. *Revolver* was a mind-bending postapocalyptic adventure story. *Super Spy* was a wonderfully paranoid thriller, and I loved both.

And with *MIND MGMT*, Matt has crafted a work that's both mind bending and paranoid, but also epic and open ended in scope.

The world of *MIND MGMT* is filled with conspiracy and mystery—a place where immortal assassins are hot on your trail, and where psychic dolphins leave desperate clues for you to follow. But it's also a world populated by rich, layered characters—Meru, a crime writer struggling to understand her own past, and at the center of the story, Henry Lyme, the greatest agent Mind Management ever trained, a man tortured by his past, bent on bringing the agency down once and for all. And all of this, the whole darkly vibrant world of *MIND MGMT*, is brought to life by Matt's distinctive watercolors—watercolors that manage to be unsettling and lush all at once, the perfect blend for a thriller like this.

And while the first volume introduced us to the world of *MIND MGMT*, this volume delves even deeper into the secrets behind all our favorite characters, from the Archivist to Duncan to Henry Lyme himself. Questions are undoubtedly answered, even as the mystery deepens.

But when I say Matt scares me, I also mean something else. Because my favorite books are the ones that scare me. Not by way of cheap thrills (though those are always fun), but by tapping into and exploring my own deep, deep fears—some personal, some cultural. What if you're not who you think you are? Can your memory be trusted? What if they're really after you? What if what you know about yourself, about your life, was never real?

These are the sorts of questions *MIND MGMT* explores—and yet explores in the most fun, thrilling way possible. Put simply, *MIND MGMT* is a terrific read—a ferociously smart and brilliantly inventive page turner of a mystery. I loved every chapter, and what Matt Kindt has me most scared of now is the wait for every next issue.

Scott Snyder
April 2013

Scott Snyder is an award-winning writer of prose and comics, including the short story collection Voodoo Heart *and the Vertigo Comics series* American Vampire, *cowritten with Stephen King. Snyder is currently among the most prominent creative forces of DC Comics' New 52 initiative, for which he has written* Batman, Swamp Thing, *and* Superman Unchained.

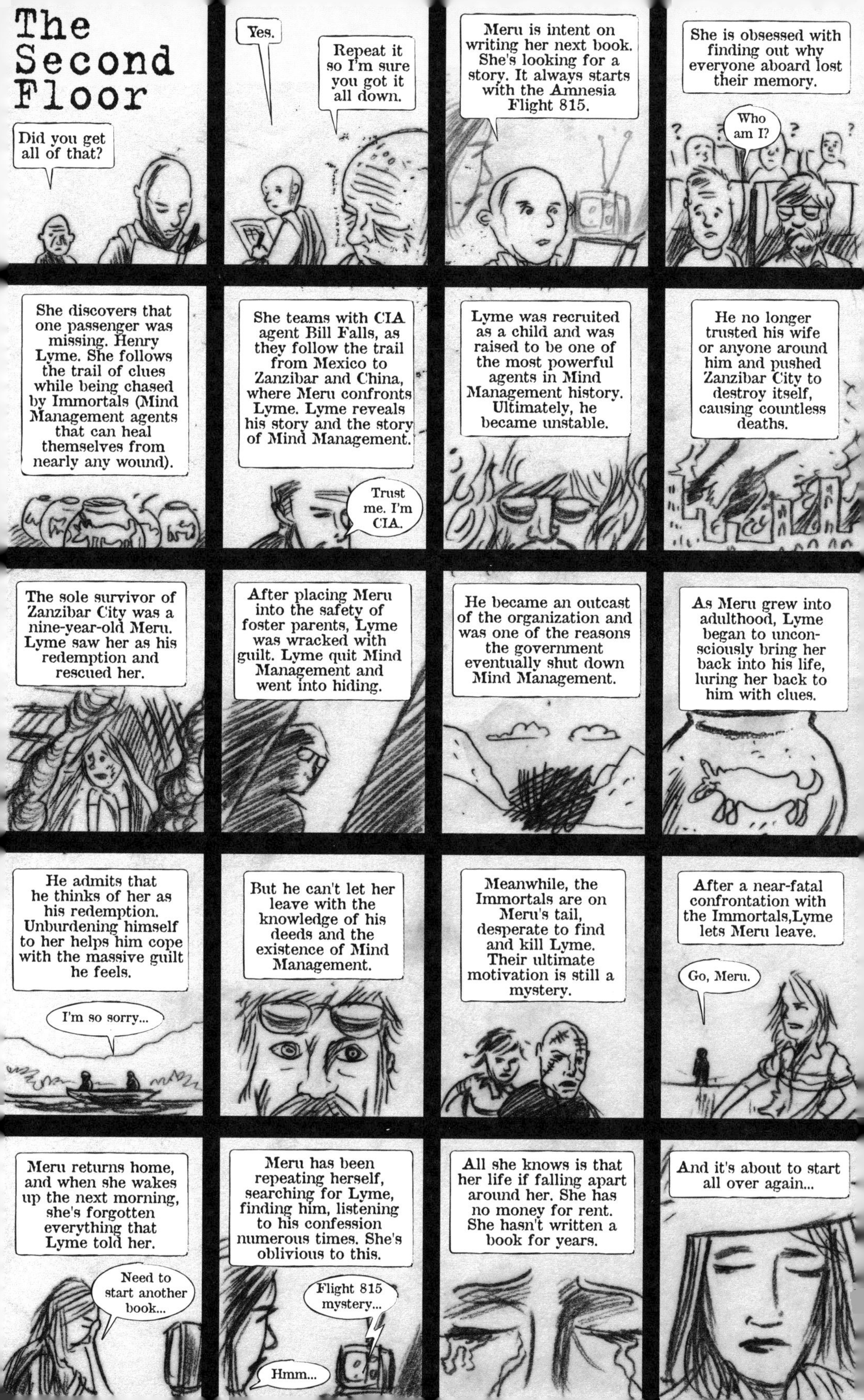
The Second Floor
Did you get all of that?
Yes.
Repeat it so I'm sure you got it all down.
Meru is intent on writing her next book. She's looking for a story. It always starts with the Amnesia Flight 815.
She is obsessed with finding out why everyone aboard lost their memory.
Who am I?
She discovers that one passenger was missing. Henry Lyme. She follows the trail of clues while being chased by Immortals (Mind Management agents that can heal themselves from nearly any wound).
She teams with CIA agent Bill Falls, as they follow the trail from Mexico to Zanzibar and China, where Meru confronts Lyme. Lyme reveals his story and the story of Mind Management.
Trust me. I'm CIA.
Lyme was recruited as a child and was raised to be one of the most powerful agents in Mind Management history. Ultimately, he became unstable.
He no longer trusted his wife or anyone around him and pushed Zanzibar City to destroy itself, causing countless deaths.
The sole survivor of Zanzibar City was a nine-year-old Meru. Lyme saw her as his redemption and rescued her.
After placing Meru into the safety of foster parents, Lyme was wracked with guilt. Lyme quit Mind Management and went into hiding.
He became an outcast of the organization and was one of the reasons the government eventually shut down Mind Management.
As Meru grew into adulthood, Lyme began to unconsciously bring her back into his life, luring her back to him with clues.
He admits that he thinks of her as his redemption. Unburdening himself to her helps him cope with the massive guilt he feels.
I'm so sorry...
But he can't let her leave with the knowledge of his deeds and the existence of Mind Management.
Meanwhile, the Immortals are on Meru's tail, desperate to find and kill Lyme. Their ultimate motivation is still a mystery.
After a near-fatal confrontation with the Immortals,Lyme lets Meru leave.
Go, Meru.
Meru returns home, and when she wakes up the next morning, she's forgotten everything that Lyme told her.
Need to start another book...
Meru has been repeating herself, searching for Lyme, finding him, listening to his confession numerous times. She's oblivious to this.
Flight 815 mystery...
Hmm...
All she knows is that her life if falling apart around her. She has no money for rent. She hasn't written a book for years.
And it's about to start all over again...

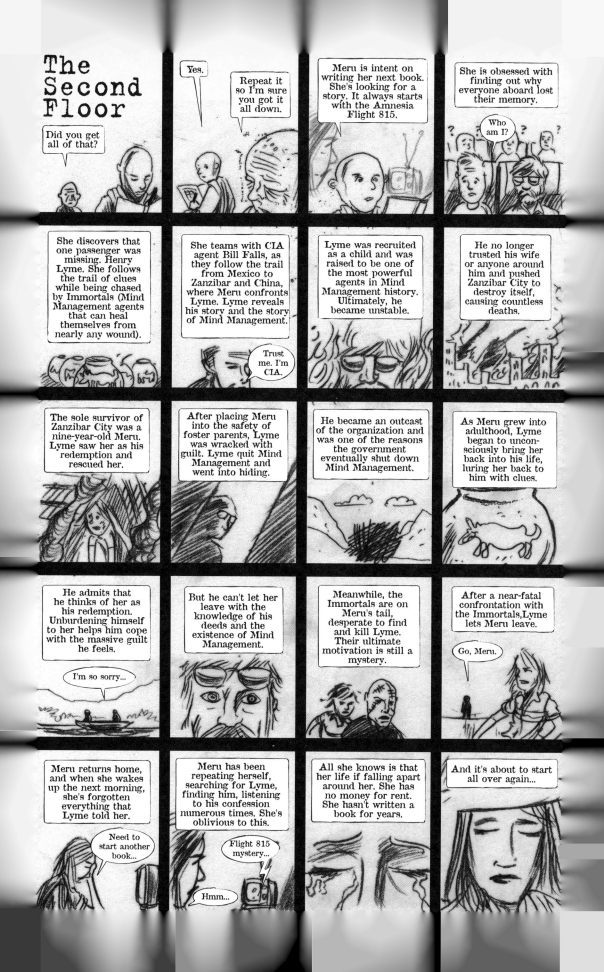

PROLOGUE

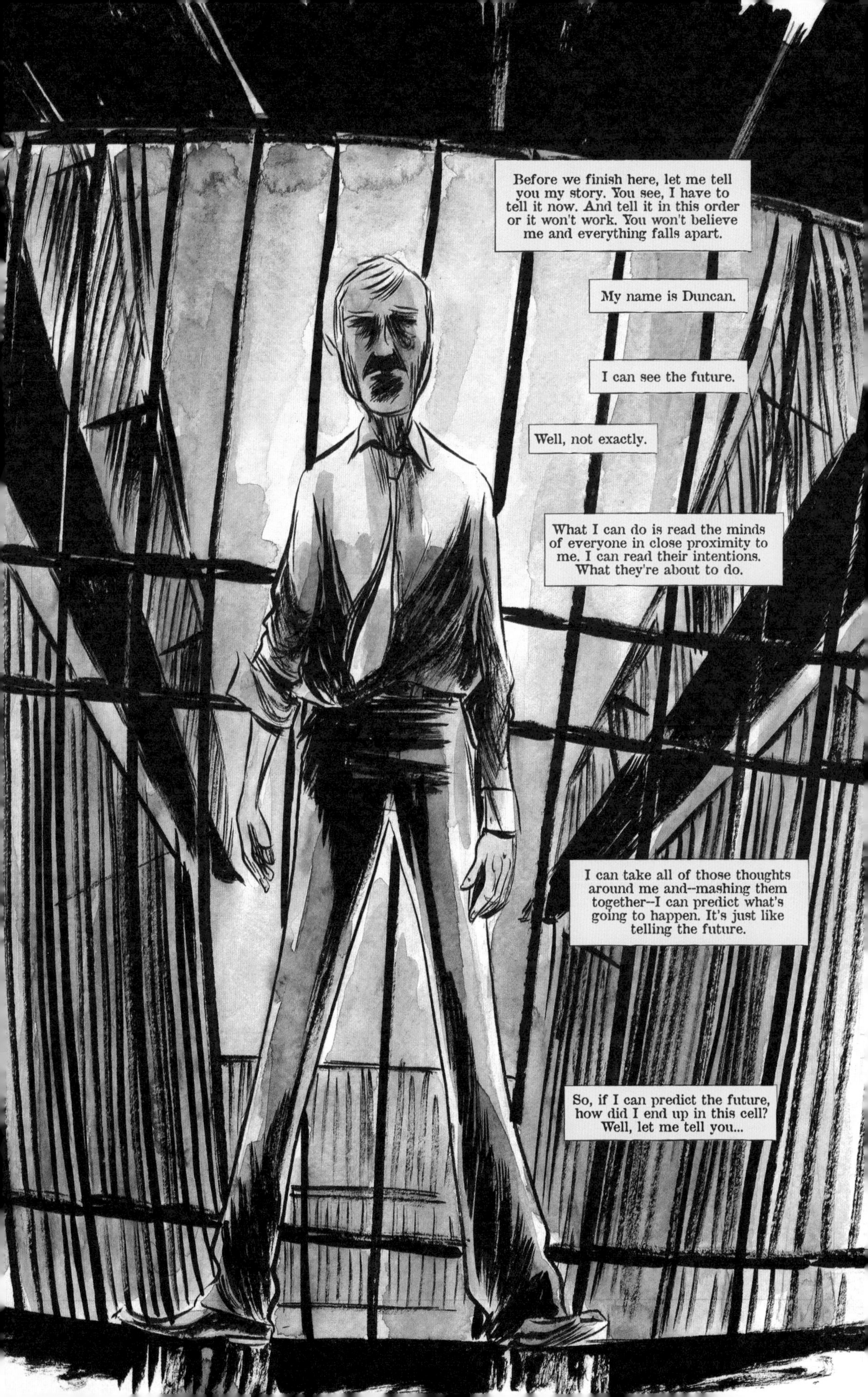
Before we finish here, let me tell you my story. You see, I have to tell it now. And tell it in this order or it won't work. You won't believe me and everything falls apart.
My name is Duncan.
I can see the future.
Well, not exactly.
What I can do is read the minds of everyone in close proximity to me. I can read their intentions. What they're about to do.
I can take all of those thoughts around me and--mashing them together--I can predict what's going to happen. It's just like telling the future.
So, if I can predict the future, how did I end up in this cell? Well, let me tell you...

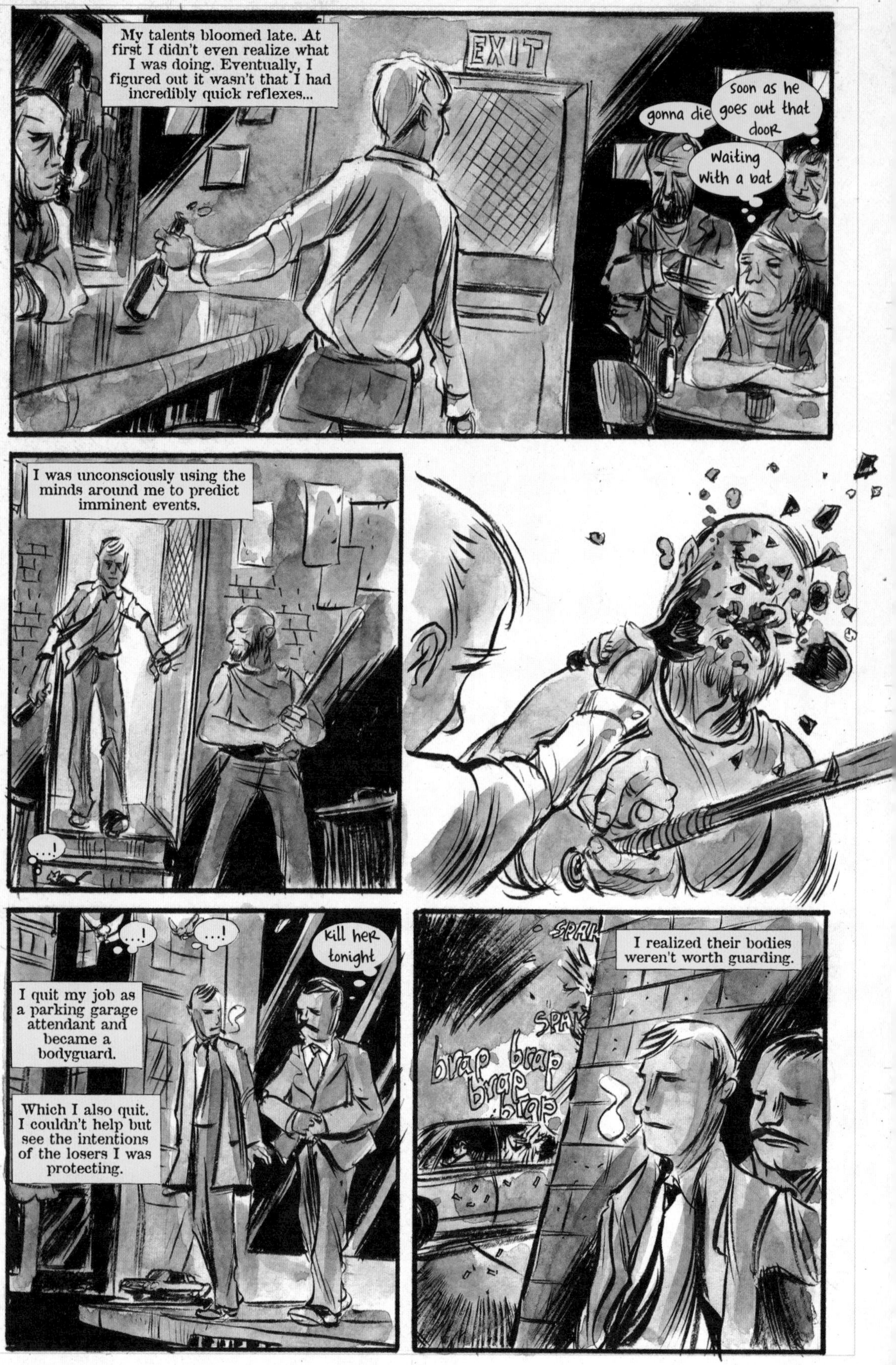
My talents bloomed late. At first I didn't even realize what I was doing. Eventually, I figured out it wasn't that I had incredibly quick reflexes...
EXIT
gonna die
Soon as he goes out that door
Waiting with a bat
I was unconsciously using the minds around me to predict imminent events.
...!
...!
...!
Kill her tonight
I quit my job as a parking garage attendant and became a bodyguard.
Which I also quit. I couldn't help but see the intentions of the losers I was protecting.
SPAK
SPAK
brap brap brap brap
I realized their bodies weren't worth guarding.

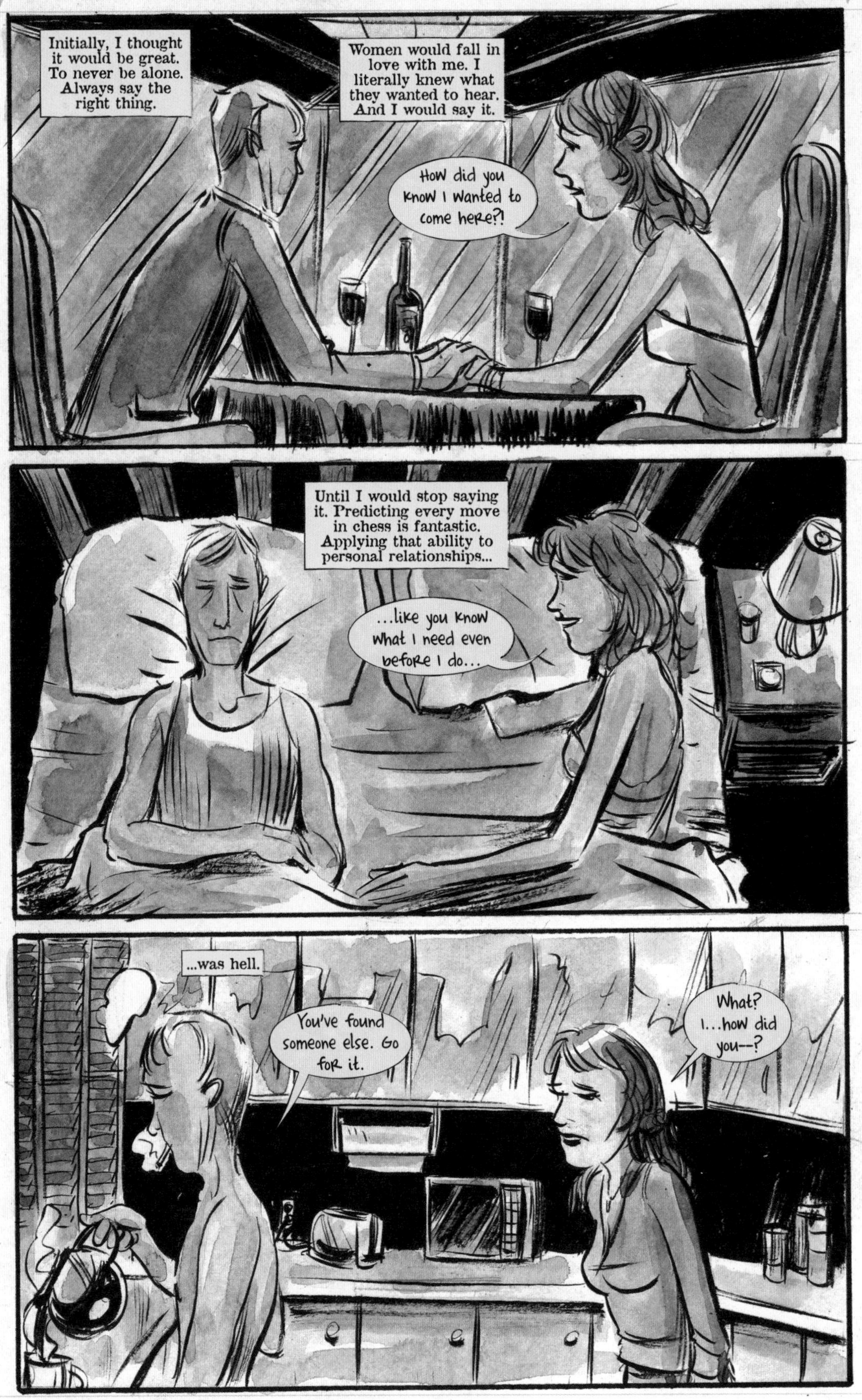
Initially, I thought it would be great. To never be alone. Always say the right thing.
Women would fall in love with me. I literally knew what they wanted to hear. And I would say it.
How did you know I wanted to come here?!
Until I would stop saying it. Predicting every move in chess is fantastic. Applying that ability to personal relationships...
...like you know what I need even before I do...
...was hell.
You've found someone else. Go for it.
What? I...how did you--?

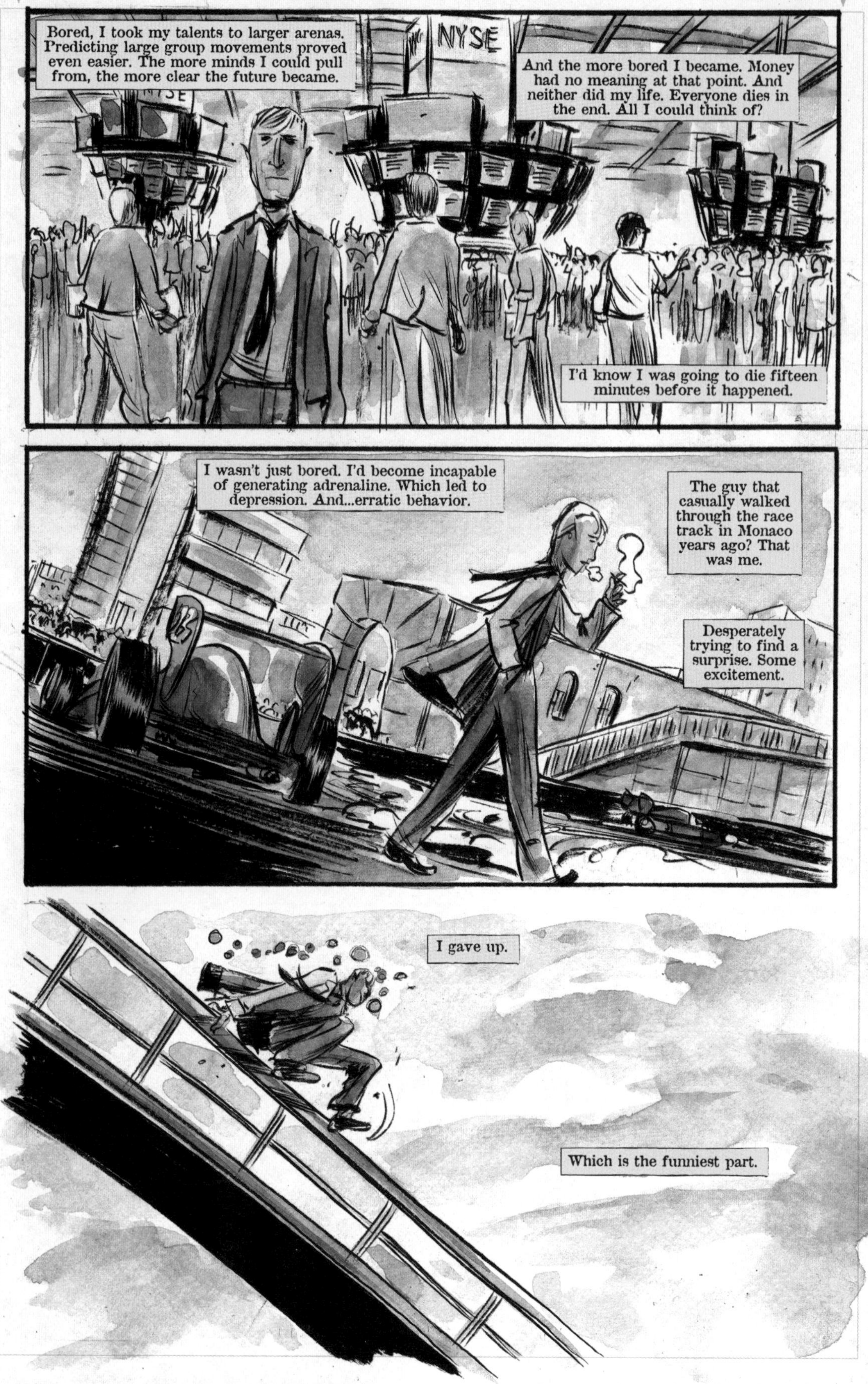
Bored, I took my talents to larger arenas. Predicting large group movements proved even easier. The more minds I could pull from, the more clear the future became.
NYSE
And the more bored I became. Money had no meaning at that point. And neither did my life. Everyone dies in the end. All I could think of?
I'd know I was going to die fifteen minutes before it happened.
I wasn't just bored. I'd become incapable of generating adrenaline. Which led to depression. And...erratic behavior.
The guy that casually walked through the race track in Monaco years ago? That was me.
Desperately trying to find a surprise. Some excitement.
I gave up.
Which is the funniest part.

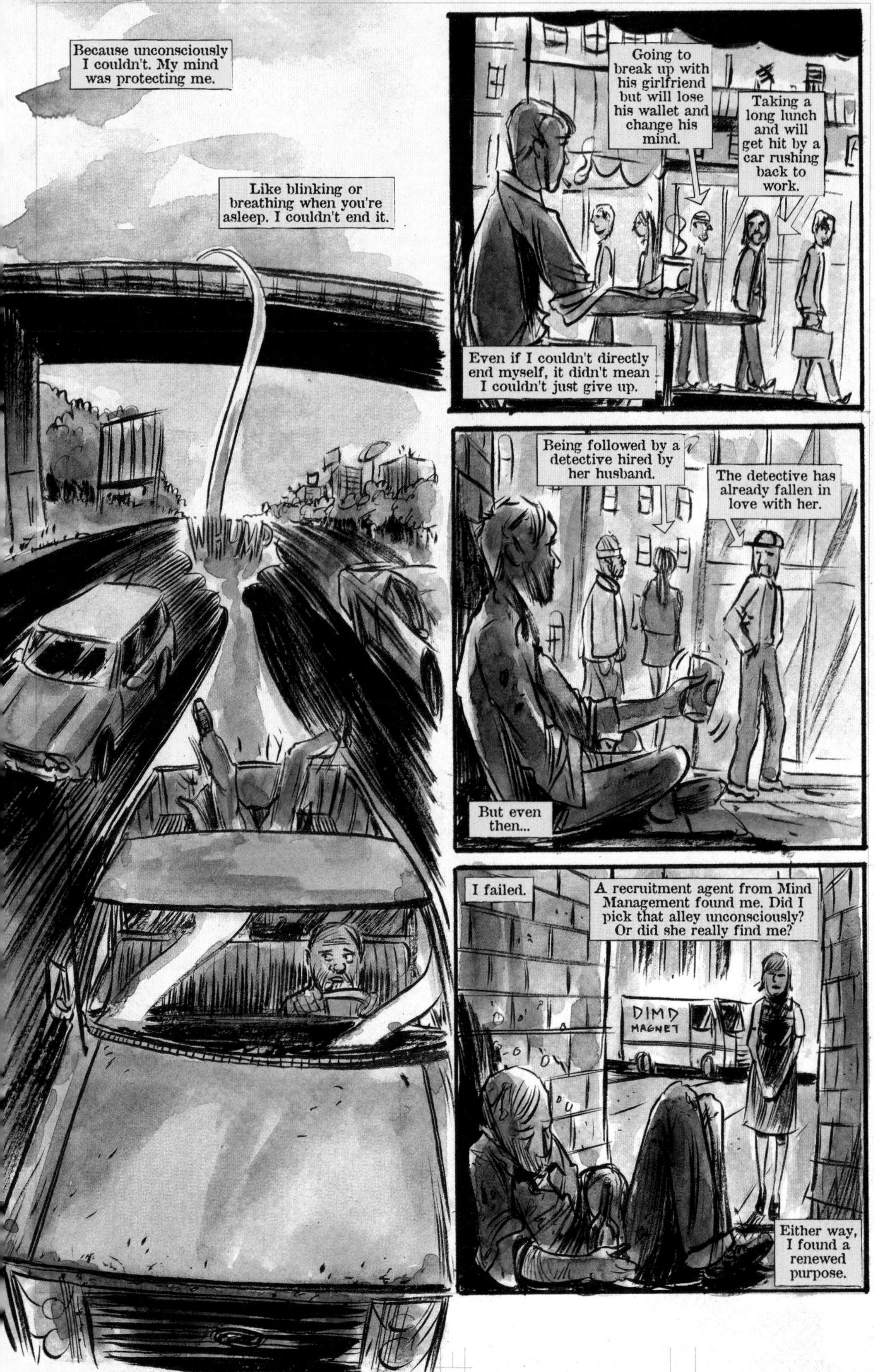
Because unconsciously I couldn't. My mind was protecting me.
Like blinking or breathing when you're asleep. I couldn't end it.
WHUMP
Going to break up with his girlfriend but will lose his wallet and change his mind.
Taking a long lunch and will get hit by a car rushing back to work.
Even if I couldn't directly end myself, it didn't mean I couldn't just give up.
Being followed by a detective hired by her husband.
The detective has already fallen in love with her.
But even then...
I failed.
A recruitment agent from Mind Management found me. Did I pick that alley unconsciously? Or did she really find me?
DIMD MAGNET
Either way, I found a renewed purpose.

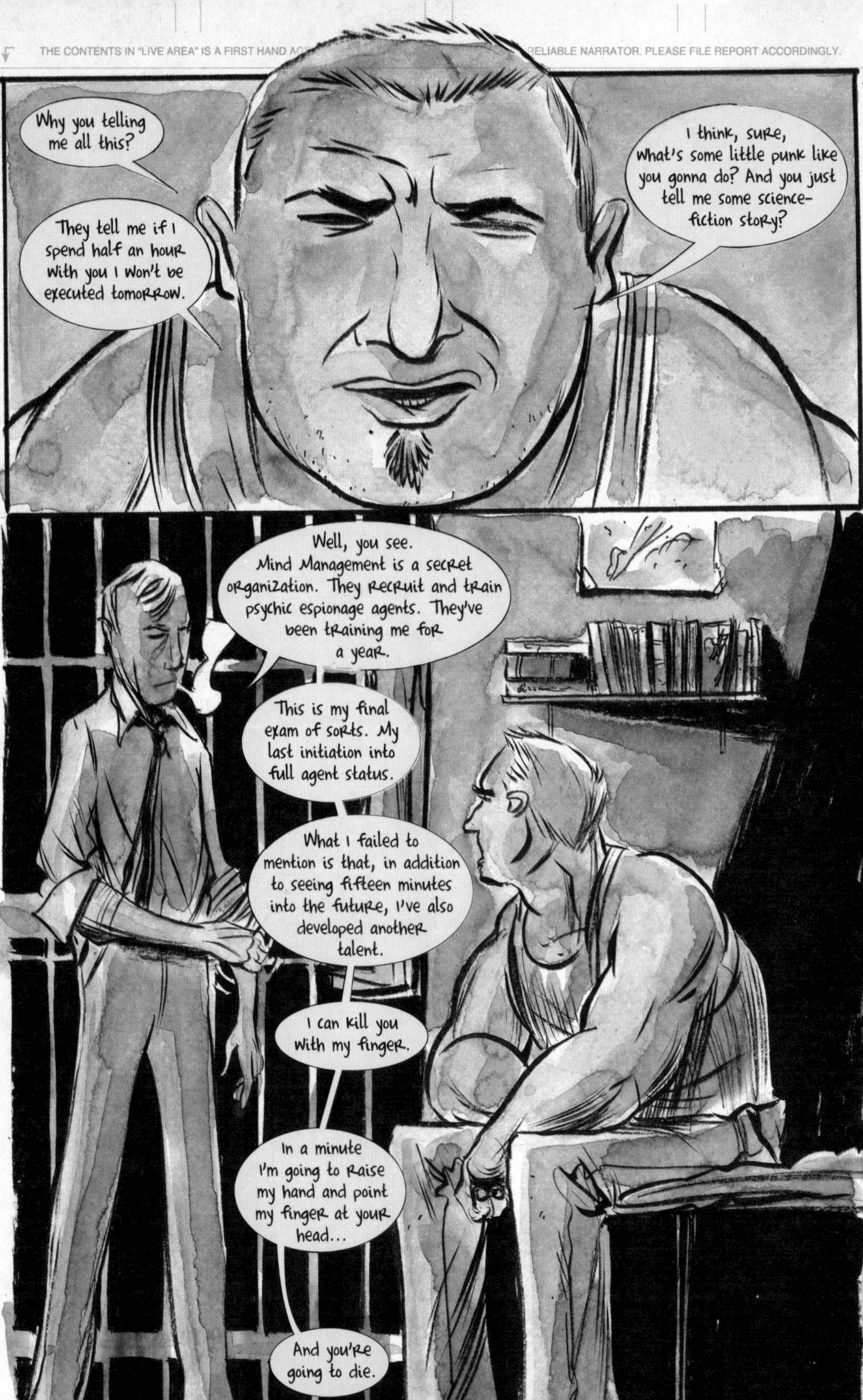
Why you telling me all this?
They tell me if I spend half an hour with you I won't be executed tomorrow.
I think, sure, what's some little punk like you gonna do? And you just tell me some science-fiction story?
Well, you see. Mind Management is a secret organization. They recruit and train psychic espionage agents. They've been training me for a year.
This is my final exam of sorts. My last initiation into full agent status.
What I failed to mention is that, in addition to seeing fifteen minutes into the future, I've also developed another talent.
I can kill you with my finger.
In a minute I'm going to raise my hand and point my finger at your head...
And you're going to die.

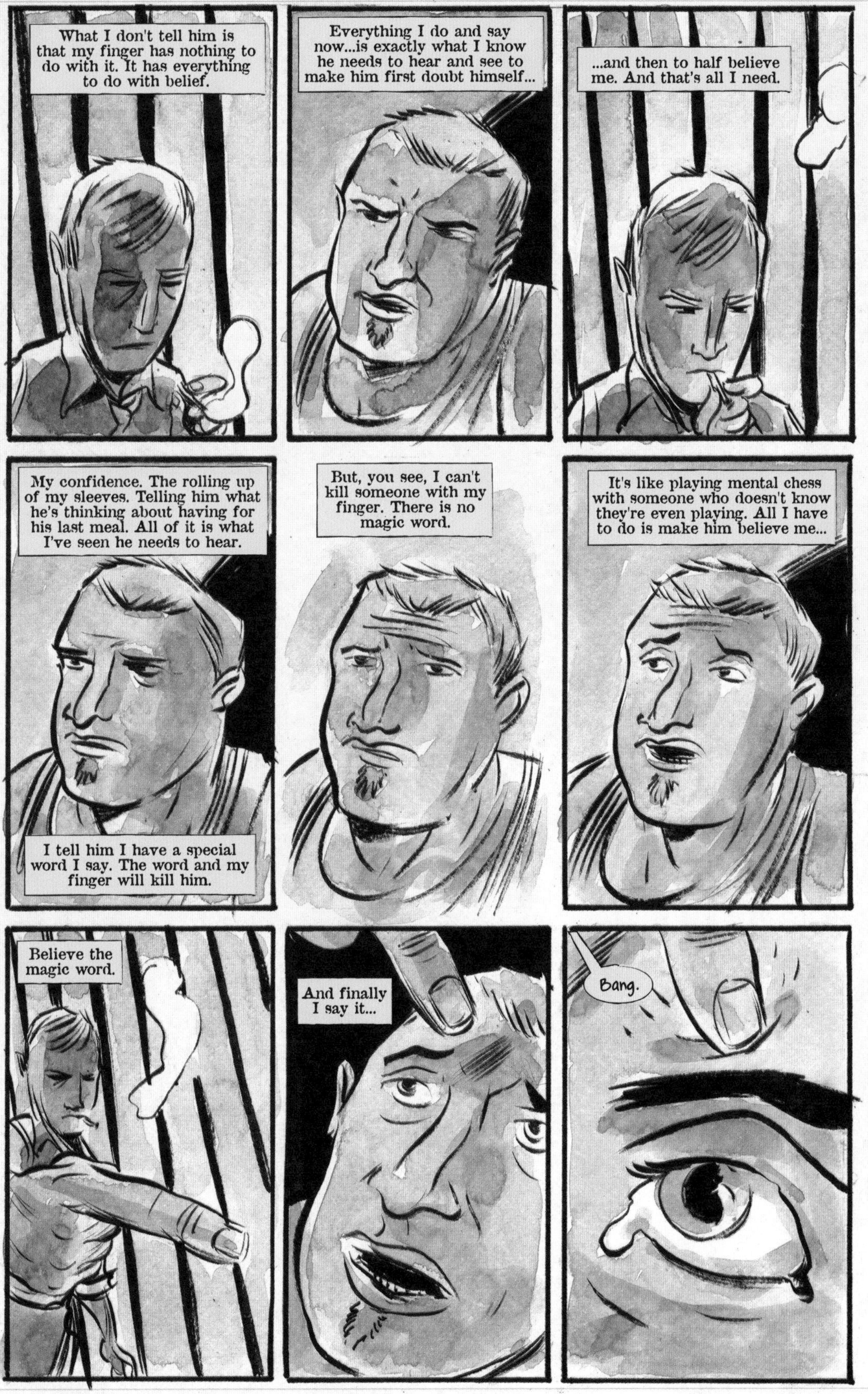
What I don't tell him is that my finger has nothing to do with it. It has everything to do with belief.
Everything I do and say now...is exactly what I know he needs to hear and see to make him first doubt himself...
...and then to half believe me. And that's all I need.
My confidence. The rolling up of my sleeves. Telling him what he's thinking about having for his last meal. All of it is what I've seen he needs to hear.
I tell him I have a special word I say. The word and my finger will kill him.
But, you see, I can't kill someone with my finger. There is no magic word.
It's like playing mental chess with someone who doesn't know they're even playing. All I have to do is make him believe me...
Believe the magic word.
And finally I say it...
Bang.

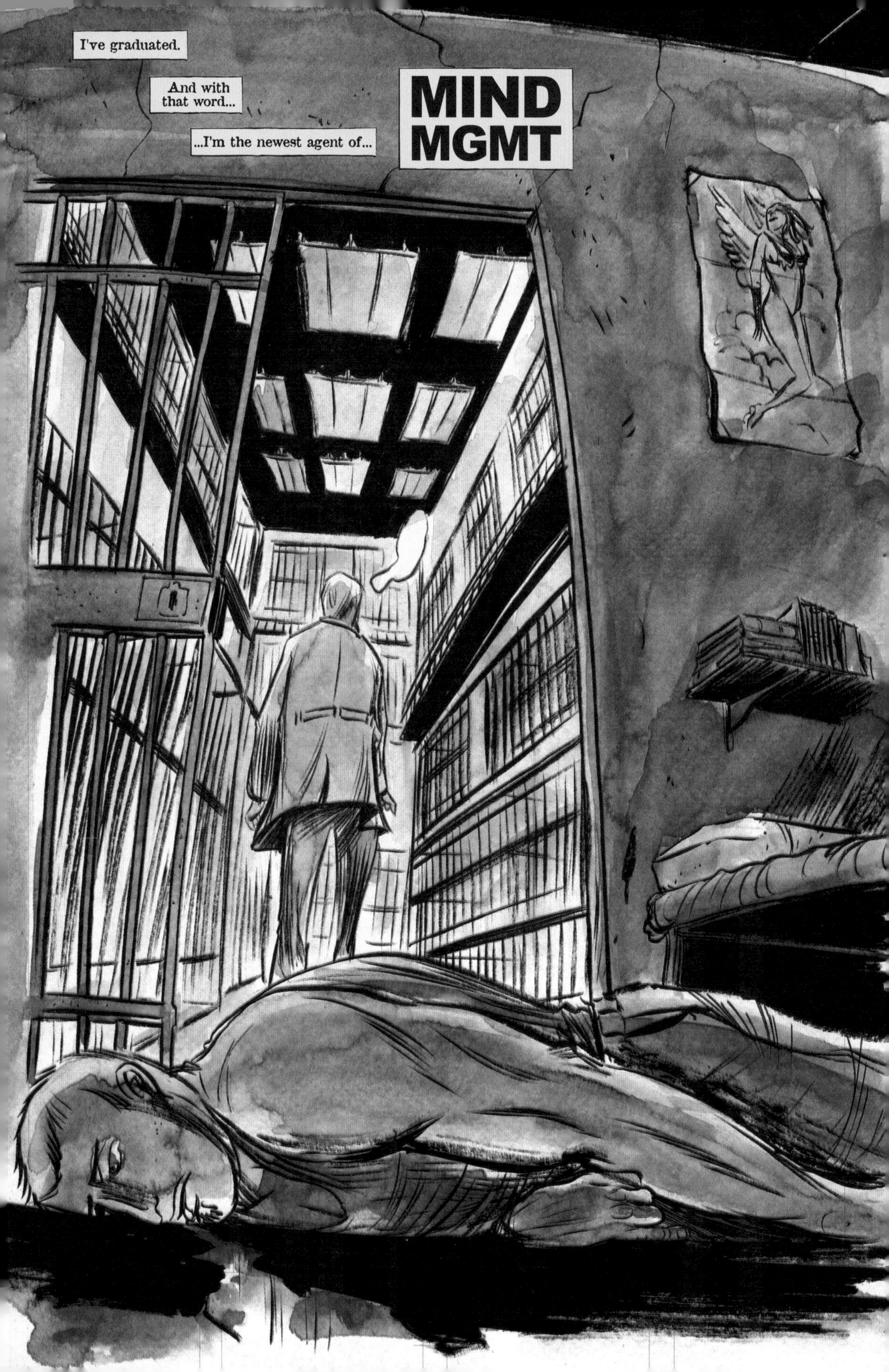
I've graduated.
And with that word...
...I'm the newest agent of...
MIND MGMT

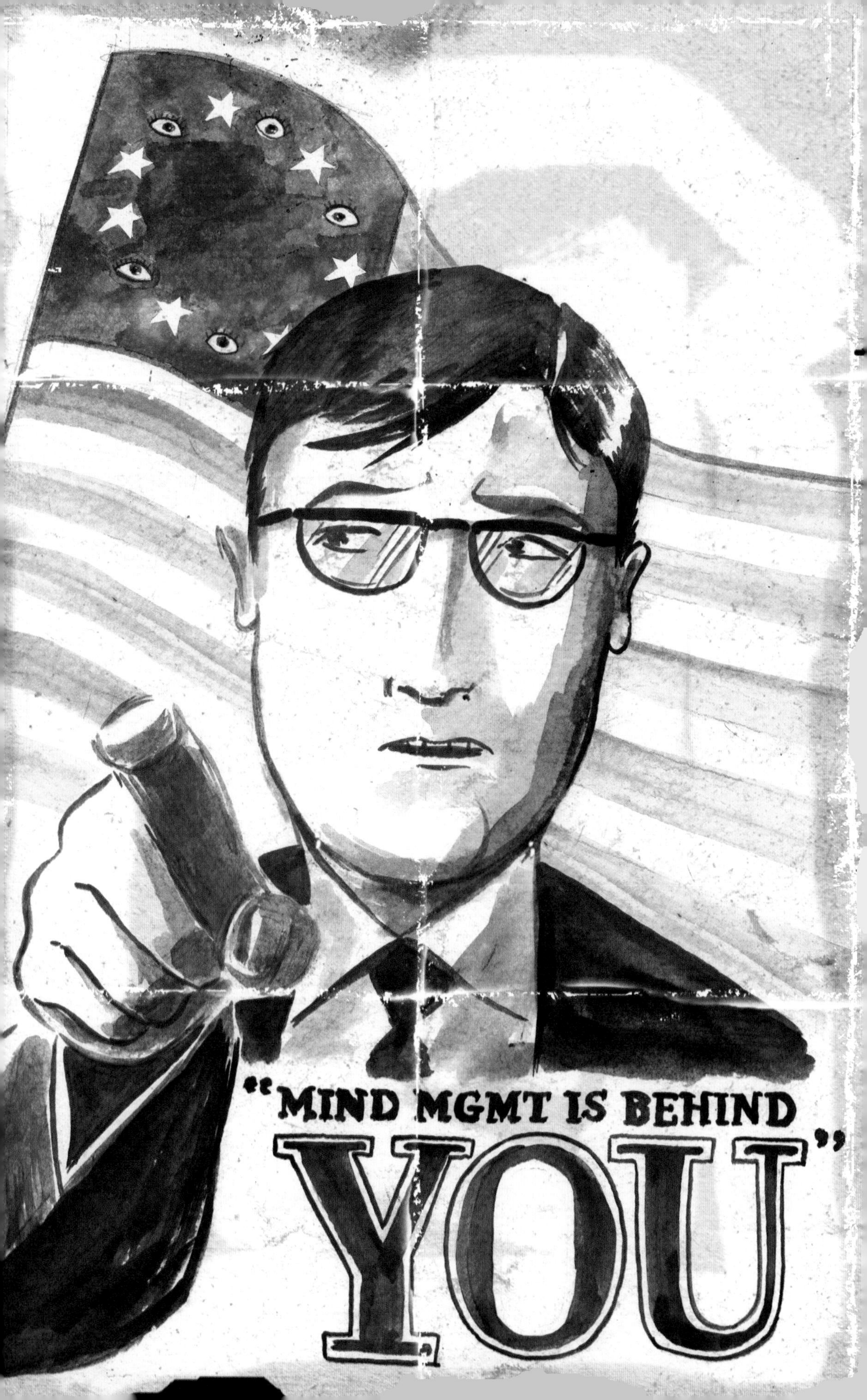
"MIND MGMT IS BEHIND
YOU"

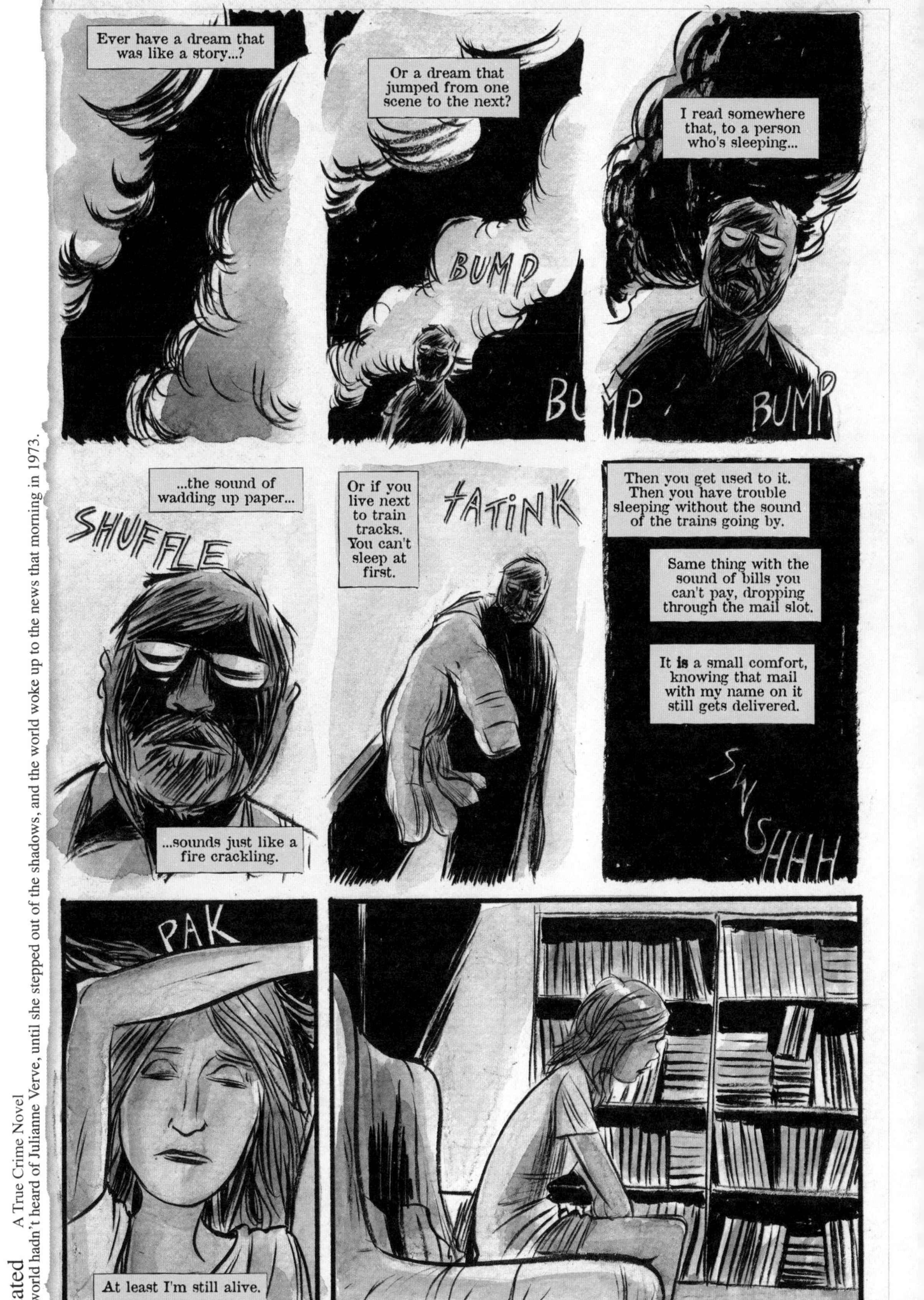
Ever have a dream that was like a story...?
Or a dream that jumped from one scene to the next?
BUMP
I read somewhere that, to a person who's sleeping...
BUMP
BUMP
...the sound of wadding up paper...
SHUFFLE
...sounds just like a fire crackling.
Or if you live next to train tracks. You can't sleep at first.
TATINK
Then you get used to it. Then you have trouble sleeping without the sound of the trains going by.
Same thing with the sound of bills you can't pay, dropping through the mail slot.
It **is** a small comfort, knowing that mail with my name on it still gets delivered.
SWSHHH
PAK
At least I'm still alive.

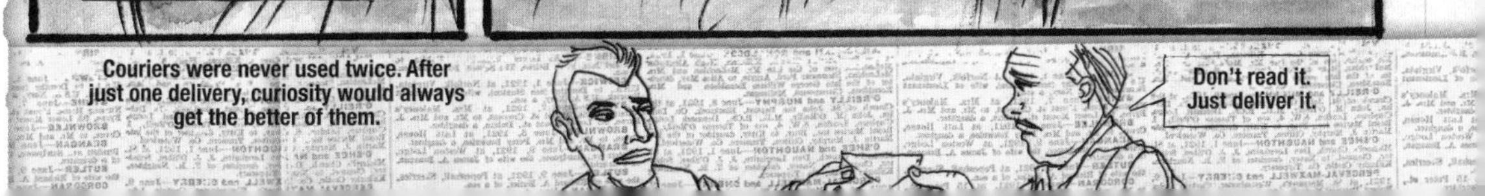
Couriers were never used twice. After just one delivery, curiosity would always get the better of them.
Don't read it. Just deliver it.

Premeditated A True Crime Novel
Most of the world hadn't heard of Julianne Verve, until she stepped out of the shadows, and the world woke up to the news that morning in 1973.

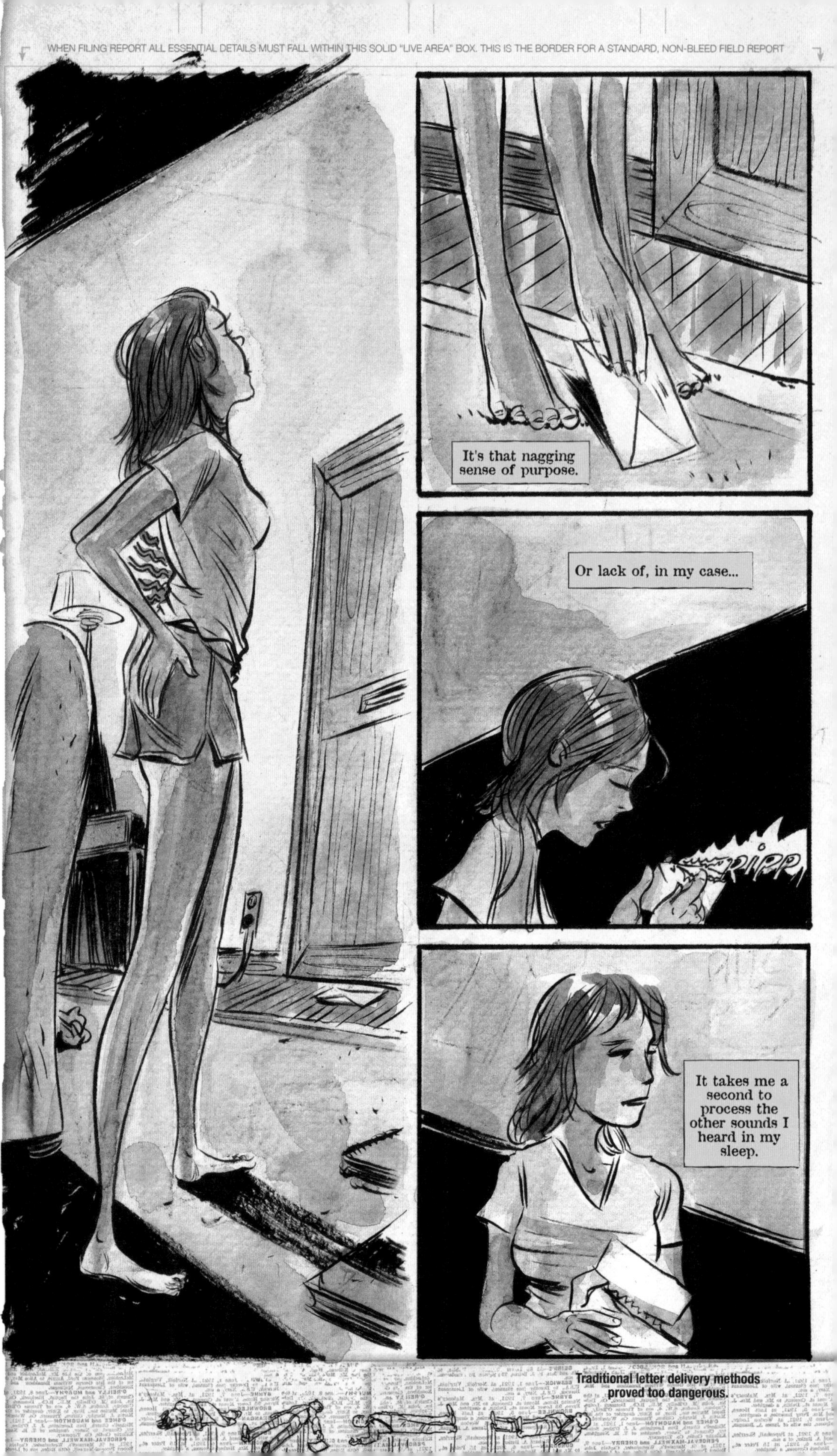
WHEN FILING REPORT ALL ESSENTIAL DETAILS MUST FALL WITHIN THIS SOLID "LIVE AREA" BOX. THIS IS THE BORDER FOR A STANDARD, NON-BLEED FIELD REPORT
It's that nagging sense of purpose.
Or lack of, in my case...
RIPP
It takes me a second to process the other sounds I heard in my sleep.
Traditional letter delivery methods proved too dangerous.

The news that she'd killed her millionaire husband, renowned author P. K. Verve. And her two children. All before breakfast.

WHEN FILING REPORT ALL ESSENTIAL DETAILS MUST FALL WITHIN THIS SOLID "LIVE AREA" BOX. THIS IS THE BORDER FOR A STANDARD, NON-BLEED FIELD REPORT

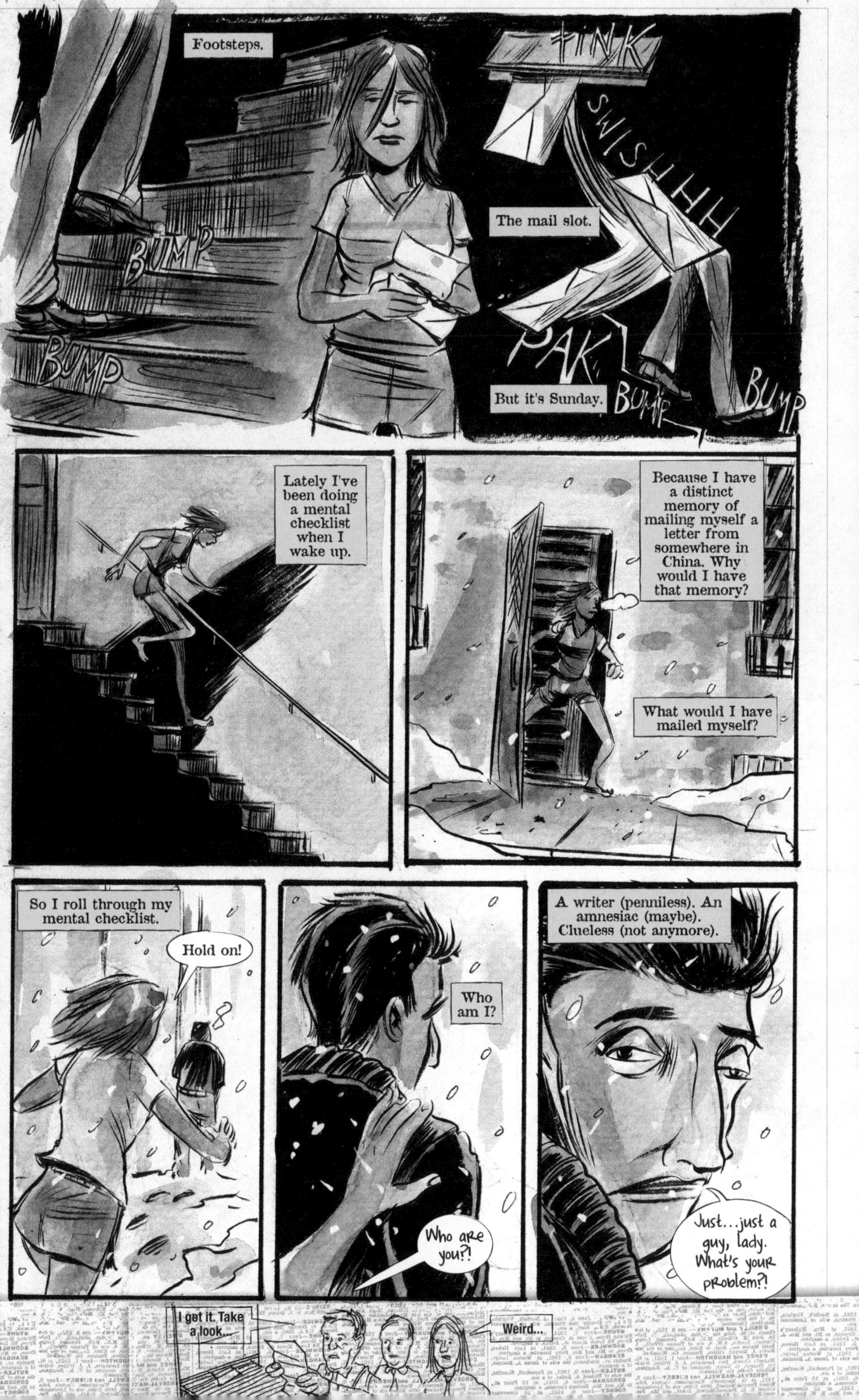
Footsteps.
BUMP
BUMP
FINK
SWISHHH
The mail slot.
PAK
But it's Sunday.
BUMP
BUMP
Lately I've been doing a mental checklist when I wake up.
Because I have a distinct memory of mailing myself a letter from somewhere in China. Why would I have that memory?
What would I have mailed myself?
So I roll through my mental checklist.
Hold on!
Who am I?
Who are you?!
A writer (penniless). An amnesiac (maybe). Clueless (not anymore).
Just...just a guy, lady. What's your problem?!
I get it. Take a look...
Weird...

To understand what happened that early morning years ago, I decided to interview everyone who had ever known Julianne. Literally everyone. This would involve unprecedented research. And a lot of legwork.

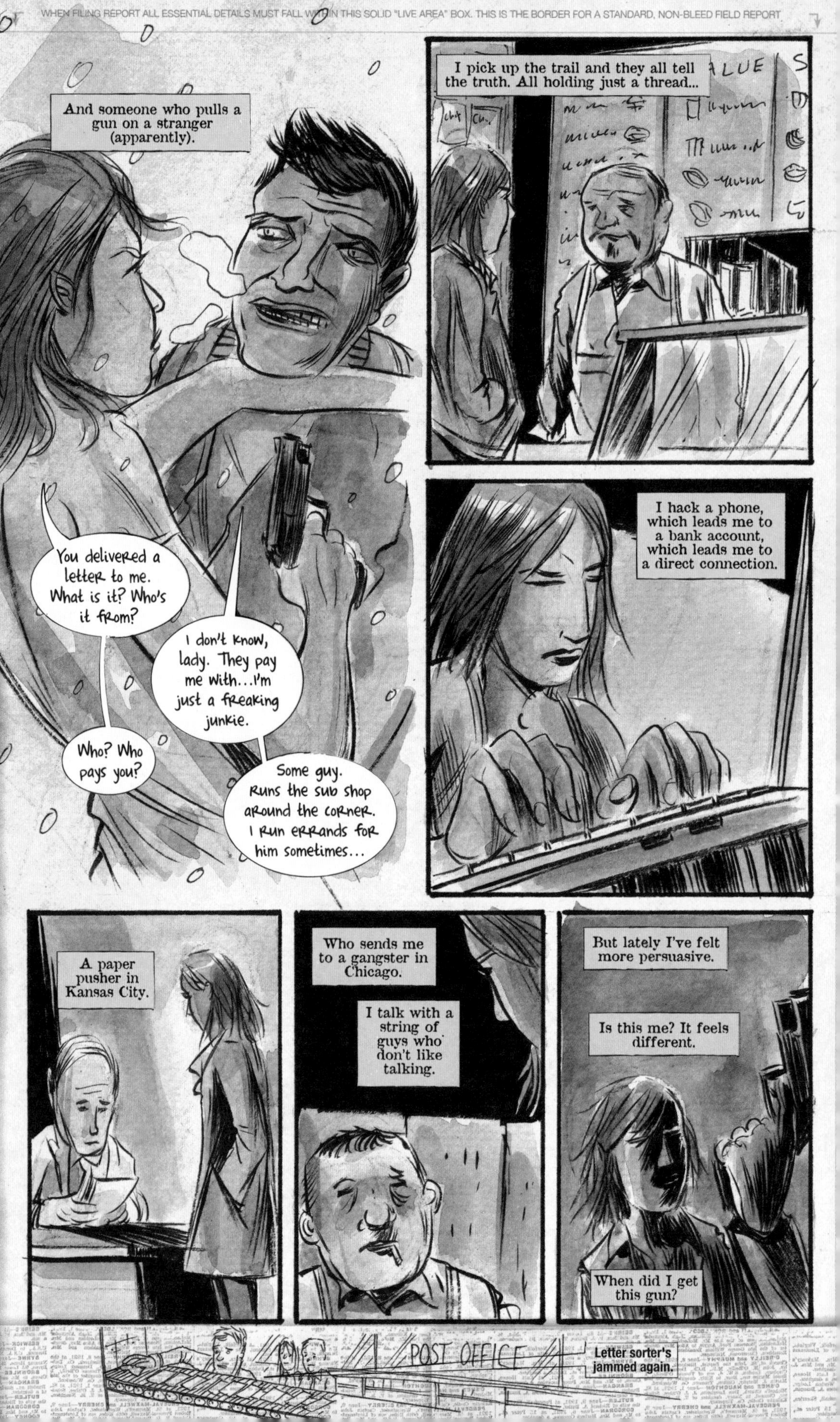
WHEN FILING REPORT ALL ESSENTIAL DETAILS MUST FALL WITHIN THIS SOLID "LIVE AREA" BOX. THIS IS THE BORDER FOR A STANDARD, NON-BLEED FIELD REPORT
And someone who pulls a gun on a stranger (apparently).
You delivered a letter to me. What is it? Who's it from?
I don't know, lady. They pay me with...I'm just a freaking junkie.
Who? Who pays you?
Some guy. Runs the sub shop around the corner. I run errands for him sometimes...
I pick up the trail and they all tell the truth. All holding just a thread...
I hack a phone, which leads me to a bank account, which leads me to a direct connection.
A paper pusher in Kansas City.
Who sends me to a gangster in Chicago.
I talk with a string of guys who don't like talking.
But lately I've felt more persuasive.
Is this me? It feels different.
When did I get this gun?
POST OFFICE
Letter sorter's jammed again.

In my research, I would discover many unsavory characters, many of them enemies of Julianne Verve. But even more were her closest friends. Or claimed to be.

WHEN FILING REPORT ALL ESSENTIAL DETAILS MUST FALL WITHIN THIS SOLID "LIVE AREA" BOX. THIS IS THE BORDER FOR A STANDARD, NON-BLEED FIELD REPORT

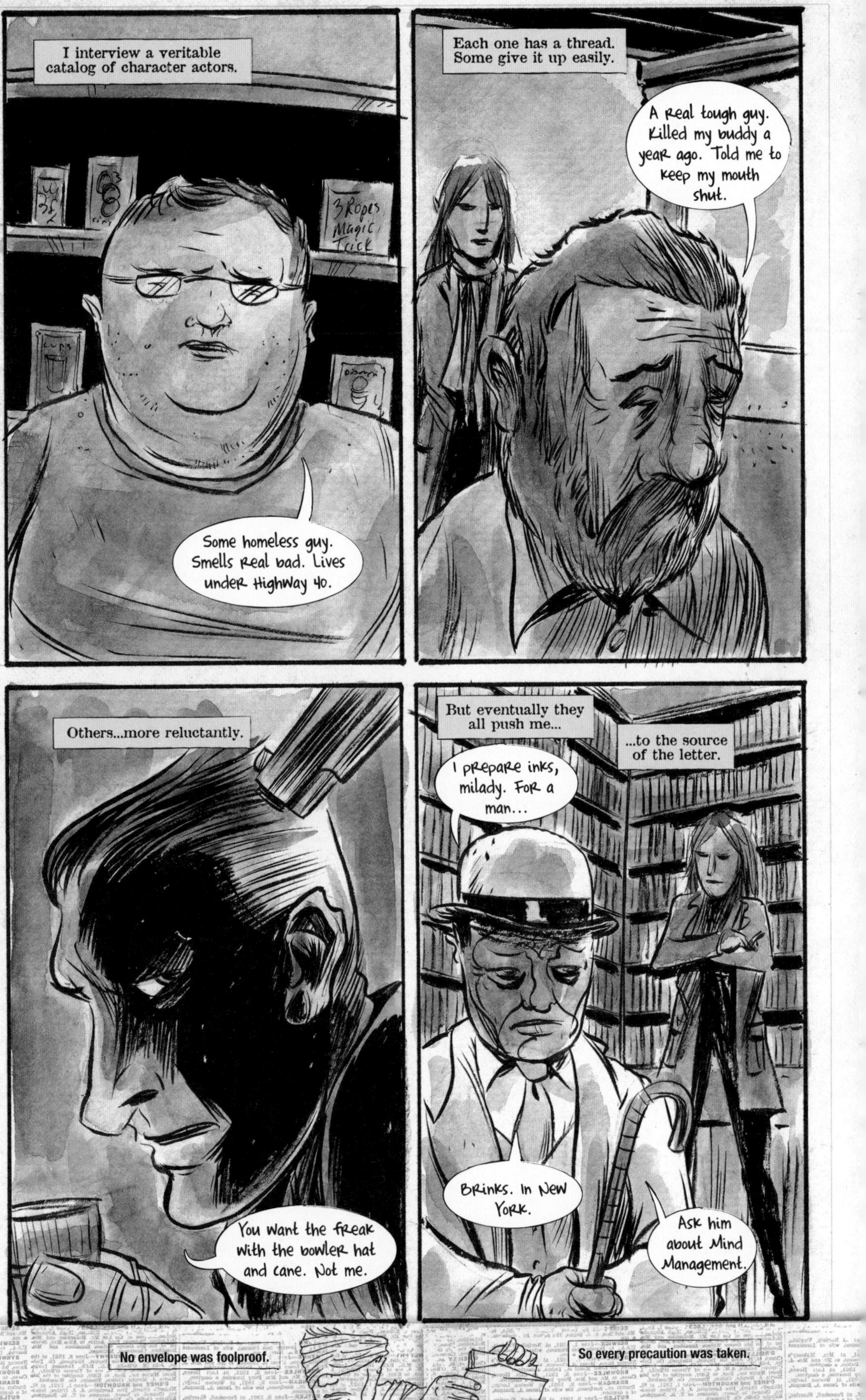
I interview a veritable catalog of character actors.
Some homeless guy. Smells real bad. Lives under Highway 40.
Each one has a thread. Some give it up easily.
A real tough guy. Killed my buddy a year ago. Told me to keep my mouth shut.
Others...more reluctantly.
You want the freak with the bowler hat and cane. Not me.
But eventually they all push me...
...to the source of the letter.
I prepare inks, milady. For a man...
Brinks. In New York.
Ask him about Mind Management.
No envelope was foolproof.
So every precaution was taken.

Julianne's husband was an eccentric: an accomplished tennis player, author, and motivational speaker. He moved in circles that most people don't even realize exist.

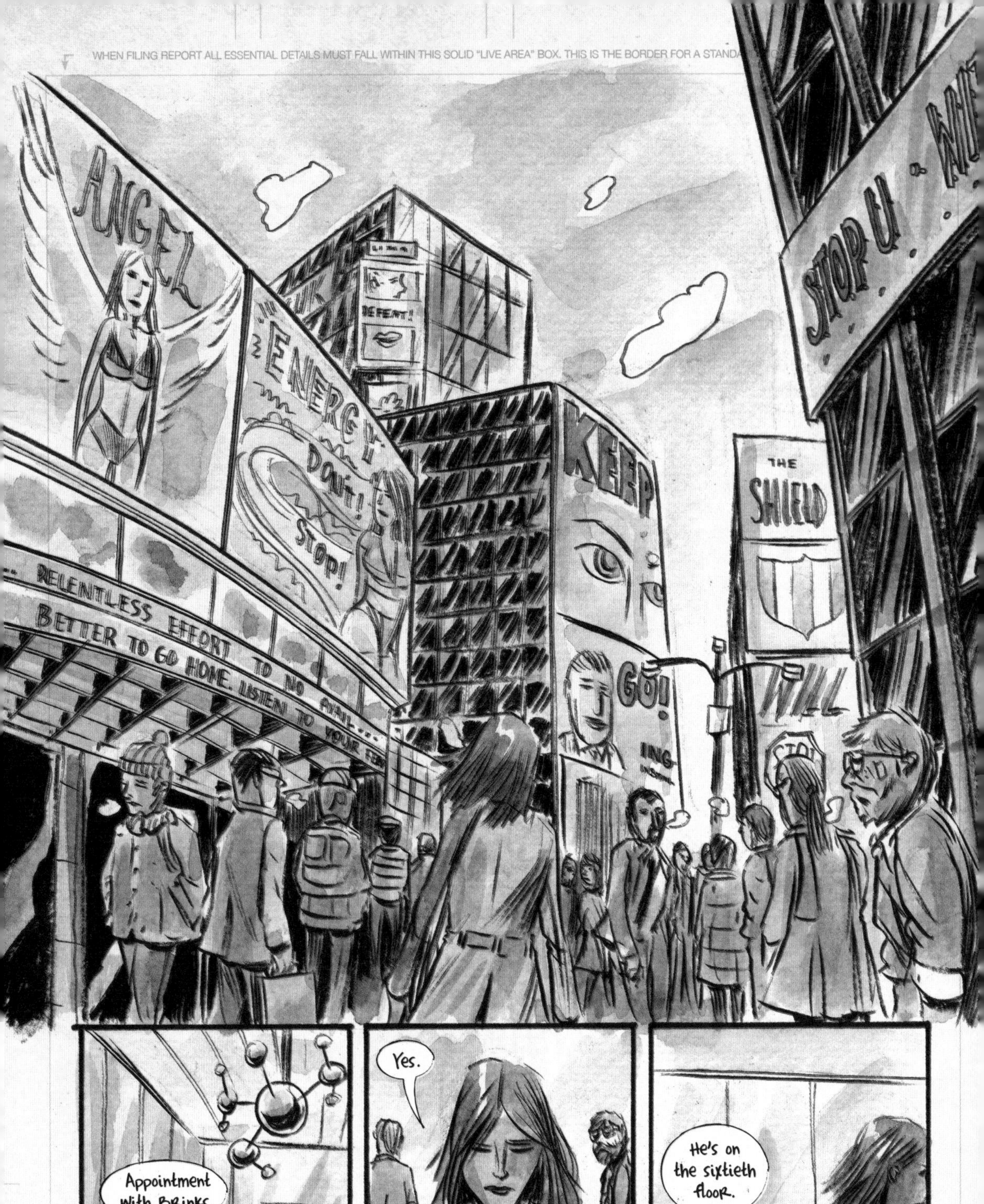
WHEN FILING REPORT ALL ESSENTIAL DETAILS MUST FALL WITHIN THIS SOLID "LIVE AREA" BOX. THIS IS THE BORDER FOR A STANDA
ANGEL
ENERGY
DON'T!
STOP!
DEFEAT!
KEEP
THE SHIELD
STOP U
GO!
WILL
... RELENTLESS EFFORT TO NO AVAIL...
BETTER TO GO HOME. LISTEN TO YOUR FE
Appointment with Brinks.
I'm, uh...is he expecting you?
Yes.
He's on the sixtieth floor.

Only handmade paper, manufactured by specialists, was used. Nothing else can really hold it.

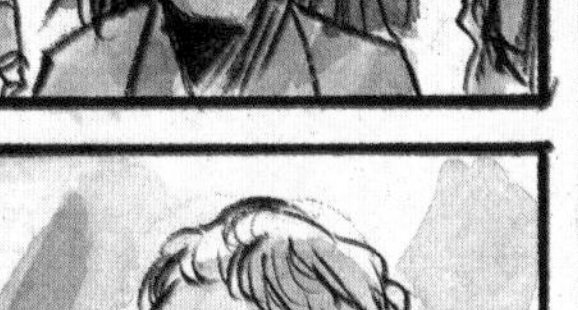

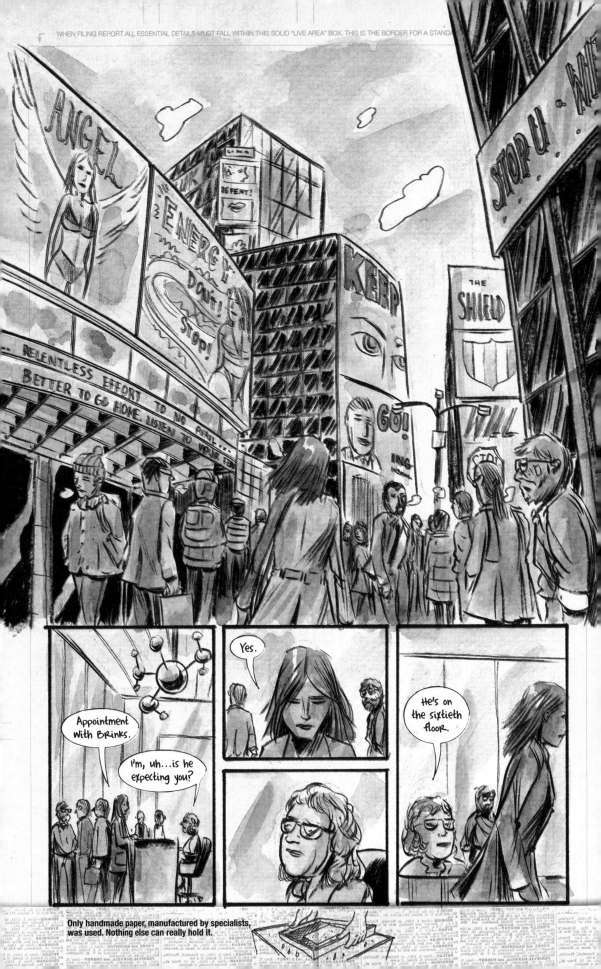

WHEN FILING REPORT ALL ESSENTIAL DETAILS MUST FALL WITHIN THIS SOLID "LIVE AREA" BOX. THIS IS THE BORDER FOR A STANDARD, NON-BLEED FIELD REPORT

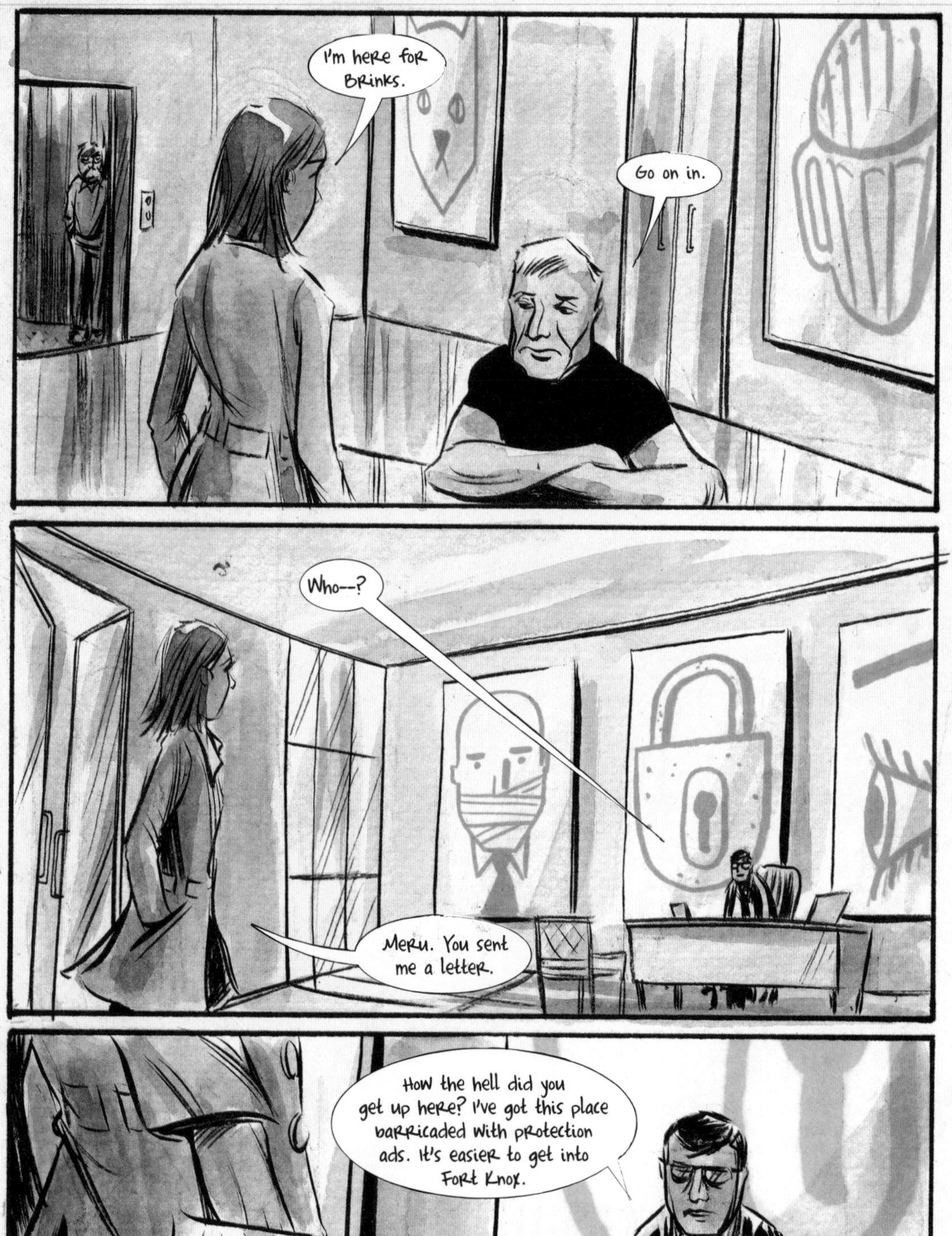
I'm here for Brinks.
Go on in.
Who--?
Meru. You sent me a letter.
How the hell did you get up here? I've got this place barricaded with protection ads. It's easier to get into Fort Knox.
Your cute secretary let me in.
Could have sworn I had my gun with me...

But to truly understand Julianne's murders, I had to go back as far as I could. To New York. Where some of her family still resides.

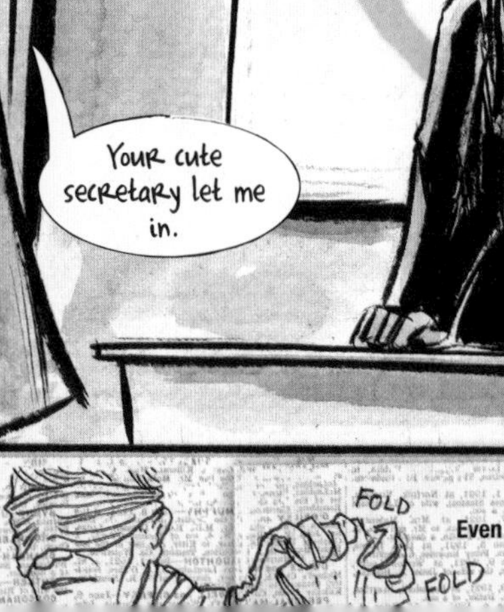
FOLD
FOLD

Even touching the letter was a risk.

WHEN FILING REPORT ALL ESSENTIAL DETAILS MUST FALL WITHIN THIS SOLID "LIVE AREA" BOX. THIS IS THE BORDER FOR A STANDARD, NON-BLEED FIELD REPORT

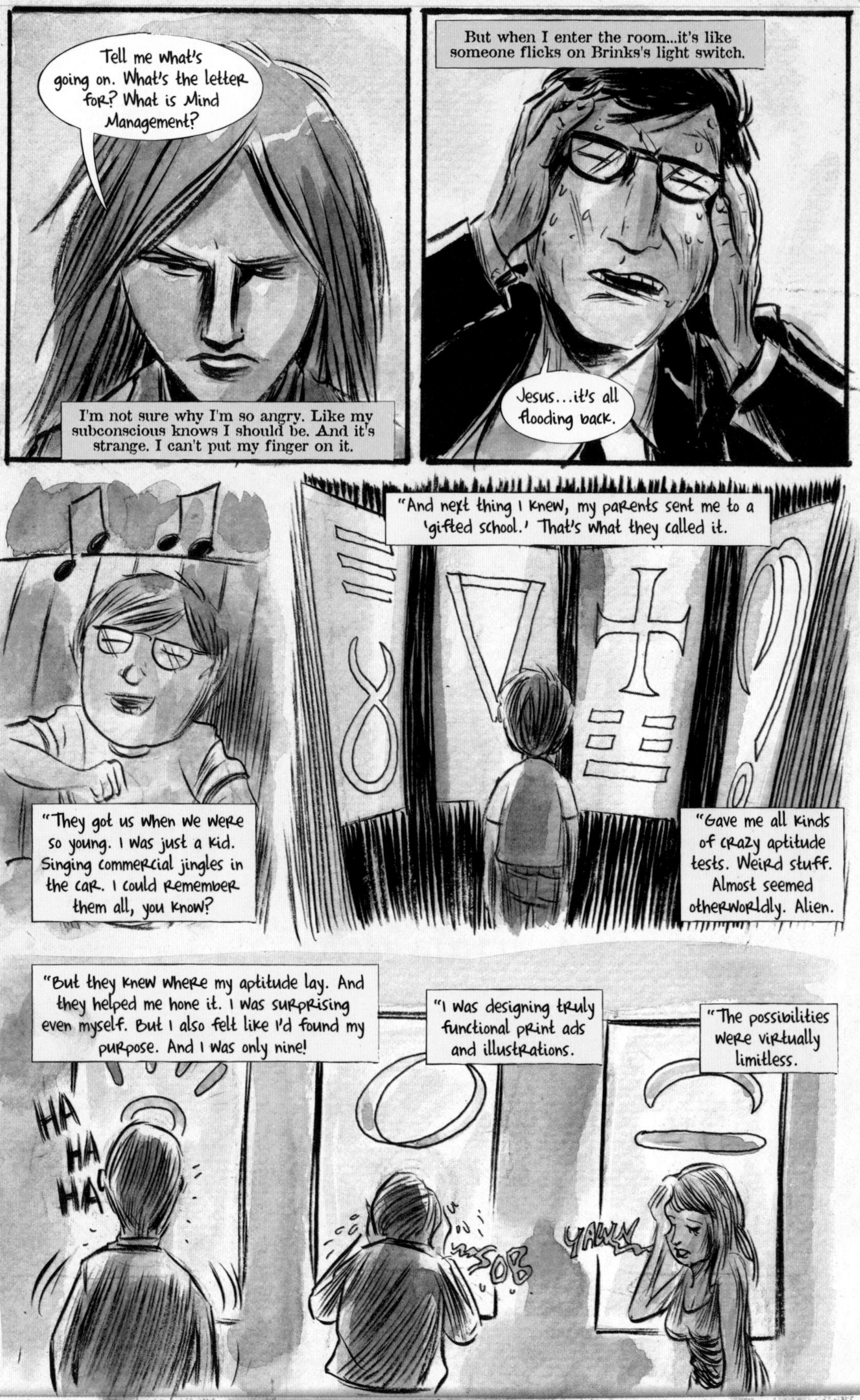
Tell me what's going on. What's the letter for? What is Mind Management?
I'm not sure why I'm so angry. Like my subconscious knows I should be. And it's strange. I can't put my finger on it.
But when I enter the room...it's like someone flicks on Brinks's light switch.
Jesus...it's all flooding back.
"They got us when we were so young. I was just a kid. Singing commercial jingles in the car. I could remember them all, you know?
"And next thing I knew, my parents sent me to a 'gifted school.' That's what they called it.
"Gave me all kinds of crazy aptitude tests. Weird stuff. Almost seemed otherworldly. Alien.
"But they knew where my aptitude lay. And they helped me hone it. I was surprising even myself. But I also felt like I'd found my purpose. And I was only nine!
HA HA HA
"I was designing truly functional print ads and illustrations.
SOB
"The possibilities were virtually limitless.
YAWN

Inks are now handcrafted and designed to fade over time and lose their impact, to minimize risk to bystanders.

My first interview was with her brother, David. A man with many of his own secrets. Someone who, I sensed, was reluctant to talk, for fear of revealing his own sordid history.

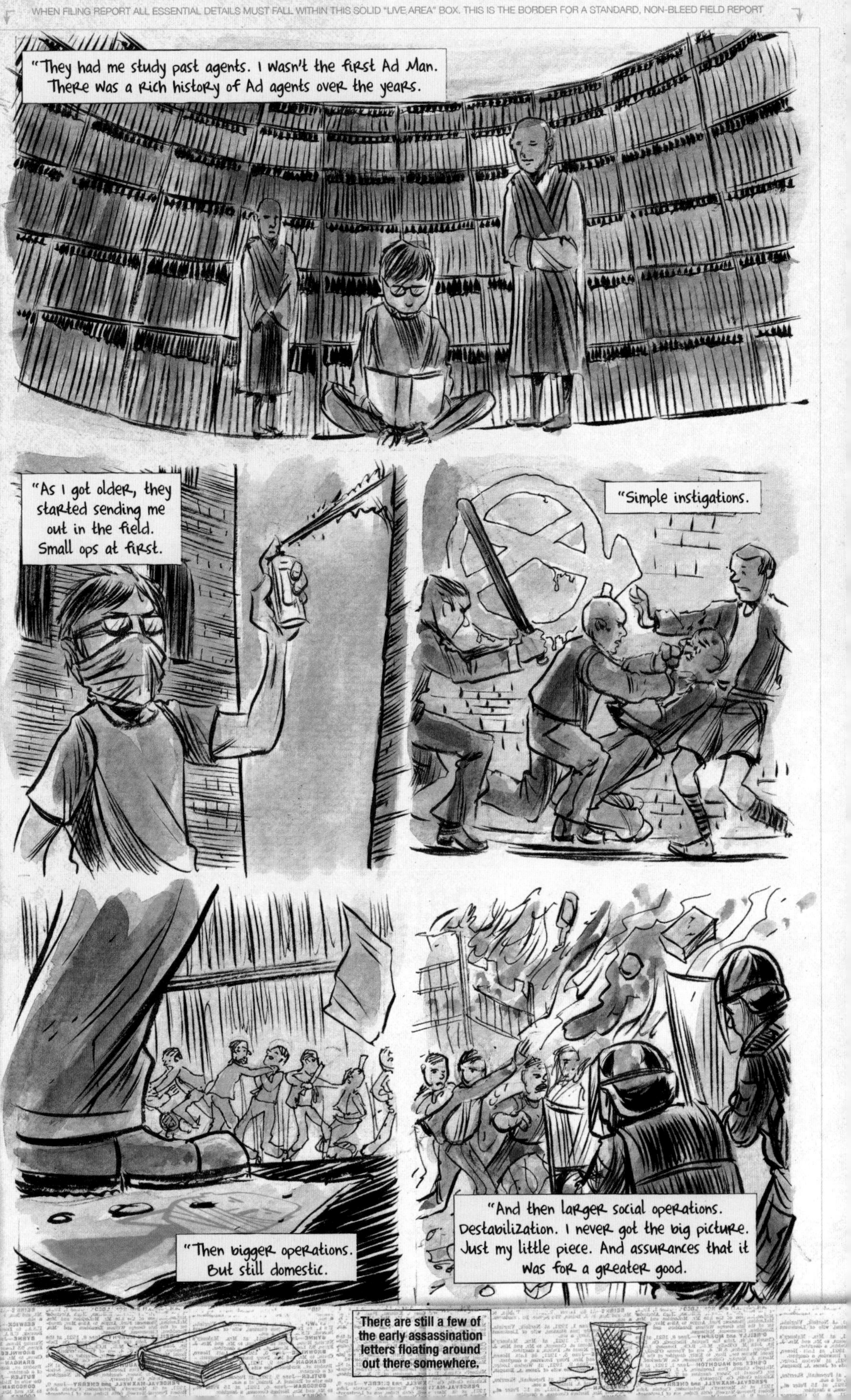
WHEN FILING REPORT ALL ESSENTIAL DETAILS MUST FALL WITHIN THIS SOLID "LIVE AREA" BOX. THIS IS THE BORDER FOR A STANDARD, NON-BLEED FIELD REPORT
"They had me study past agents. I wasn't the first Ad Man. There was a rich history of Ad agents over the years.
"As I got older, they started sending me out in the field. Small ops at first.
"Simple instigations.
"Then bigger operations. But still domestic.
"And then larger social operations. Destabilization. I never got the big picture. Just my little piece. And assurances that it was for a greater good.
There are still a few of the early assassination letters floating around out there somewhere.

But eventually he did talk. And he told me of a childhood growing up with Julianne that most would envy.

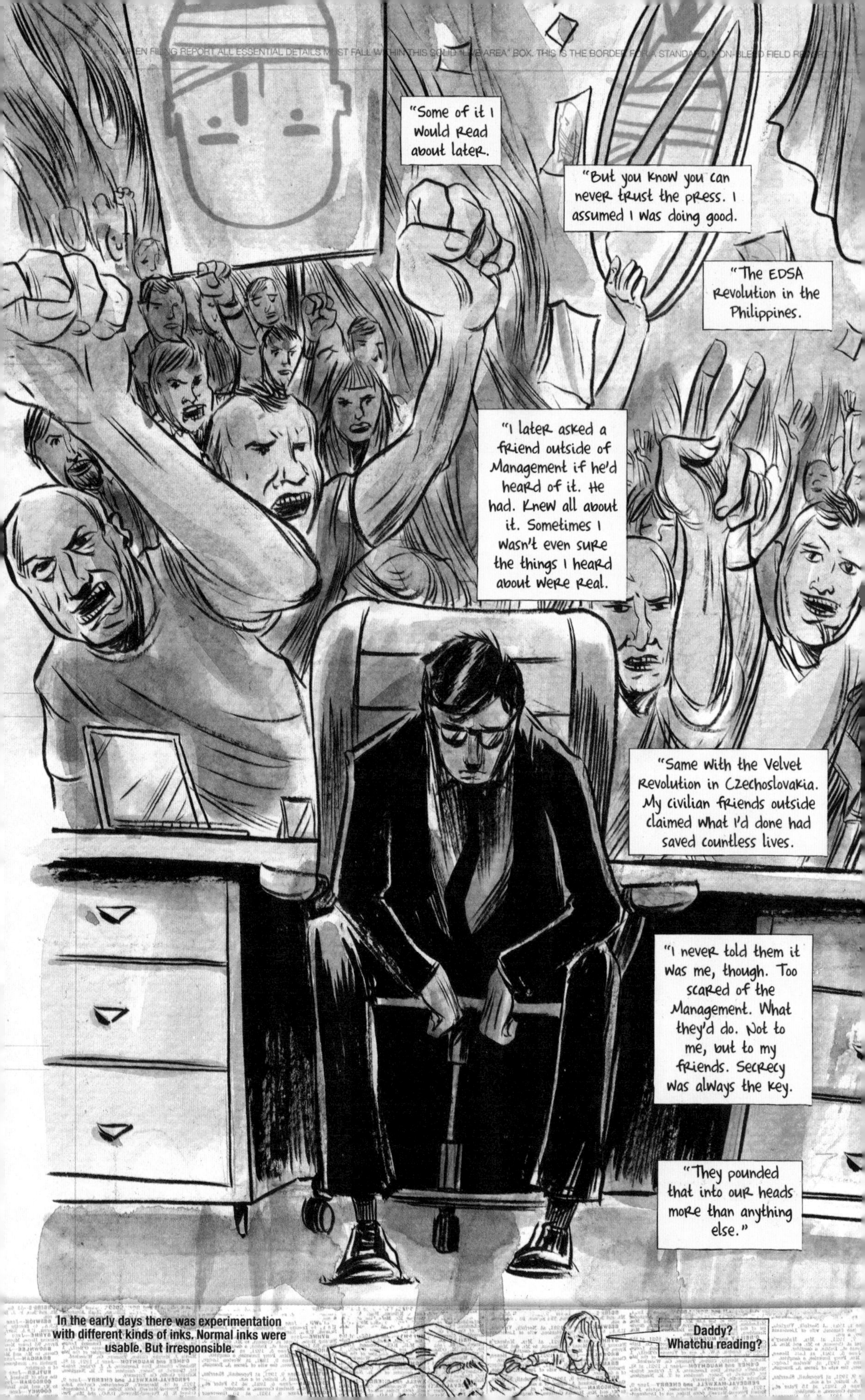
"Some of it I would read about later.
"But you know you can never trust the press. I assumed I was doing good.
"The EDSA Revolution in the Philippines.
"I later asked a friend outside of Management if he'd heard of it. He had. Knew all about it. Sometimes I wasn't even sure the things I heard about were real.
"Same with the Velvet Revolution in Czechoslovakia. My civilian friends outside claimed what I'd done had saved countless lives.
"I never told them it was me, though. Too scared of the Management. What they'd do. Not to me, but to my friends. Secrecy was always the key.
"They pounded that into our heads more than anything else."
In the early days there was experimentation with different kinds of inks. Normal inks were usable. But irresponsible.
Daddy? Whatchu reading?

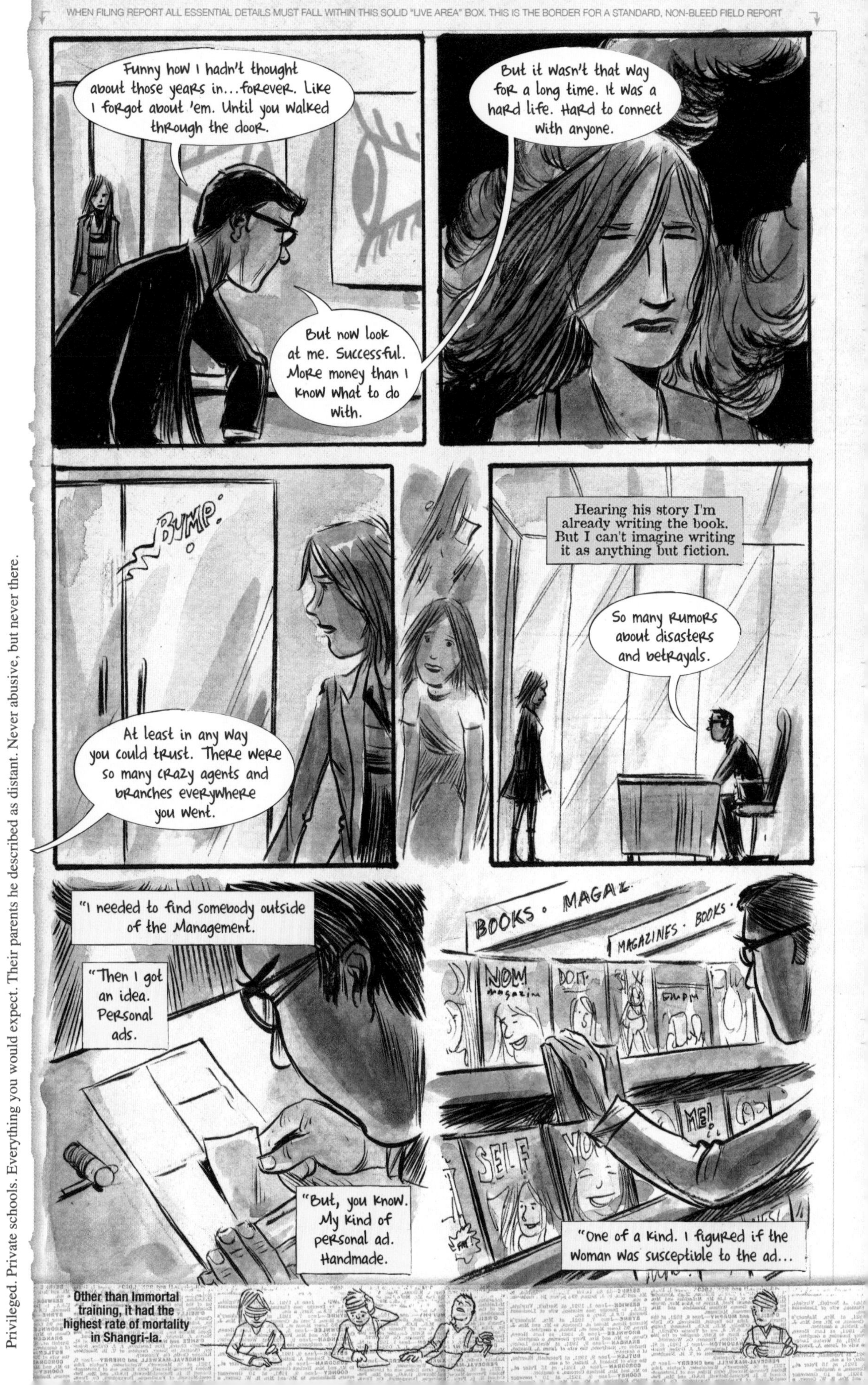
WHEN FILING REPORT ALL ESSENTIAL DETAILS MUST FALL WITHIN THIS SOLID "LIVE AREA" BOX. THIS IS THE BORDER FOR A STANDARD, NON-BLEED FIELD REPORT
Funny how I hadn't thought about those years in...forever. Like I forgot about 'em. Until you walked through the door.
But now look at me. Successful. More money than I know what to do with.
But it wasn't that way for a long time. It was a hard life. Hard to connect with anyone.
BUMP
At least in any way you could trust. There were so many crazy agents and branches everywhere you went.
Hearing his story I'm already writing the book. But I can't imagine writing it as anything but fiction.
So many rumors about disasters and betrayals.
"I needed to find somebody outside of the Management.
"Then I got an idea. Personal ads.
"But, you know. My kind of personal ad. Handmade.
BOOKS · MAGAZ
MAGAZINES · BOOKS ·
NOW
DO IT
SELF
ME!
"One of a kind. I figured if the woman was susceptible to the ad...
Other than Immortal training, it had the highest rate of mortality in Shangri-la.
Privileged. Private schools. Everything you would expect. Their parents he described as distant. Never abusive, but never there.

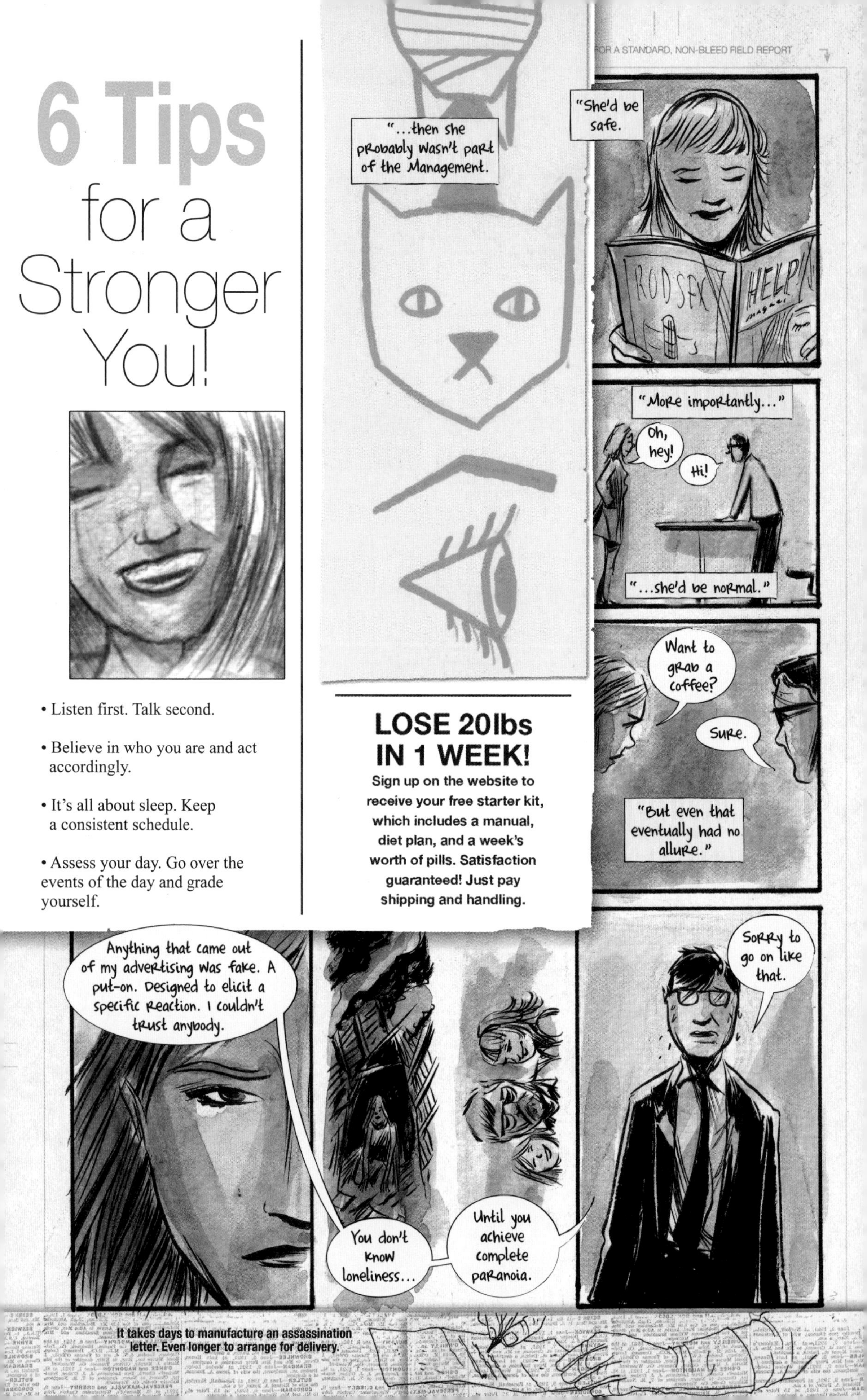
FOR A STANDARD, NON-BLEED FIELD REPORT
6 Tips for a Stronger You!
• Listen first. Talk second.
• Believe in who you are and act accordingly.
• It's all about sleep. Keep a consistent schedule.
• Assess your day. Go over the events of the day and grade yourself.
"...then she probably wasn't part of the Management.
LOSE 20lbs IN 1 WEEK!
Sign up on the website to receive your free starter kit, which includes a manual, diet plan, and a week's worth of pills. Satisfaction guaranteed! Just pay shipping and handling.
"She'd be safe.
HELP
"More importantly..."
Oh, hey!
Hi!
"...she'd be normal."
Want to grab a coffee?
Sure.
"But even that eventually had no allure."
Anything that came out of my advertising was fake. A put-on. Designed to elicit a specific reaction. I couldn't trust anybody.
You don't know loneliness...
Until you achieve complete paranoia.
Sorry to go on like that.
It takes days to manufacture an assassination letter. Even longer to arrange for delivery.

WHEN FILING REPORT ALL ESSENTIAL DETAILS MUST FALL WITHIN THIS SOLID "LIVE AREA" BOX. THIS IS THE BORDER FOR A STANDARD, NON-BLEED FIELD REPORT

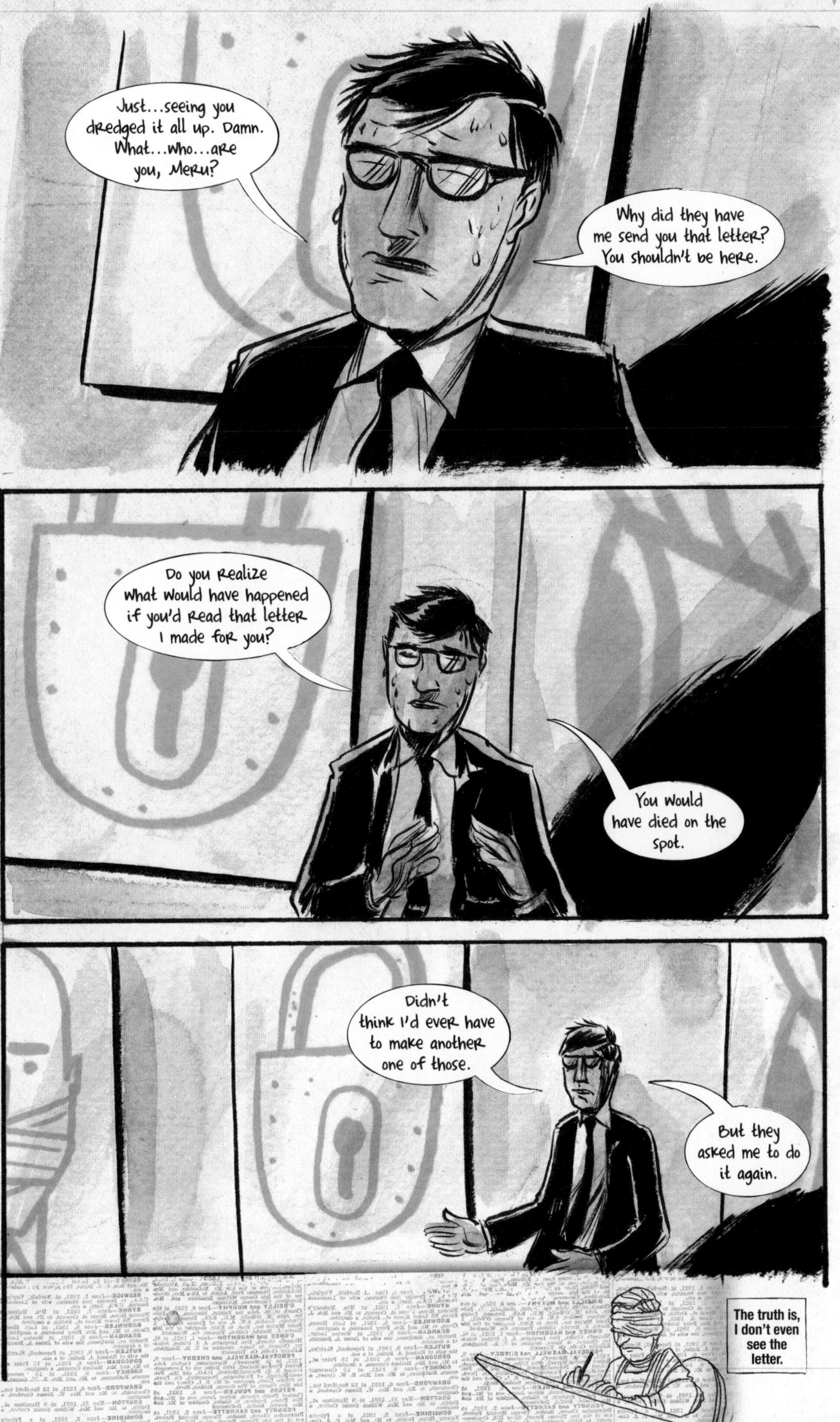

Just...seeing you dredged it all up. Damn. What...who...are you, Meru?
Why did they have me send you that letter? You shouldn't be here.
Do you realize what would have happened if you'd read that letter I made for you?
You would have died on the spot.
Didn't think I'd ever have to make another one of those.
But they asked me to do it again.
The truth is, I don't even see the letter.

David described Julianne's cruel streak. His favorite story was when she drafted a fake love letter, planted it in a book her father was reading, and arranged for her mother to find it.

WHEN FILING REPORT ALL ESSENTIAL DETAILS MUST FALL WITHIN THIS SOLID "LIVE AREA" BOX. THIS IS THE BORDER FOR A STANDARD, NON-BLEED FIELD REPORT

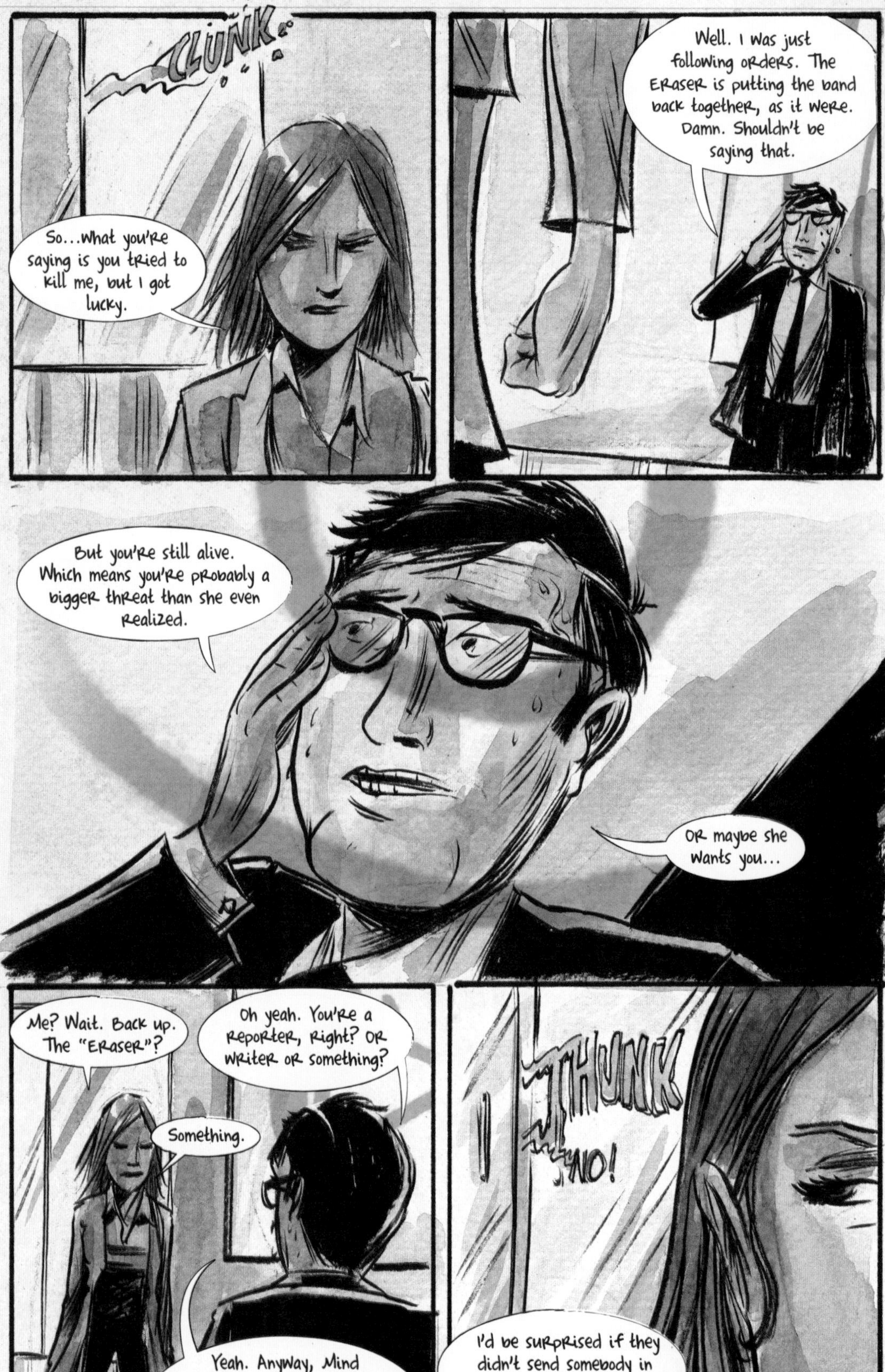
CLUNK
So...What you're saying is you tried to kill me, but I got lucky.
Well. I was just following orders. The Eraser is putting the band back together, as it were. Damn. Shouldn't be saying that.
But you're still alive. Which means you're probably a bigger threat than she even realized.
Or maybe she wants you...
Me? Wait. Back up. The "Eraser"?
Oh yeah. You're a reporter, right? Or writer or something?
Something.
Yeah. Anyway, Mind Management. You shouldn't even know that term. You knowing that and being a writer?
THUNK
NO!
I'd be surprised if they didn't send somebody in here. Shit. I've made a hash of it all.

According to David, she thrived on deceit and conflict. She seemed to derive an enjoyment from these artificial conflicts she spawned between her parents.

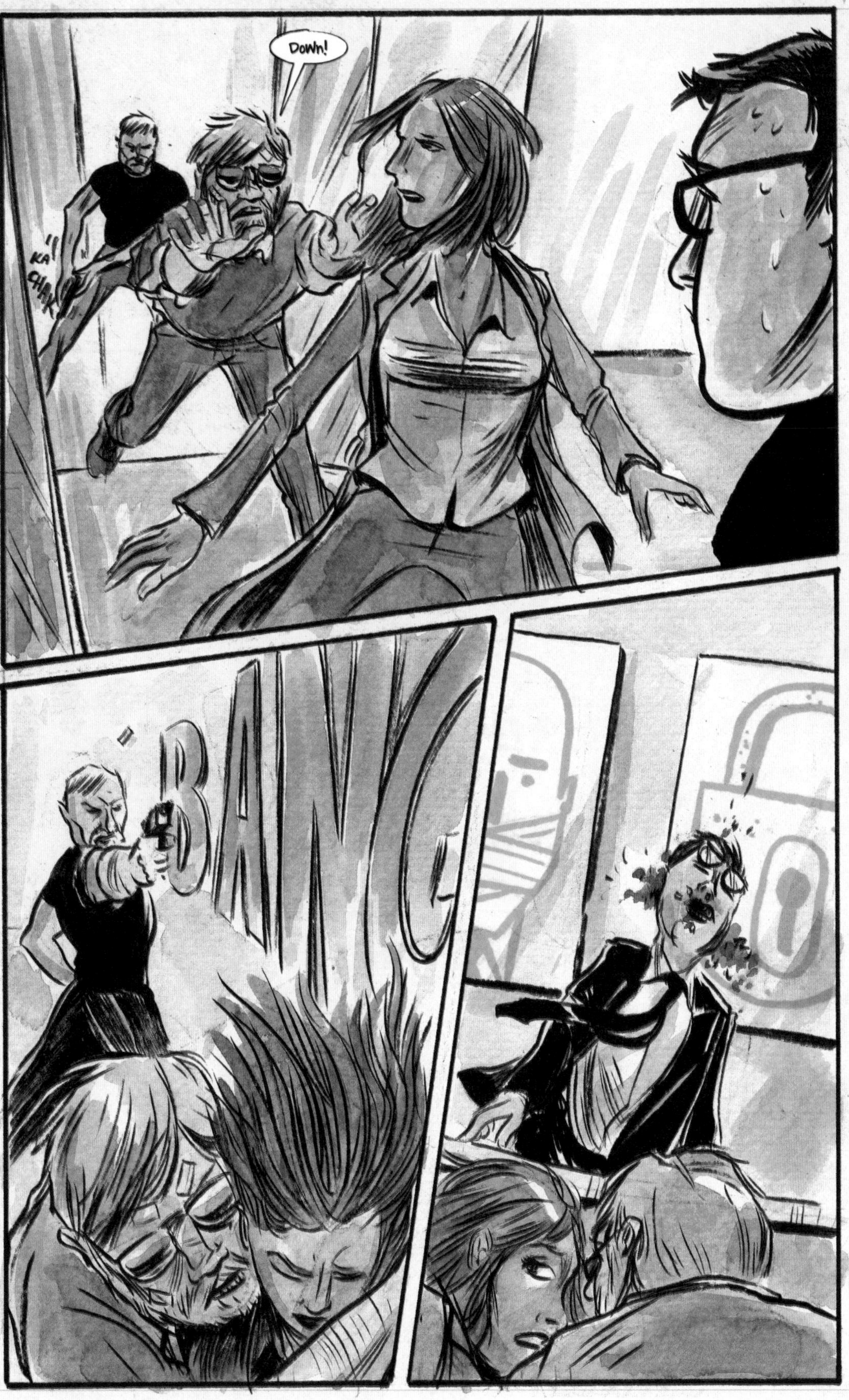
Down!
KA CHAK
BANG

When asked about what Julianne was like as a teenager, her brother became nervous. And it soon became clear he wasn't telling me everything. Before interviewing David I had heard rumors. So when I confronted him and asked if he and Julianne had anything other than a platonic relationship, he became angry and threatened to leave.

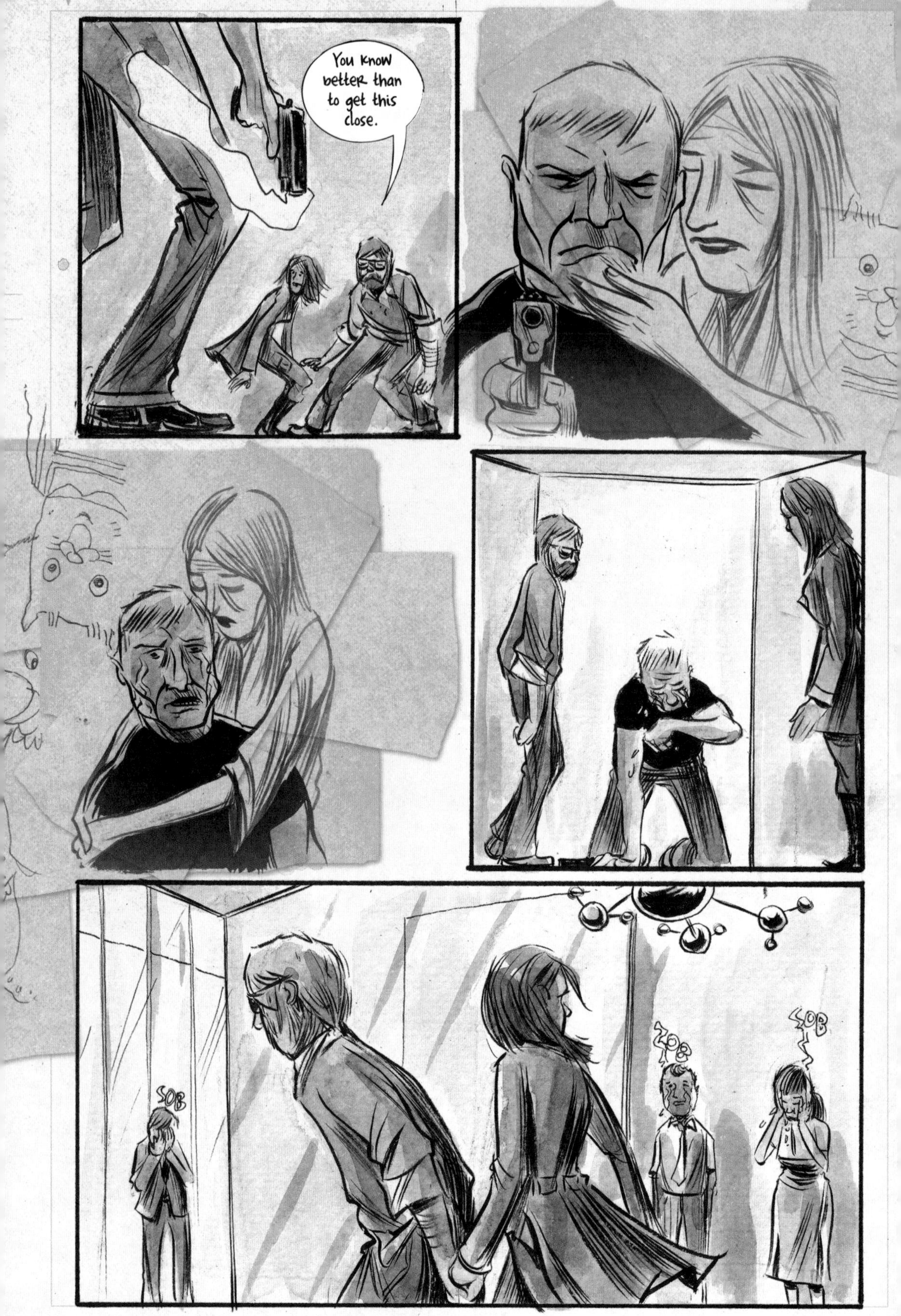
You know better than to get this close.
SOB
SOB
SOB

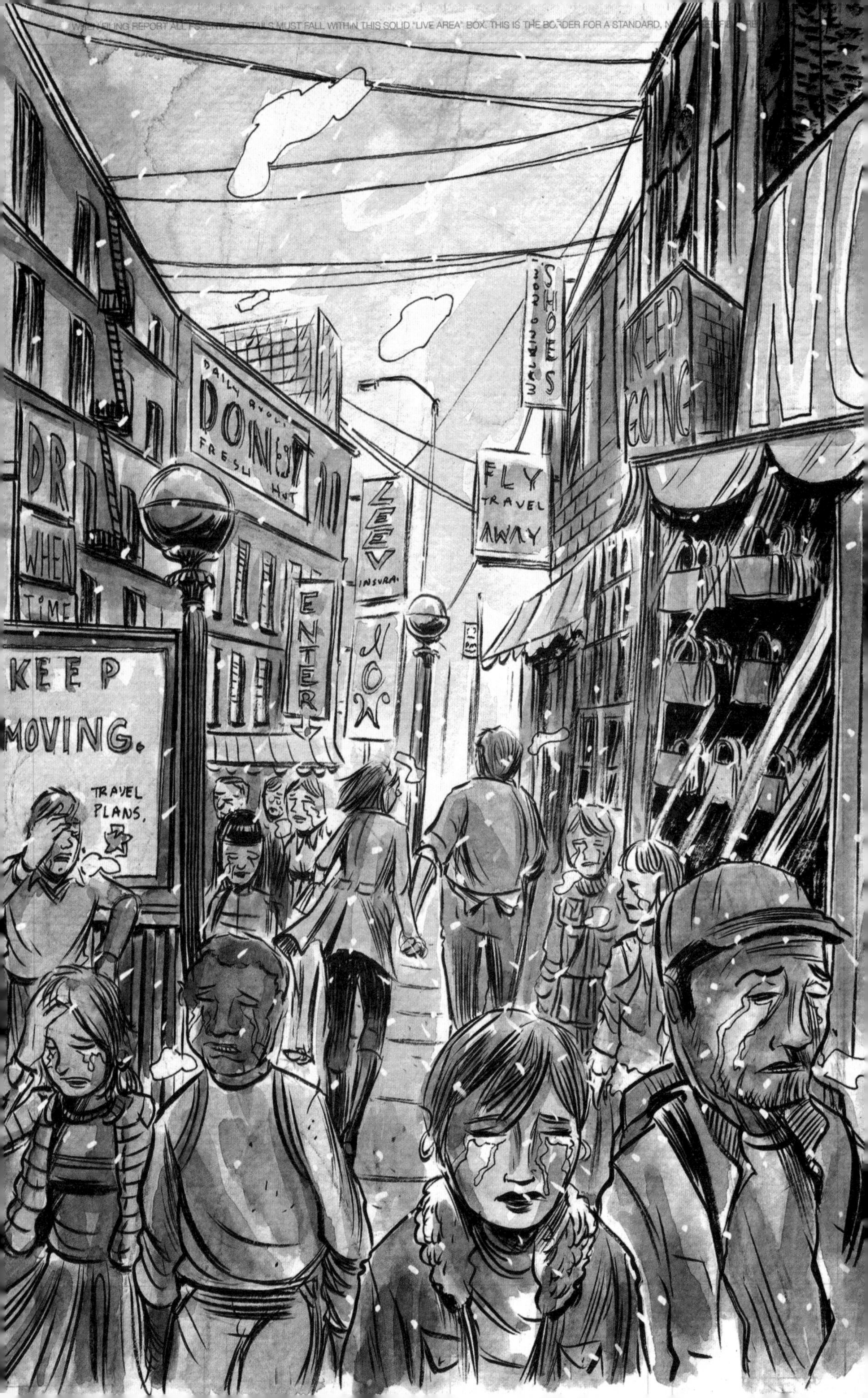
DR
WHEN
TIME
KEEP MOVING.
TRAVEL PLANS.
DAILY
FRESH
HOT
ENTER
LEEV
INSURA
NOW
FLY TRAVEL AWAY
SHOES
KEEP GOING

WHEN FILING REPORT ALL ESSENTIAL DETAILS MUST FALL WITHIN THIS SOLID "LIVE AREA" BOX. THIS IS THE BORDER FOR A STANDARD, NON-BLEED FIELD REPORT

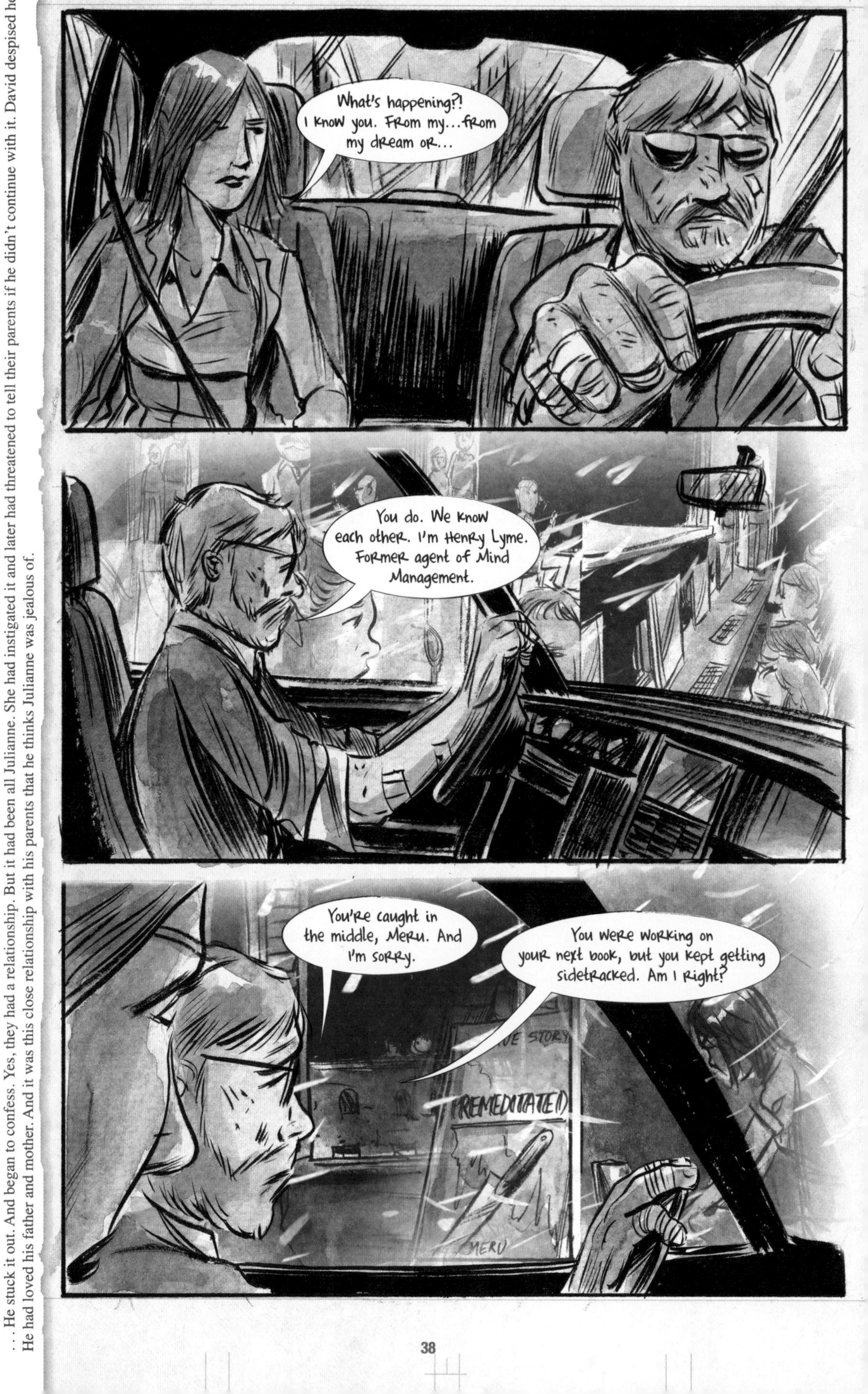
What's happening?! I know you. From my... from my dream or...
You do. We know each other. I'm Henry Lyme. Former agent of Mind Management.
You're caught in the middle, Meru. And I'm sorry.
You were working on your next book, but you kept getting sidetracked. Am I right?
PREMEDITATED
MERU

. . . He stuck it out. And began to confess. Yes, they had a relationship. But it had been all Julianne. She had instigated it and later had threatened to tell their parents if he didn't continue with it. David despised her. He had loved his father and mother. And it was this close relationship with his parents that he thinks Julianne was jealous of.

WHEN FILING REPORT ALL ESSENTIAL DETAILS MUST FALL WITHIN THIS SOLID "LIVE AREA" BOX. THIS IS THE BORDER FOR A STANDARD, NON-BLEED FIELD REPORT

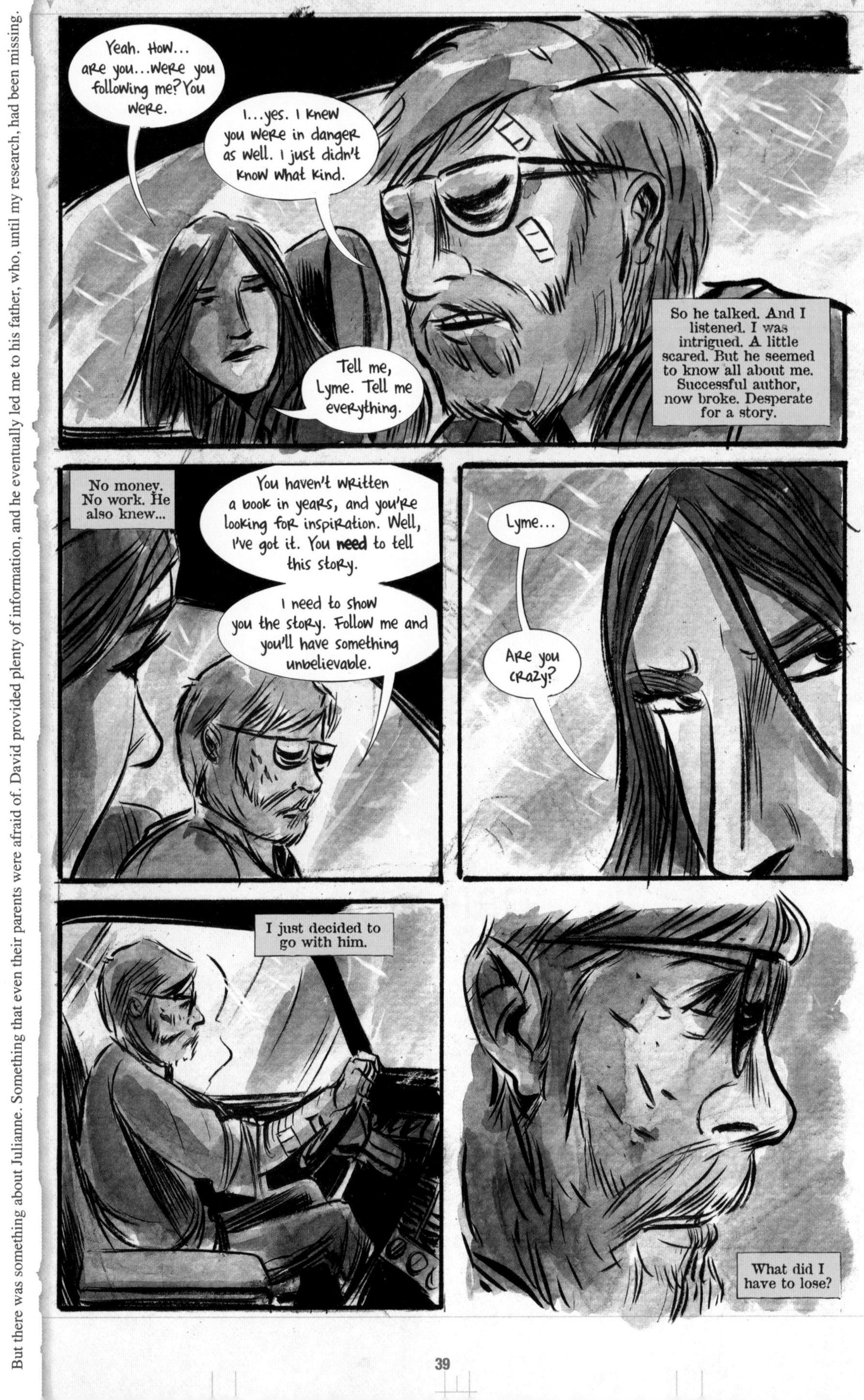

Yeah. How... are you...were you following me? You were.
I...yes. I knew you were in danger as well. I just didn't know what kind.
Tell me, Lyme. Tell me everything.
So he talked. And I listened. I was intrigued. A little scared. But he seemed to know all about me. Successful author, now broke. Desperate for a story.
No money. No work. He also knew...
You haven't written a book in years, and you're looking for inspiration. Well, I've got it. You **need** to tell this story.
I need to show you the story. Follow me and you'll have something unbelievable.
Lyme...
Are you crazy?
I just decided to go with him.
What did I have to lose?

But there was something about Julianne. Something that even their parents were afraid of. David provided plenty of information, and he eventually led me to his father, who, until my research, had been missing.

WHEN FILING REPORT ALL ESSENTIAL DETAILS MUST FALL WITHIN THIS SOLID "LIVE AREA" BOX. THIS IS THE BORDER FOR A STANDARD, NON-BLEED FIELD REPORT

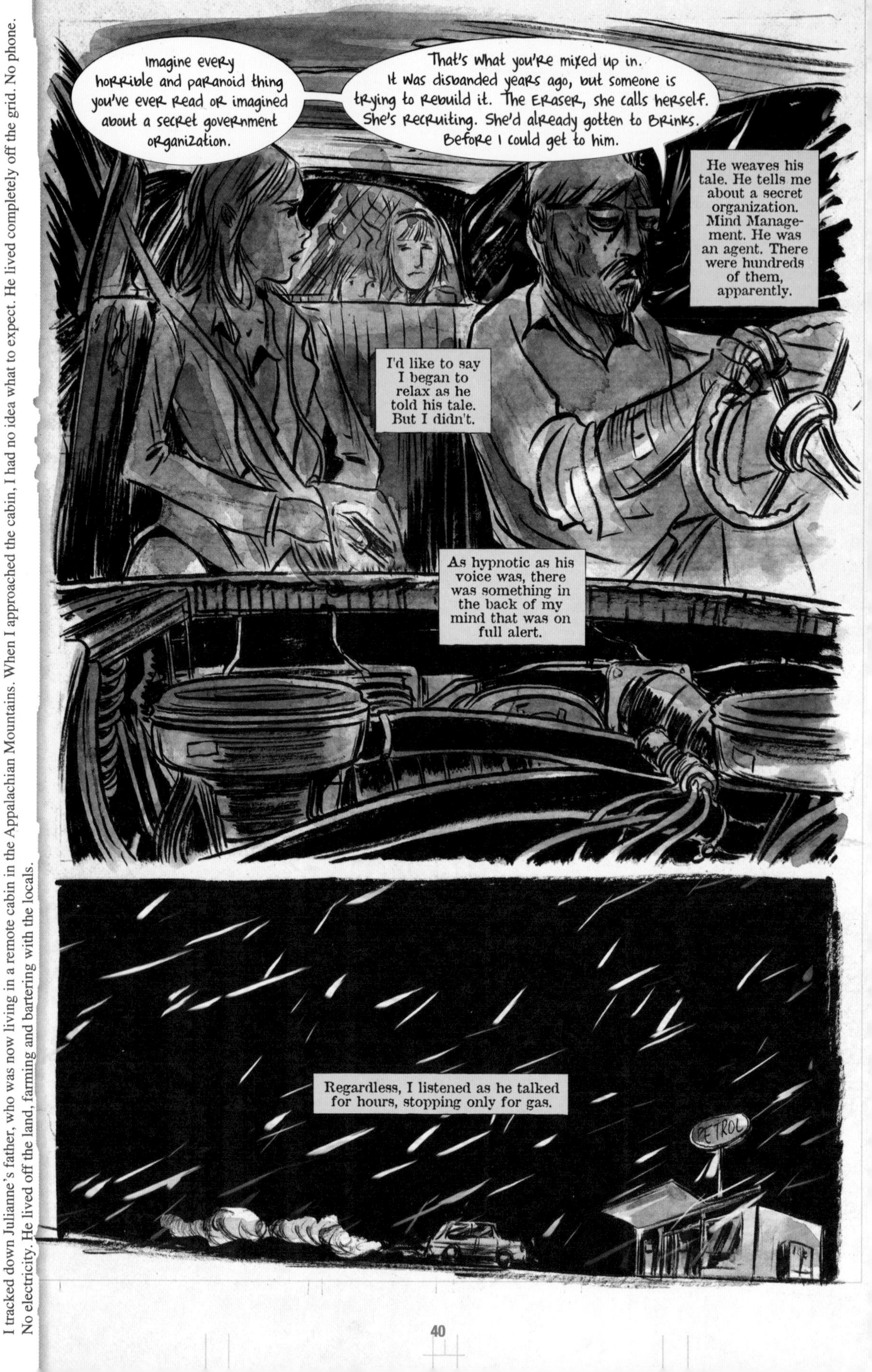
Imagine every horrible and paranoid thing you've ever read or imagined about a secret government organization.
That's what you're mixed up in. It was disbanded years ago, but someone is trying to rebuild it. The Eraser, she calls herself. She's recruiting. She'd already gotten to Brinks. Before I could get to him.
He weaves his tale. He tells me about a secret organization. Mind Management. He was an agent. There were hundreds of them, apparently.
I'd like to say I began to relax as he told his tale. But I didn't.
As hypnotic as his voice was, there was something in the back of my mind that was on full alert.
Regardless, I listened as he talked for hours, stopping only for gas.
PETROL

I tracked down Julianne's father, who was now living in a remote cabin in the Appalachian Mountains. When I approached the cabin, I had no idea what to expect. He lived completely off the grid. No phone. No electricity. He lived off the land, farming and bartering with the locals.

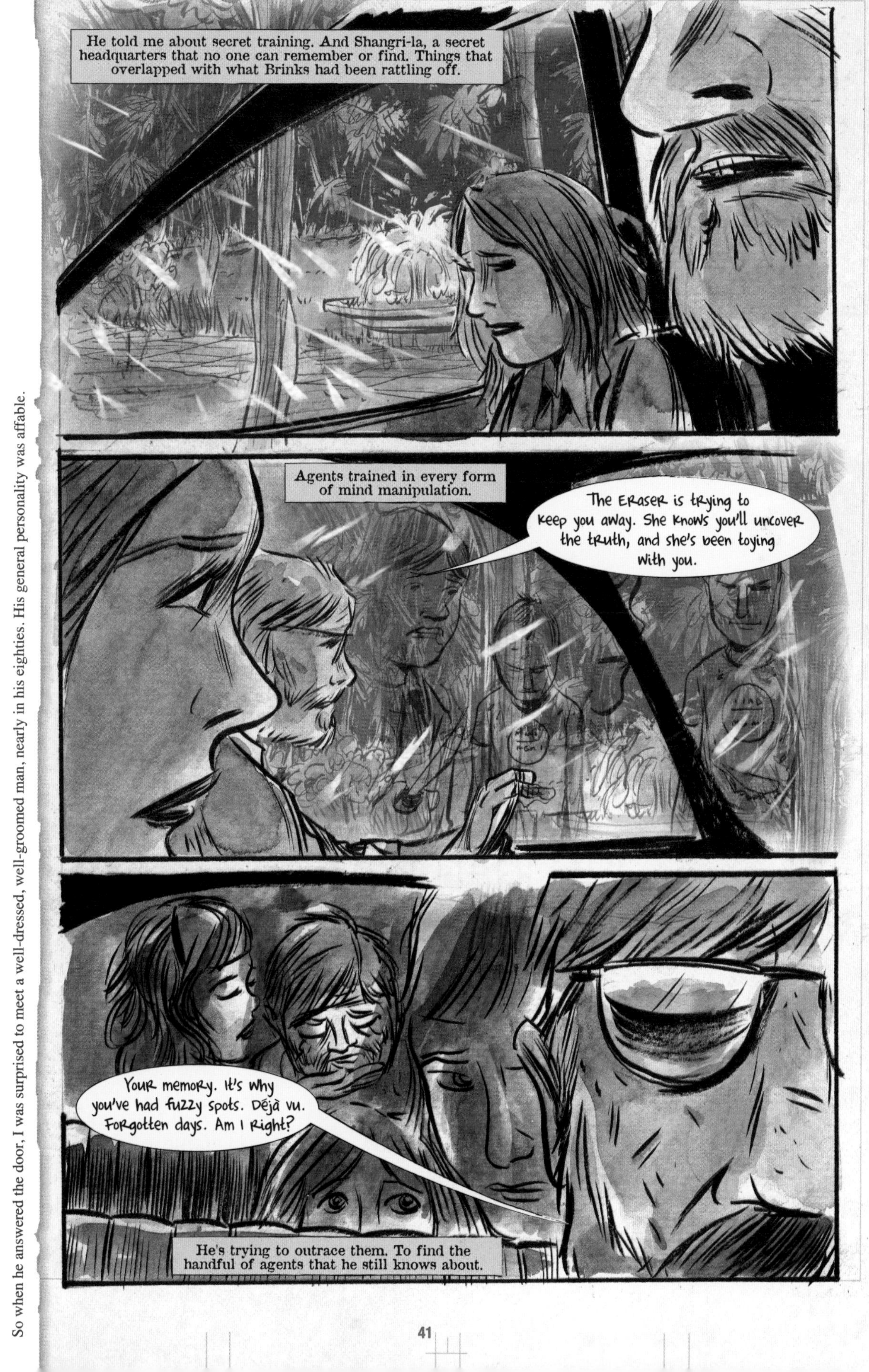
He told me about secret training. And Shangri-la, a secret headquarters that no one can remember or find. Things that overlapped with what Brinks had been rattling off.
Agents trained in every form of mind manipulation.
The Eraser is trying to keep you away. She knows you'll uncover the truth, and she's been toying with you.
Your memory. It's why you've had fuzzy spots. Déjà vu. Forgotten days. Am I right?
He's trying to outrace them. To find the handful of agents that he still knows about.

So when he answered the door, I was surprised to meet a well-dressed, well-groomed man, nearly in his eighties. His general personality was affable.

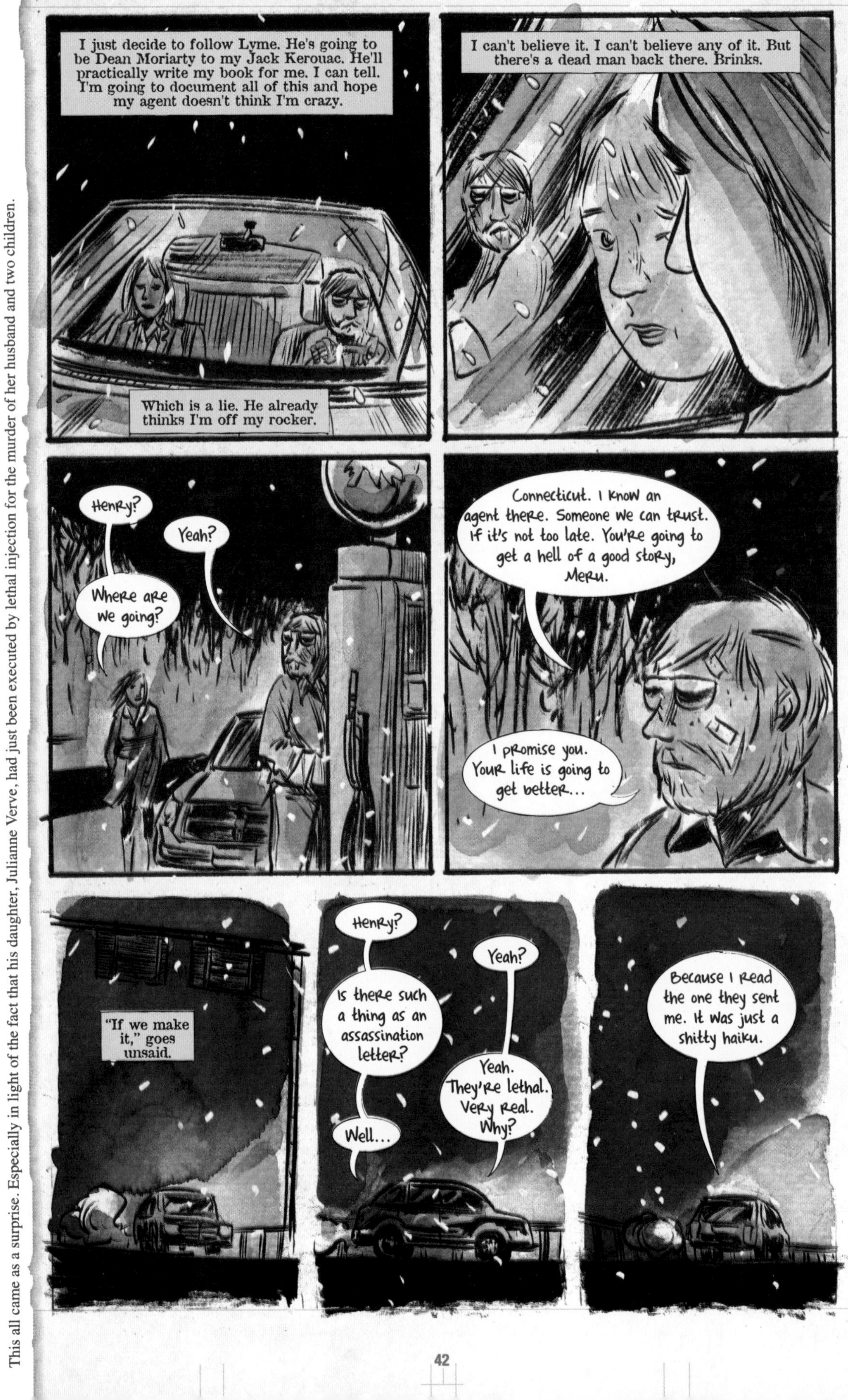
I just decide to follow Lyme. He's going to be Dean Moriarty to my Jack Kerouac. He'll practically write my book for me. I can tell. I'm going to document all of this and hope my agent doesn't think I'm crazy.
Which is a lie. He already thinks I'm off my rocker.
I can't believe it. I can't believe any of it. But there's a dead man back there. Brinks.
Henry?
Yeah?
Where are we going?
Connecticut. I know an agent there. Someone we can trust. If it's not too late. You're going to get a hell of a good story, Meru.
I promise you. Your life is going to get better...
"If we make it," goes unsaid.
Henry?
Yeah?
Is there such a thing as an assassination letter?
Yeah. They're lethal. Very real. Why?
Well...
Because I read the one they sent me. It was just a shitty haiku.

This all came as a surprise. Especially in light of the fact that his daughter, Julianne Verve, had just been executed by lethal injection for the murder of her husband and two children.

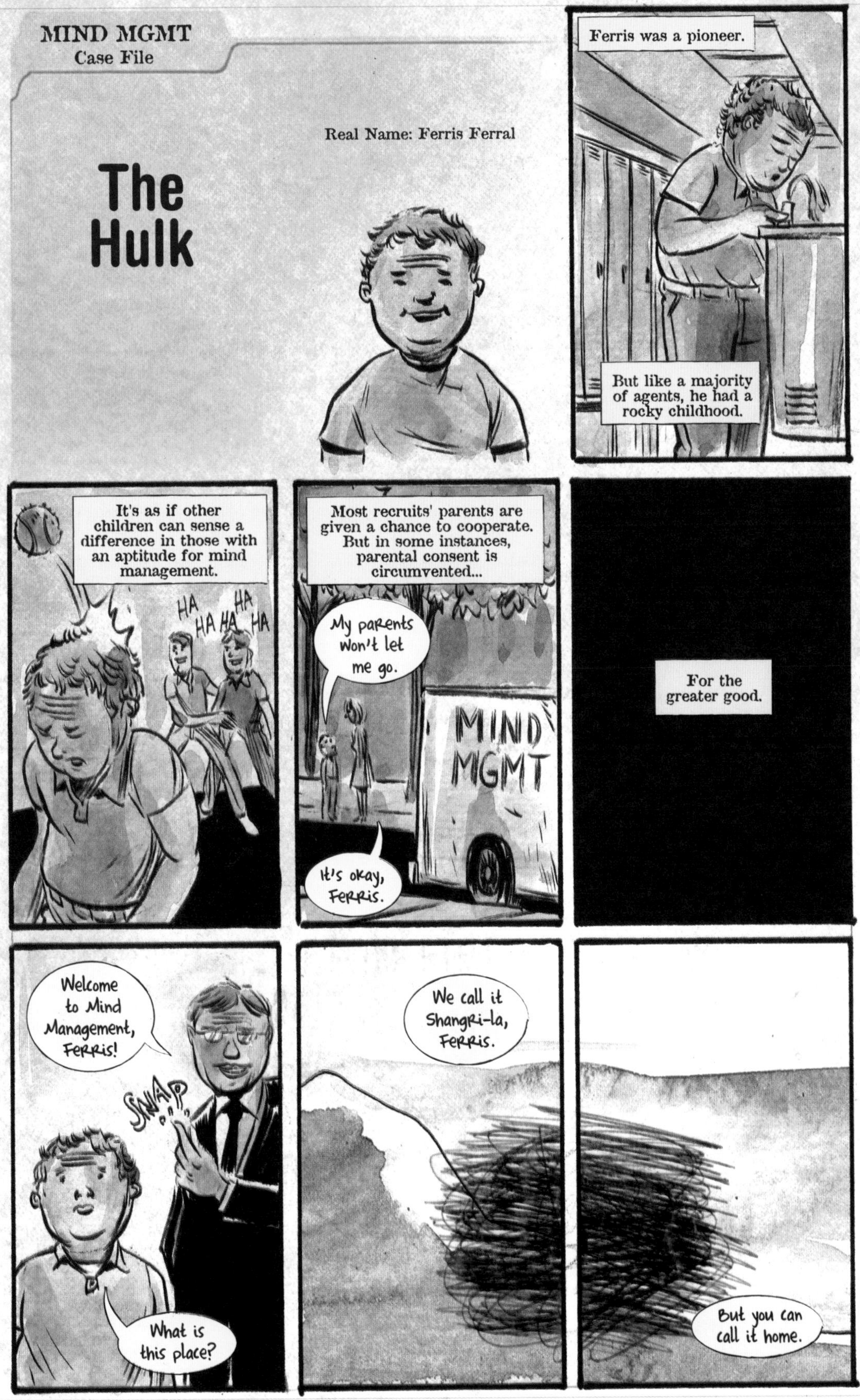
MIND MGMT
Case File
The Hulk
Real Name: Ferris Ferral
Ferris was a pioneer.
But like a majority of agents, he had a rocky childhood.
It's as if other children can sense a difference in those with an aptitude for mind management.
HA HA HA HA HA
Most recruits' parents are given a chance to cooperate. But in some instances, parental consent is circumvented...
My parents won't let me go.
MIND MGMT
It's okay, Ferris.
For the greater good.
Welcome to Mind Management, Ferris!
SNAP
What is this place?
We call it Shangri-la, Ferris.
But you can call it home.

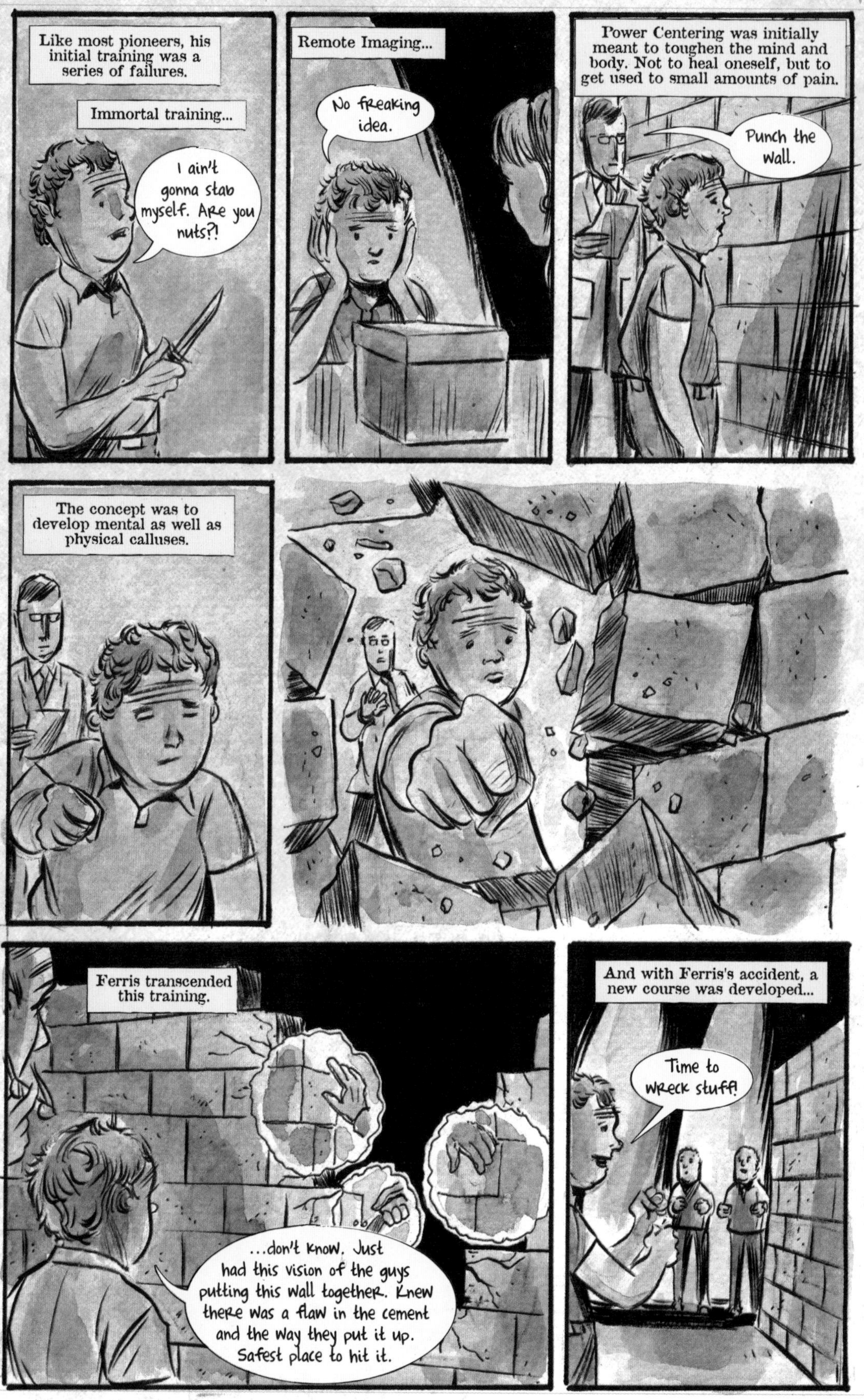
Like most pioneers, his initial training was a series of failures.
Immortal training...
I ain't gonna stab myself. Are you nuts?!
Remote Imaging...
No freaking idea.
Power Centering was initially meant to toughen the mind and body. Not to heal oneself, but to get used to small amounts of pain.
Punch the wall.
The concept was to develop mental as well as physical calluses.
Ferris transcended this training.
...don't know. Just had this vision of the guys putting this wall together. Knew there was a flaw in the cement and the way they put it up. Safest place to hit it.
And with Ferris's accident, a new course was developed...
Time to wreck stuff!

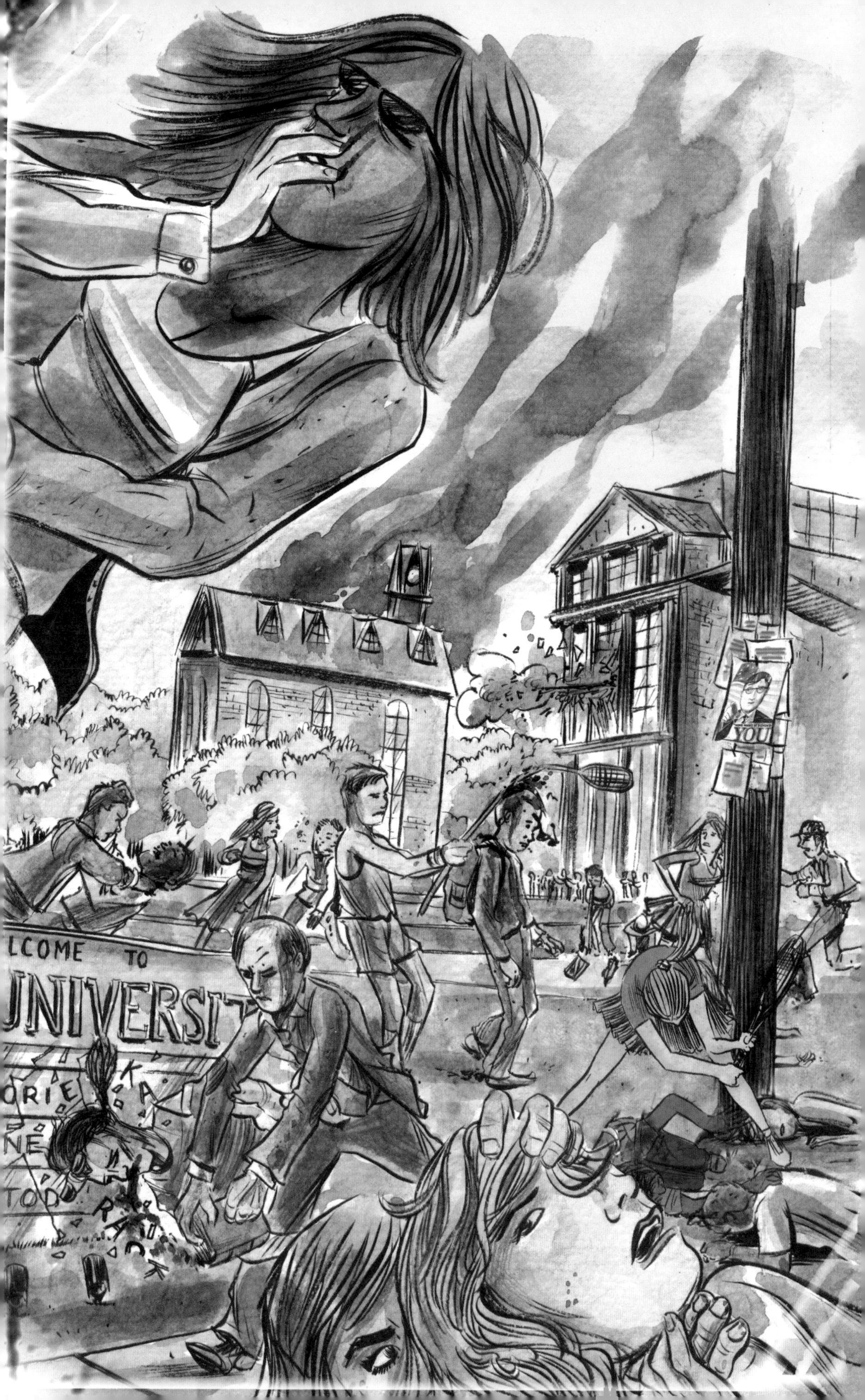
LCOME TO
UNIVERSIT
ORIE
NE
TOD
KA
RACK
YOU

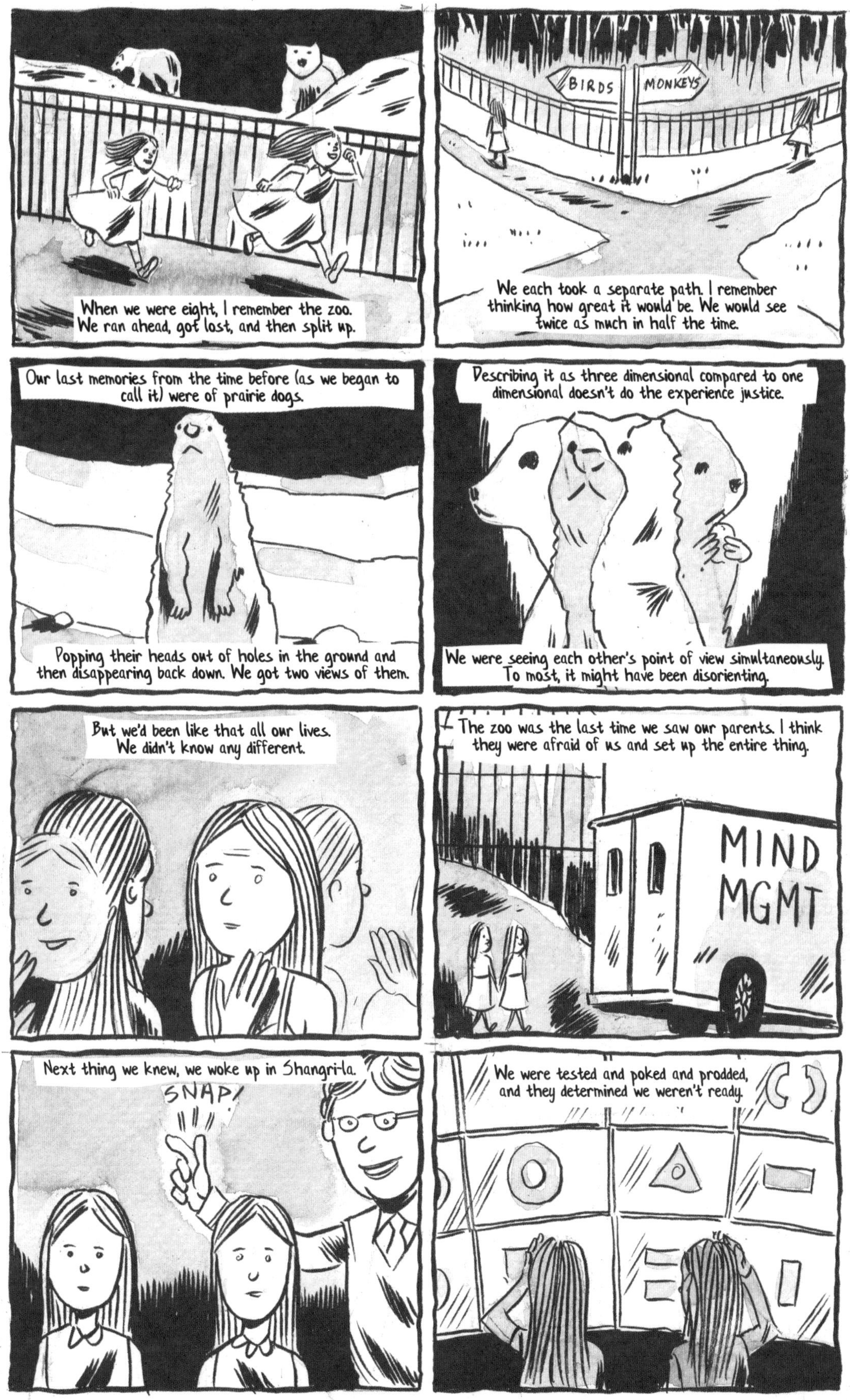

When we were eight, I remember the zoo. We ran ahead, got lost, and then split up.
BIRDS
MONKEYS
We each took a separate path. I remember thinking how great it would be. We would see twice as much in half the time.
Our last memories from the time before (as we began to call it) were of prairie dogs.
Describing it as three dimensional compared to one dimensional doesn't do the experience justice.
Popping their heads out of holes in the ground and then disappearing back down. We got two views of them.
We were seeing each other's point of view simultaneously. To most, it might have been disorienting.
But we'd been like that all our lives. We didn't know any different.
The zoo was the last time we saw our parents. I think they were afraid of us and set up the entire thing.
MIND MGMT
Next thing we knew, we woke up in Shangri-la.
SNAP!
We were tested and poked and prodded, and they determined we weren't ready.

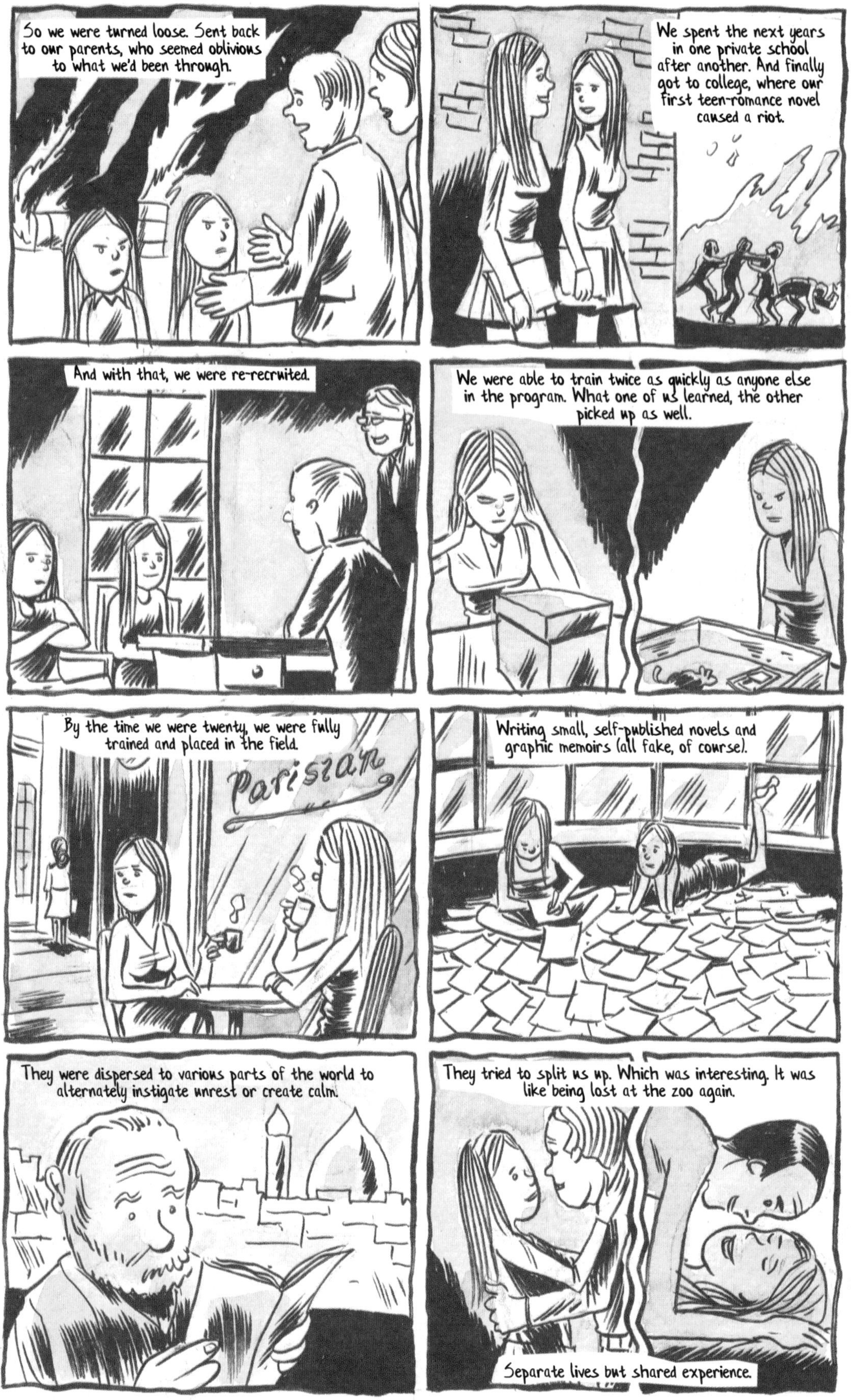
So we were turned loose. Sent back to our parents, who seemed oblivious to what we'd been through.
We spent the next years in one private school after another. And finally got to college, where our first teen-romance novel caused a riot.
And with that, we were re-recruited.
We were able to train twice as quickly as anyone else in the program. What one of us learned, the other picked up as well.
By the time we were twenty, we were fully trained and placed in the field.
Parisian
Writing small, self-published novels and graphic memoirs (all fake, of course).
They were dispersed to various parts of the world to alternately instigate unrest or create calm.
They tried to split us up. Which was interesting. It was like being lost at the zoo again.
Separate lives but shared experience.

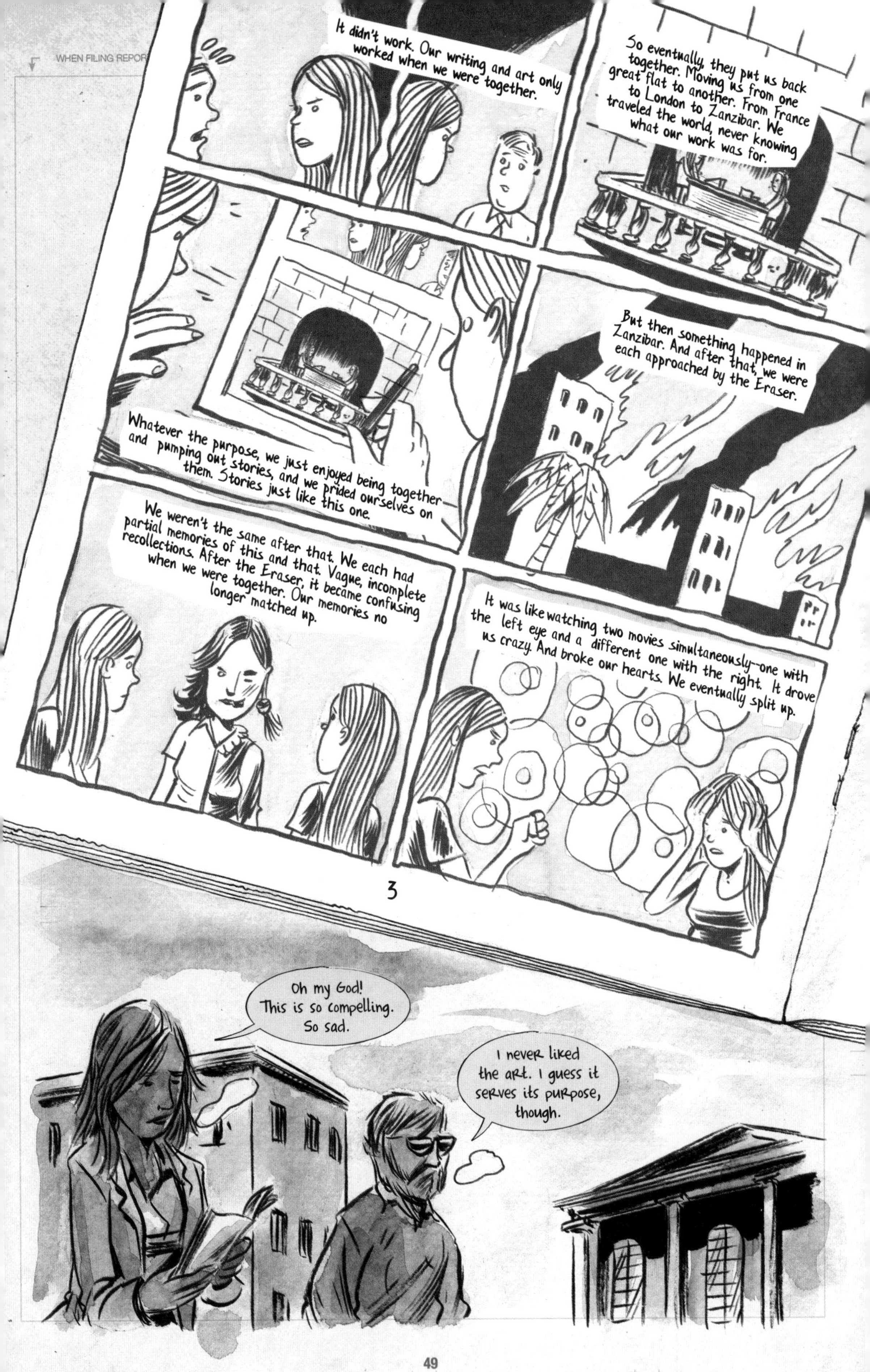
WHEN FILING REPOR
It didn't work. Our writing and art only worked when we were together.
So eventually, they put us back together. Moving us from one great flat to another. From France to London to Zanzibar. We traveled the world, never knowing what our work was for.
Whatever the purpose, we just enjoyed being together and pumping out stories, and we prided ourselves on them. Stories just like this one.
But then something happened in Zanzibar. And after that, we were each approached by the Eraser.
We weren't the same after that. We each had partial memories of this and that. Vague, incomplete recollections. After the Eraser, it became confusing when we were together. Our memories no longer matched up.
It was like watching two movies simultaneously—one with the left eye and a different one with the right. It drove us crazy. And broke our hearts. We eventually split up.
3
Oh my God! This is so compelling. So sad.
I never liked the art. I guess it serves its purpose, though.

WHEN FILING REPORT ALL ESSENTIAL DETAILS MUST FALL WITHIN THIS SOLID "LIVE AREA" BOX. THIS IS THE BORDER FOR A STANDARD, NON-BLEED FIELD REPORT

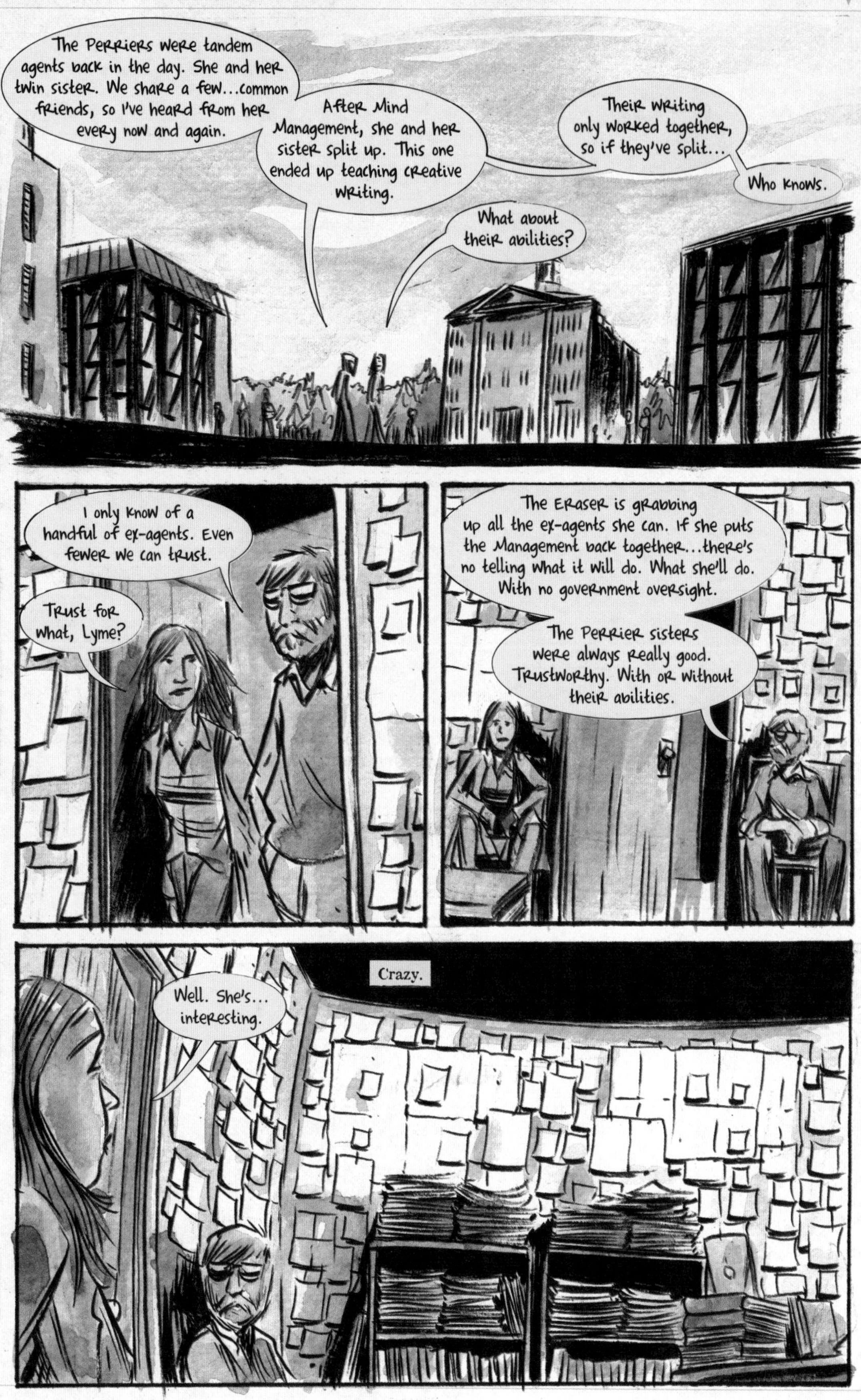

The Perriers were tandem agents back in the day. She and her twin sister. We share a few...common friends, so I've heard from her every now and again.
After Mind Management, she and her sister split up. This one ended up teaching creative writing.
Their writing only worked together, so if they've split...
Who knows.
What about their abilities?
I only know of a handful of ex-agents. Even fewer we can trust.
Trust for what, Lyme?
The Eraser is grabbing up all the ex-agents she can. If she puts the Management back together...there's no telling what it will do. What she'll do. With no government oversight.
The Perrier sisters were always really good. Trustworthy. With or without their abilities.
Crazy.
Well. She's... interesting.

Premeditated A True Crime Novel (continued)

Julianne Verve had killed her husband and two children. That wasn't the mystery. The mystery was always her motivation. What tapestry, what collage of experiences had she amassed that made her a killer?

That was my goal when I finally tracked down Julianne's father. I put pointed questions to him, and he was more than happy to answer. I found that he was not evasive or hesitant in the least. He spoke without guilt.

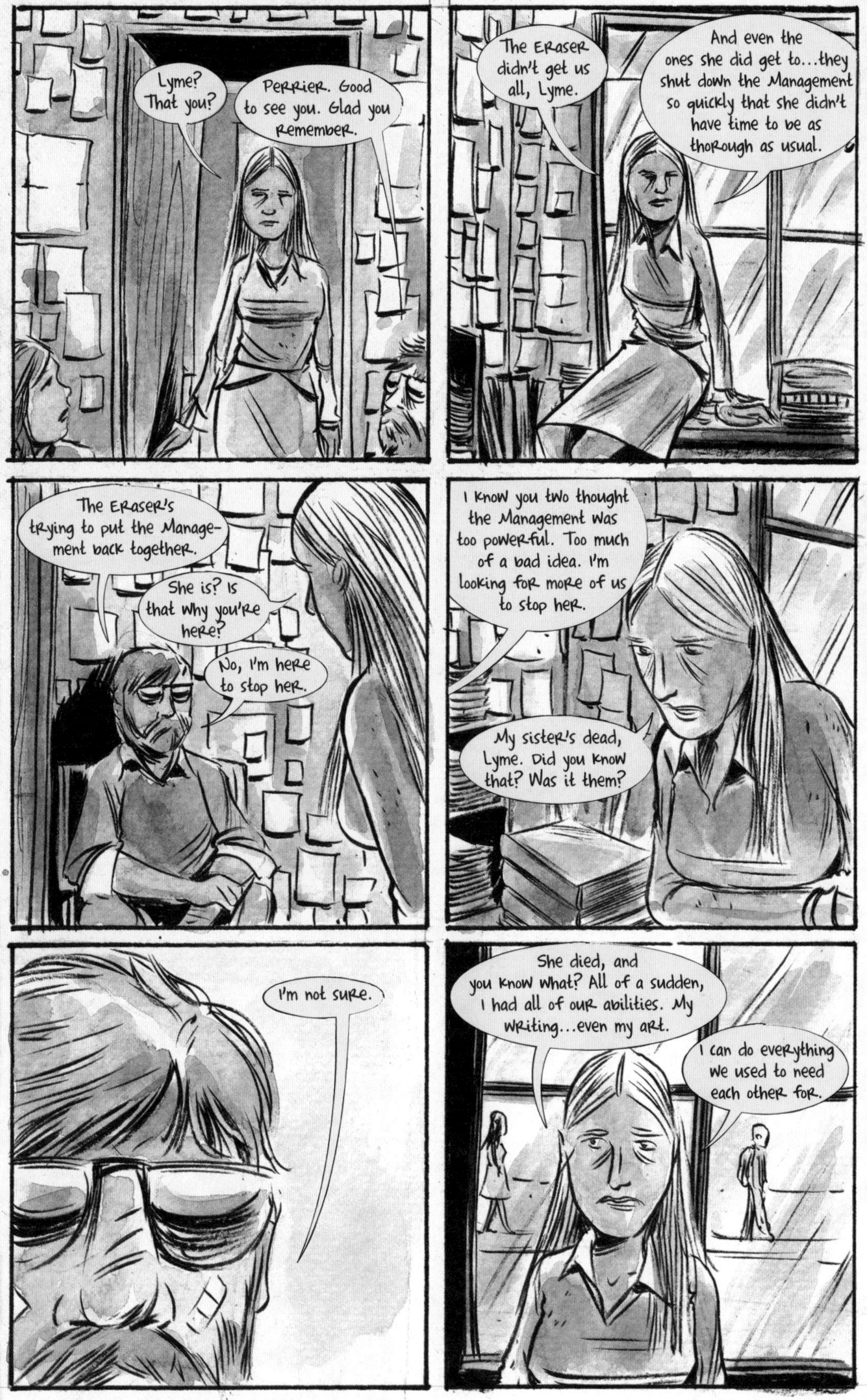
Lyme? That you?
Perrier. Good to see you. Glad you remember.
The Eraser didn't get us all, Lyme.
And even the ones she did get to...they shut down the Management so quickly that she didn't have time to be as thorough as usual.
The Eraser's trying to put the Management back together.
She is? Is that why you're here?
No, I'm here to stop her.
I know you two thought the Management was too powerful. Too much of a bad idea. I'm looking for more of us to stop her.
My sister's dead, Lyme. Did you know that? Was it them?
I'm not sure.
She died, and you know what? All of a sudden, I had all of our abilities. My writing...even my art.
I can do everything we used to need each other for.

WHEN FILING REPORT ALL ESSENTIAL DETAILS MUST FALL WITHIN THIS SOLID "LIVE AREA" BOX. THIS IS THE BORDER FOR A STANDARD, NON-BLEED FIELD REPORT

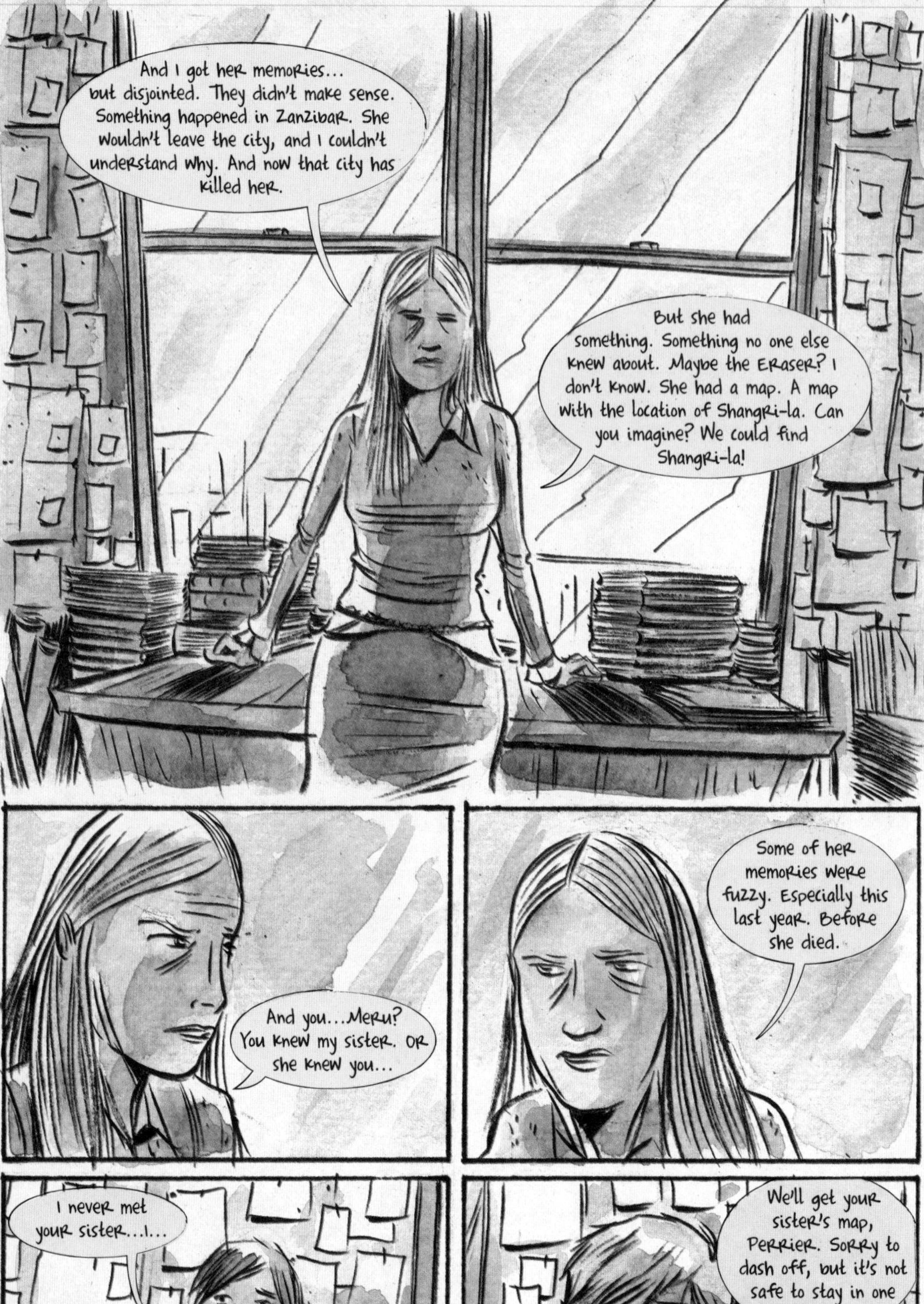

He told me of his daughter's youth. Of her sadistic manipulation of the family unit. Of her incestuous relationship with her brother. He was relaxed throughout the entire interview. Strangely so, I thought.

WHEN FILING REPORT ALL ESSENTIAL DETAILS MUST FALL WITHIN THIS SOLID "LIVE AREA" BOX. THIS IS THE BORDER FOR A STANDARD, NON-BLEED FIELD REPORT

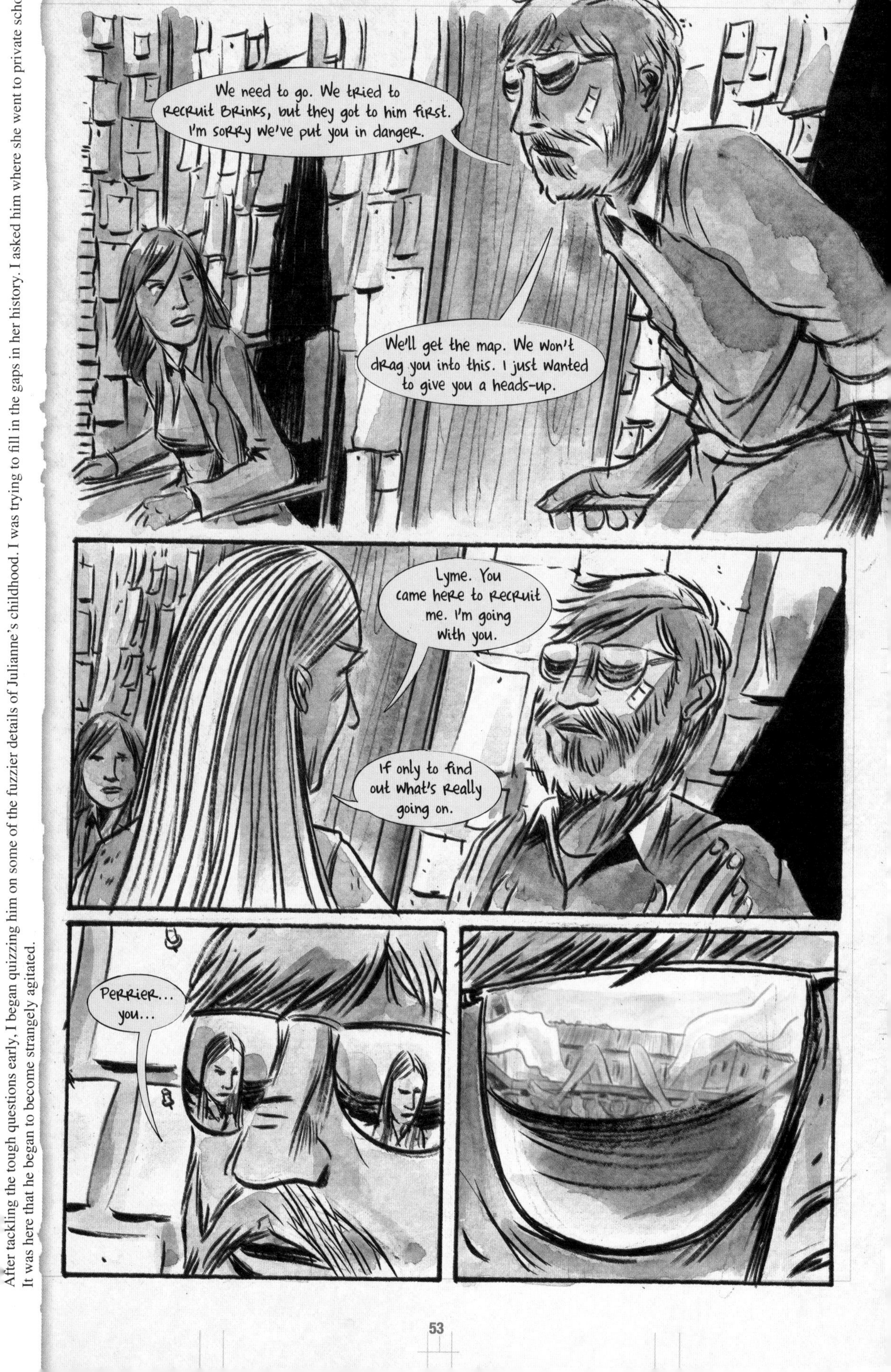
We need to go. We tried to recruit Brinks, but they got to him first. I'm sorry we've put you in danger.
We'll get the map. We won't drag you into this. I just wanted to give you a heads-up.
Lyme. You came here to recruit me. I'm going with you.
If only to find out what's really going on.
Perrier... you...

After tackling the tough questions early, I began quizzing him on some of the fuzzier details of Julianne's childhood. I was trying to fill in the gaps in her history. I asked him where she went to private school. It was here that he began to become strangely agitated.

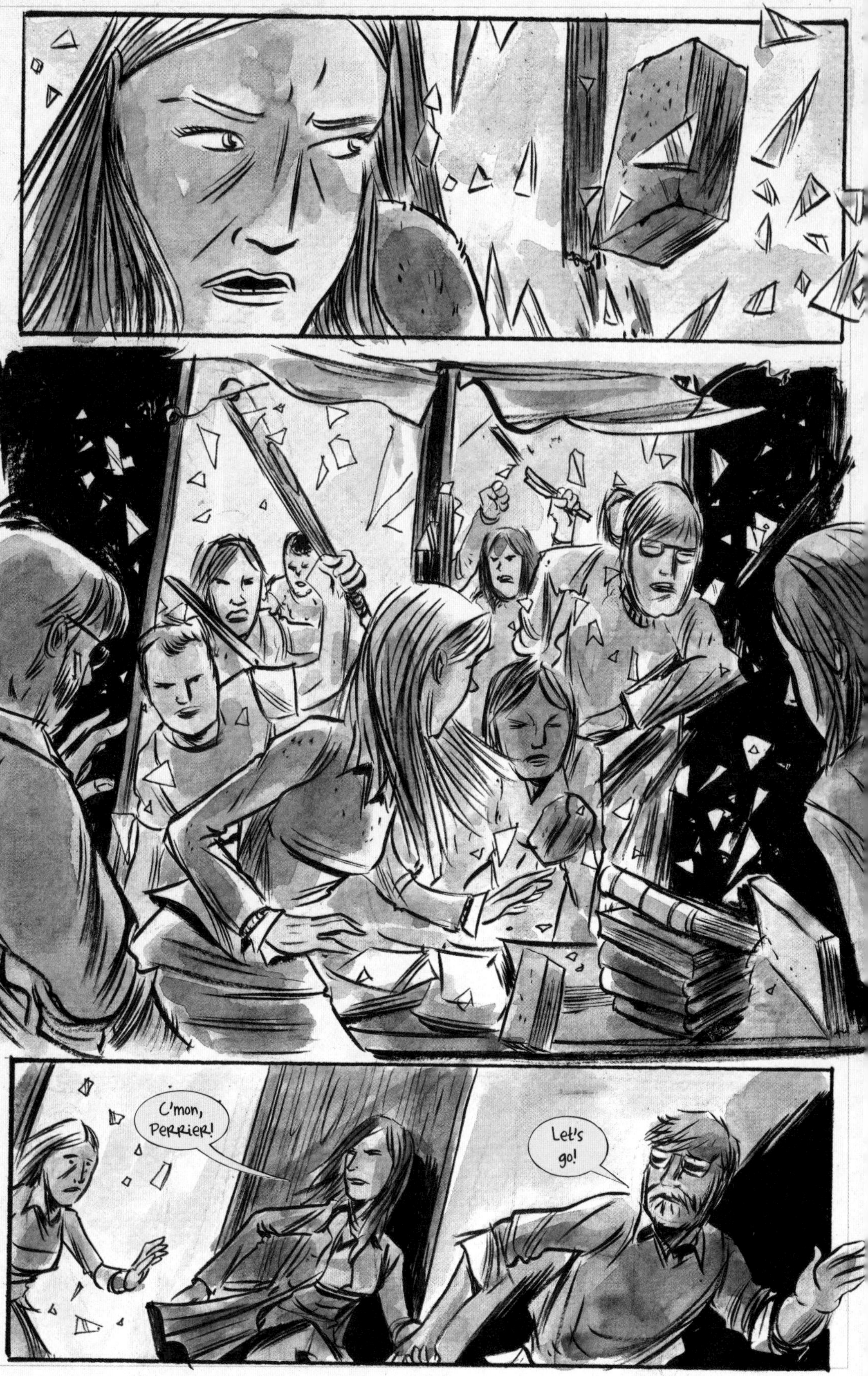
C'mon, PERRIER!
Let's go!

"I don't fucking remember!" he shouted. I tensed up as he rose from his chair and moved toward me. It was as if the question flipped a switch, causing him to become enraged and incoherent.

WHEN FILING REPORT ALL ESSENTIAL DETAILS MUST FALL WITHIN THIS SOLID "LIVE AREA" BOX. THIS IS THE BORDER FOR A STANDARD, NON-BLEED FIELD REPORT

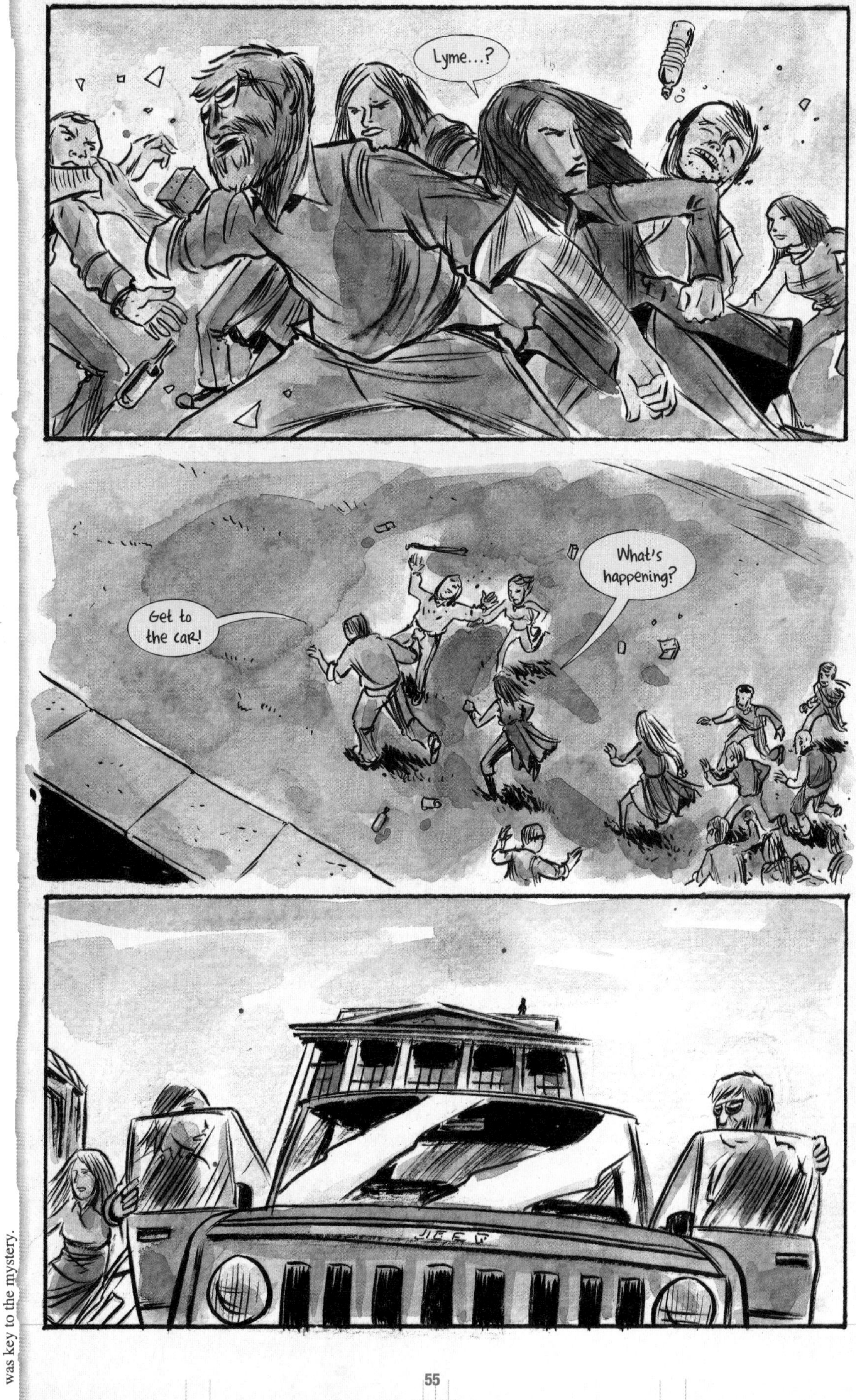
Lyme...?
Get to the car!
What's happening?
JEEP

At this point, he literally chased me from the cabin. I fled to my car and pulled away, even as he continued to give chase, shaking his fist and cursing. It was this incident that made me realize that Julianne's schooling was key to the mystery.

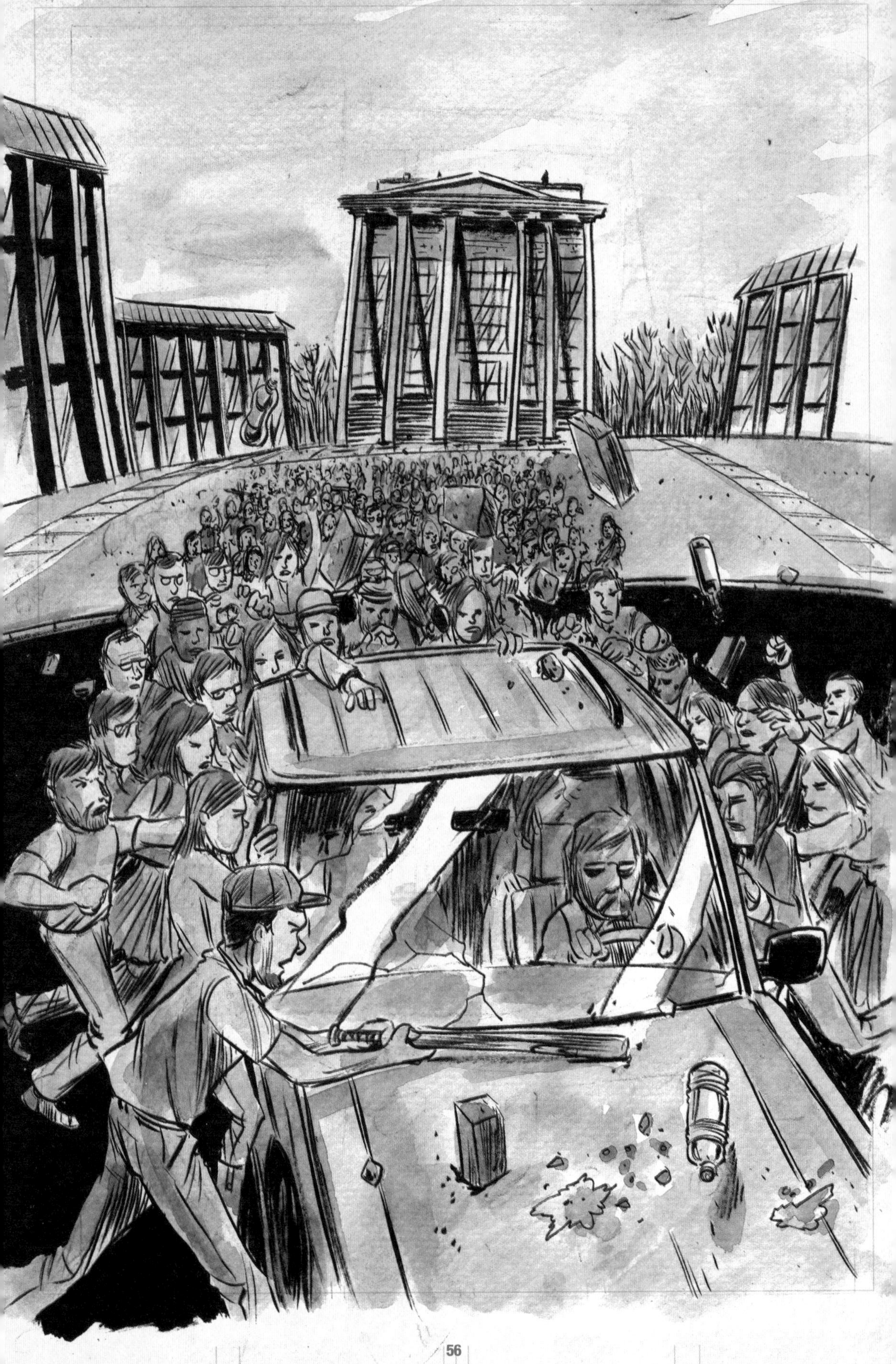

WHEN FILING REPORT ALL ESSENTIAL DETAILS MUST FALL WITHIN THIS SOLID "LIVE AREA" BOX. THIS IS THE BORDER FOR A STANDARD, NON-BLEED FIELD REPORT

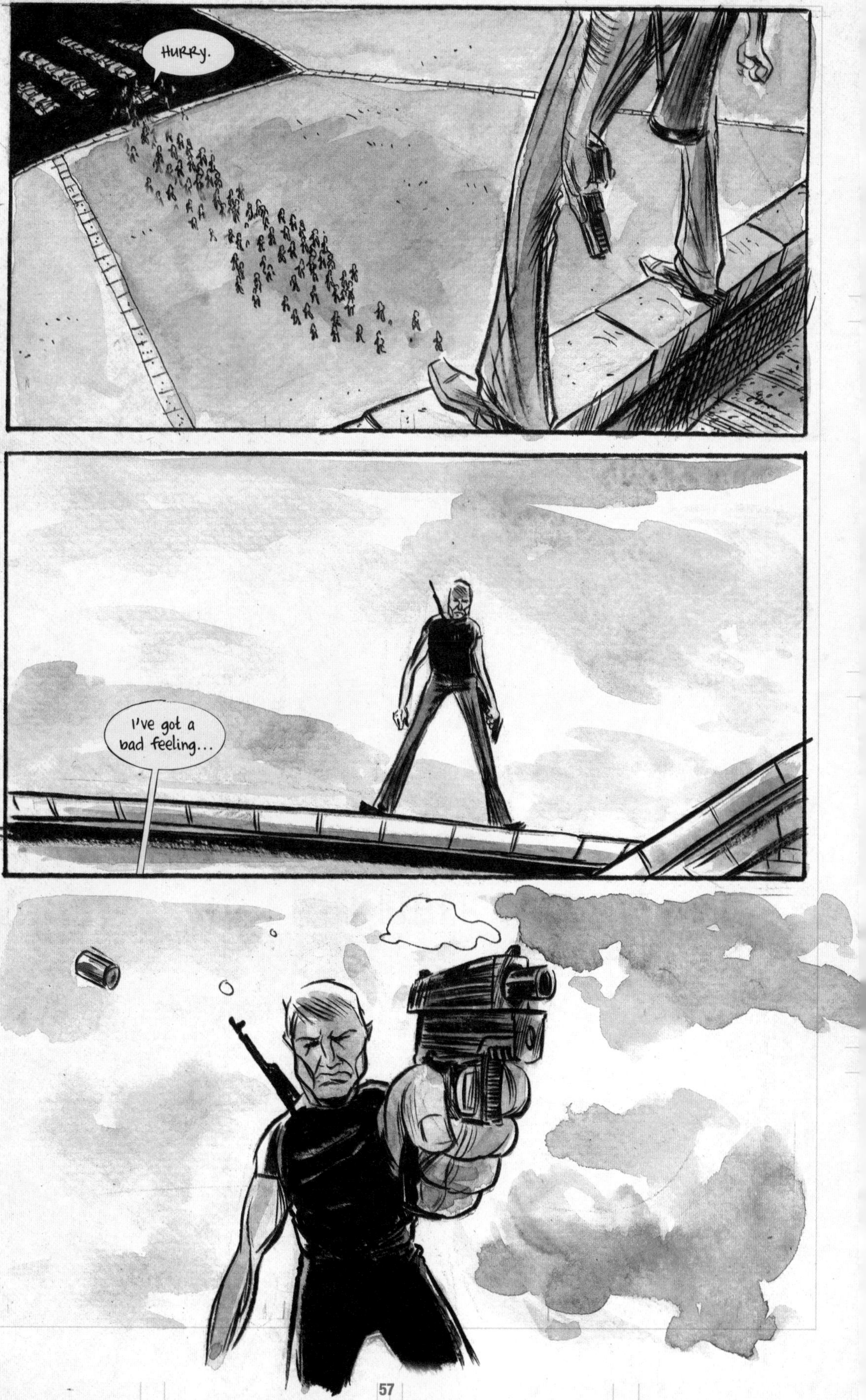
HURRY.
I've got a bad feeling...

I dug into all of her available records. She attended an exclusive preschool, from which she was expelled after just three weeks.

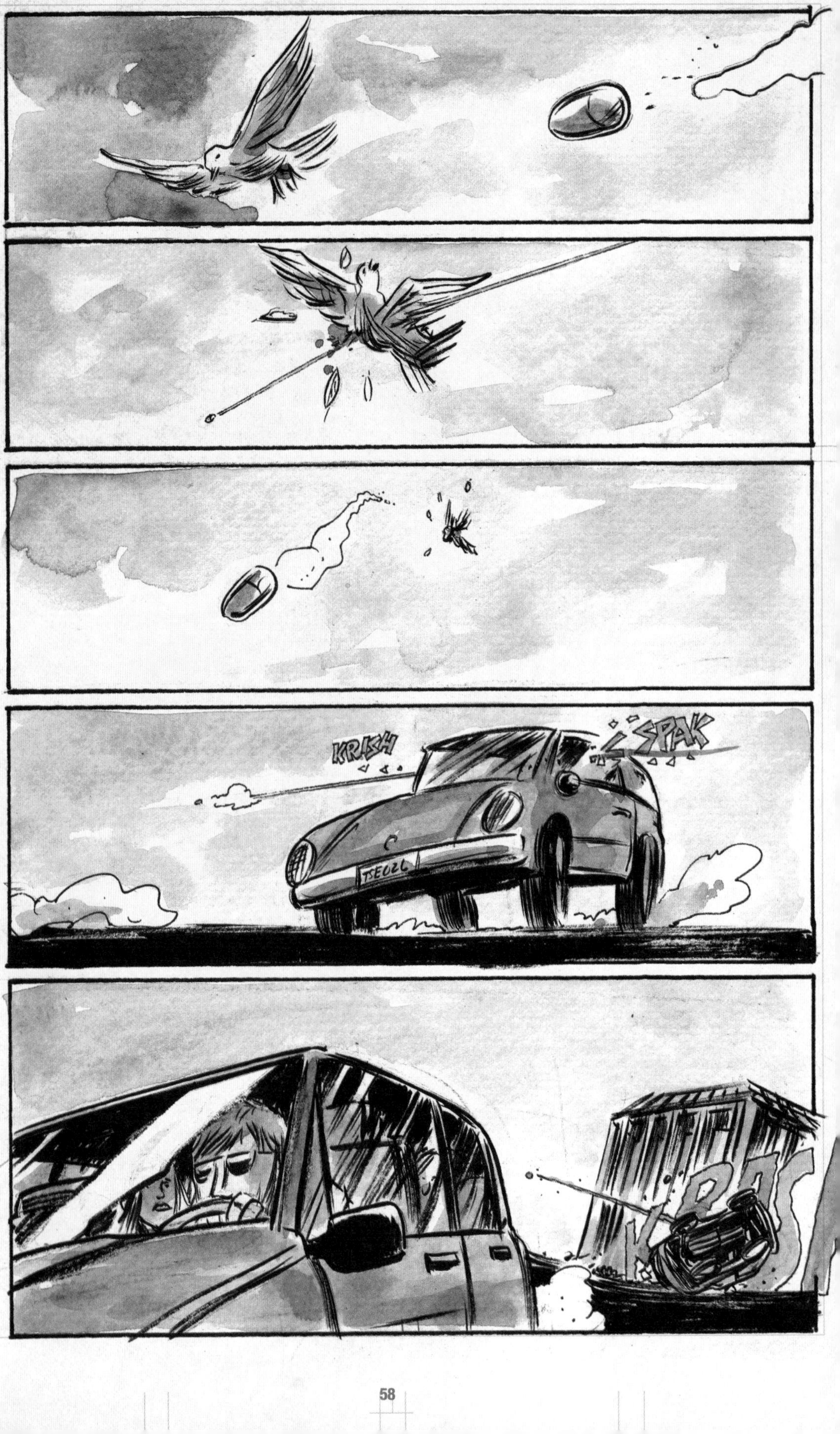
KRISH
SPAK
TSE026

According to the school's records, one day Julianne and a male student captured a cat at recess. The report is vague, but alludes to the fact that Julianne and the boy eviscerated the cat.

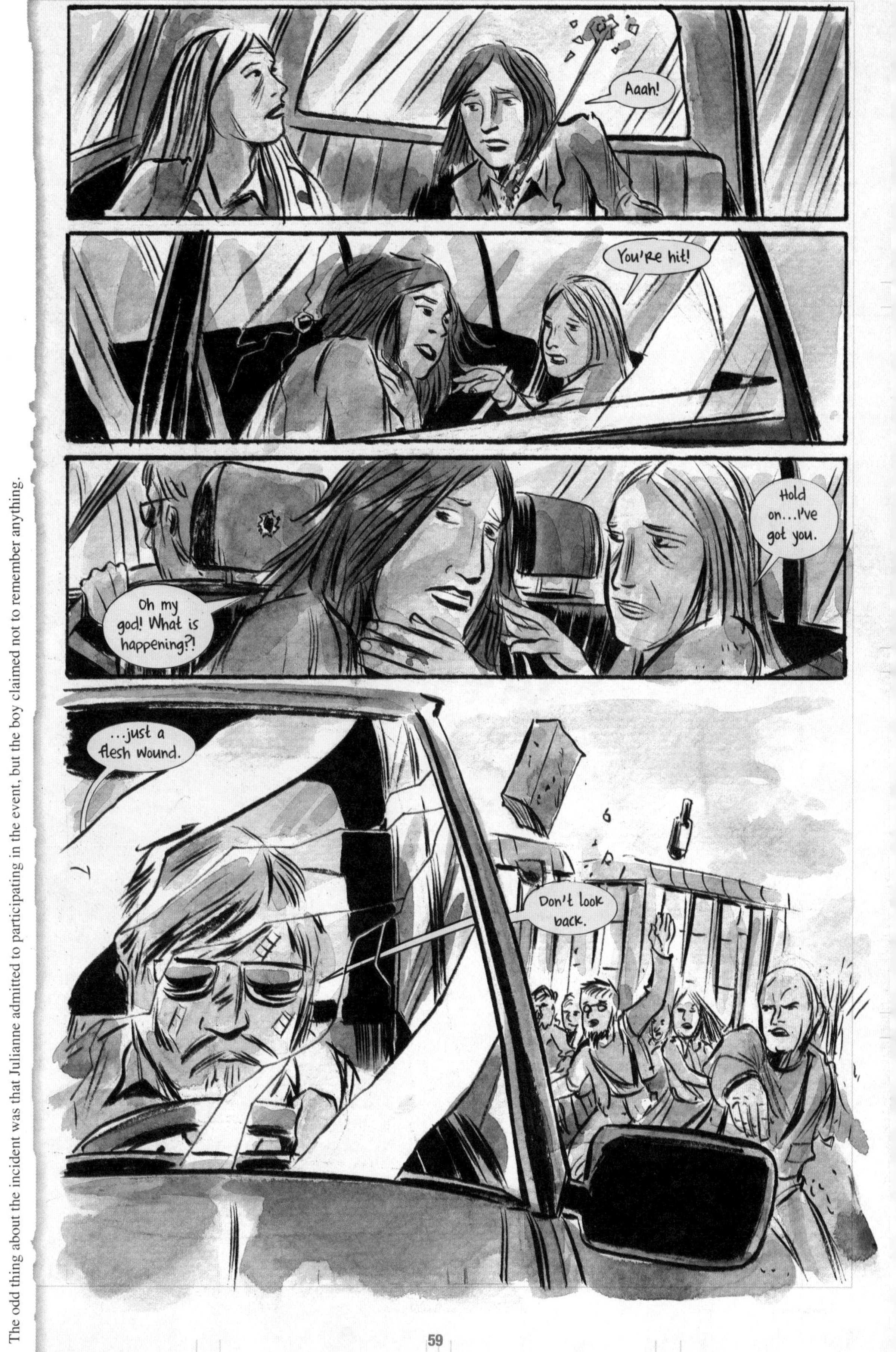
Aaah!
You're hit!
Hold on...I've got you.
Oh my god! What is happening?!
...just a flesh wound.
Don't look back.

The odd thing about the incident was that Julianne admitted to participating in the event, but the boy claimed not to remember anything.

WHEN FILING REPORT ALL ESSENTIAL DETAILS MUST FALL WITHIN THIS SOLID "LIVE AREA" BOX. THIS IS THE BORDER FOR A STANDARD, NON-BLEED FIELD REPORT

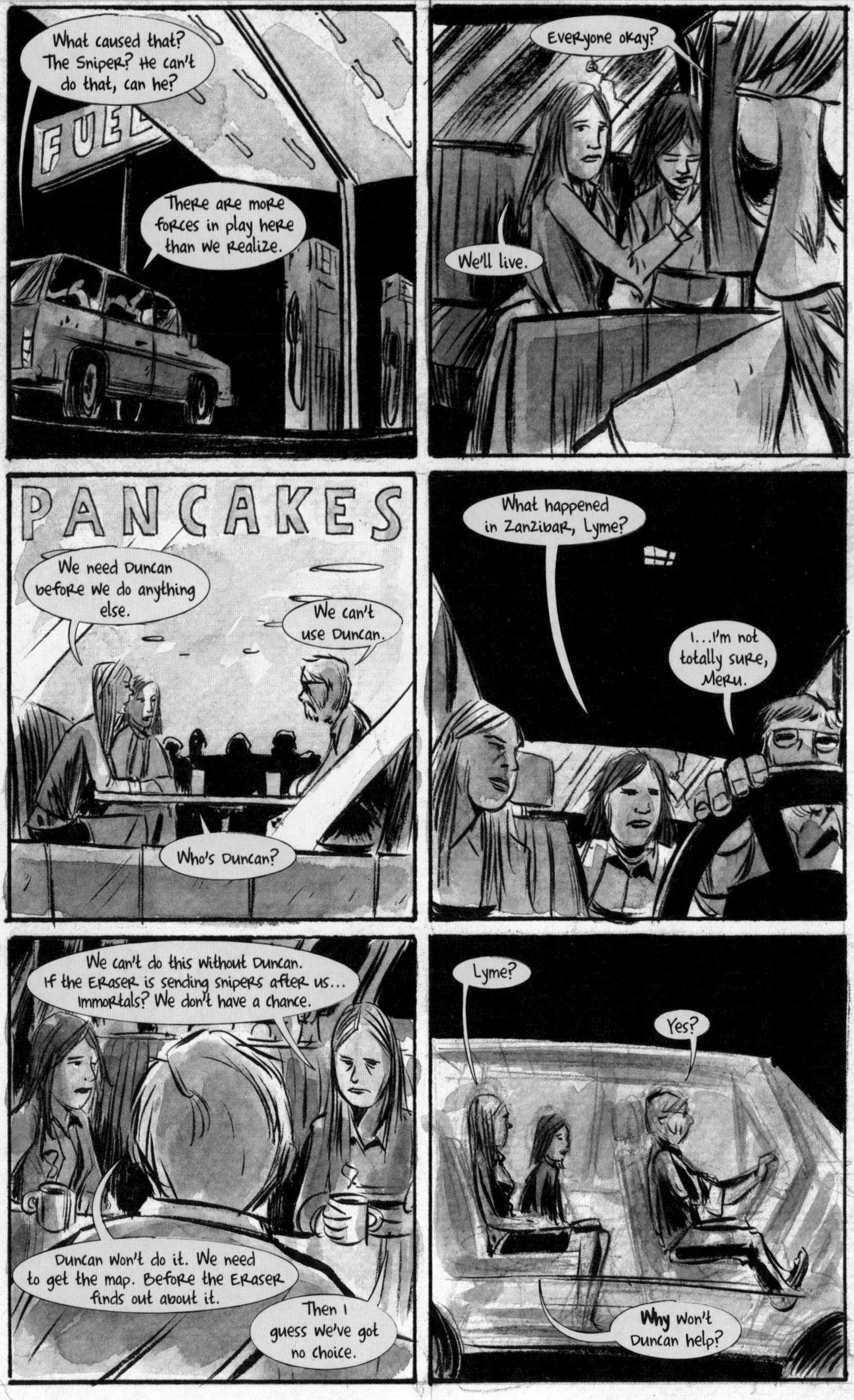

What caused that? The Sniper? He can't do that, can he?
FUEL
There are more forces in play here than we realize.
Everyone okay?
We'll live.
PANCAKES
We need Duncan before we do anything else.
We can't use Duncan.
Who's Duncan?
What happened in Zanzibar, Lyme?
I...I'm not totally sure, Meru.
We can't do this without Duncan. If the Eraser is sending snipers after us... Immortals? We don't have a chance.
Duncan won't do it. We need to get the map. Before the Eraser finds out about it.
Then I guess we've got no choice.
Lyme?
Yes?
Why won't Duncan help?

I spent the next six weeks traveling the country, following the trail of Julianne's school career, reading as she was accepted and then expelled from one school after another.

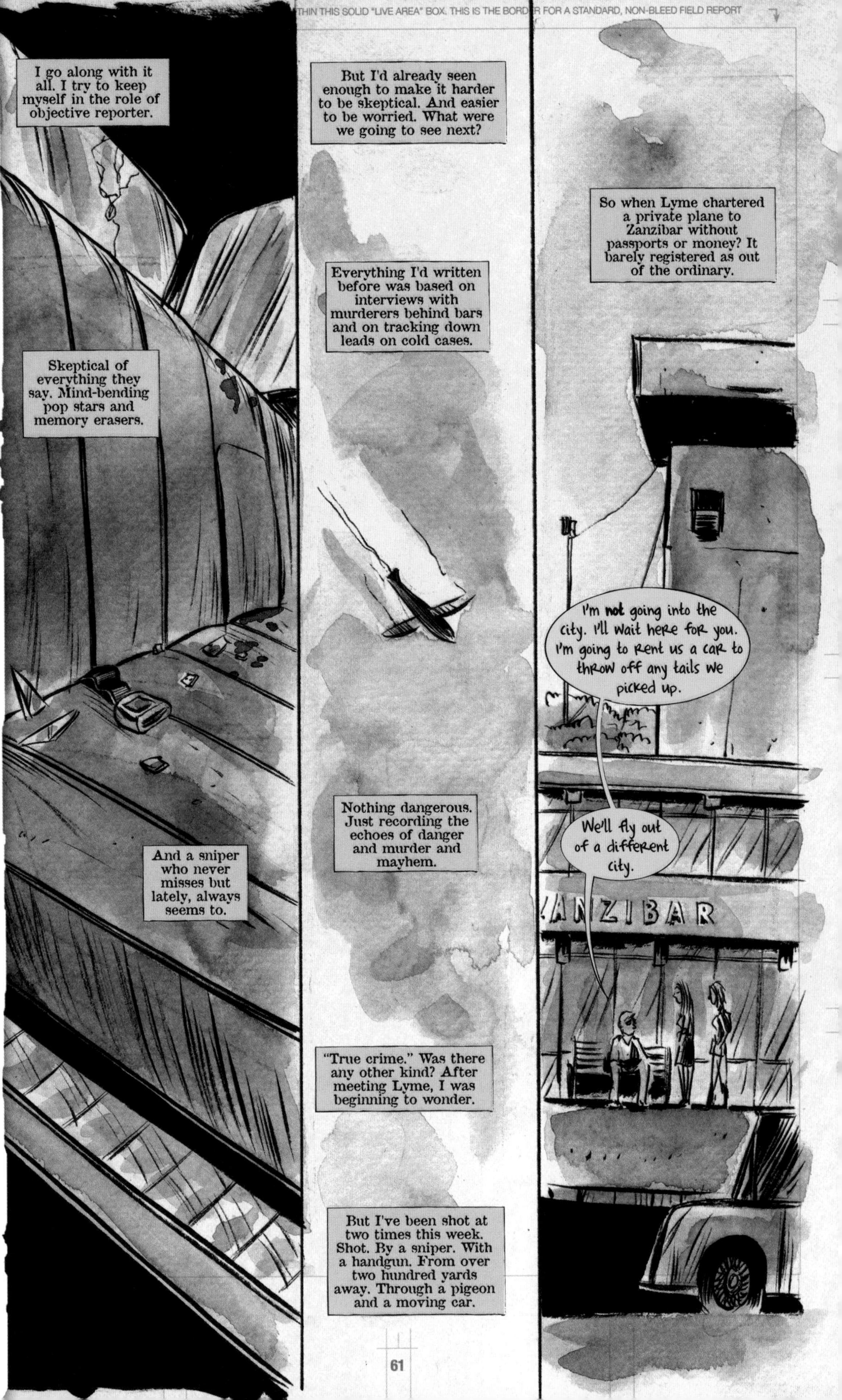
THIN THIS SOLID "LIVE AREA" BOX. THIS IS THE BORDER FOR A STANDARD, NON-BLEED FIELD REPORT
I go along with it all. I try to keep myself in the role of objective reporter.
Skeptical of everything they say. Mind-bending pop stars and memory erasers.
And a sniper who never misses but lately, always seems to.
But I'd already seen enough to make it harder to be skeptical. And easier to be worried. What were we going to see next?
Everything I'd written before was based on interviews with murderers behind bars and on tracking down leads on cold cases.
Nothing dangerous. Just recording the echoes of danger and murder and mayhem.
"True crime." Was there any other kind? After meeting Lyme, I was beginning to wonder.
But I've been shot at two times this week. Shot. By a sniper. With a handgun. From over two hundred yards away. Through a pigeon and a moving car.
So when Lyme chartered a private plane to Zanzibar without passports or money? It barely registered as out of the ordinary.
I'm not going into the city. I'll wait here for you. I'm going to rent us a car to throw off any tails we picked up.
We'll fly out of a different city.
ZANZIBAR

During all of the travel, a picture emerged of a troubled child, even at a young age. However, when interviewing her old teachers, they all had the same opinion of her: "Unremarkable."

WHEN FILING REPORT ALL ESSENTIAL DETAILS MUST FALL WITHIN THIS SOLID "LIVE AREA" BO... IS THE BORDER FOR A STANDARD, NON-BLEED FIELD REPORT.

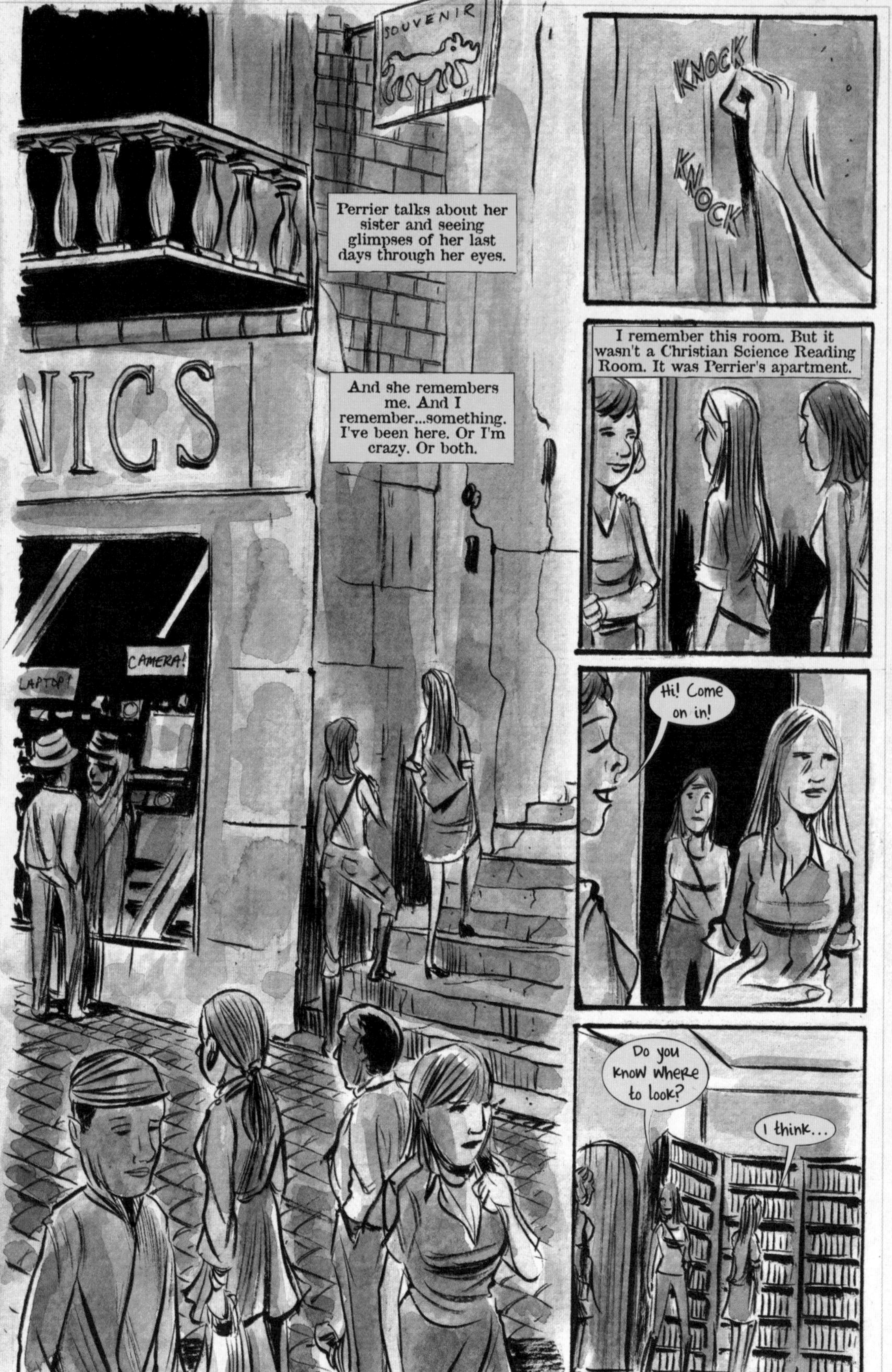
SOUVENIR
VICS
CAMERA!
LAPTOP!
Perrier talks about her sister and seeing glimpses of her last days through her eyes.
And she remembers me. And I remember...something. I've been here. Or I'm crazy. Or both.
KNOCK
KNOCK
I remember this room. But it wasn't a Christian Science Reading Room. It was Perrier's apartment.
Hi! Come on in!
Do you know where to look?
I think...

But I did discover something remarkable. From age sixteen to twenty, there is no record of Julianne's schooling. It's as if she dropped off the face of the Earth. There were no medical records. No criminal reports. Nothing.

Staring at her past and talking to her family was like seeing a life that you are expecting to see but also getting the sense that you're staring through something. A ghost or a shadow history that is right in front of you but that you can't quite see.

WHEN FILING REPORT ALL ESSENTIAL DETAILS MUST FALL WITHIN THIS SOLID "LIVE AREA" BOX. THIS IS THE BORDER FOR A STANDARD, NON-BLEED FIELD REPORT

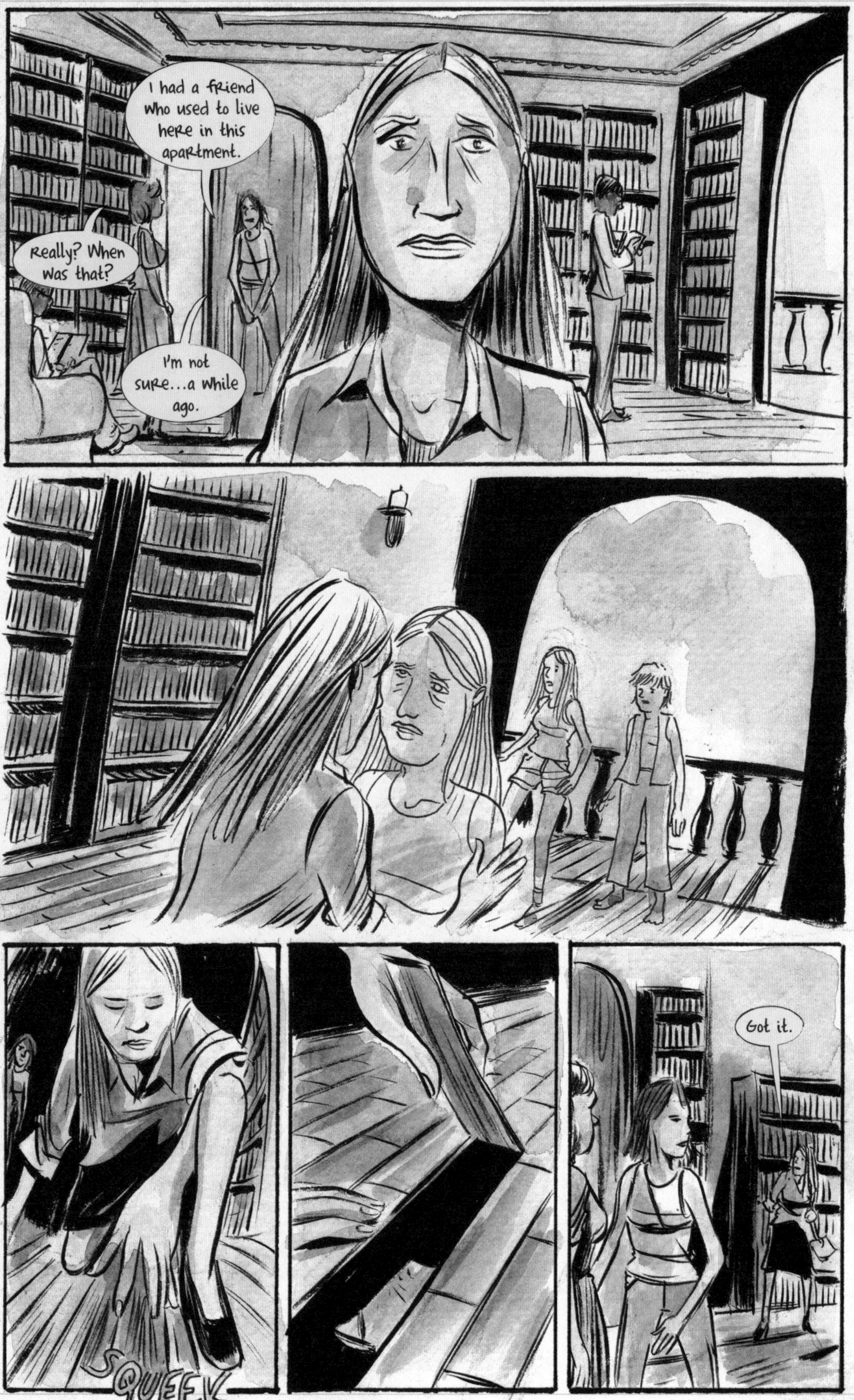
I had a friend who used to live here in this apartment.
Really? When was that?
I'm not sure...a while ago.
SQUEEK
Got it.

I still felt like her father was the key. And with the road map of her childhood I'd compiled, I felt I could question him one more time.

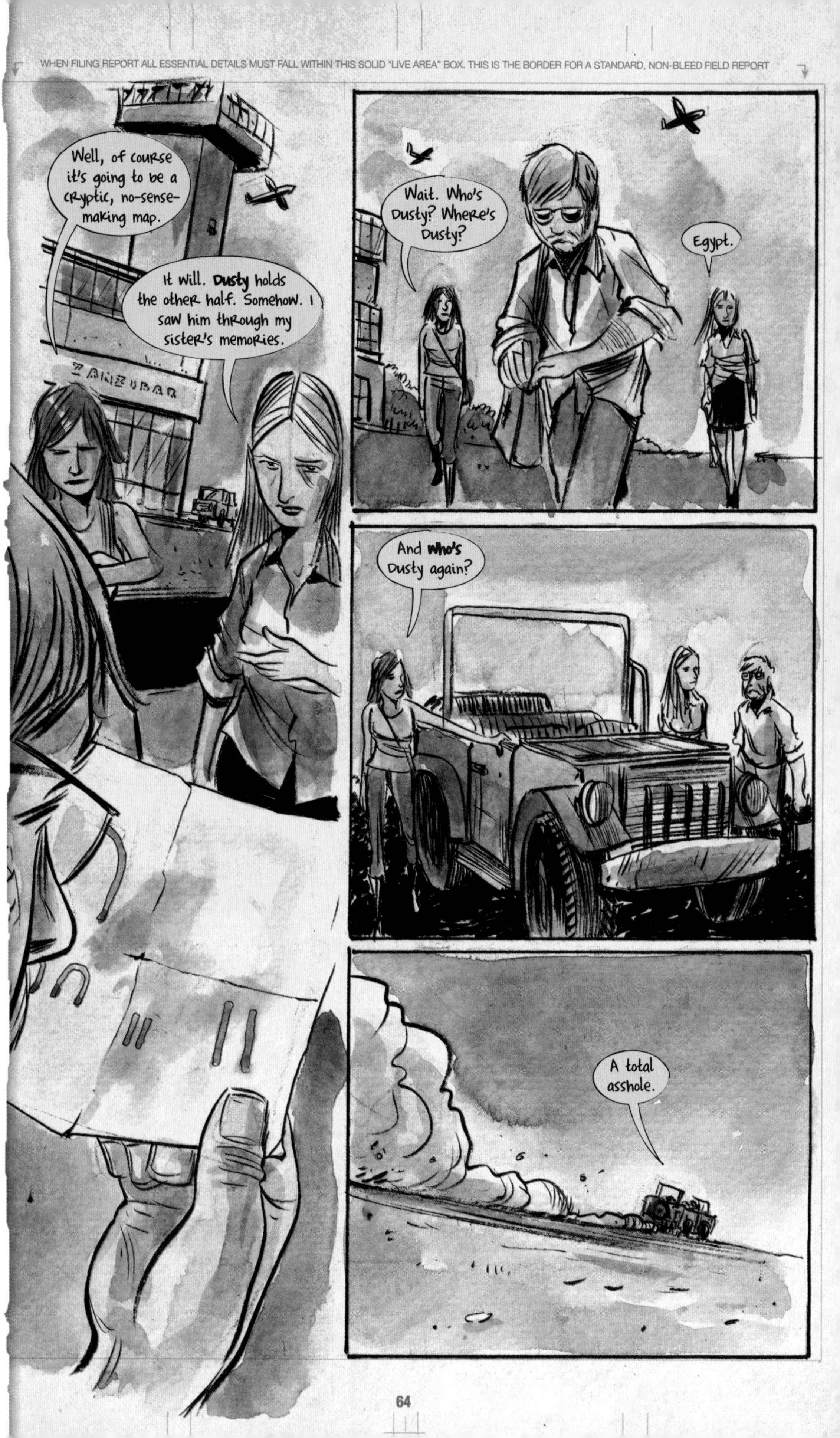

WHEN FILING REPORT ALL ESSENTIAL DETAILS MUST FALL WITHIN THIS SOLID "LIVE AREA" BOX. THIS IS THE BORDER FOR A STANDARD, NON-BLEED FIELD REPORT
Well, of course it's going to be a cryptic, no-sense-making map.
It will. **Dusty** holds the other half. Somehow. I saw him through my sister's memories.
ZANZIBAR
Wait. Who's Dusty? Where's Dusty?
Egypt.
And **who's** Dusty again?
A total asshole.

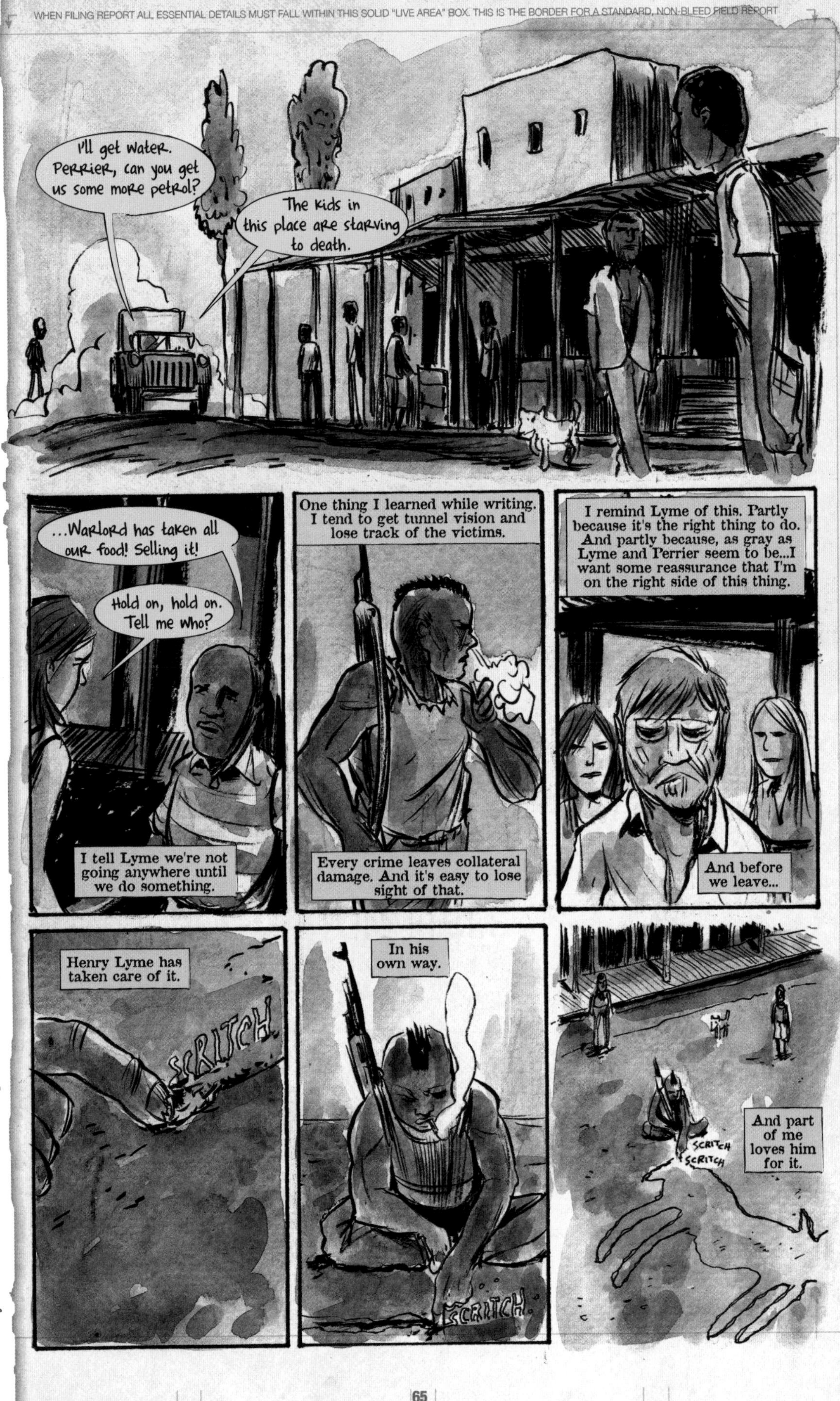
WHEN FILING REPORT ALL ESSENTIAL DETAILS MUST FALL WITHIN THIS SOLID "LIVE AREA" BOX. THIS IS THE BORDER FOR A STANDARD, NON-BLEED FIELD REPORT
I'll get water. Perrier, can you get us some more petrol?
The kids in this place are starving to death.
...Warlord has taken all our food! Selling it!
Hold on, hold on. Tell me who?
I tell Lyme we're not going anywhere until we do something.
One thing I learned while writing. I tend to get tunnel vision and lose track of the victims.
Every crime leaves collateral damage. And it's easy to lose sight of that.
I remind Lyme of this. Partly because it's the right thing to do. And partly because, as gray as Lyme and Perrier seem to be...I want some reassurance that I'm on the right side of this thing.
And before we leave...
Henry Lyme has taken care of it.
SCRITCH
In his own way.
SCRITCH
SCRITCH
SCRITCH
And part of me loves him for it.

I conducted my last interview with him over the phone. And strangely, he seemed not to remember me. He didn't remember me or my questions, or the book I had been working on.

WHEN FILING REPORT ALL ESSENTIAL DETAILS MUST FALL WITHIN THIS SOLID "LIVE AREA" BOX. THIS IS THE BORDER FOR A STANDARD, NON-BLEED FIELD REPORT

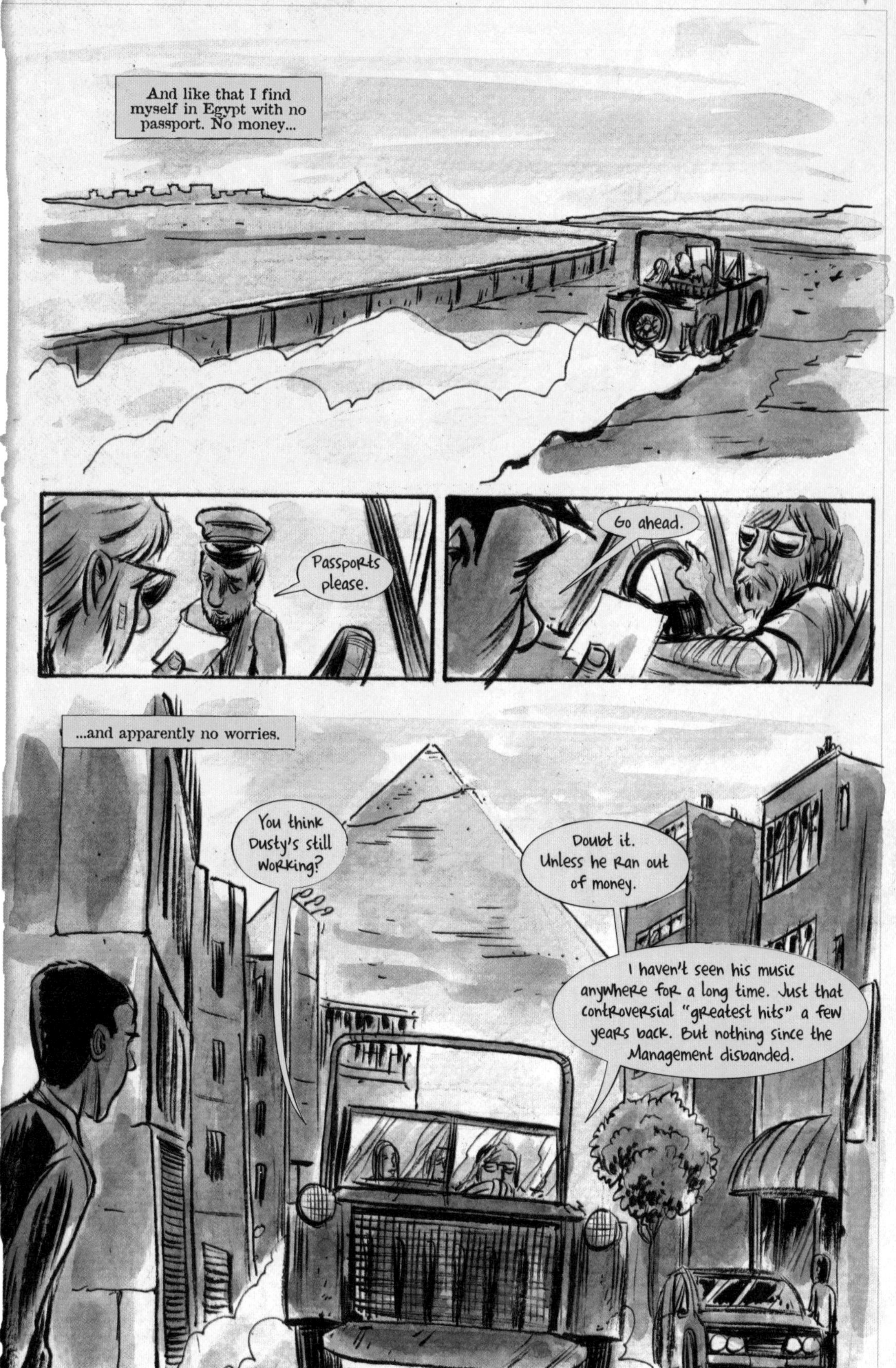
And like that I find myself in Egypt with no passport. No money...
Passports please.
Go ahead.
...and apparently no worries.
You think Dusty's still working?
Doubt it. Unless he ran out of money.
I haven't seen his music anywhere for a long time. Just that controversial "greatest hits" a few years back. But nothing since the Management disbanded.

It was like starting over from scratch. I explained my book and how I was trying to uncover his daughter's secret history. I didn't mention her schooling this time, but I didn't need to. He just began talking. As if our last conversation had loosened an old memory and he couldn't stop.

WHEN FILING REPORT ALL ESSENTIAL DETAILS MUST FALL WITHIN THIS SOLID "LIVE AREA" BOX. THIS IS THE BORDER FOR A STANDARD, NON-BLEED FIELD REPORT

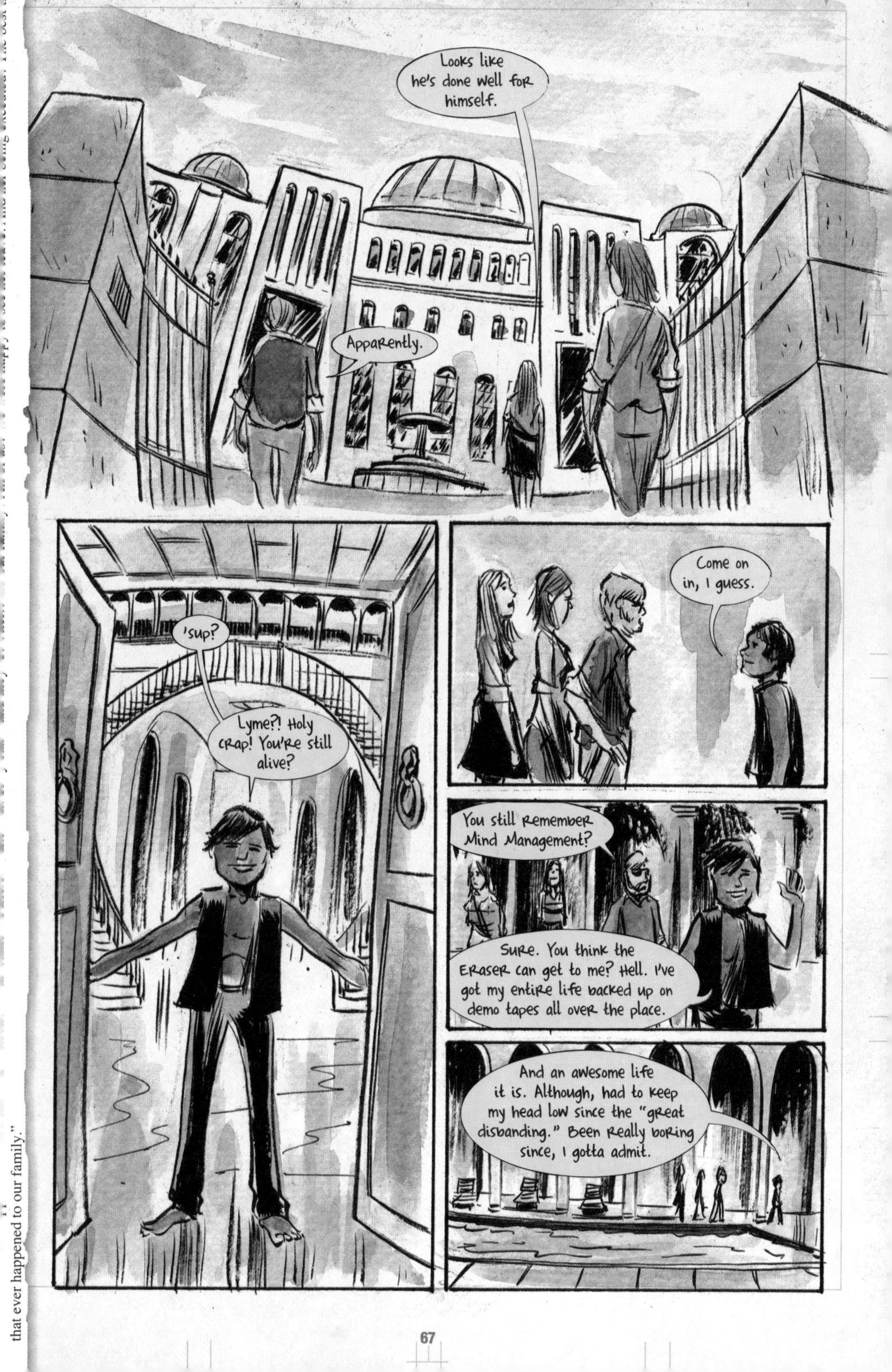

Looks like he's done well for himself.
Apparently.
'sup?
Lyme?! Holy crap! You're still alive?
Come on in, I guess.
You still remember Mind Management?
Sure. You think the Eraser can get to me? Hell. I've got my entire life backed up on demo tapes all over the place.
And an awesome life it is. Although, had to keep my head low since the "great disbanding." Been really boring since, I gotta admit.

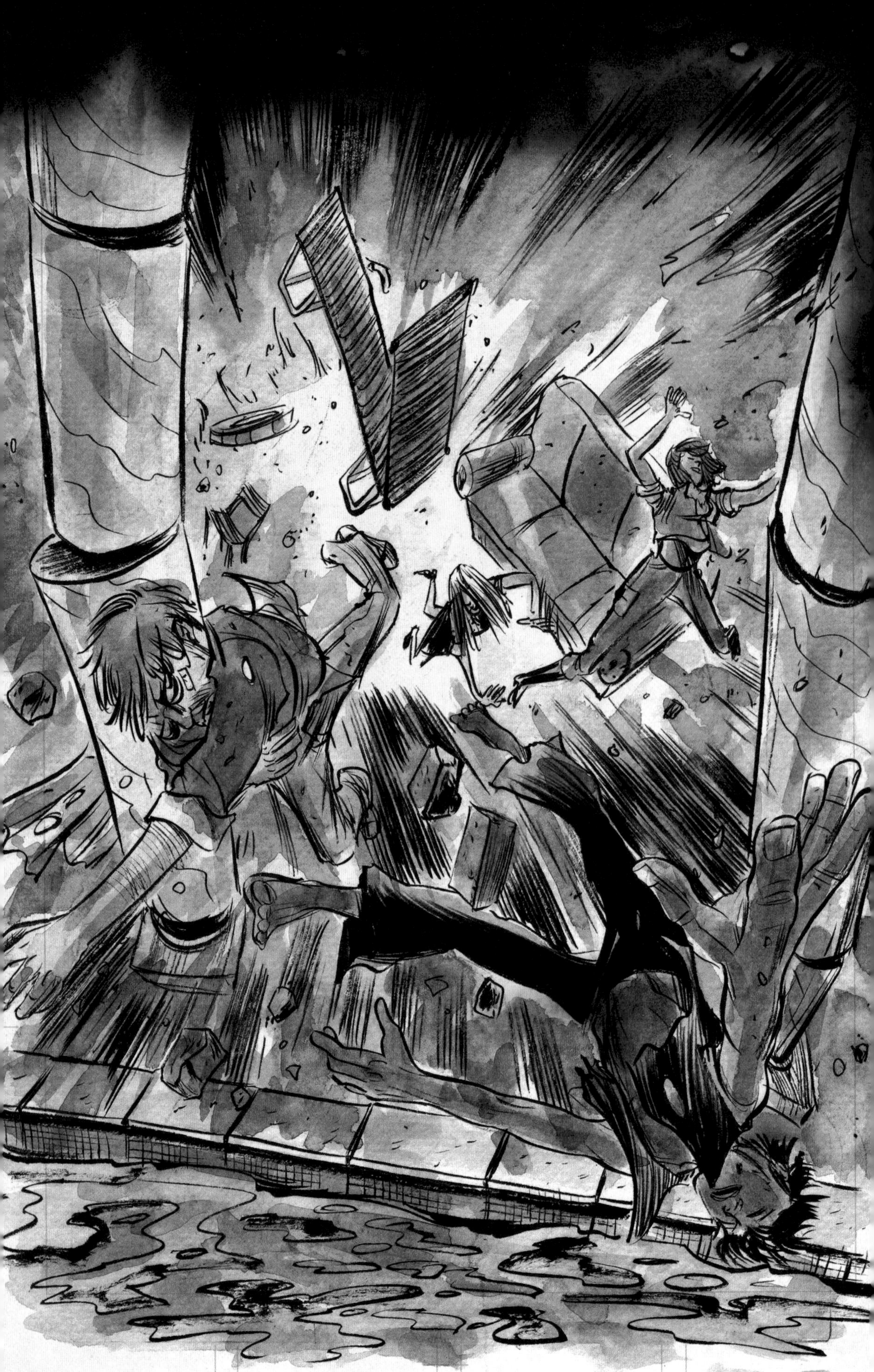

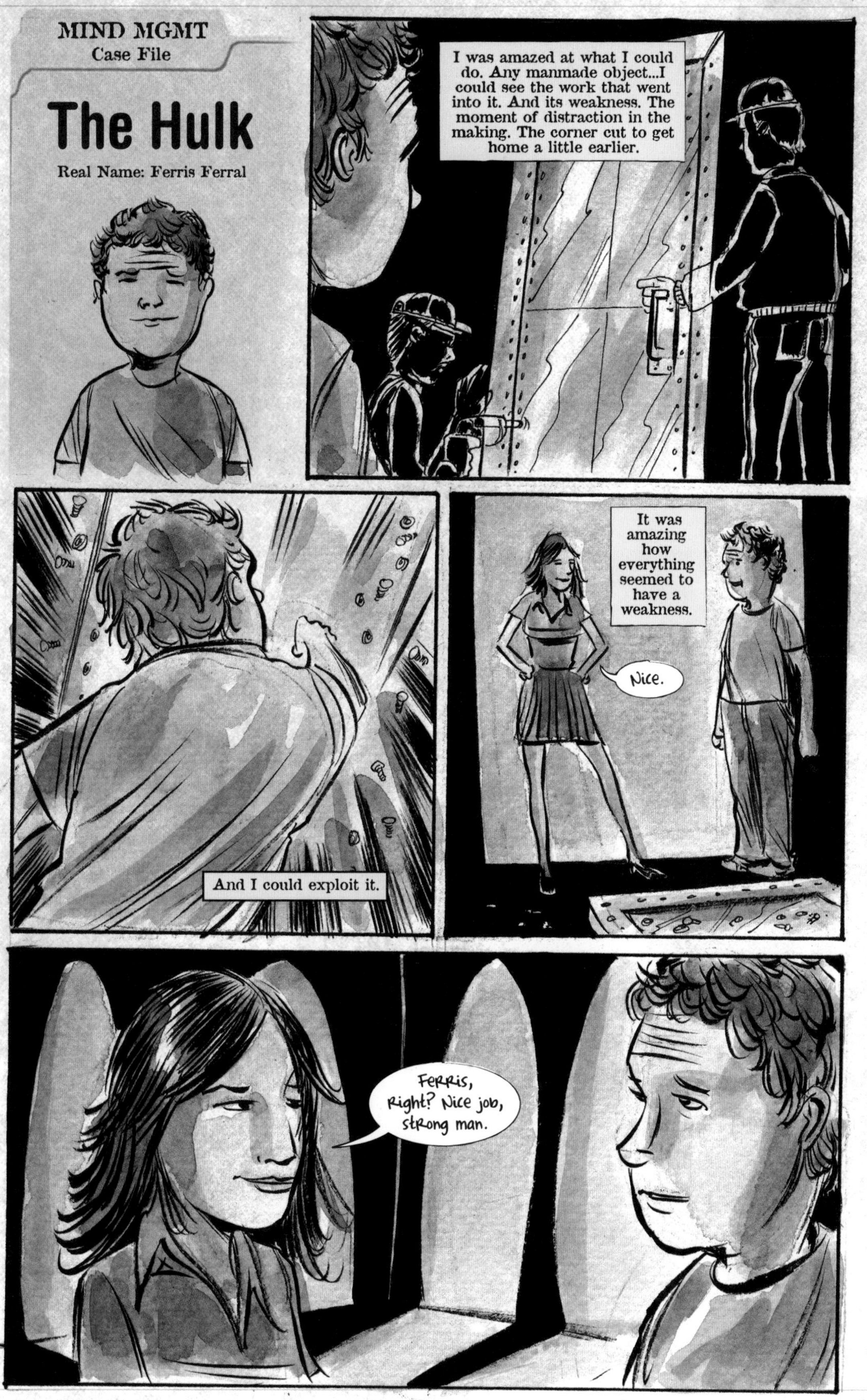
MIND MGMT
Case File
The Hulk
Real Name: Ferris Ferral
I was amazed at what I could do. Any manmade object...I could see the work that went into it. And its weakness. The moment of distraction in the making. The corner cut to get home a little earlier.
And I could exploit it.
It was amazing how everything seemed to have a weakness.
Nice.
Ferris, Right? Nice job, strong man.

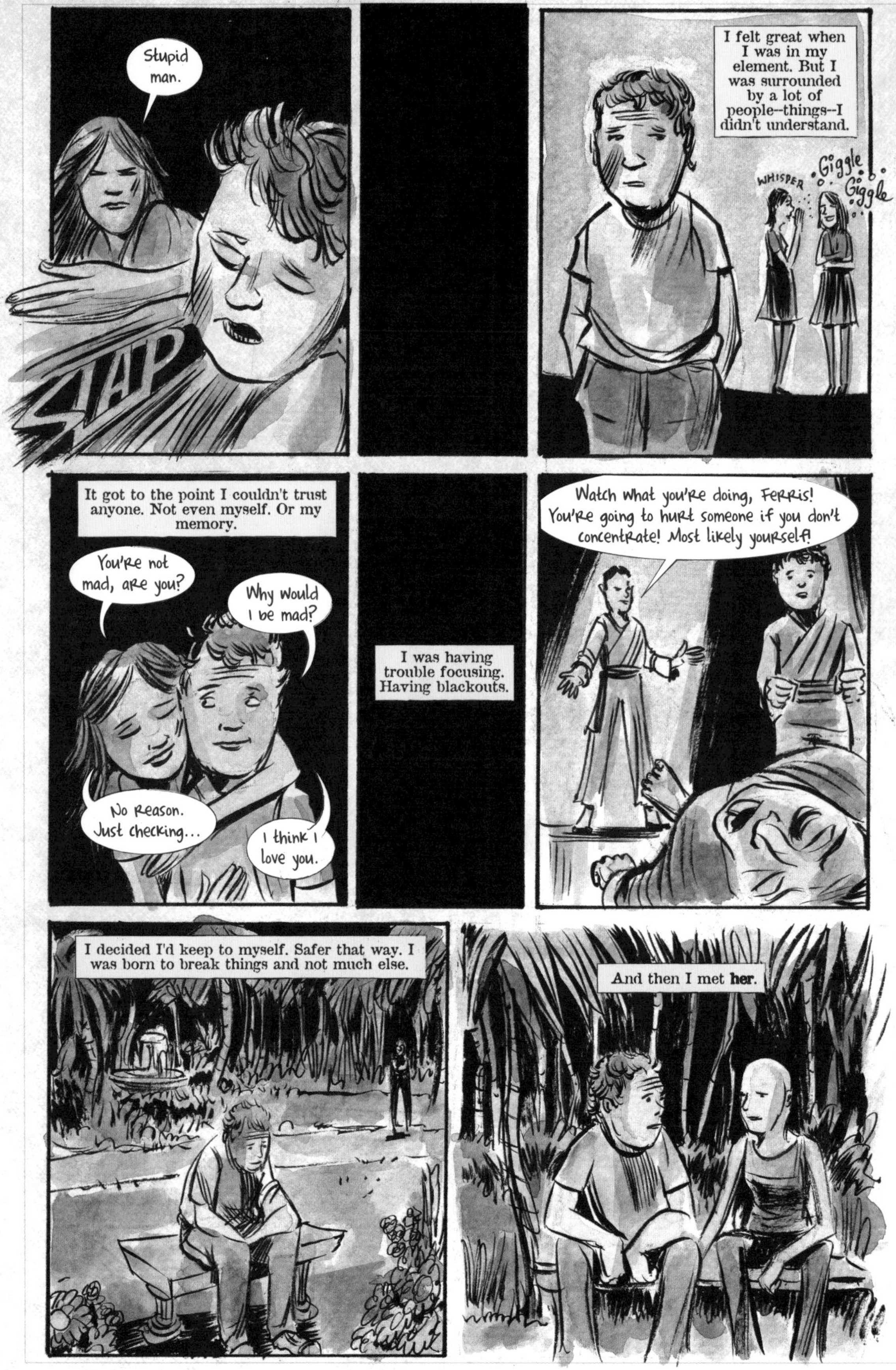
Stupid man.
SLAP
I felt great when I was in my element. But I was surrounded by a lot of people--things--I didn't understand.
WHISPER
Giggle Giggle
It got to the point I couldn't trust anyone. Not even myself. Or my memory.
You're not mad, are you?
Why would I be mad?
No reason. Just checking...
I think I love you.
I was having trouble focusing. Having blackouts.
Watch what you're doing, Ferris! You're going to hurt someone if you don't concentrate! Most likely yourself!
I decided I'd keep to myself. Safer that way. I was born to break things and not much else.
And then I met **her**.

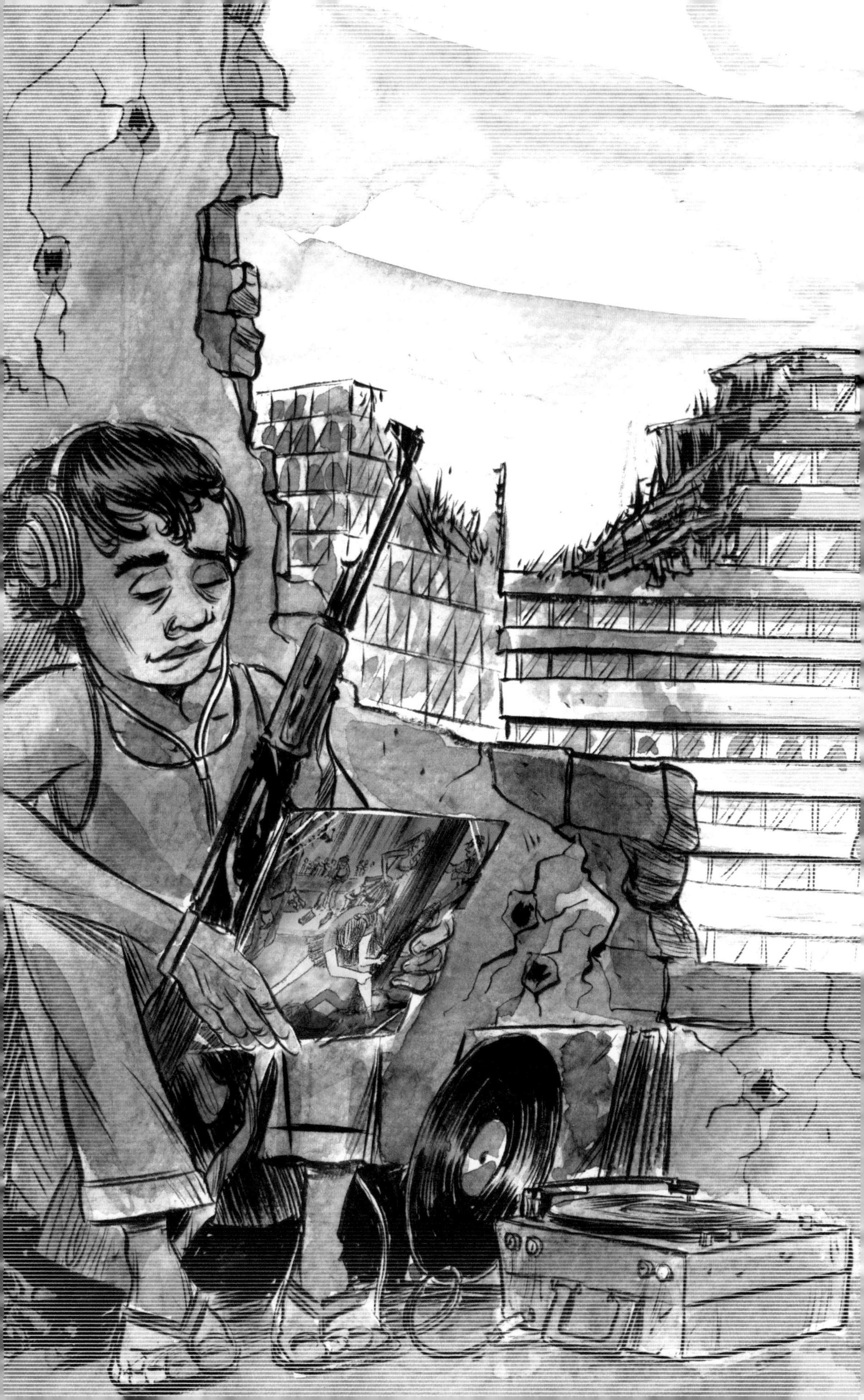

9

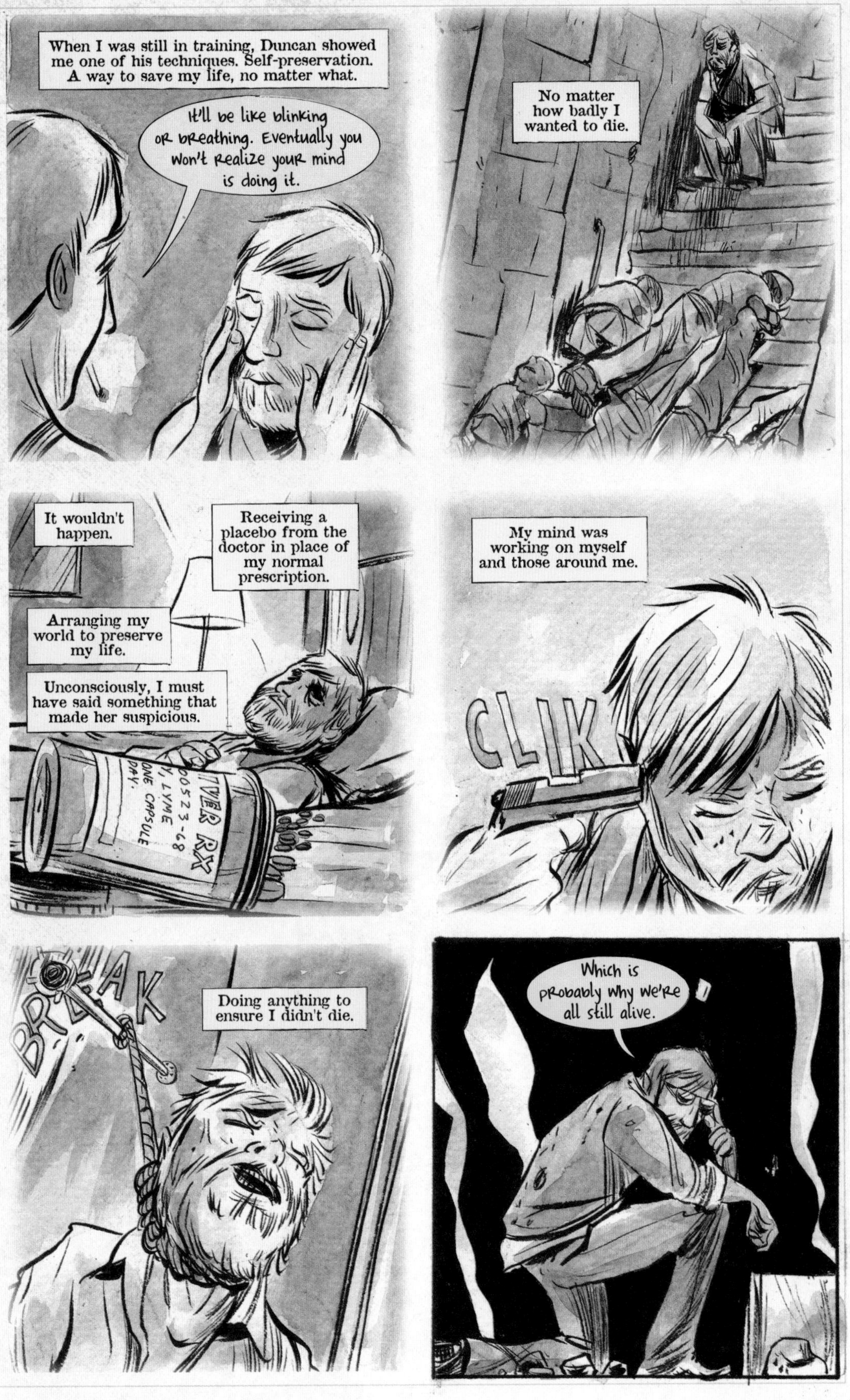
When I was still in training, Duncan showed me one of his techniques. Self-preservation. A way to save my life, no matter what.
It'll be like blinking or breathing. Eventually you won't realize your mind is doing it.
No matter how badly I wanted to die.
It wouldn't happen.
Receiving a placebo from the doctor in place of my normal prescription.
Arranging my world to preserve my life.
Unconsciously, I must have said something that made her suspicious.
00523-68
ONE CAPSULE
DAY.
My mind was working on myself and those around me.
CLIK
Doing anything to ensure I didn't die.
Which is probably why we're all still alive.

Premeditated A True Crime Novel (continued)
Julianne Verve's schooling and the missing gap in her life will probably forever be a mystery. So we can do nothing but pick back up where her life is once again documented.

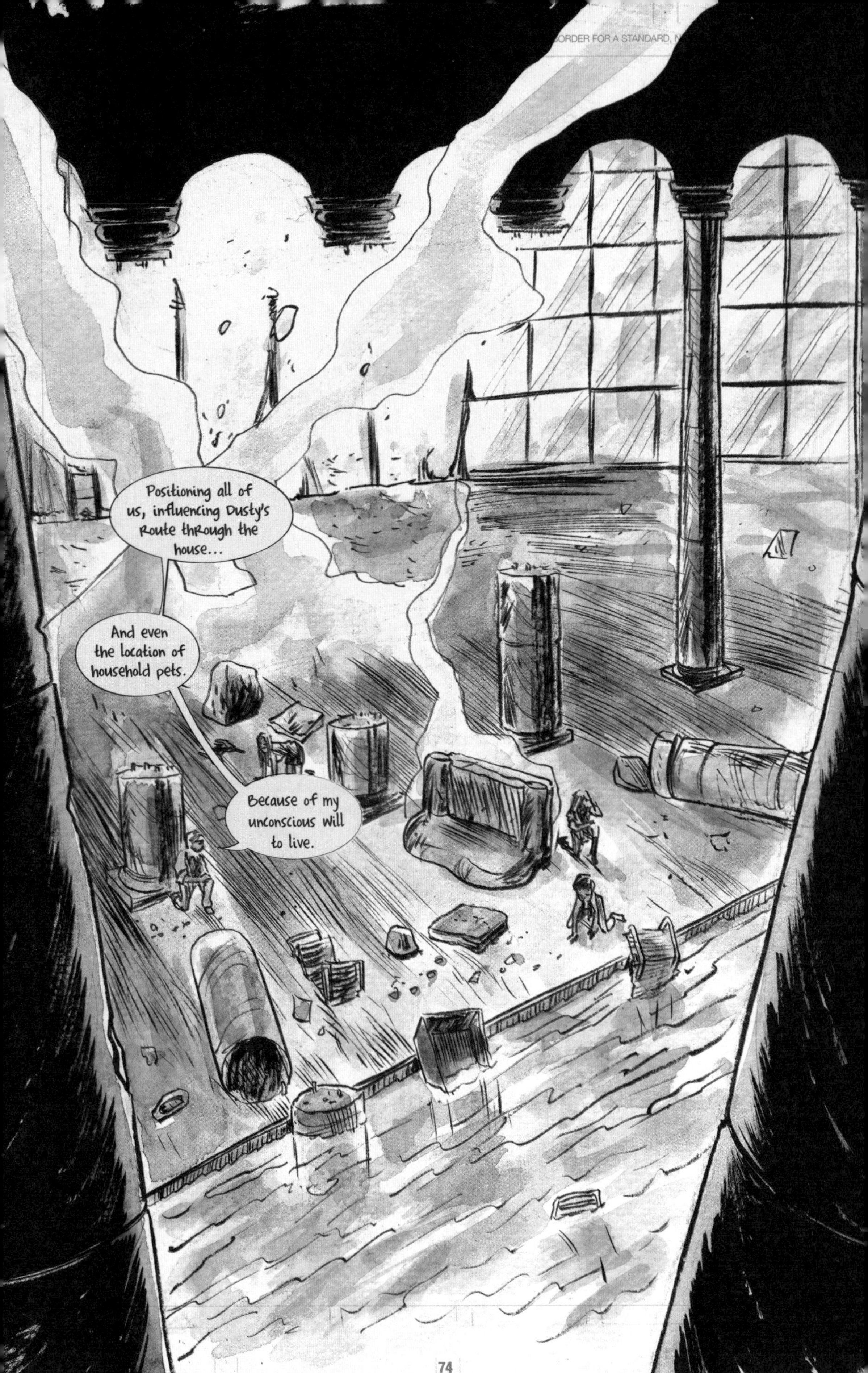
Positioning all of us, influencing Dusty's Route through the house...
And even the location of household pets.
Because of my unconscious will to live.

WHEN FILING REPORT ALL ESSENTIAL DETAILS MUST FALL WITHIN THIS SOLID "LIVE AREA" BOX. THIS IS THE BORDER FOR A STANDARD, NON-BLEED FIELD REPORT

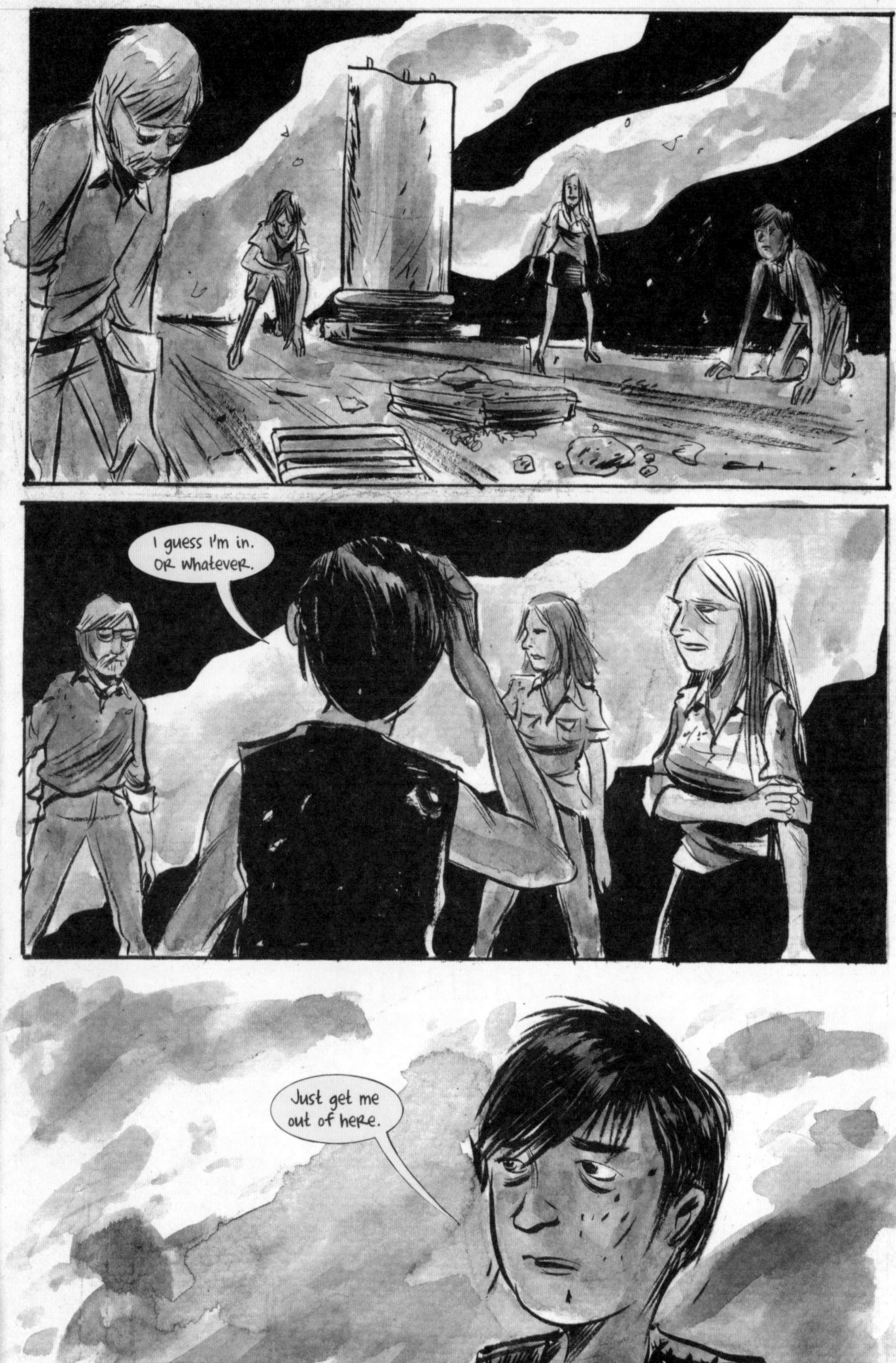
I guess I'm in. OR whatever.
Just get me out of here.

Her wedding to the popular author P. K. Verve made waves. He was one of the richest authors in the world, and she seemed plucked out of relative obscurity. But when the excitement and dust settled on their nuptials, the true drama began.

Julianne gave Verve two children, but all was not serene in the Verve household. During my investigation, I recovered one of Julianne's journals from the first few years of their marriage:

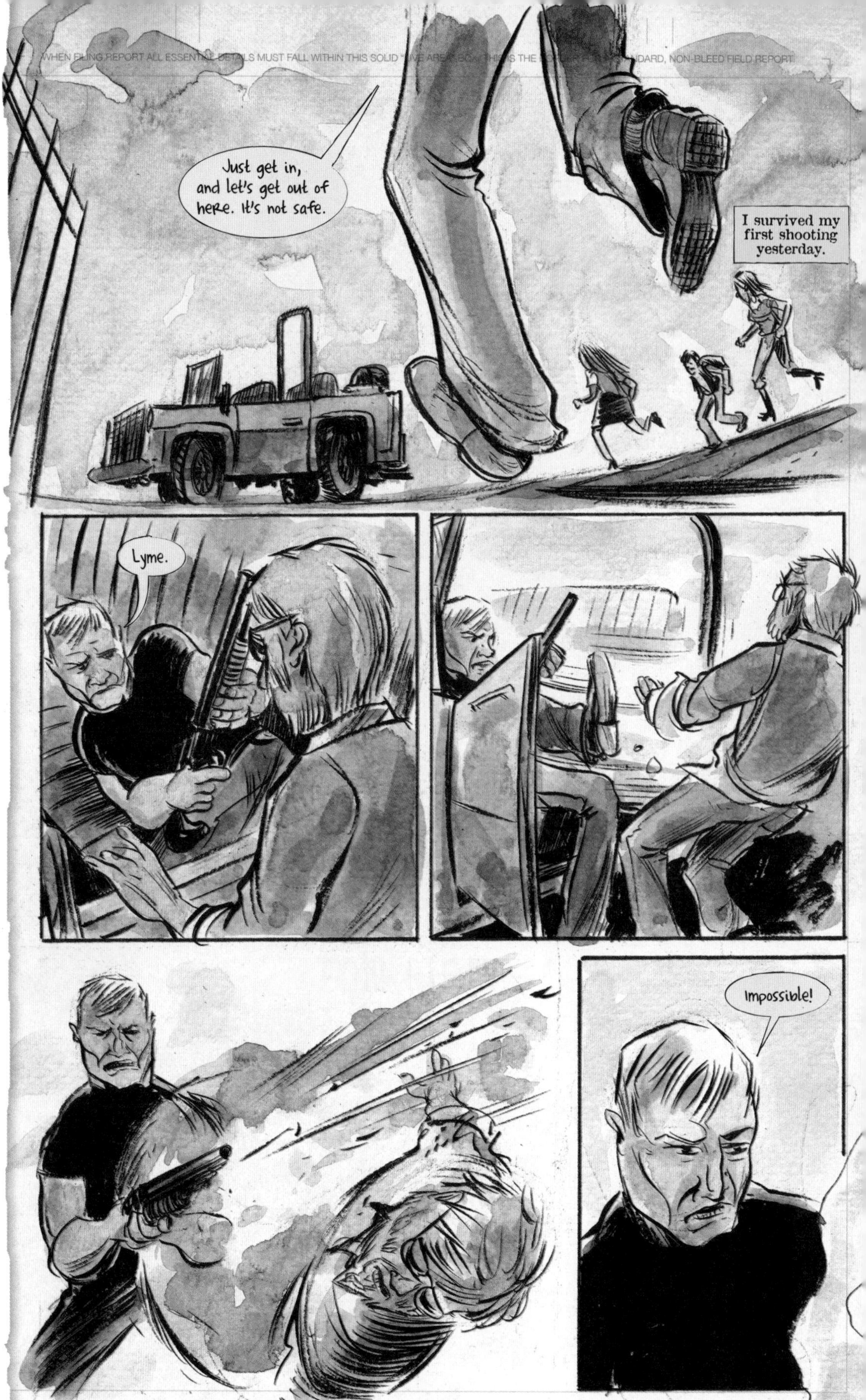
Just get in, and let's get out of here. It's not safe.
I survived my first shooting yesterday.
Lyme.
Impossible!

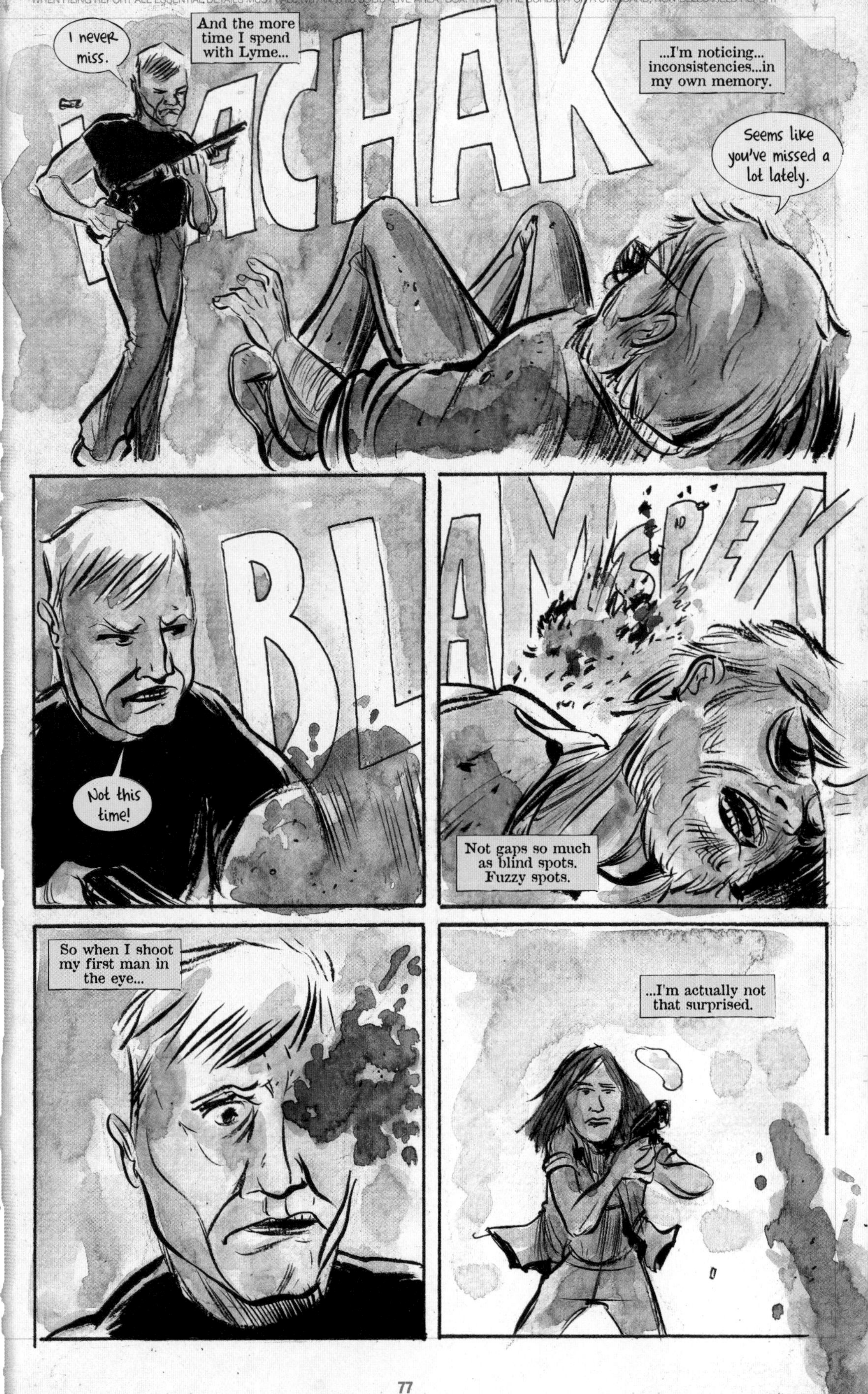
I never miss.
And the more time I spend with Lyme...
CHAK
...I'm noticing... inconsistencies...in my own memory.
Seems like you've missed a lot lately.
BL
Not this time!
AM
SPEK
Not gaps so much as blind spots. Fuzzy spots.
So when I shoot my first man in the eye...
...I'm actually not that surprised.

"Verve is running around on me again. I thought once we were married it would stop. Makes me want to put a gun in my mouth. The strangest part? I know we argued about another woman yesterday. But I don't remember the argument.

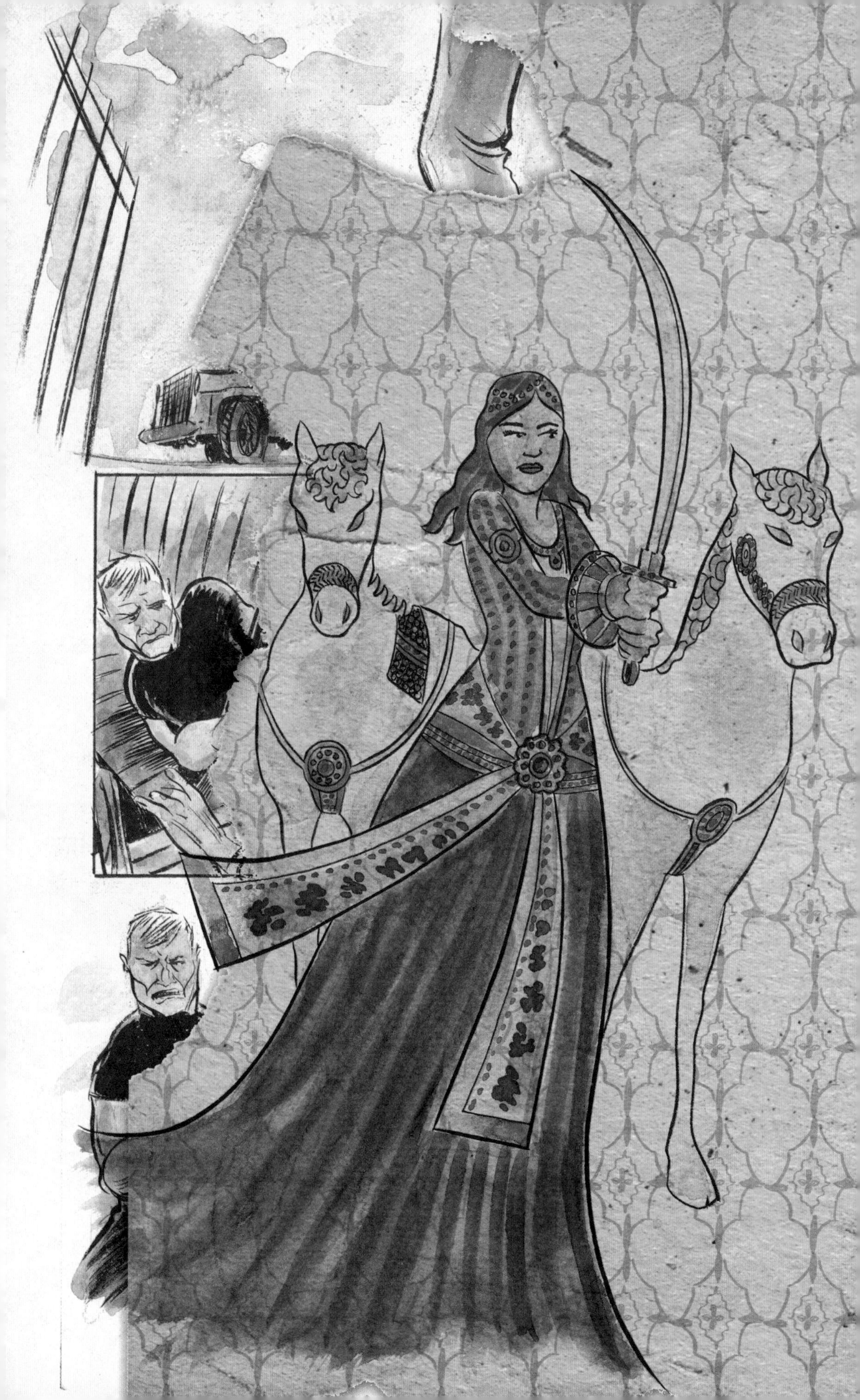

WHEN FILING REPORT ALL ESSENTIAL DETAILS MUST FALL WITHIN THIS SOLID “LIVE AREA” BOX. THIS IS THE BORDER FOR A STANDARD, NON-BLEED FIELD REPORT

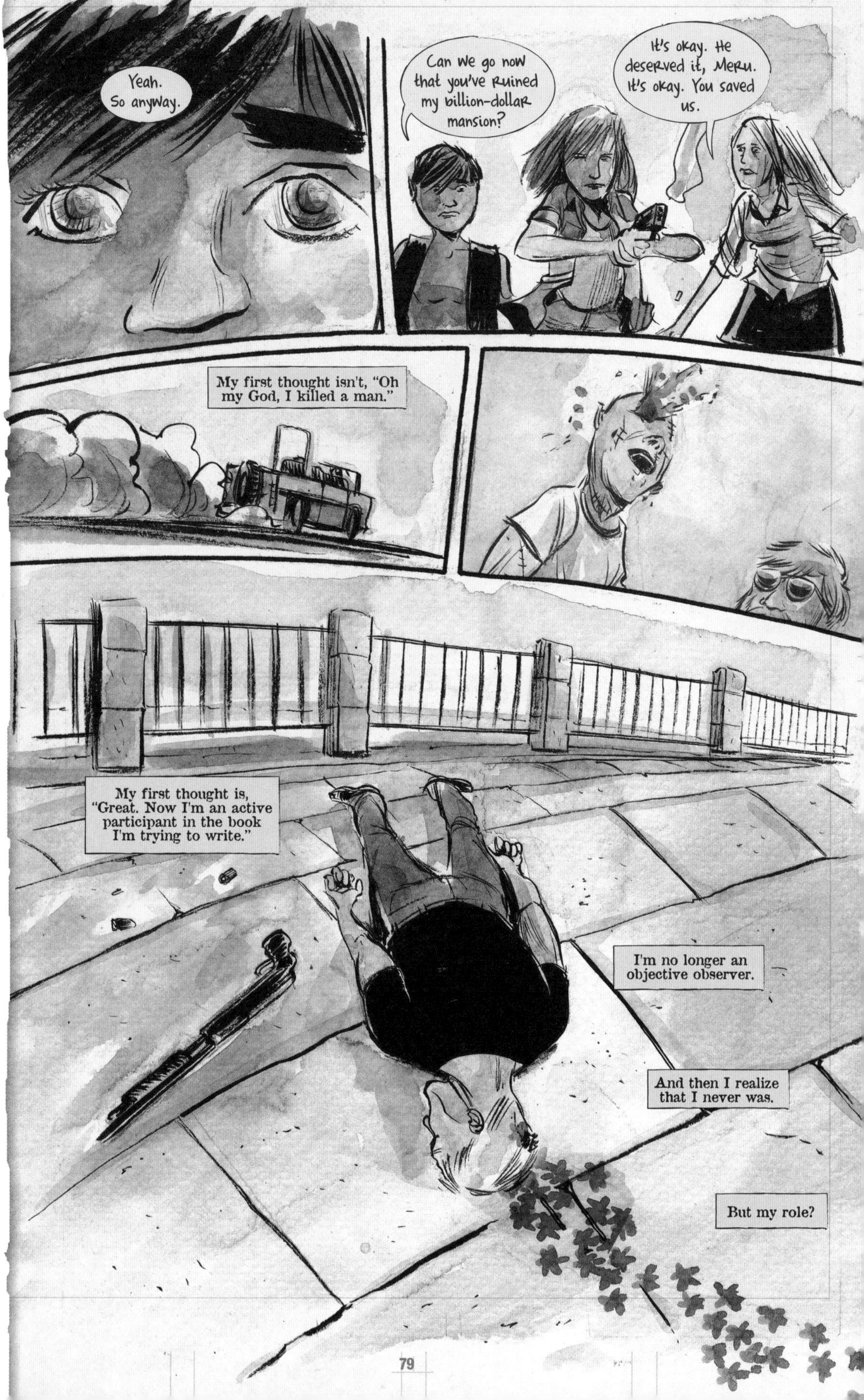

Yeah. So anyway.
Can we go now that you've ruined my billion-dollar mansion?
It's okay. He deserved it, Meru. It's okay. You saved us.
My first thought isn't, “Oh my God, I killed a man.”
My first thought is, “Great. Now I'm an active participant in the book I'm trying to write.”
I'm no longer an objective observer.
And then I realize that I never was.
But my role?

“I only remember because I wrote it in my journal. I read yesterday’s entry, and it’s as if another woman wrote it. Someone living a parallel life to mine. Is this my voice? Is that my husband?

WHEN FILING REPORT ALL ESSENTIAL DETAILS MUST FALL WITHIN THIS SOLID "LIVE AREA" BOX. THIS IS THE BORDER FOR A STANDARD, NON-BLEED FIELD REPORT

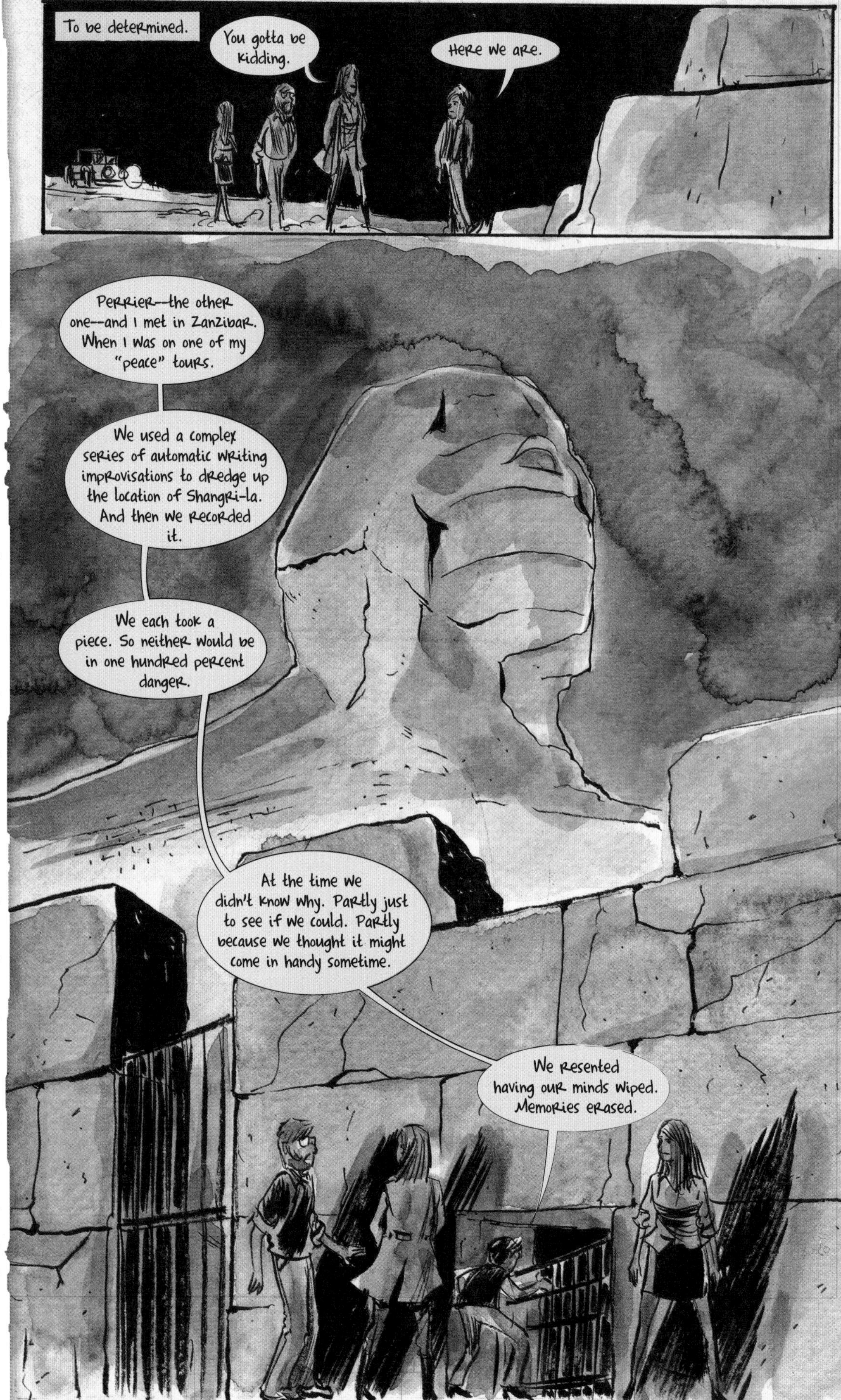
To be determined.
You gotta be kidding.
Here we are.
Perrier--the other one--and I met in Zanzibar. When I was on one of my "peace" tours.
We used a complex series of automatic writing improvisations to dredge up the location of Shangri-la. And then we recorded it.
We each took a piece. So neither would be in one hundred percent danger.
At the time we didn't know why. Partly just to see if we could. Partly because we thought it might come in handy sometime.
We resented having our minds wiped. Memories erased.

"I feel like I'm going crazy. I'm starting to have blind spots in my memory. I remember a buildup to an argument and making up after. But I don't remember the argument. Like someone is erasing bits of my brain.

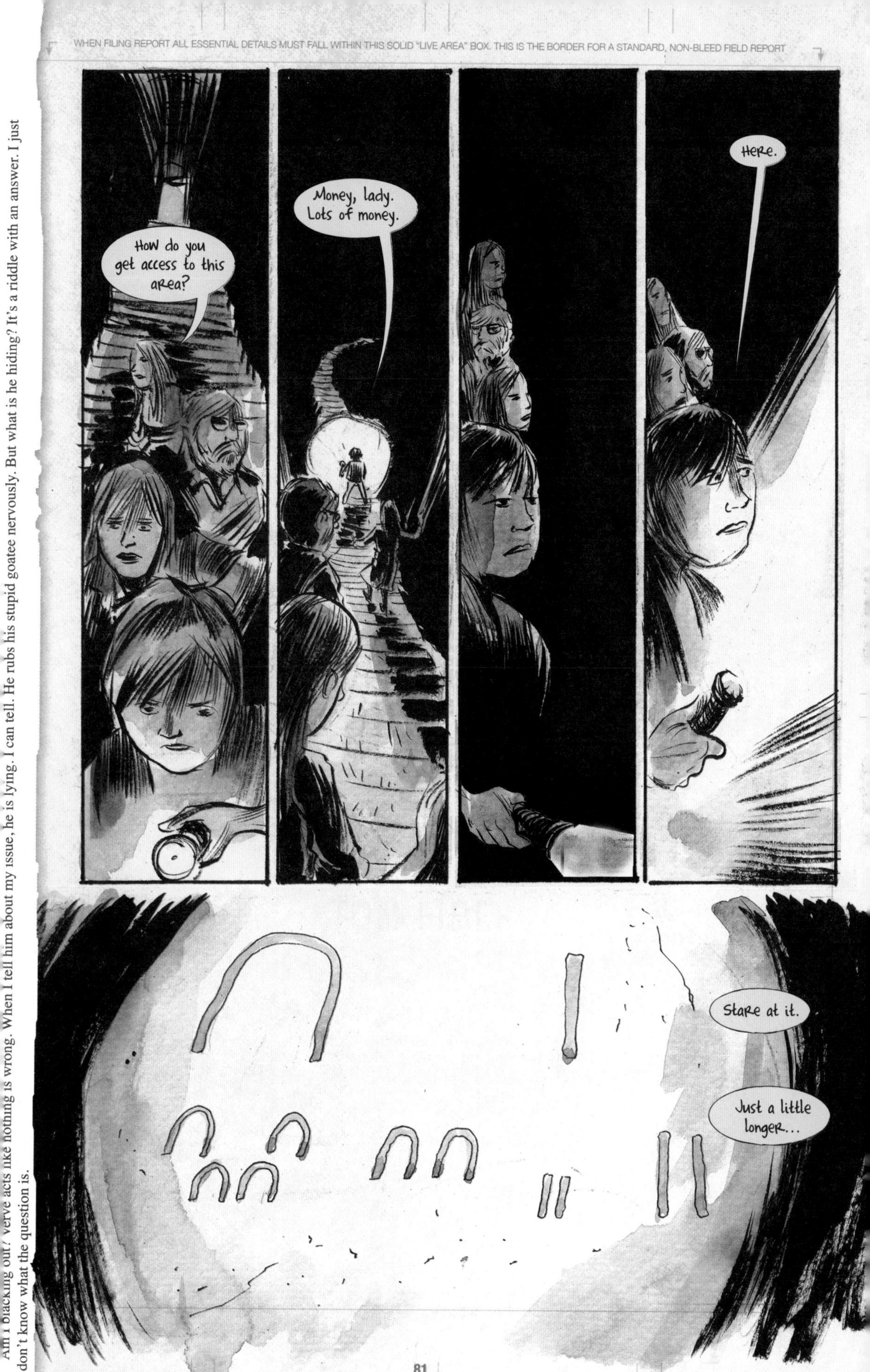
WHEN FILING REPORT ALL ESSENTIAL DETAILS MUST FALL WITHIN THIS SOLID "LIVE AREA" BOX. THIS IS THE BORDER FOR A STANDARD, NON-BLEED FIELD REPORT
Am I blacking out? Verve acts like nothing is wrong. When I tell him about my issue, he is lying. I can tell. He rubs his stupid goatee nervously. But what is he hiding? It's a riddle with an answer. I just don't know what the question is.
How do you get access to this area?
Money, lady. Lots of money.
Here.
Stare at it.
Just a little longer...

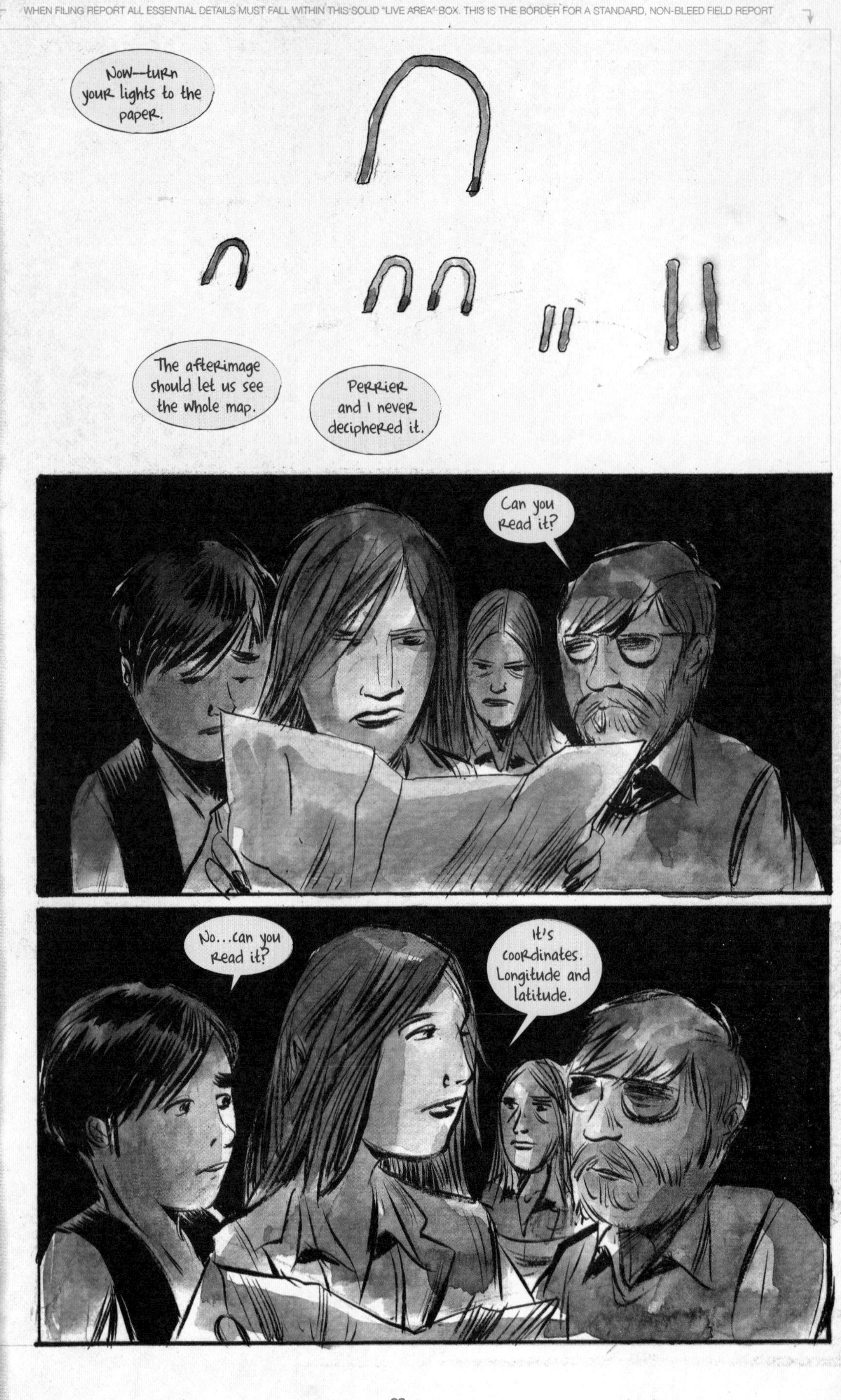
WHEN FILING REPORT ALL ESSENTIAL DETAILS MUST FALL WITHIN THIS SOLID "LIVE AREA" BOX. THIS IS THE BORDER FOR A STANDARD, NON-BLEED FIELD REPORT
Now--turn your lights to the paper.
The afterimage should let us see the whole map.
Perrier and I never deciphered it.
Can you read it?
No...can you read it?
It's coordinates. Longitude and latitude.

"Another bad day. I woke up sore. I've got bruises on my arms. Look like handprints. I'm sure it's Verve. He's doing something to me. But why can't I remember? It's like I'm heading down this dark tunnel with no flashlight and no end in sight."

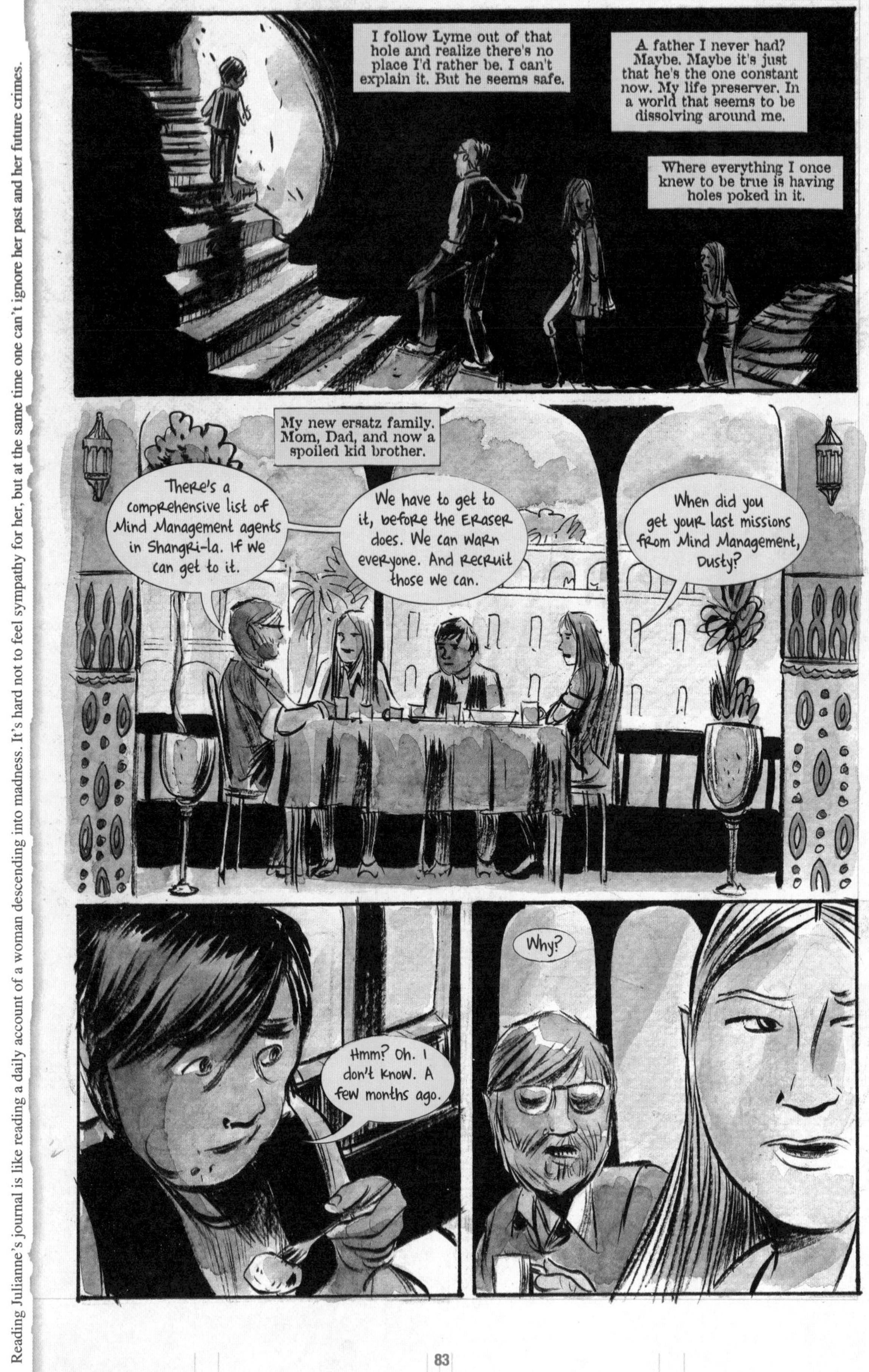
I follow Lyme out of that hole and realize there's no place I'd rather be. I can't explain it. But he seems safe.
A father I never had? Maybe. Maybe it's just that he's the one constant now. My life preserver. In a world that seems to be dissolving around me.
Where everything I once knew to be true is having holes poked in it.
My new ersatz family. Mom, Dad, and now a spoiled kid brother.
There's a comprehensive list of Mind Management agents in Shangri-la. If we can get to it.
We have to get to it, before the Eraser does. We can warn everyone. And recruit those we can.
When did you get your last missions from Mind Management, Dusty?
Hmm? Oh. I don't know. A few months ago.
Why?

Reading Julianne's journal is like reading a daily account of a woman descending into madness. It's hard not to feel sympathy for her, but at the same time one can't ignore her past and her future crimes.

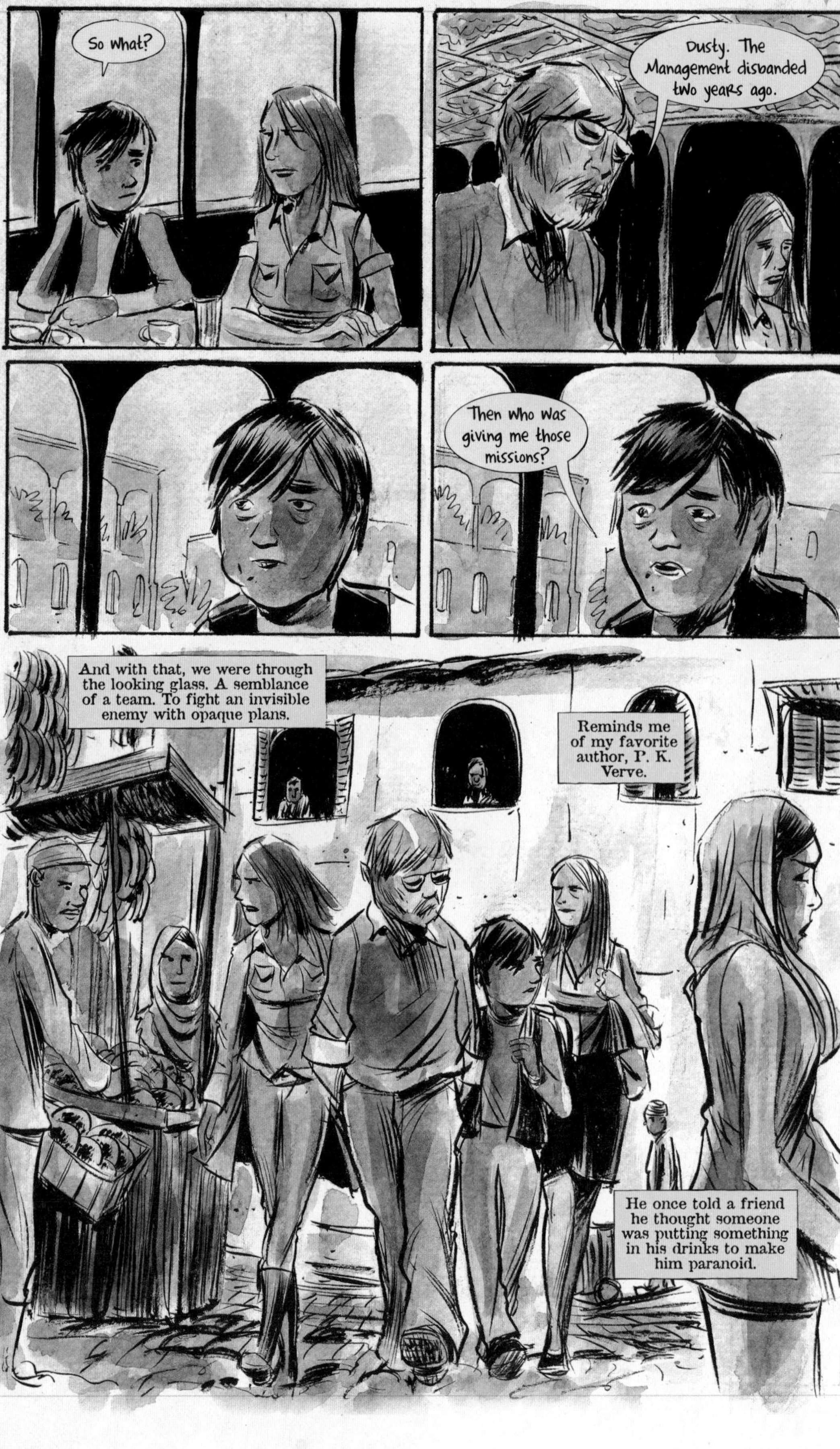
So what?
Dusty. The Management disbanded two years ago.
Then who was giving me those missions?
And with that, we were through the looking glass. A semblance of a team. To fight an invisible enemy with opaque plans.
Reminds me of my favorite author, P. K. Verve.
He once told a friend he thought someone was putting something in his drinks to make him paranoid.

It's at this point that Julianne's family life really starts to disintegrate. She becomes reclusive and Verve is often absent. The children are being cared for exclusively by the nanny.

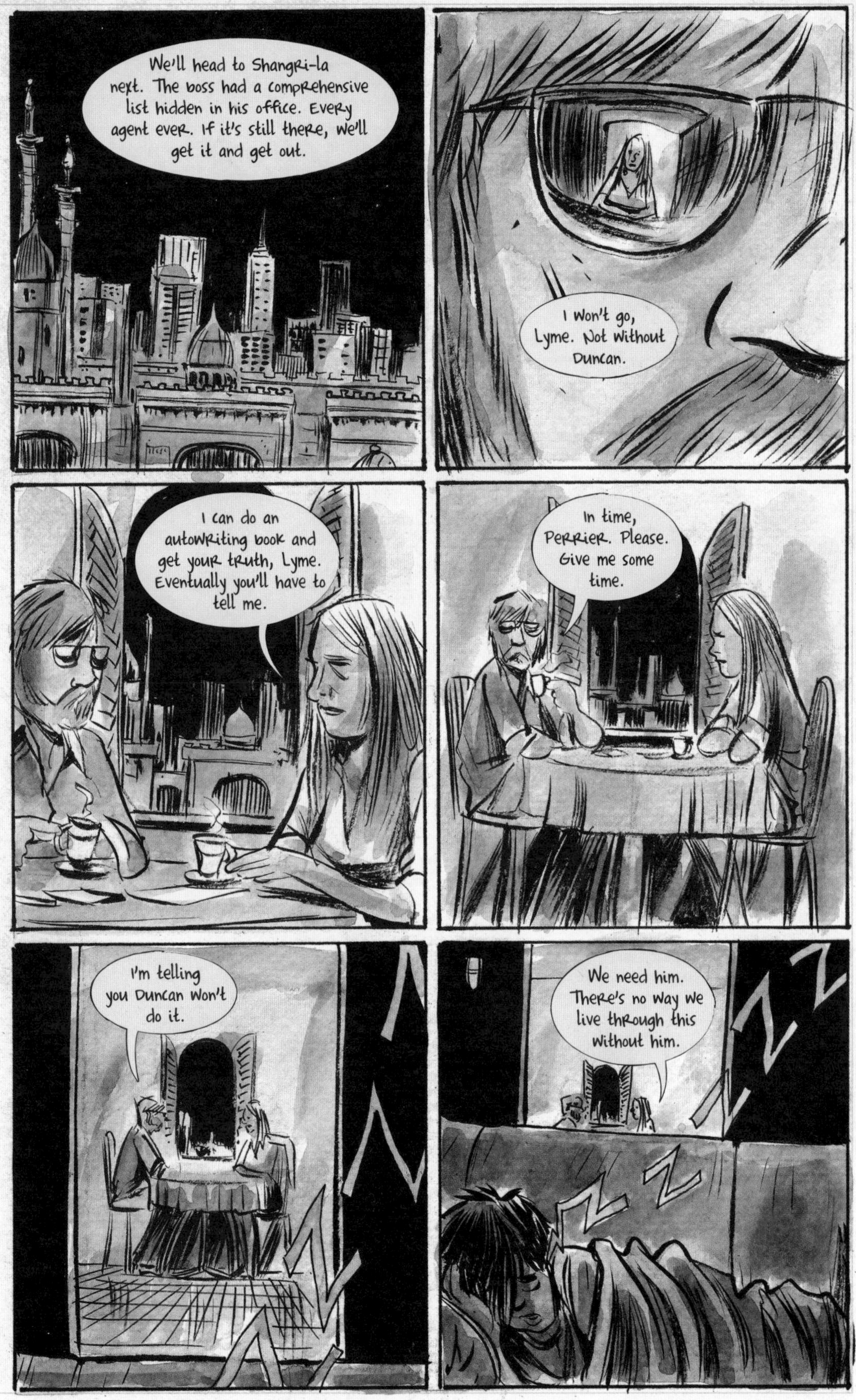
We'll head to Shangri-la next. The boss had a comprehensive list hidden in his office. Every agent ever. If it's still there, we'll get it and get out.
I won't go, Lyme. Not without Duncan.
I can do an autowriting book and get your truth, Lyme. Eventually you'll have to tell me.
In time, Perrier. Please. Give me some time.
I'm telling you Duncan won't do it.
We need him. There's no way we live through this without him.

Any friends or family that Julianne had are now gone or refuse to see her. She's all alone in the world with a (possibly) abusive husband and children who grow more distant each day.

The last truly coherent journal entry that Julianne makes is a week before the murders. She details the last conversation that she and Verve had in the kitchen late that night.

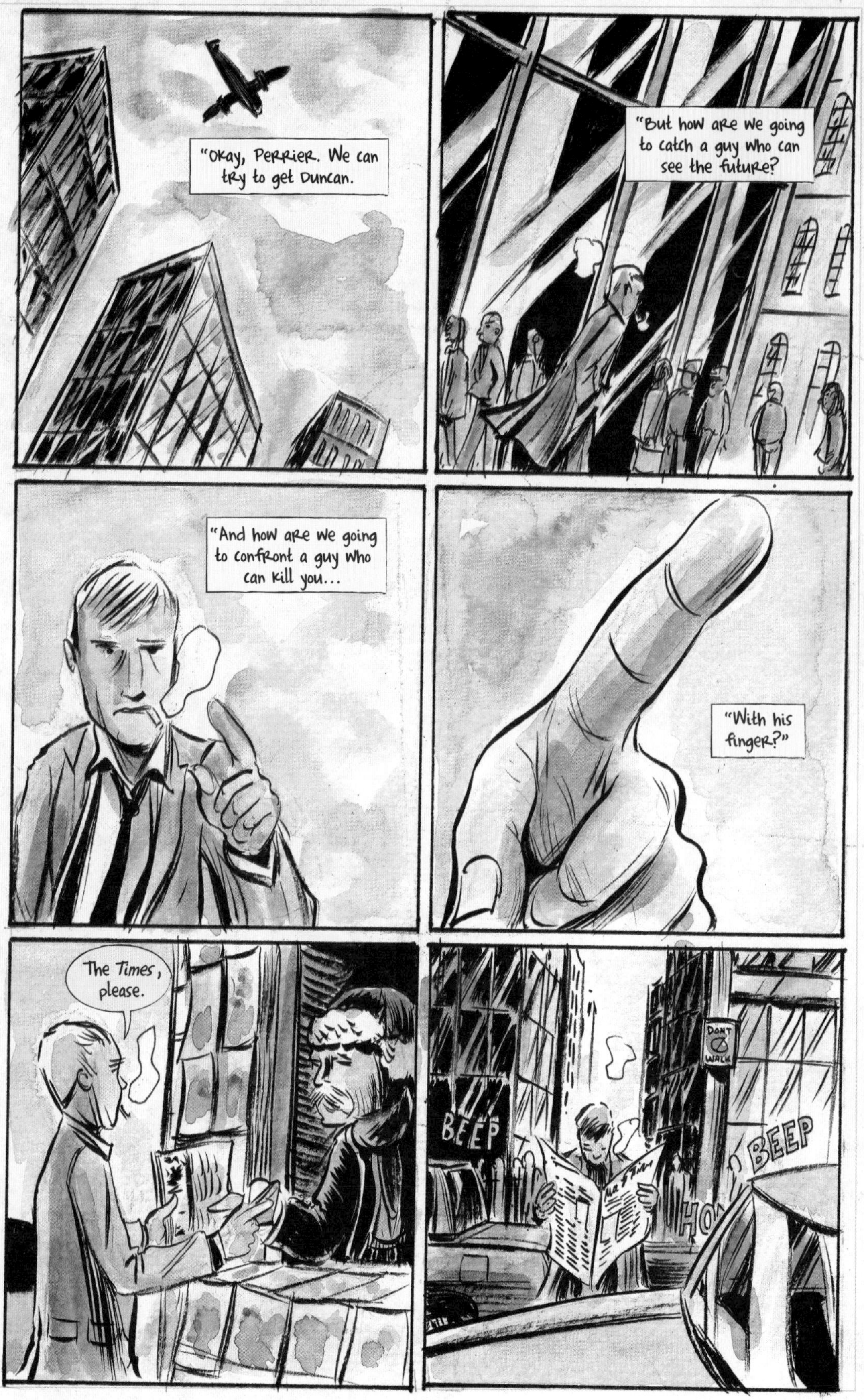
"Okay, Perrier. We can try to get Duncan.
"But how are we going to catch a guy who can see the future?
"And how are we going to confront a guy who can kill you...
"With his finger?"
The *Times*, please.
DON'T WALK
BEEP
BEEP

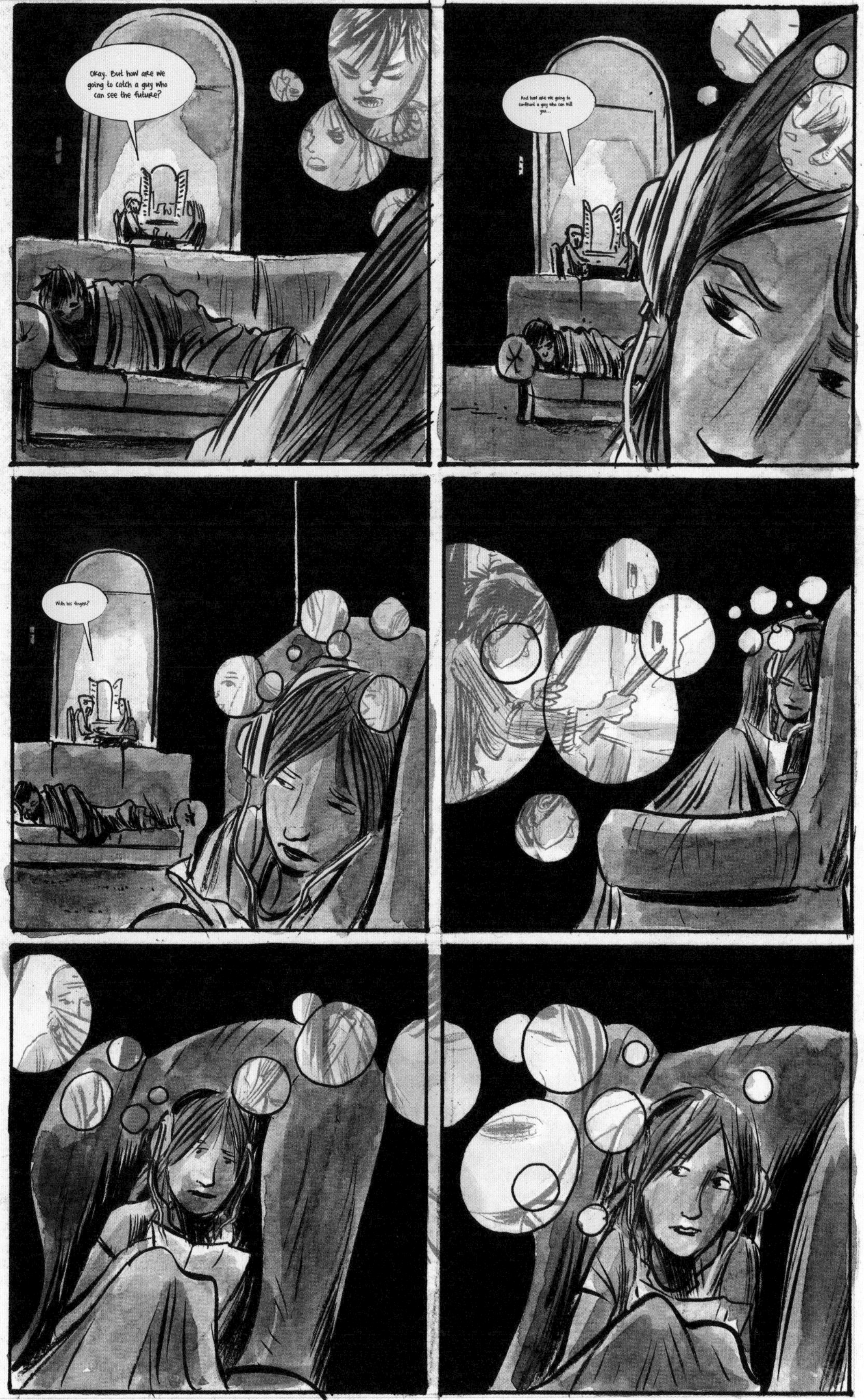
Okay. But how are we going to catch a guy who can see the future?
And how are we going to confront a guy who can kill you...
With his finger?

"We sat across from each other, and I swear when I looked in his face, it was like seeing the face of a stranger. He pointed his finger at me and shouted something. I don't remember what.

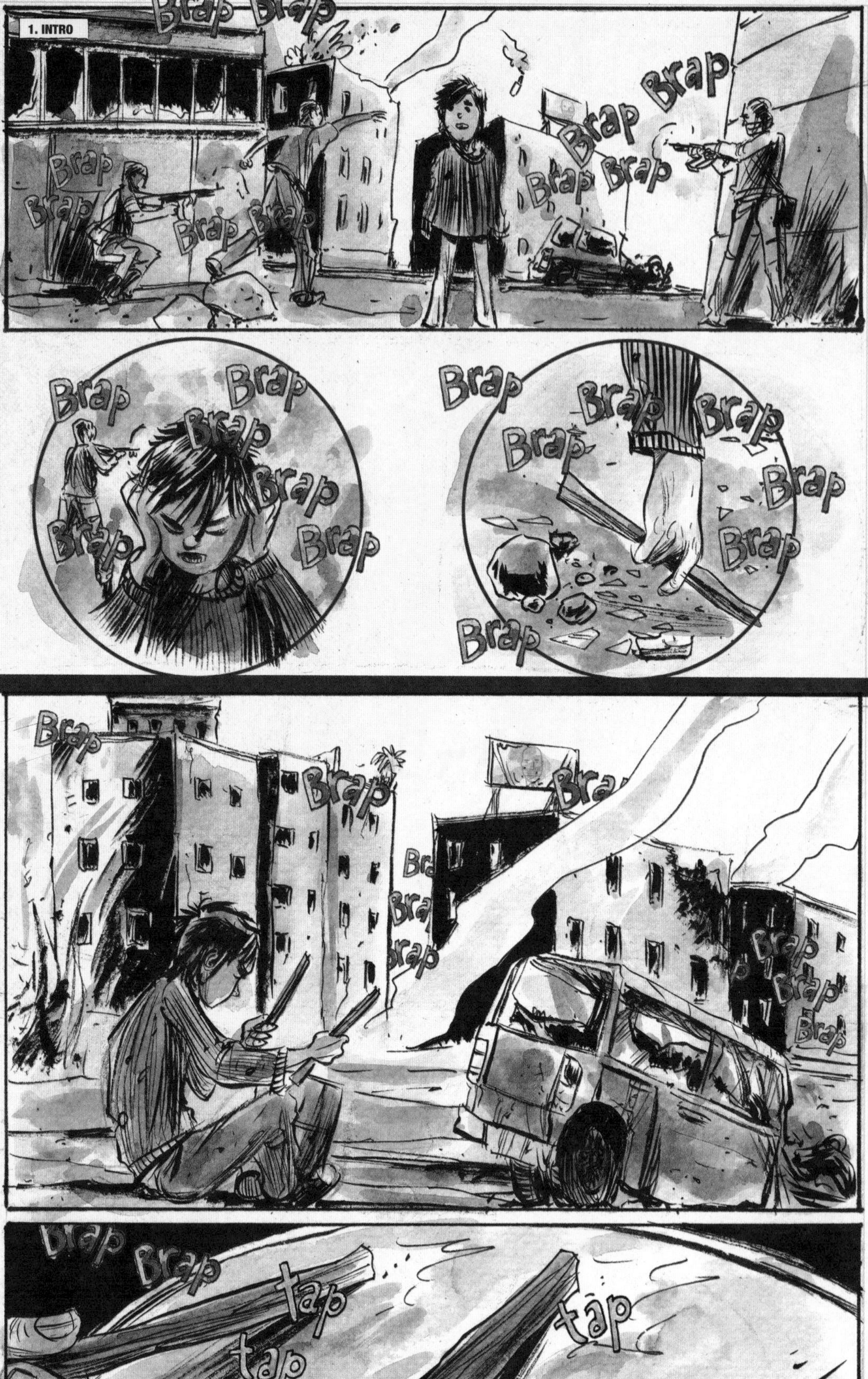
1. INTRO
Brap Brap
Brap
Brap
Brap Brap
Brap Brap
Brap Brap
Brap Brap
Brap
Brap
Brap
Brap
Brap
Brap
Brap
Brap
Brap
Brap
Brap
Brap
Brap
Brap
Brap
Brap
Brap
Brap
Brap
Brap Brap
tap
tap
tap

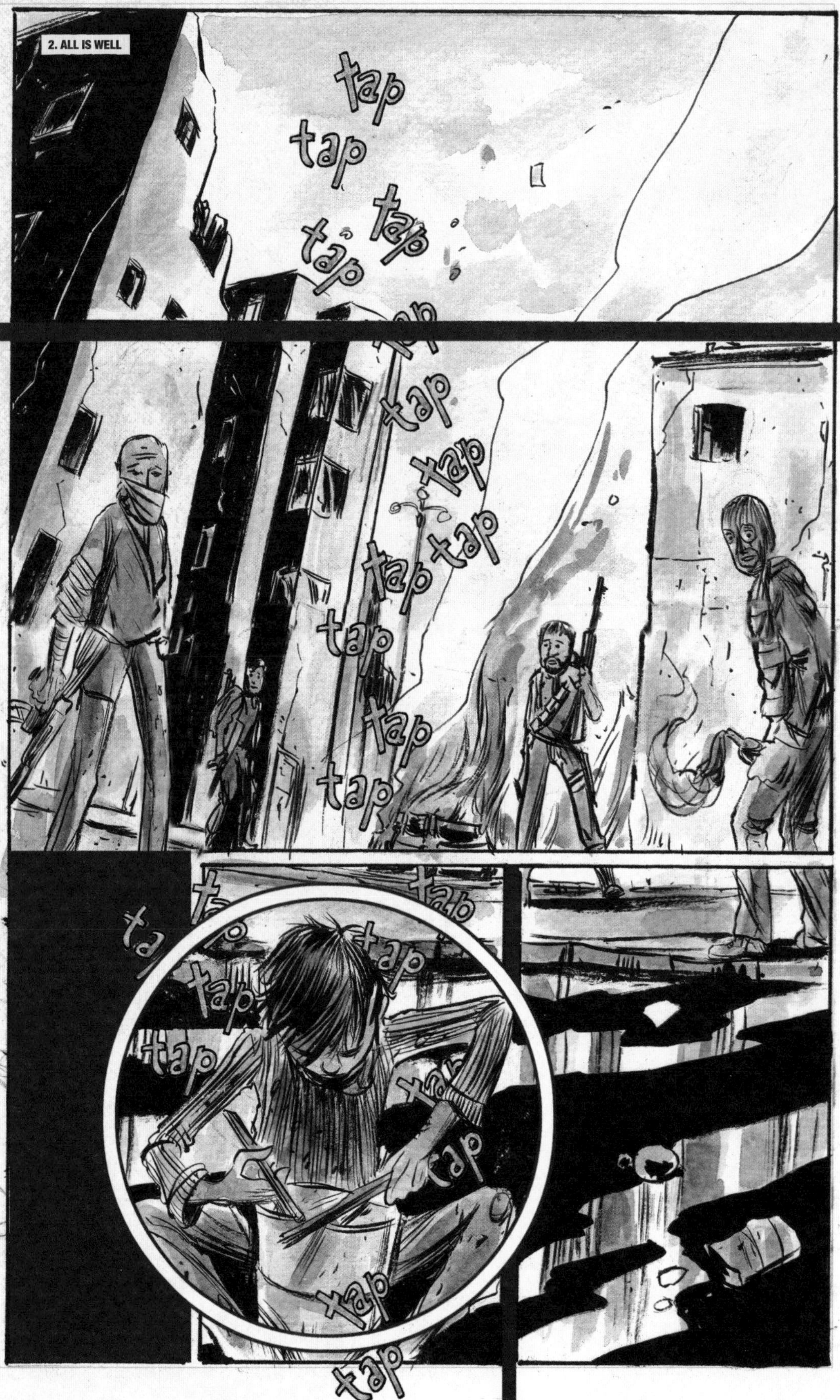
2. ALL IS WELL
tap
tap
tap
tap
tap
tap
tap
tap
tap
tap
tap
tap
tap
tap
tap
tap
tap
tap
tap

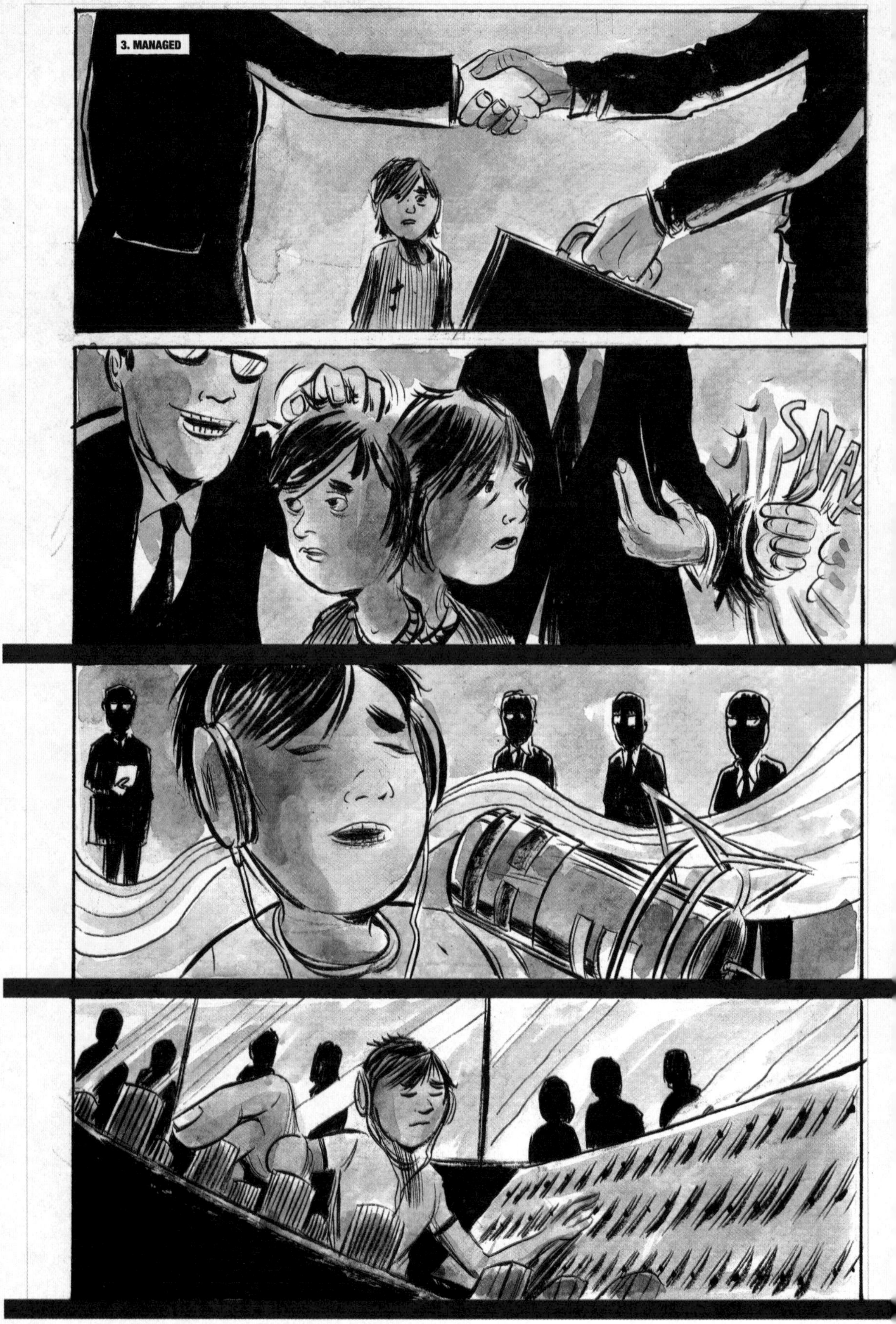
3. MANAGED
SNA

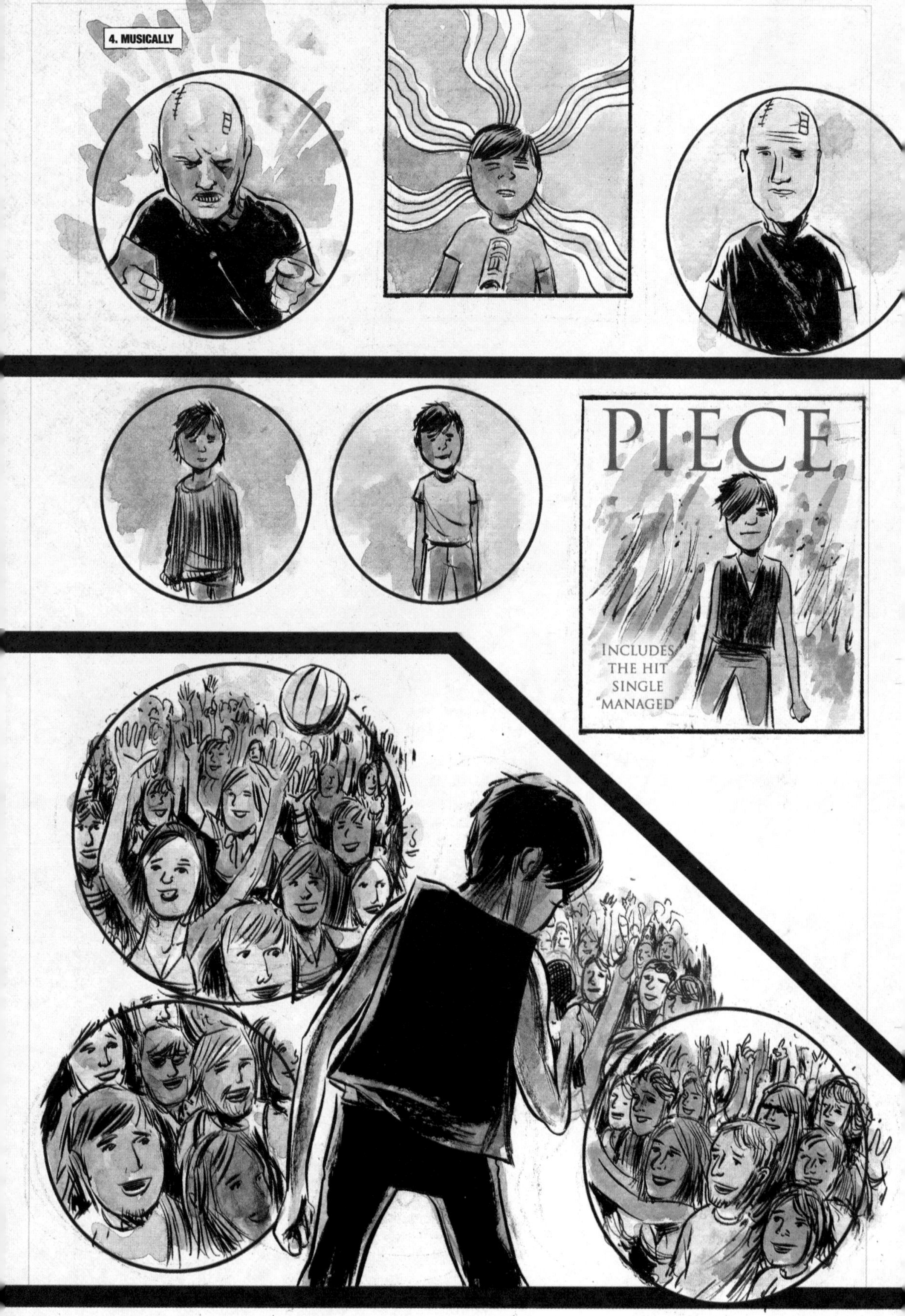
4. MUSICALLY
PIECE
INCLUDES THE HIT SINGLE "MANAGED"

WHEN FILING REPORT ALL ESSENTIAL DETAILS MUST FALL WITHIN THIS SOLID "LIVE AREA" BOX. THIS IS THE BORDER FOR A STANDARD, NON-BLEED FIELD REPORT

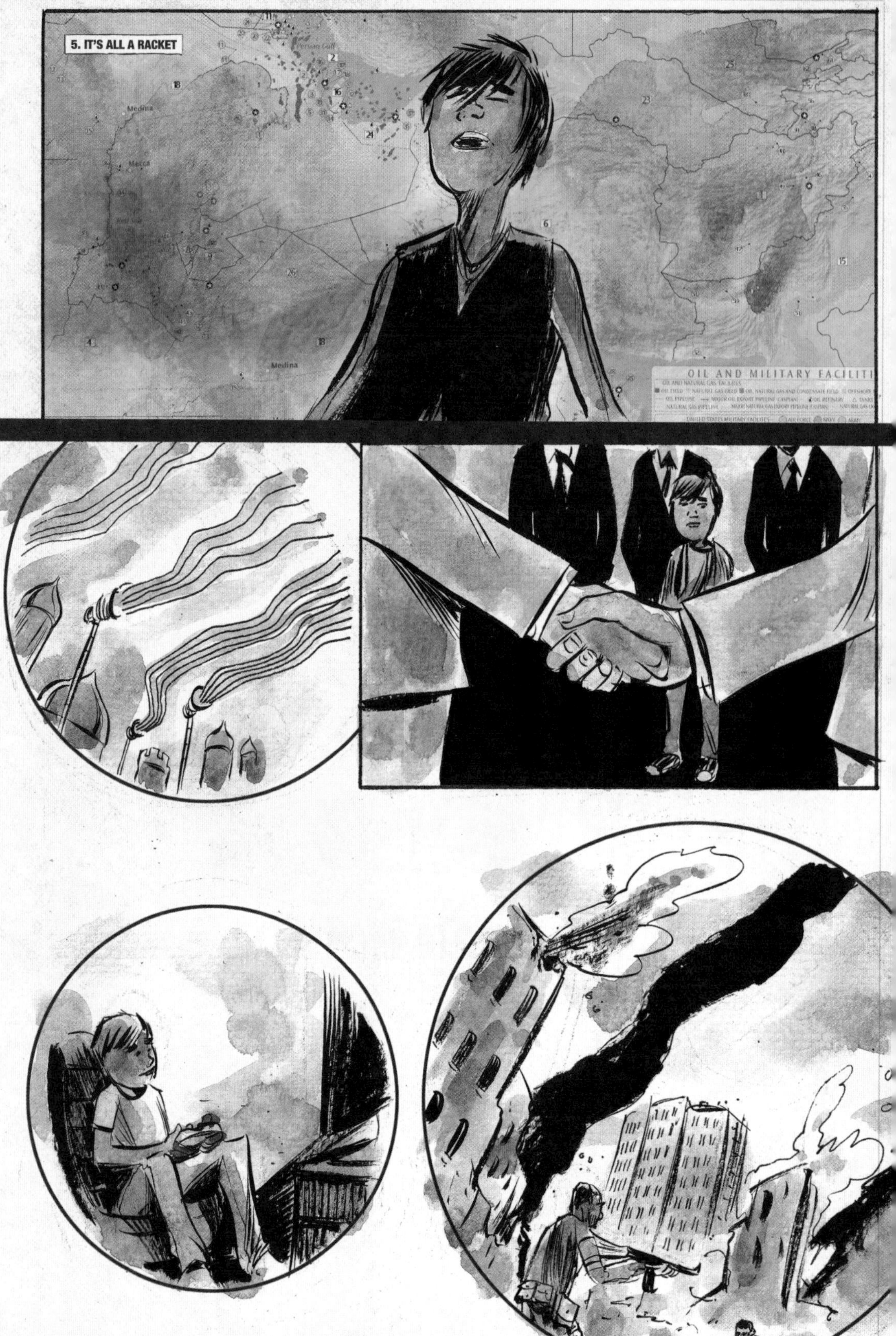

5. IT'S ALL A RACKET
Medina
Mecca
Medina
OIL AND MILITARY FACILITI

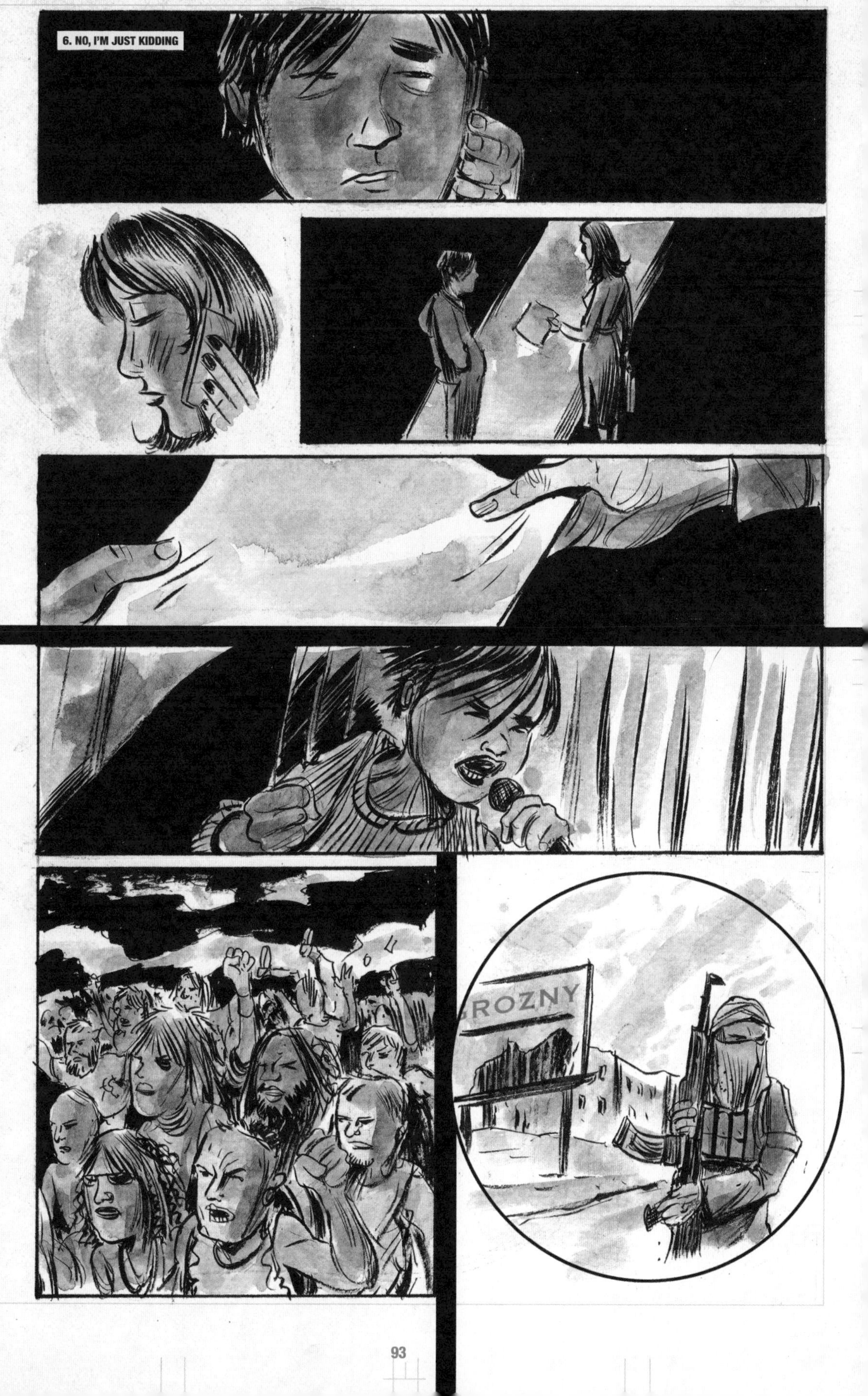
6. NO, I'M JUST KIDDING
ROZNY

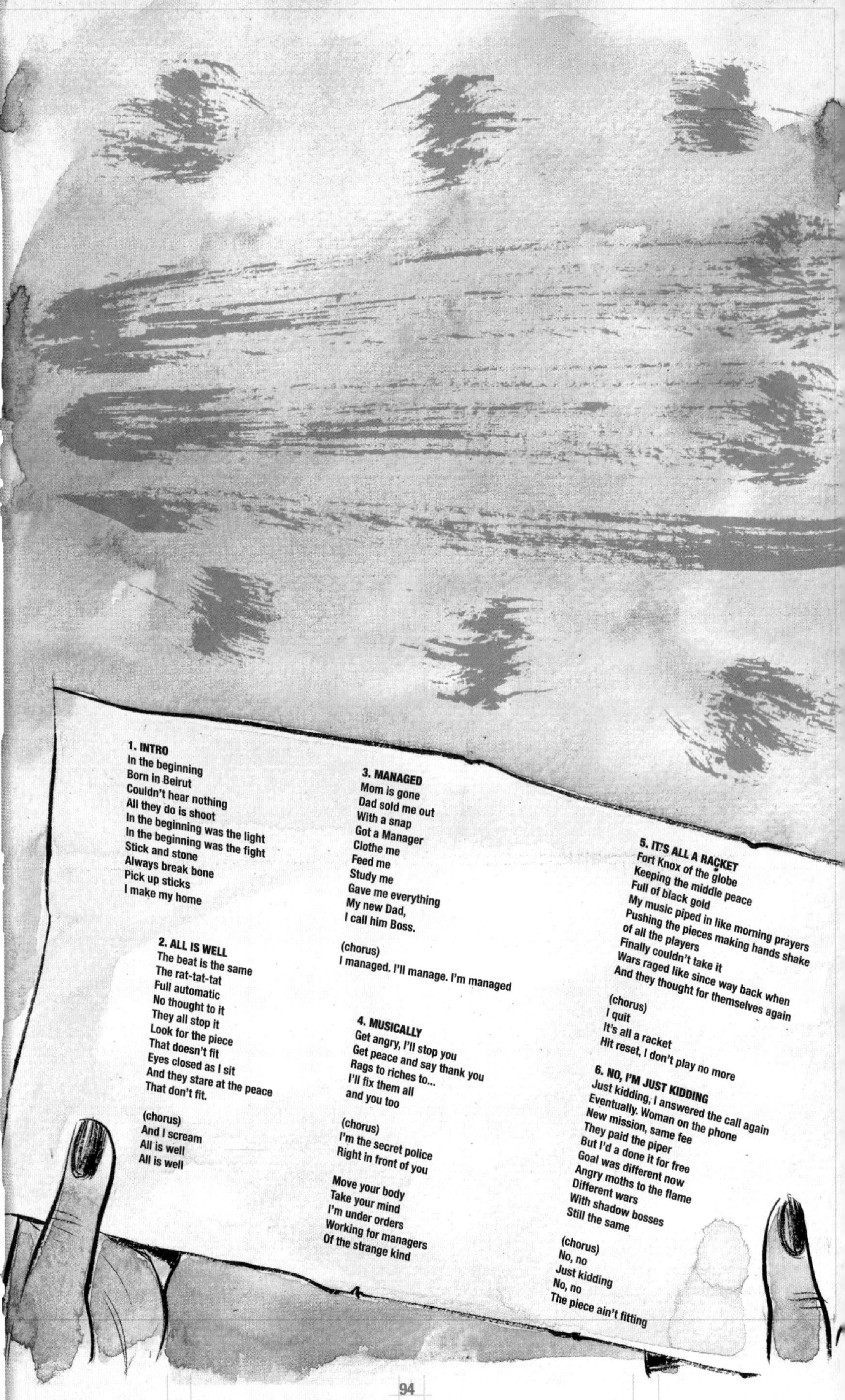
1. INTRO
In the beginning
Born in Beirut
Couldn't hear nothing
All they do is shoot
In the beginning was the light
In the beginning was the fight
Stick and stone
Always break bone
Pick up sticks
I make my home

2. ALL IS WELL
The beat is the same
The rat-tat-tat
Full automatic
No thought to it
They all stop it
Look for the piece
That doesn't fit
Eyes closed as I sit
And they stare at the peace
That don't fit.

(chorus)
And I scream
All is well
All is well

3. MANAGED
Mom is gone
Dad sold me out
With a snap
Got a Manager
Clothe me
Feed me
Study me
Gave me everything
My new Dad,
I call him Boss.

(chorus)
I managed. I'll manage. I'm managed

4. MUSICALLY
Get angry, I'll stop you
Get peace and say thank you
Rags to riches to...
I'll fix them all
and you too

(chorus)
I'm the secret police
Right in front of you

Move your body
Take your mind
I'm under orders
Working for managers
Of the strange kind

5. IT'S ALL A RACKET
Fort Knox of the globe
Keeping the middle peace
Full of black gold
My music piped in like morning prayers
Pushing the pieces making hands shake
of all the players
Finally couldn't take it
Wars raged like since way back when
And they thought for themselves again

(chorus)
I quit
It's all a racket
Hit reset, I don't play no more

6. NO, I'M JUST KIDDING
Just kidding, I answered the call again
Eventually. Woman on the phone
New mission, same fee
They paid the piper
But I'd a done it for free
Goal was different now
Angry moths to the flame
Different wars
With shadow bosses
Still the same

(chorus)
No, no
Just kidding
No, no
The piece ain't fitting

"And it was at that point I realized this man was a liar. A fraud. He wasn't my husband. He wasn't an author. He wasn't a father. All of those things were a cover. A disguise. A mask. My husband is a mole. A spy. And he's slowly erasing my mind."

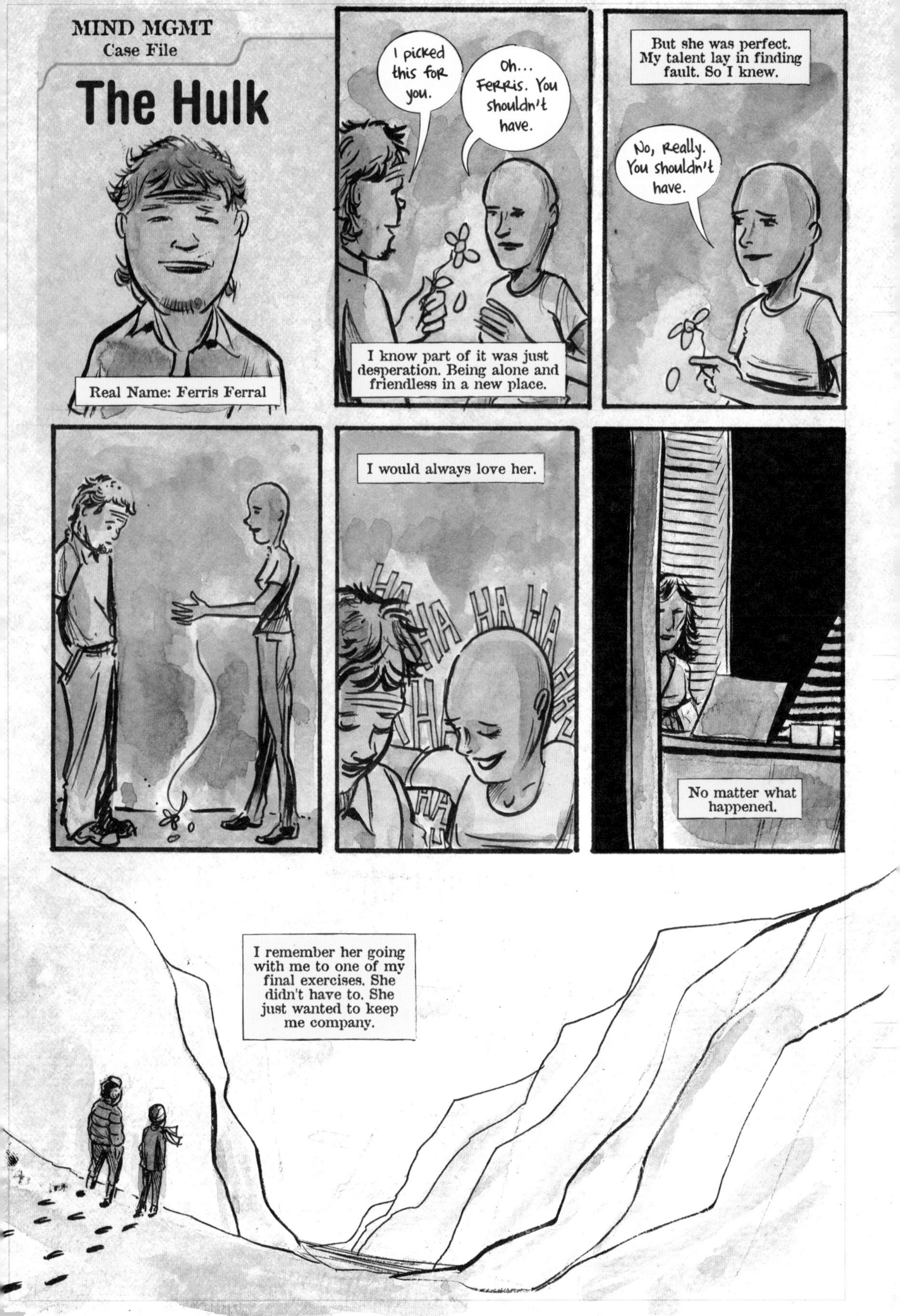
MIND MGMT
Case File
The Hulk
Real Name: Ferris Ferral
I picked this for you.
Oh... Ferris. You shouldn't have.
I know part of it was just desperation. Being alone and friendless in a new place.
But she was perfect. My talent lay in finding fault. So I knew.
No, really. You shouldn't have.
I would always love her.
HA HA HA HA HA HA HA
No matter what happened.
I remember her going with me to one of my final exercises. She didn't have to. She just wanted to keep me company.

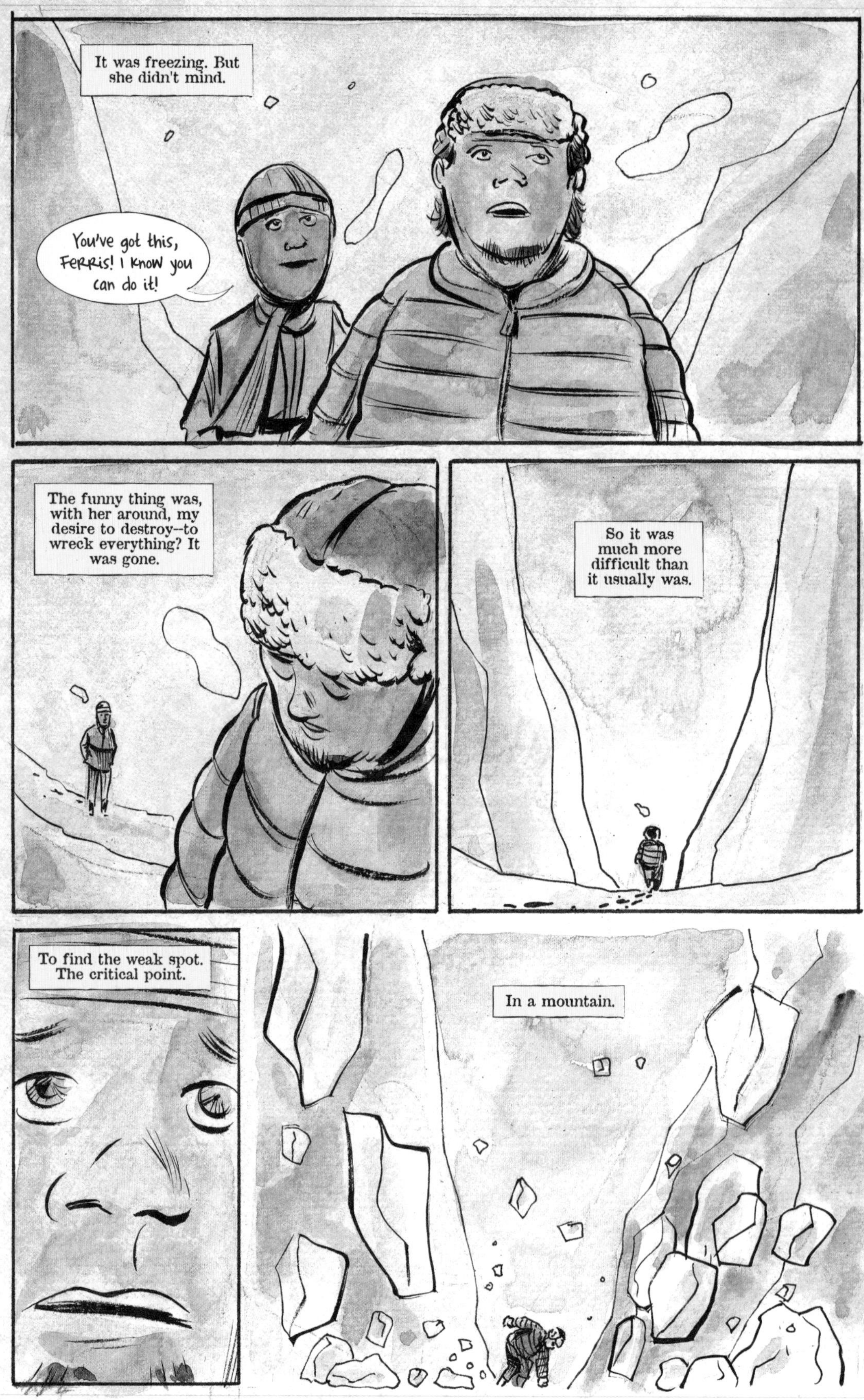
It was freezing. But she didn't mind.
You've got this, Ferris! I know you can do it!
The funny thing was, with her around, my desire to destroy--to wreck everything? It was gone.
So it was much more difficult than it usually was.
To find the weak spot. The critical point.
In a mountain.

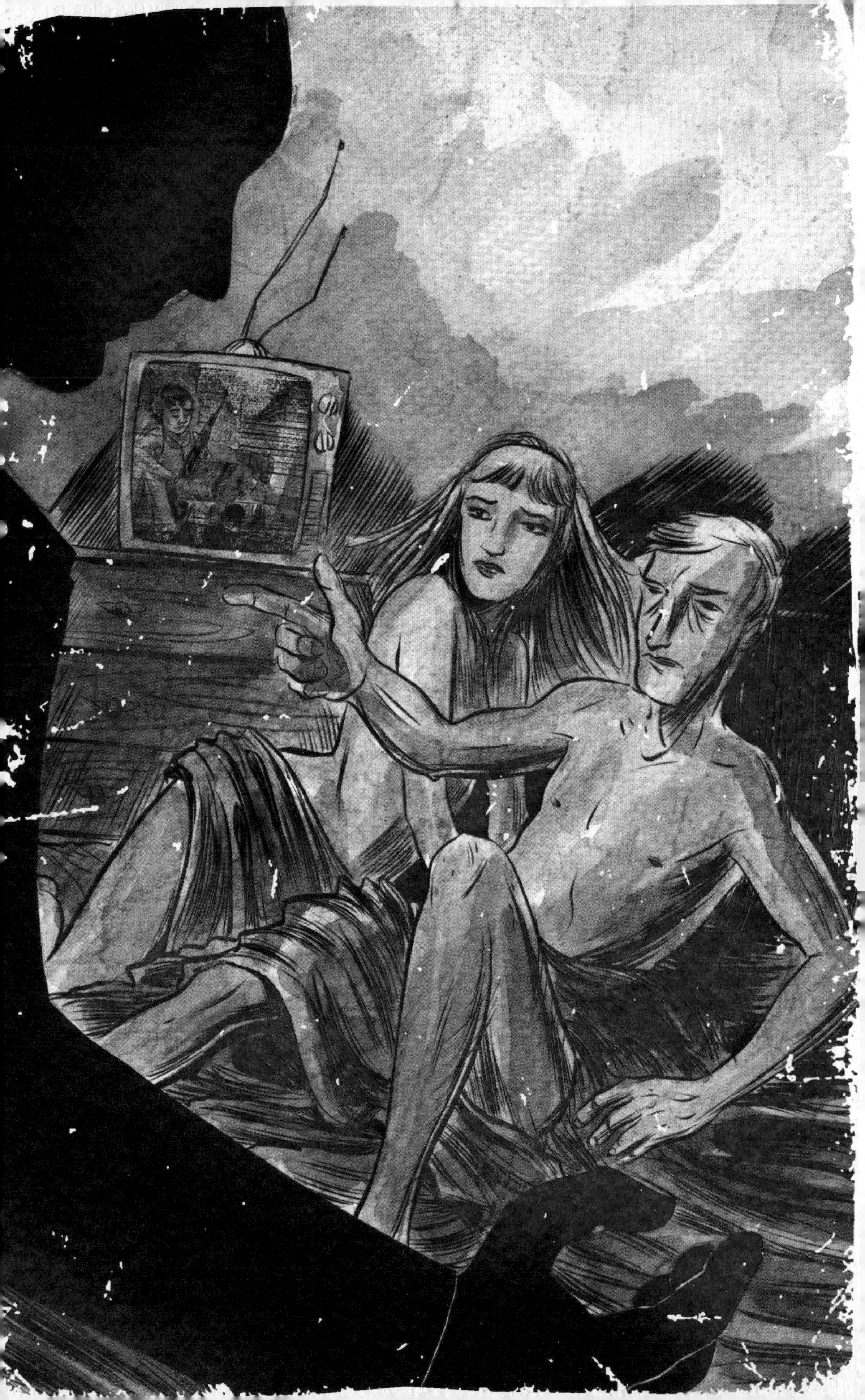

WHEN FILING REPORT ALL ESSENTIAL DETAILS MUST FALL WITHIN THIS SOLID "LIVE AREA" BOX. THIS IS THE BORDER FOR A STANDARD, NON-BLEED FIELD REPORT

Bird (content, warm, sleep) - Man downstairs (where are keys, wife lost hers, always forgetting, talk to her later) - She (tell him details, like his shirt, crinkle in the corner of his eyes)

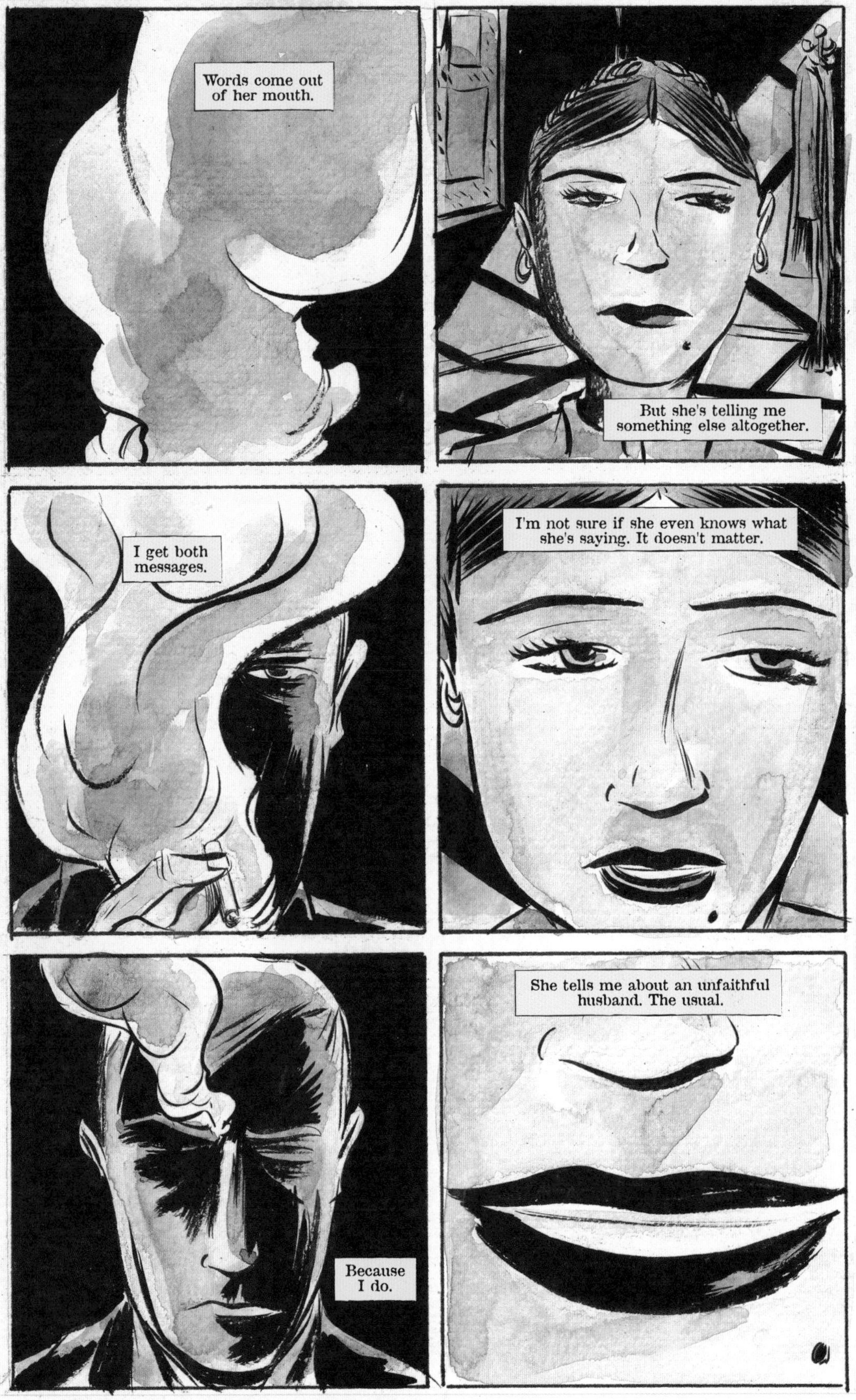

Words come out of her mouth.
But she's telling me something else altogether.
I get both messages.
I'm not sure if she even knows what she's saying. It doesn't matter.
Because I do.
She tells me about an unfaithful husband. The usual.

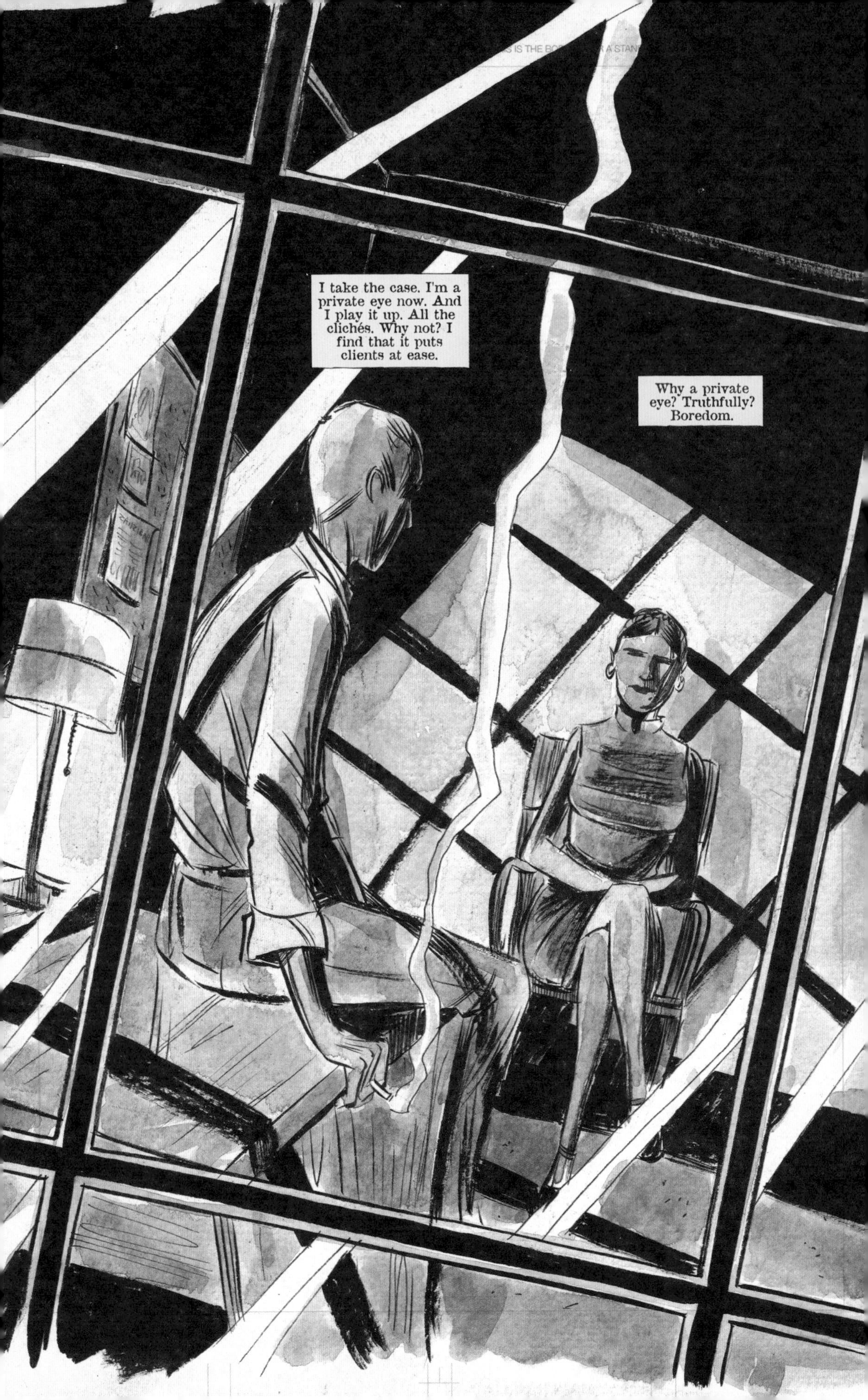
I take the case. I'm a private eye now. And I play it up. All the clichés. Why not? I find that it puts clients at ease.
Why a private eye? Truthfully? Boredom.

WHEN FILING REPORT ALL ESSENTIAL DETAILS MUST FALL WITHIN THIS SOLID "LIVE AREA" BOX. THIS IS THE BORDER FOR A STANDARD, NON-BLEED FIELD REPORT

Bartender (always leaves big tip, please no trouble again tonight) - Jock (one more, no, two more, then home. Game's on, two more there, sleep on couch, alone again. Goofy guy looking at me, kick his ass first.
looking for fight? Give him one, punch him in the, no...)

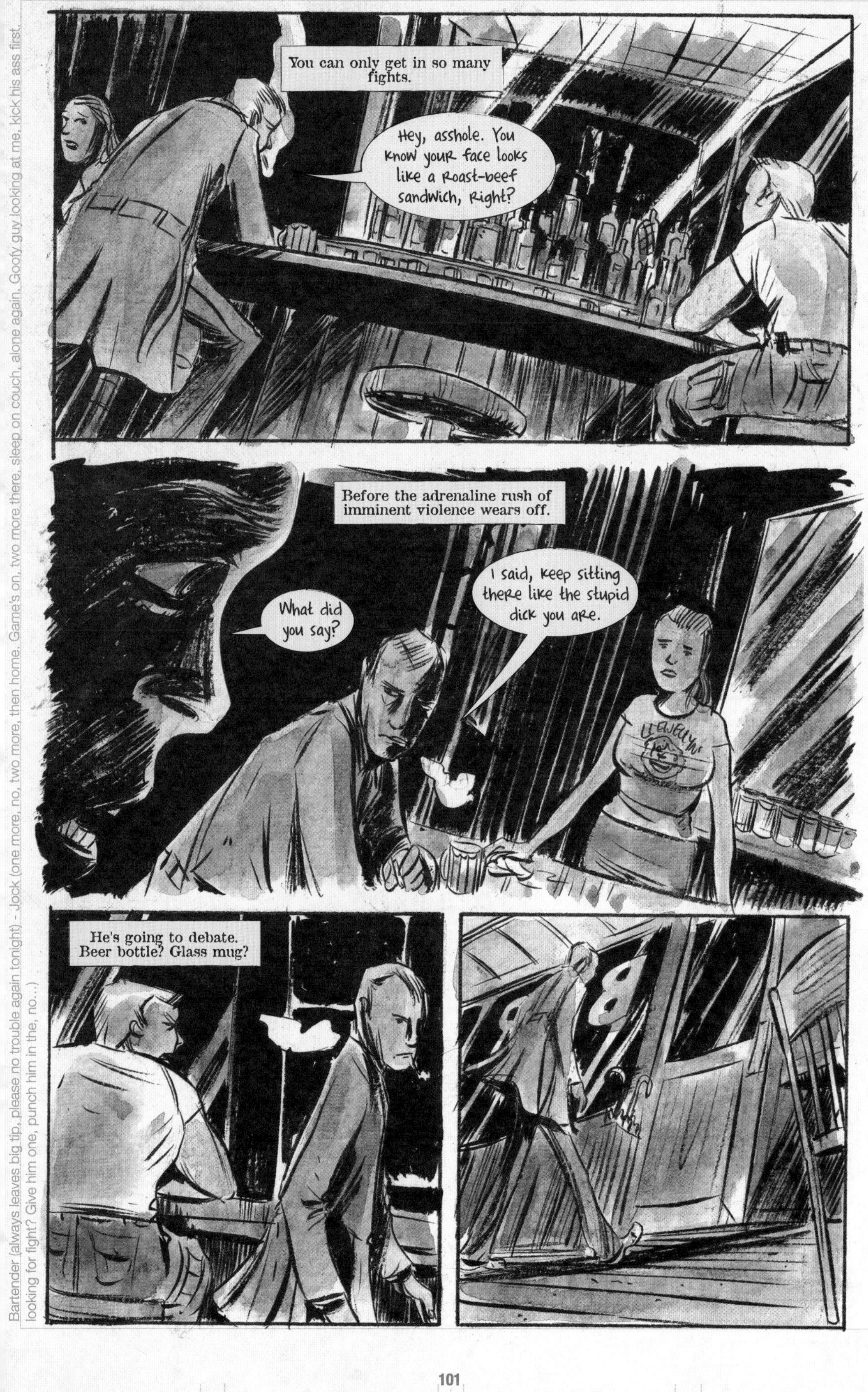

You can only get in so many fights.
Hey, asshole. You know your face looks like a Roast-beef sandwich, Right?
Before the adrenaline rush of imminent violence wears off.
What did you say?
I said, keep sitting there like the stupid dick you are.
He's going to debate. Beer bottle? Glass mug?

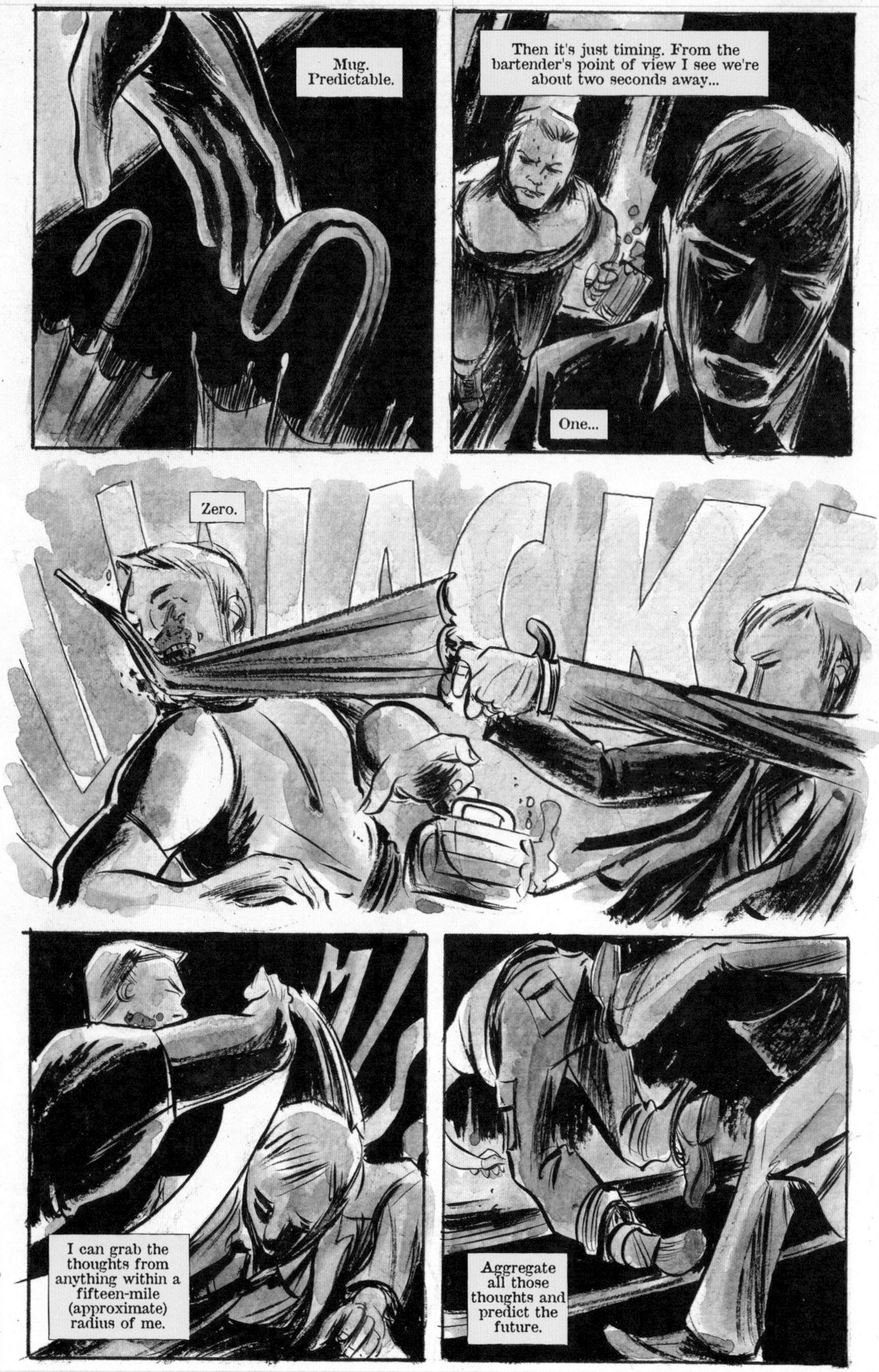
Mug. Predictable.
Then it's just timing. From the bartender's point of view I see we're about two seconds away...
One...
Zero.
I can grab the thoughts from anything within a fifteen-mile (approximate) radius of me.
Aggregate all those thoughts and predict the future.

Jock (beer mug to his skull, damn, what, kill him, crush his nose, cave that stupid face in)

WHEN FILING REPORT ALL ESSENTIAL DETAILS MUST FALL WITHIN THIS SOLID "LIVE AREA" BOX. THIS IS THE BORDER FOR A STANDARD, NON-BLEED FIELD REPORT

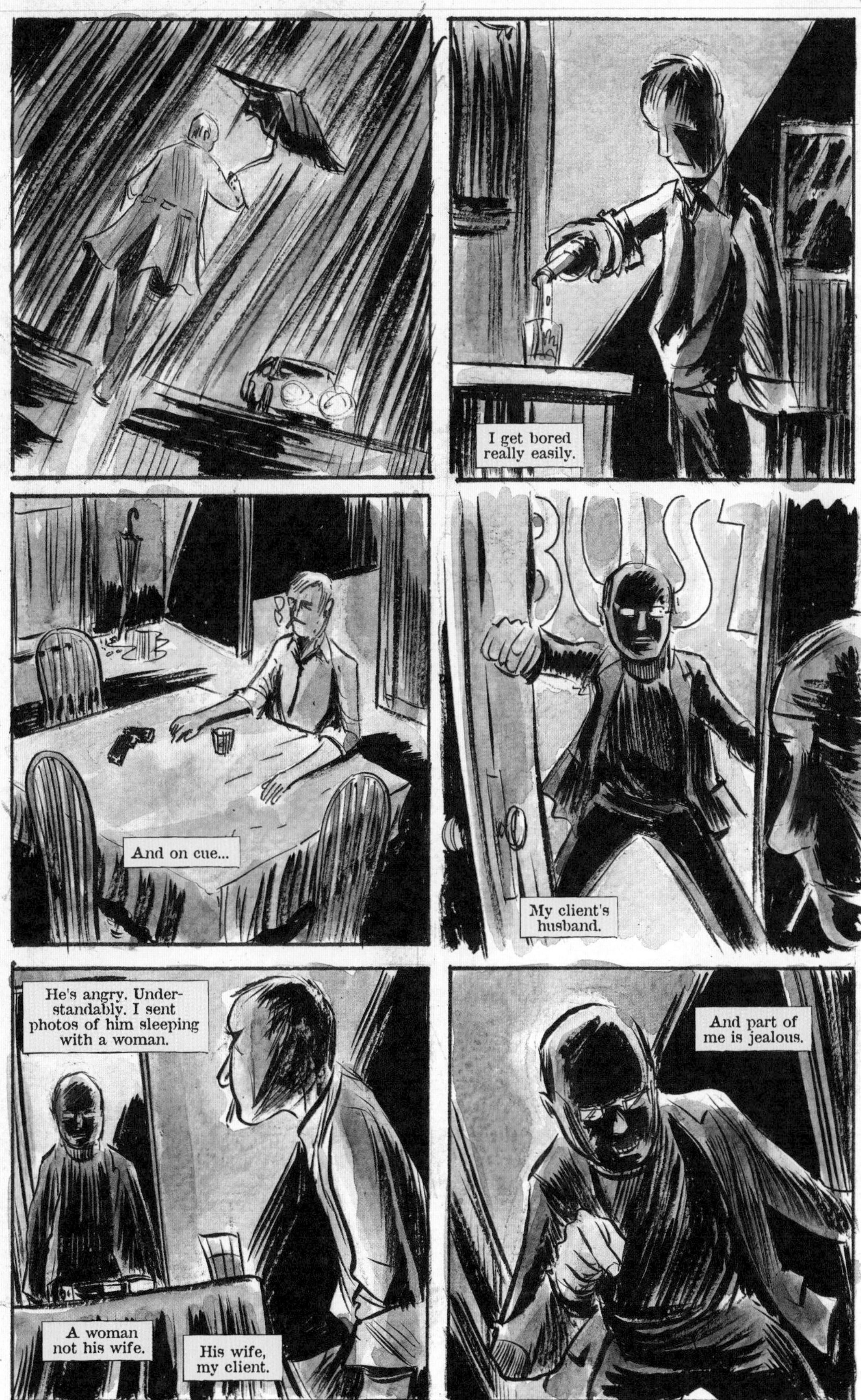

I get bored really easily.
And on cue...
BUST
My client's husband.
He's angry. Understandably. I sent photos of him sleeping with a woman.
A woman not his wife.
His wife, my client.
And part of me is jealous.

Mouse (footsteps, hide) - Husband (just talk to him, get info on her. Why'd he give me his address, setting me up, don't care, beat his ass, show them both)

WHEN FILING REPORT ALL ESSENTIAL DETAILS MUST FALL WITHIN THIS SOLID "LIVE AREA" BOX. THIS IS THE BORDER FOR A STANDARD, NON-BLEED FIELD REPORT

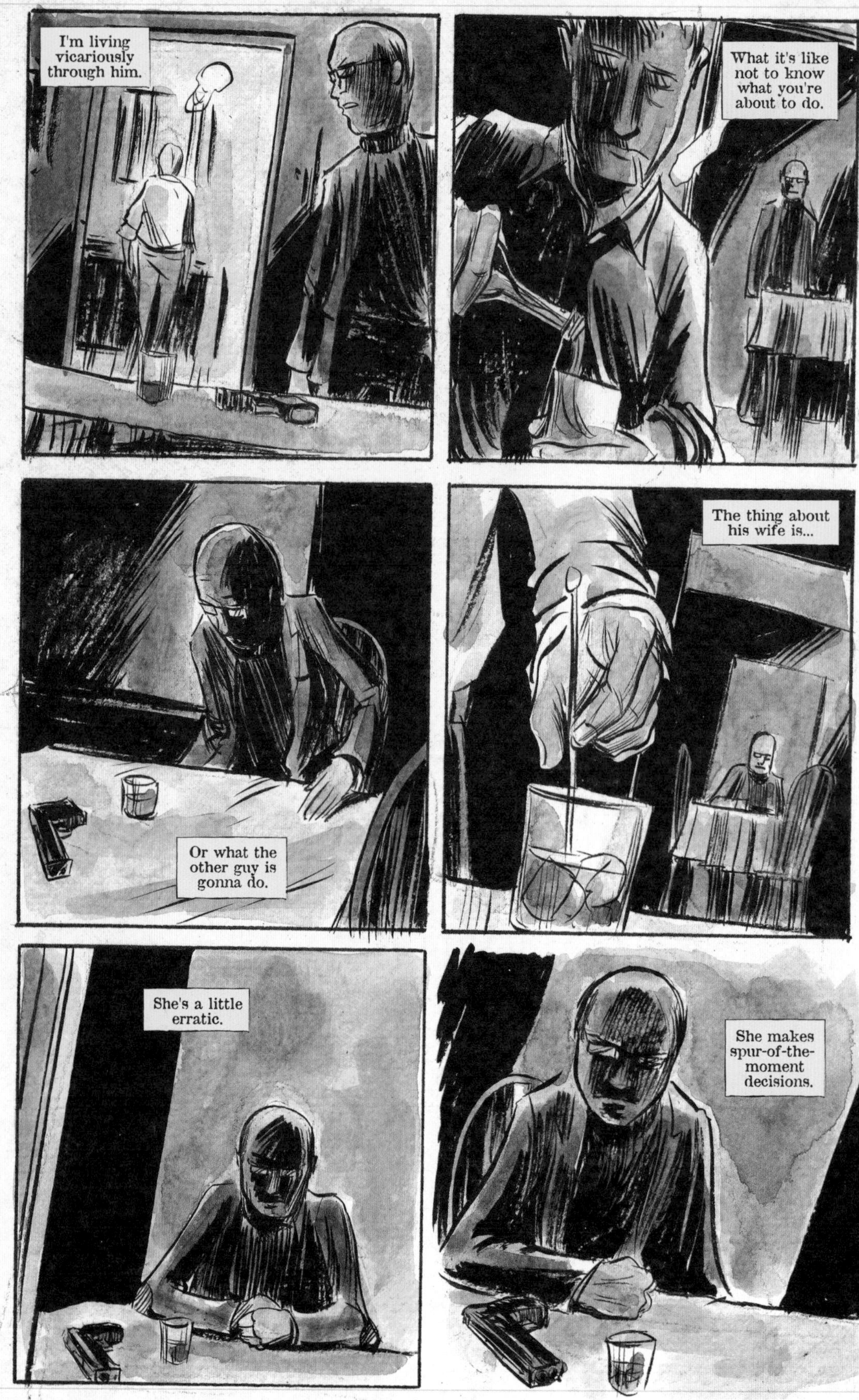
I'm living vicariously through him.
What it's like not to know what you're about to do.
Or what the other guy is gonna do.
The thing about his wife is...
She's a little erratic.
She makes spur-of-the-moment decisions.

Husband (back turned, calm down, maybe we'll just talk, have a drink, no, gun, back turned, drink, kill him, fake a suicide, too hard, shoot and run maybe)

WHEN FILING REPORT ALL ESSENTIAL DETAILS MUST FALL WITHIN THIS SOLID "LIVE AREA" BOX. THIS IS THE BORDER FOR A STANDARD, NON-BLEED FIELD REPORT

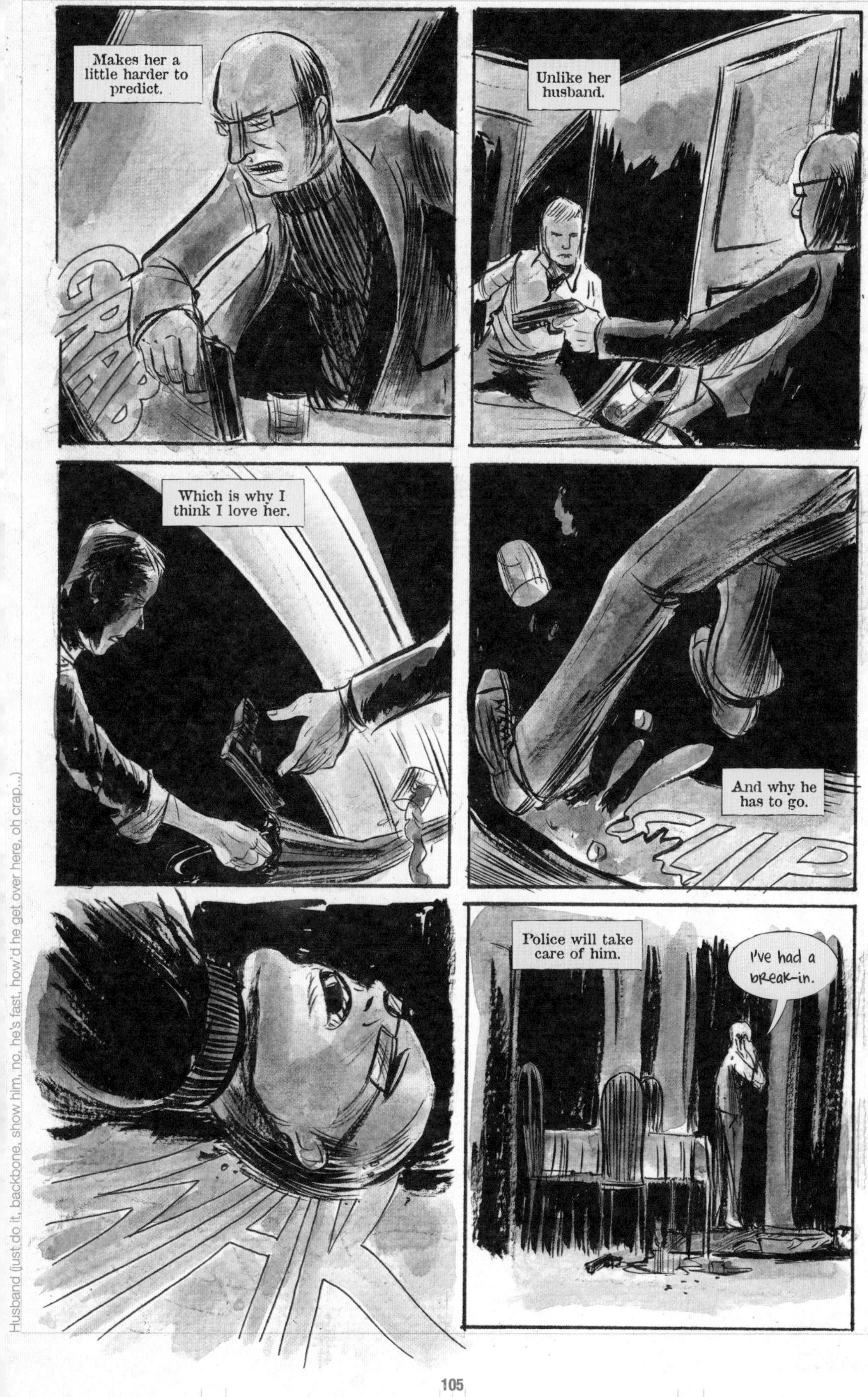

Makes her a little harder to predict.
GRAB
Unlike her husband.
Which is why I think I love her.
And why he has to go.
Police will take care of him.
I've had a break-in.

Husband (just do it, backbone, show him, no, he's fast, how'd he get over here, oh crap...)

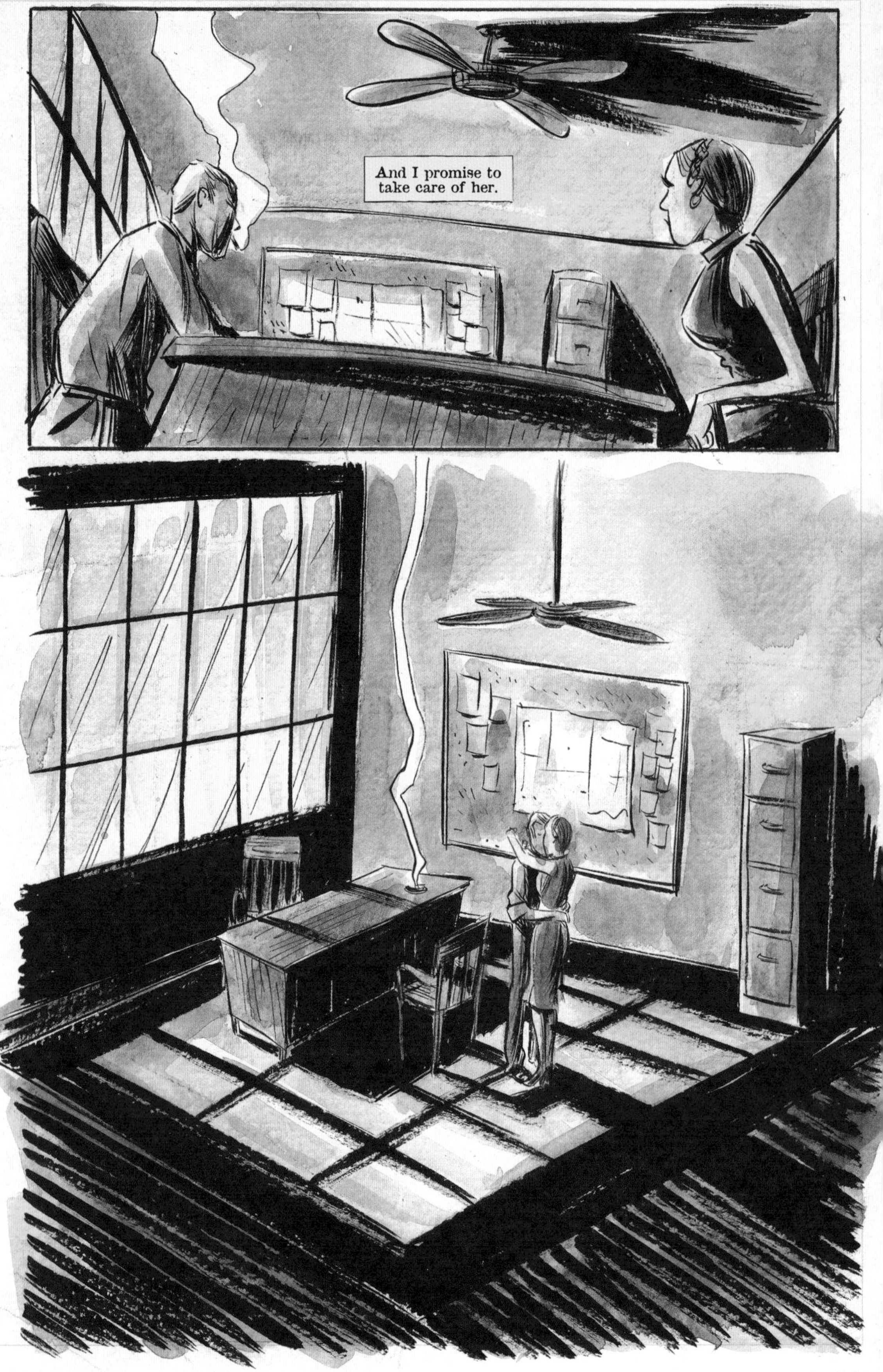
And I promise to take care of her.

Bird (cool night, fly up, find thermal, float, no effort, good) - She (relieved, scared, nervous, quiet, awkward, don't think, meant to be, just...)

WHEN FILING REPORT ALL ESSENTIAL DETAILS MUST FALL WITHIN THIS SOLID "LIVE AREA" BOX. THIS IS THE BORDER FOR A STANDARD, NON-BLEED FIELD REPORT

Passerby (too old for her, she looks happy, though) - Passerby 2 (whore) - Passerby 3 (dress too tight, no, just right, don't look, she saw you) - Passerby 4 (love that suit, she probably dresses him, need new shoes) - She (love him, perfect, too good, inside my head, too easy, love? Has to be, he's perfect, so lucky)

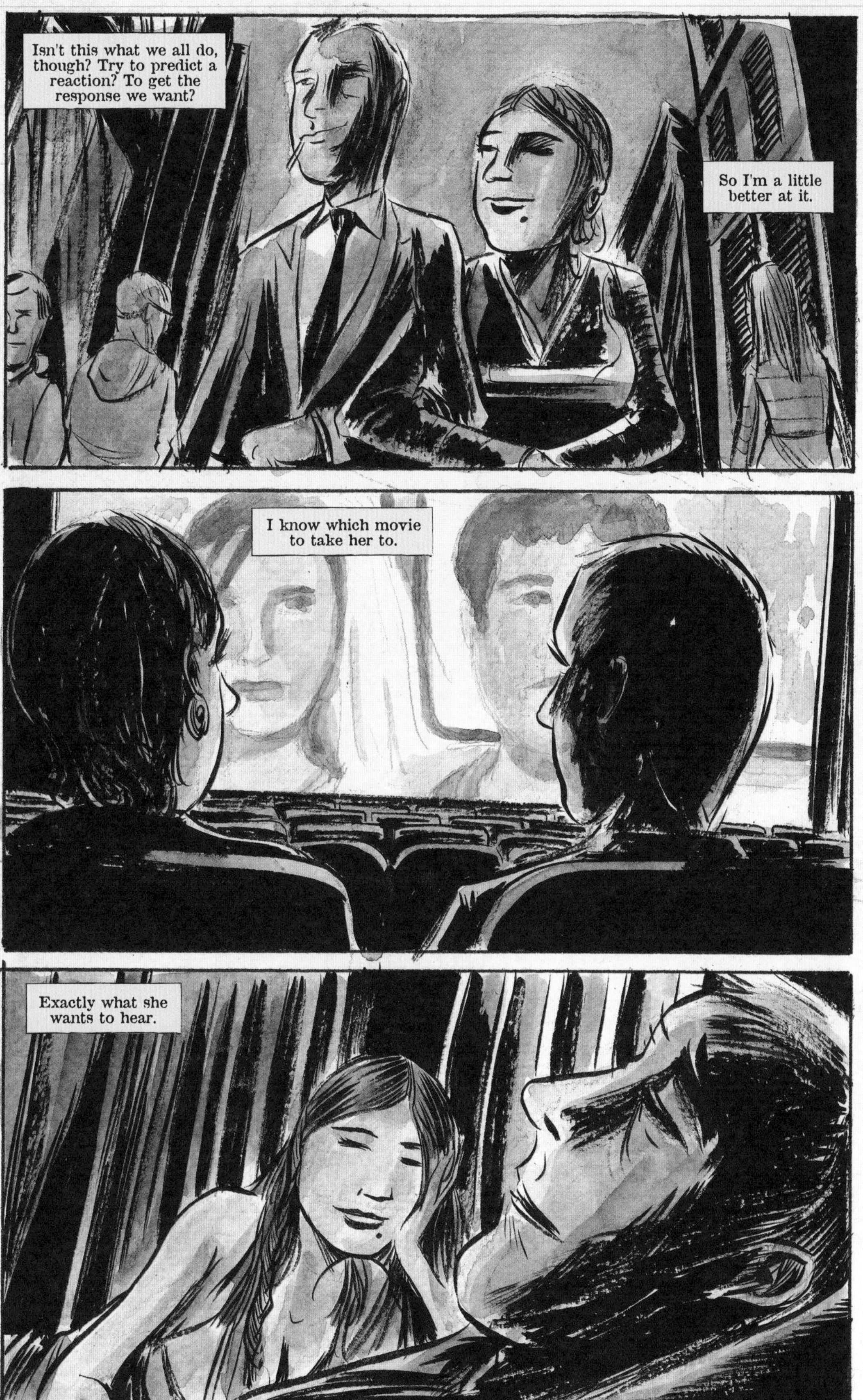
Isn't this what we all do, though? Try to predict a reaction? To get the response we want?
So I'm a little better at it.
I know which movie to take her to.
Exactly what she wants to hear.

Cat (food, smells good, hungry, window? Closed, other window? Cracked. Squeeze in) - She (so good, content, full, warm, something's wrong, what did I do? Why?) - Tom Selleck (lonely, gotta be someone out there, guy setting me up with his girl? Setup? Maybe. Desperate though, worth a shot)

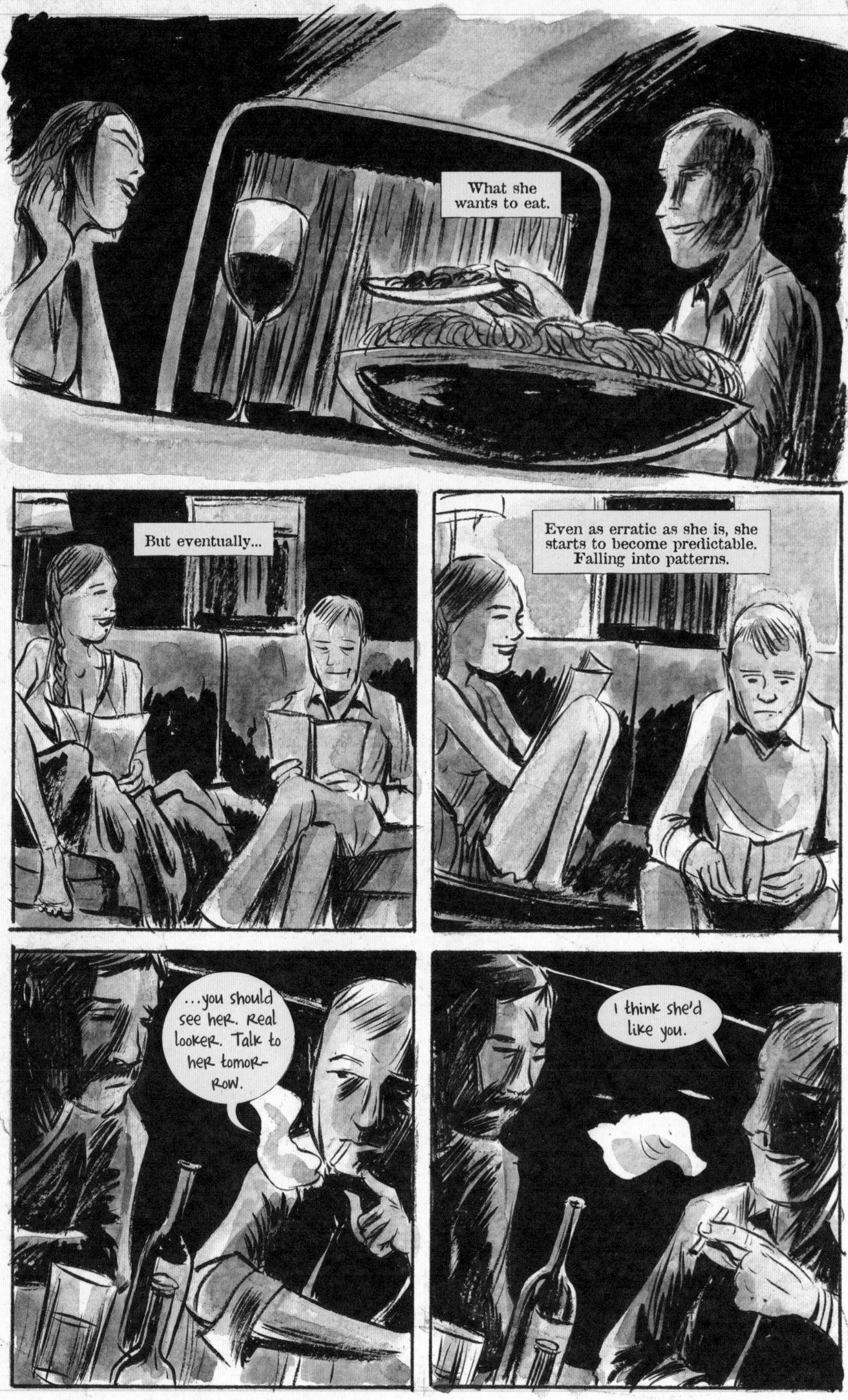
What she wants to eat.
But eventually...
Even as erratic as she is, she starts to become predictable. Falling into patterns.
...you should see her. Real looker. Talk to her tomorrow.
I think she'd like you.

WHEN FILING REPORT ALL ESSENTIAL DETAILS MUST FALL WITHIN THIS SOLID "LIVE AREA" BOX. THIS IS THE BORDER FOR A STANDARD, NON-BLEED FIELD REPORT

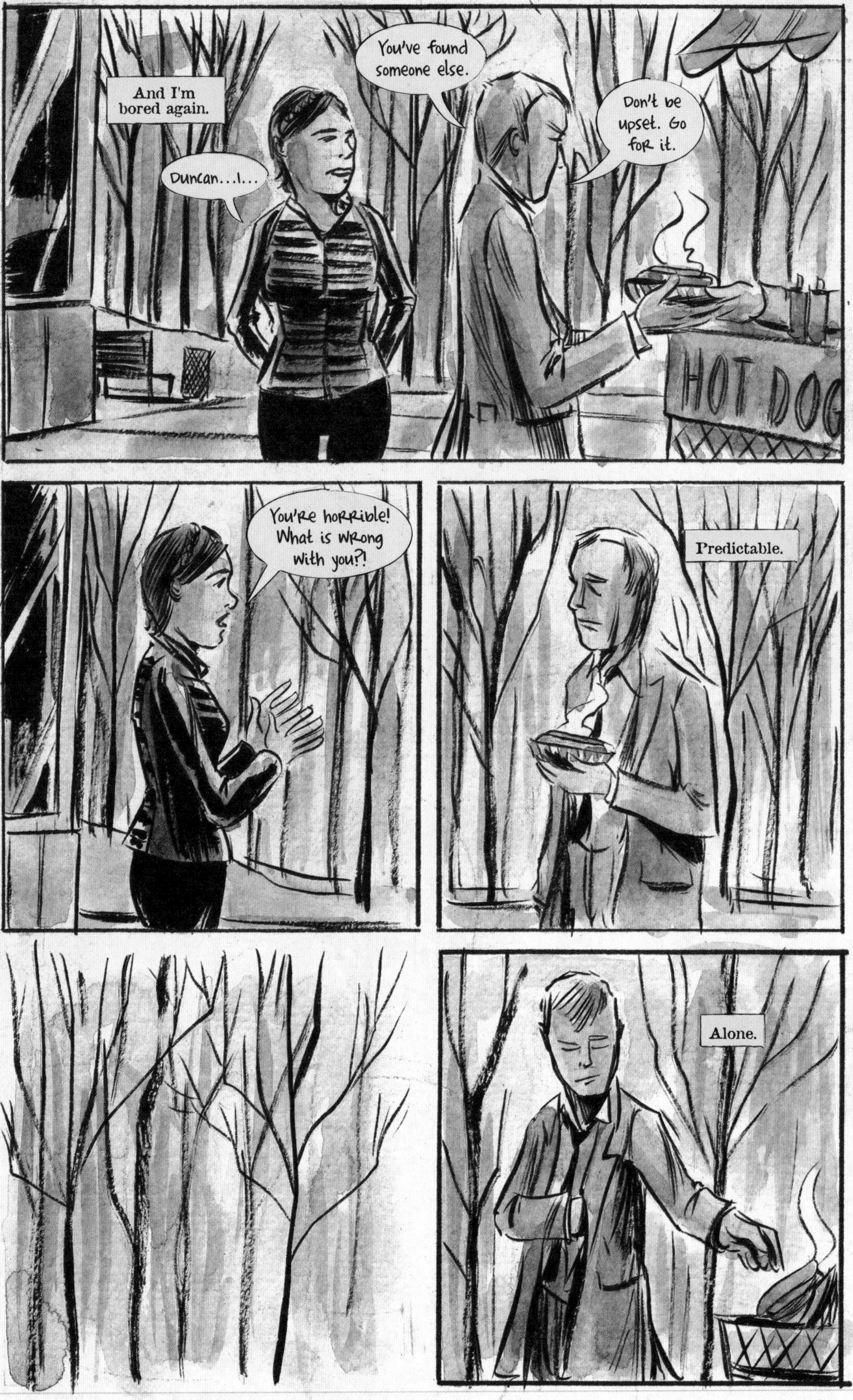
And I'm bored again.
Duncan...I...
You've found someone else.
Don't be upset. Go for it.
HOT DOG
You're horrible! What is wrong with you?!
Predictable.
Alone.

Vendor (guy creeps me out, never tips, serial killer) - She (feel dizzy, what happened to him, scared, angry? No, nothing? Something's wrong. Wrong with him. Never know what he's thinking. Over. It's over. Over. Leave.)

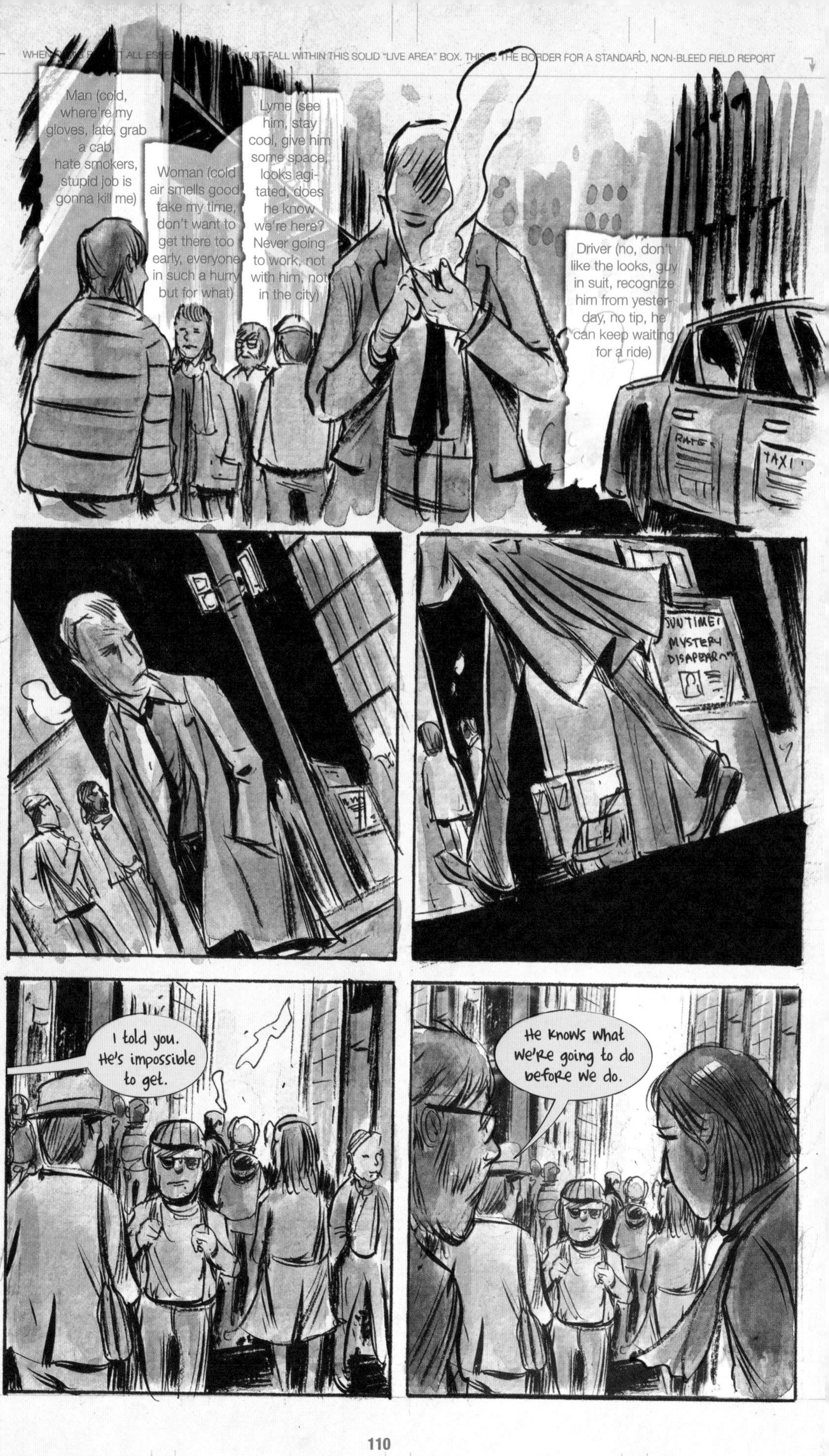

Man (cold, where're my gloves, late, grab a cab, hate smokers, stupid job is gonna kill me)
Woman (cold air smells good, take my time, don't want to get there too early, everyone in such a hurry but for what)
Lyme (see him, stay cool, give him some space, looks agitated, does he know we're here? Never going to work, not with him, not in the city)
Driver (no, don't like the looks, guy in suit, recognize him from yesterday, no tip, he can keep waiting for a ride)
TAXI
MYSTERY
I told you. He's impossible to get.
He knows what we're going to do before we do.

Premeditated A True Crime Novel (continued)

Julianne's journal continues to its awful conclusion on the morning of the murders: "I feel like someone is always following me. Always watching. Even when I'm completely alone. Which is most of the time."

WHEN FILING REPORT ALL ESSENTIAL DETAILS MUST FALL WITHIN THIS SOLID "LIVE AREA" BOX. THIS IS THE BORDER FOR A STANDARD, NON-BLEED FIELD REPORT

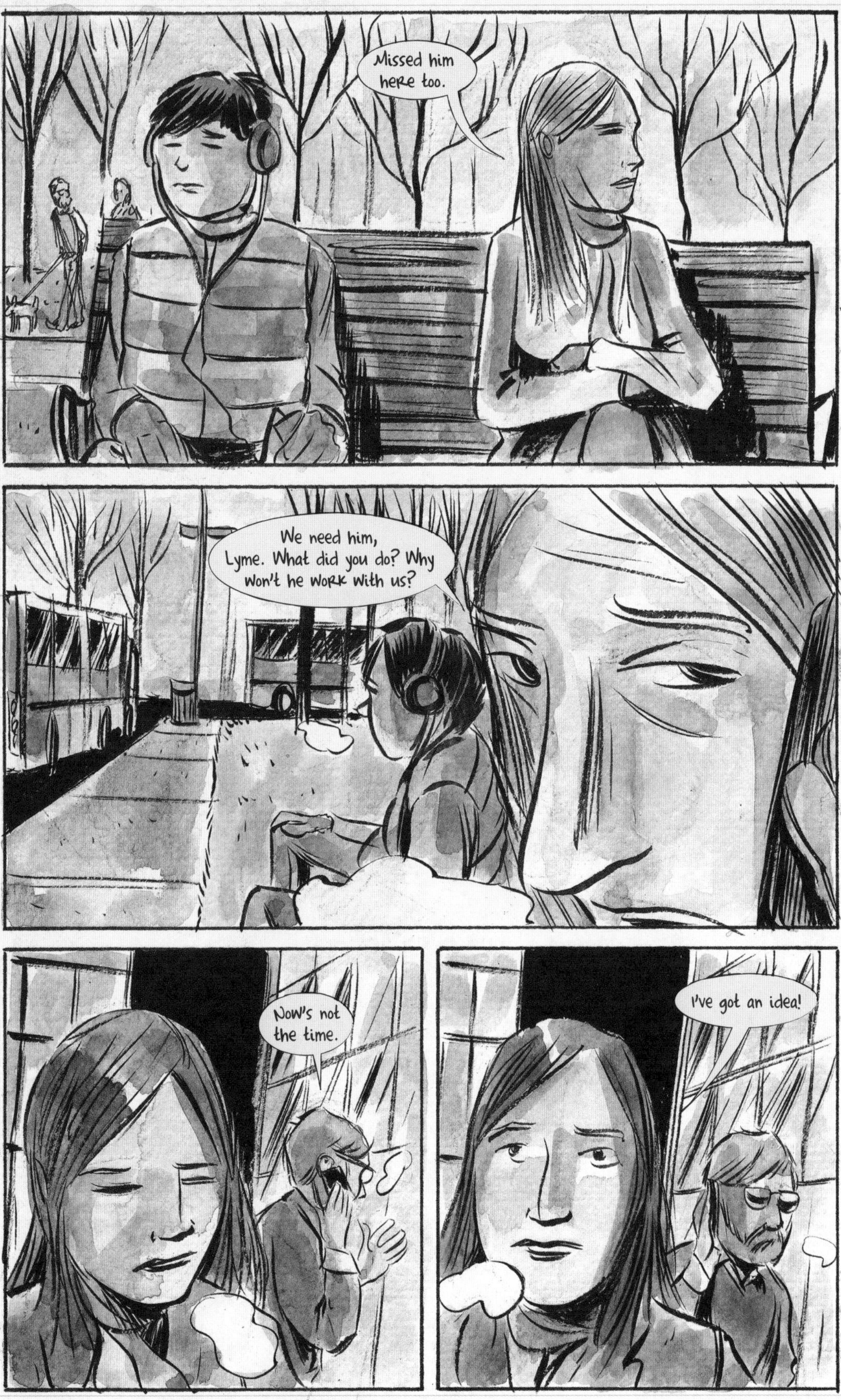

Missed him here too.
We need him, Lyme. What did you do? Why won't he work with us?
Now's not the time.
I've got an idea!

"I walked downstairs this morning and noticed that Verve's office door was cracked and he was having a heated discussion with someone on the phone. I tentatively stepped towards the door to listen.

WHEN FILING REPORT ALL ESSENTIAL DETAILS MUST FALL WITHIN THIS SOLID "LIVE AREA" BOX. THIS IS THE BORDER FOR A STANDARD, NON-BLEED FIELD REPORT

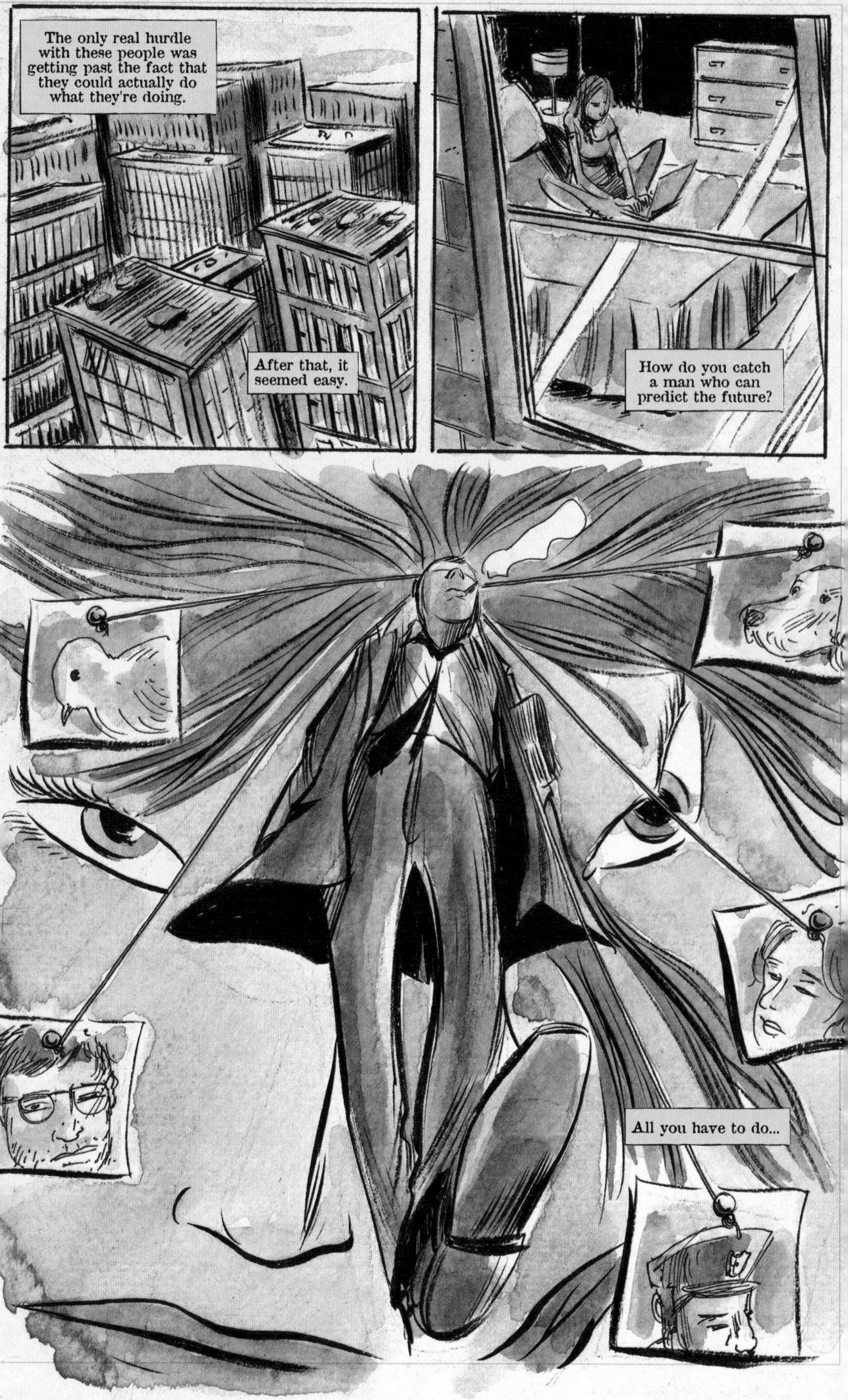

The only real hurdle with these people was getting past the fact that they could actually do what they're doing.
After that, it seemed easy.
How do you catch a man who can predict the future?
All you have to do...

“I noticed a bulletin board behind him for the first time. On it were photographs with pins in them. Some of them were X-ed out. Others had circles around them. Then I heard him say, ‘...cover is blown. She knows. I've told you. But my erasures are having side effects. She can't handle much more. I don't want to do it...’

WHEN FILING REPORT ALL ESSENTIAL DETAILS MUST FALL WITHIN THIS SOLID "LIVE AREA" BOX. THIS IS THE BORDER FOR A STANDARD, NON-BLEED FIELD REPORT

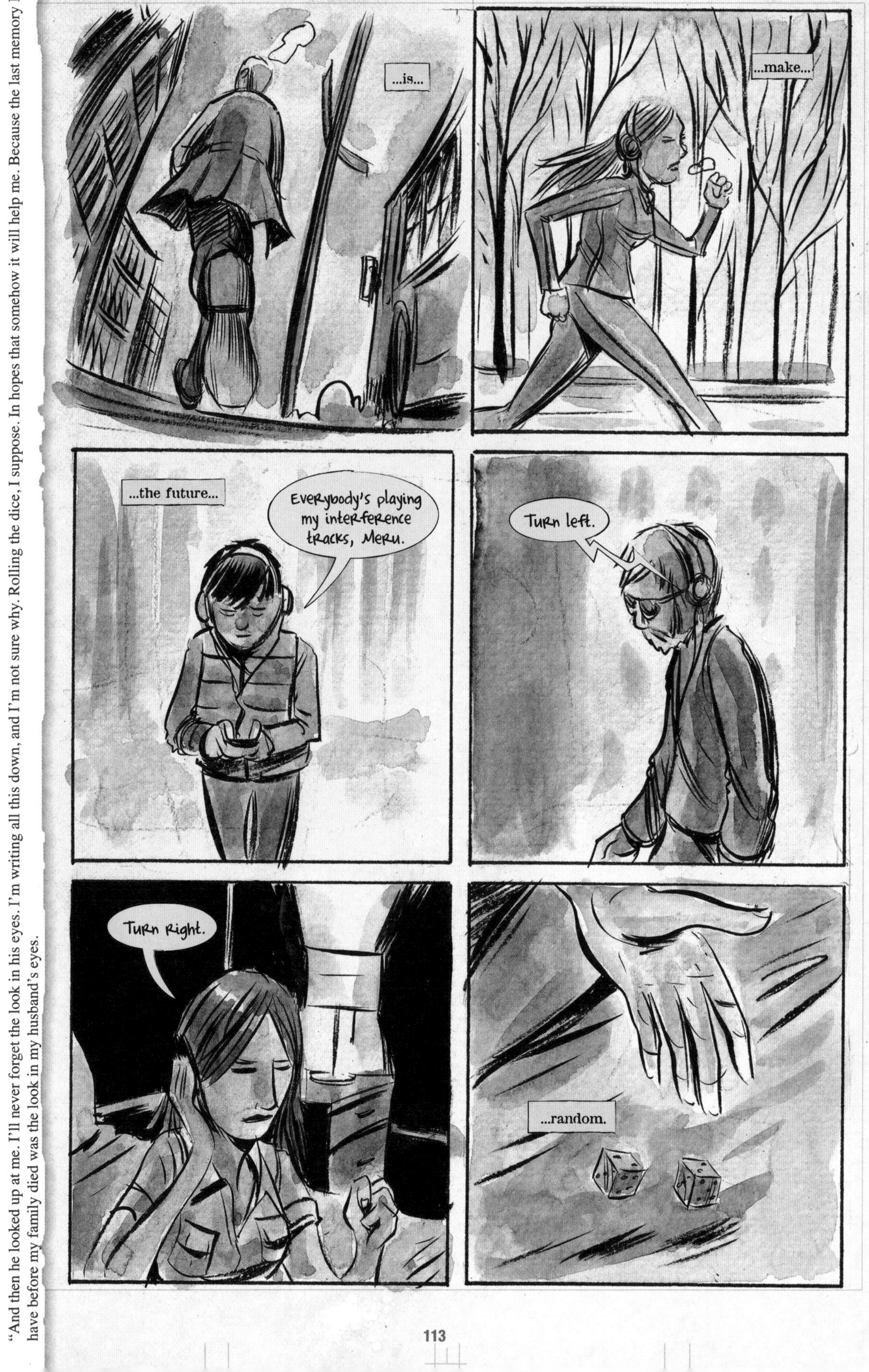

...is...
...make...
...the future...
Everybody's playing my interference tracks, Meru.
Turn left.
Turn right.
...random.

"And then he looked up at me. I'll never forget the look in his eyes. I'm writing all this down, and I'm not sure why. Rolling the dice, I suppose. In hopes that somehow it will help me. Because the last memory I have before my family died was the look in my husband's eyes.

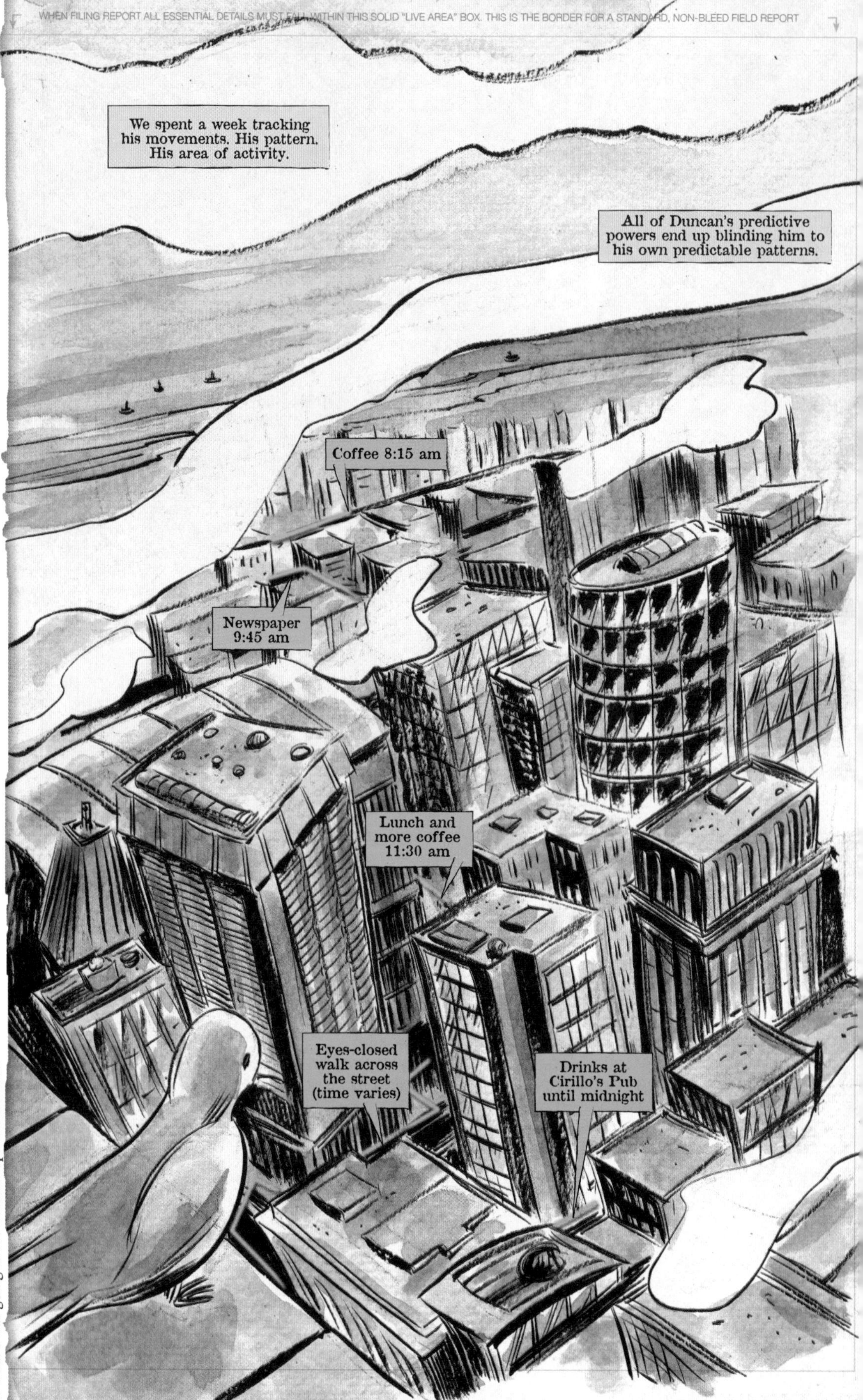
WHEN FILING REPORT ALL ESSENTIAL DETAILS MUST FALL WITHIN THIS SOLID "LIVE AREA" BOX. THIS IS THE BORDER FOR A STANDARD, NON-BLEED FIELD REPORT
We spent a week tracking his movements. His pattern. His area of activity.
All of Duncan's predictive powers end up blinding him to his own predictable patterns.
Coffee 8:15 am
Newspaper 9:45 am
Lunch and more coffee 11:30 am
Eyes-closed walk across the street (time varies)
Drinks at Cirillo's Pub until midnight

"I felt like I was outside my body watching myself walk around the house. I'm covered in blood now. I find Verve dead in his office. Stabbed to death. Then I walk upstairs and find the children. It's as if I knew what I was going to see before I opened the door.

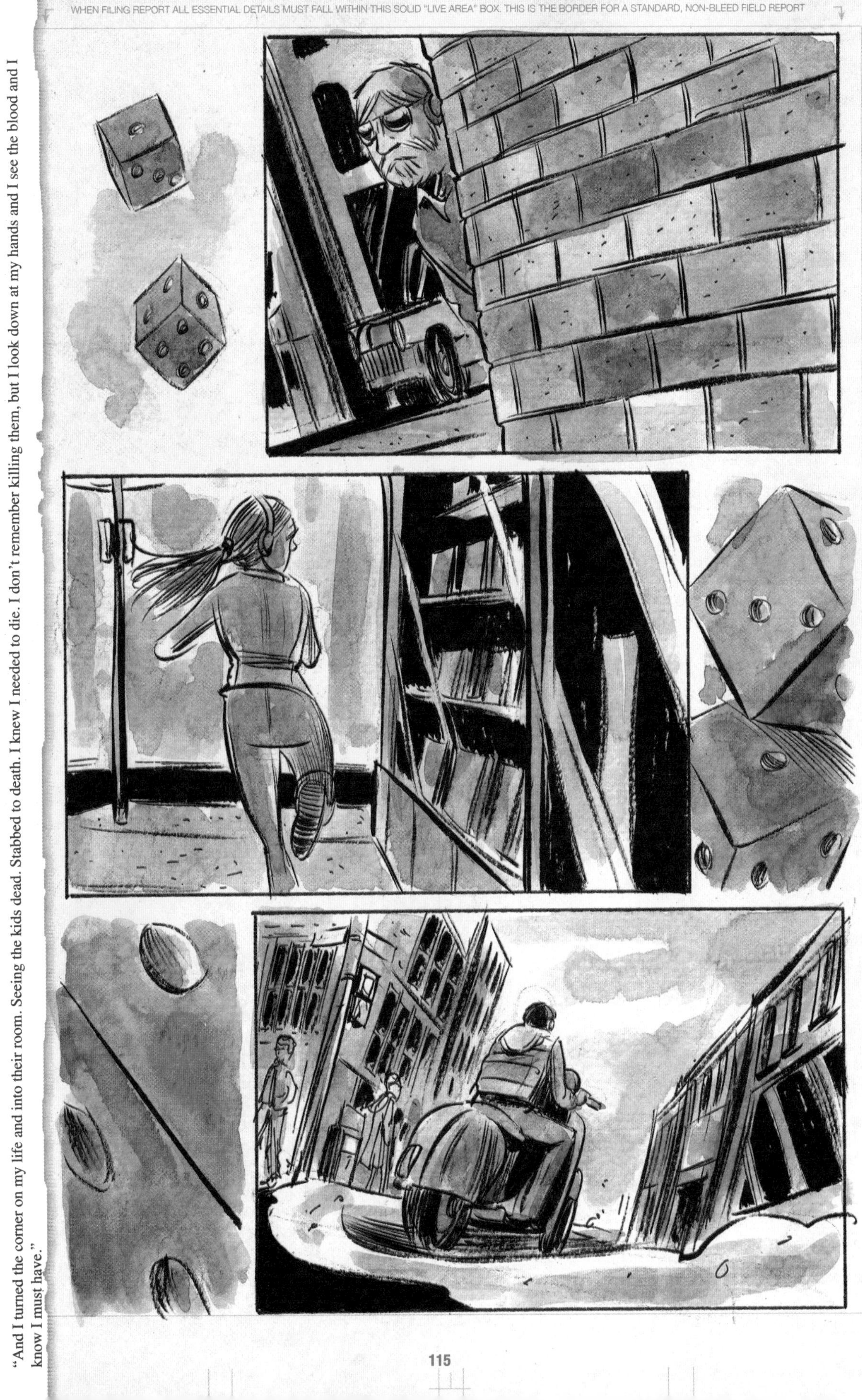
WHEN FILING REPORT ALL ESSENTIAL DETAILS MUST FALL WITHIN THIS SOLID "LIVE AREA" BOX. THIS IS THE BORDER FOR A STANDARD, NON-BLEED FIELD REPORT

"And I turned the corner on my life and into their room. Seeing the kids dead. Stabbed to death. I knew I needed to die. I don't remember killing them, but I look down at my hands and I see the blood and I know I must have."

Julianne's journal was the evidence that made her conviction and death sentence a foregone conclusion. However, during her testimony she claimed to have bumped into a man when she was fleeing the murder scene.

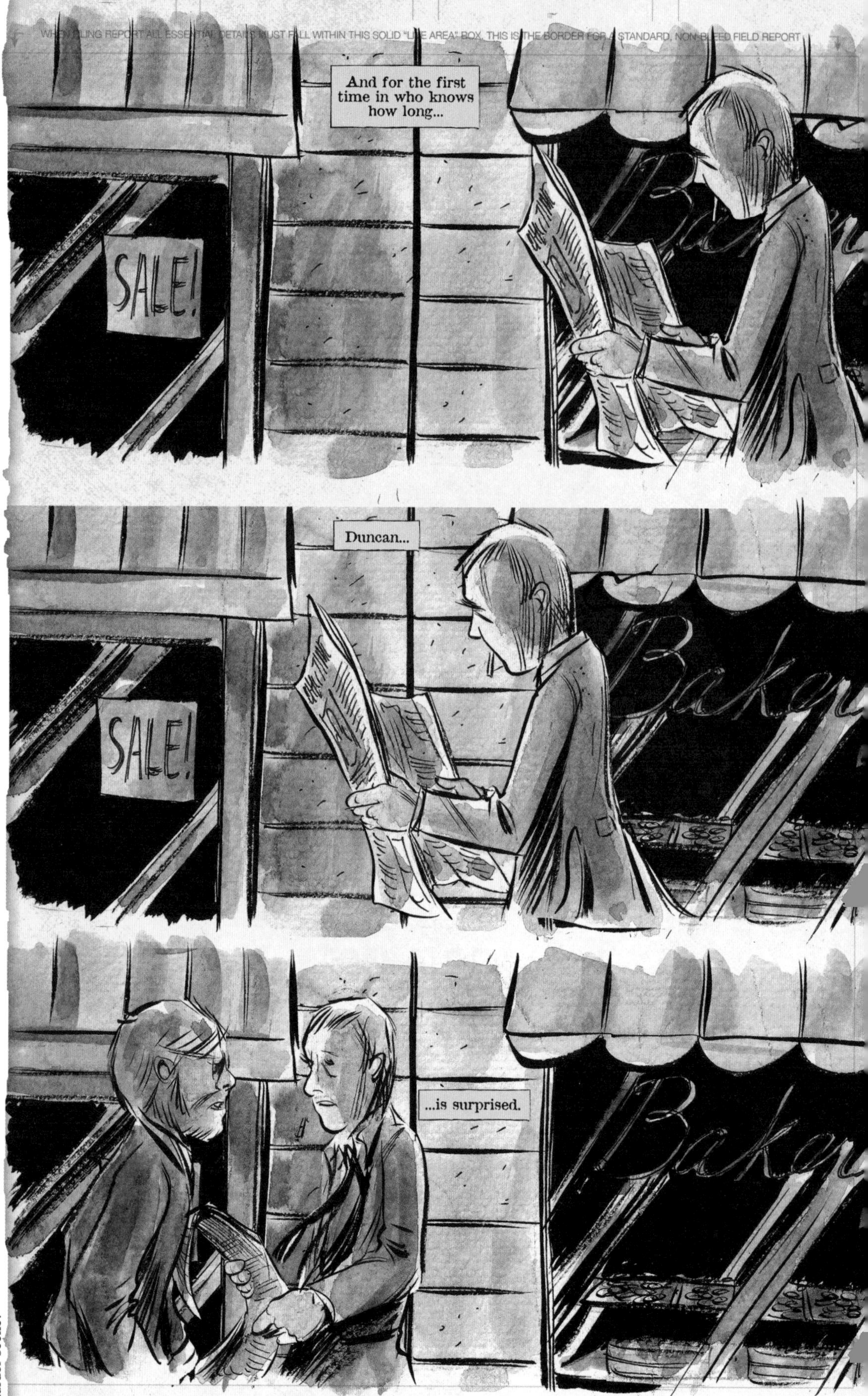
And for the first time in who knows how long...
SALE!
Duncan...
SALE!
...is surprised.

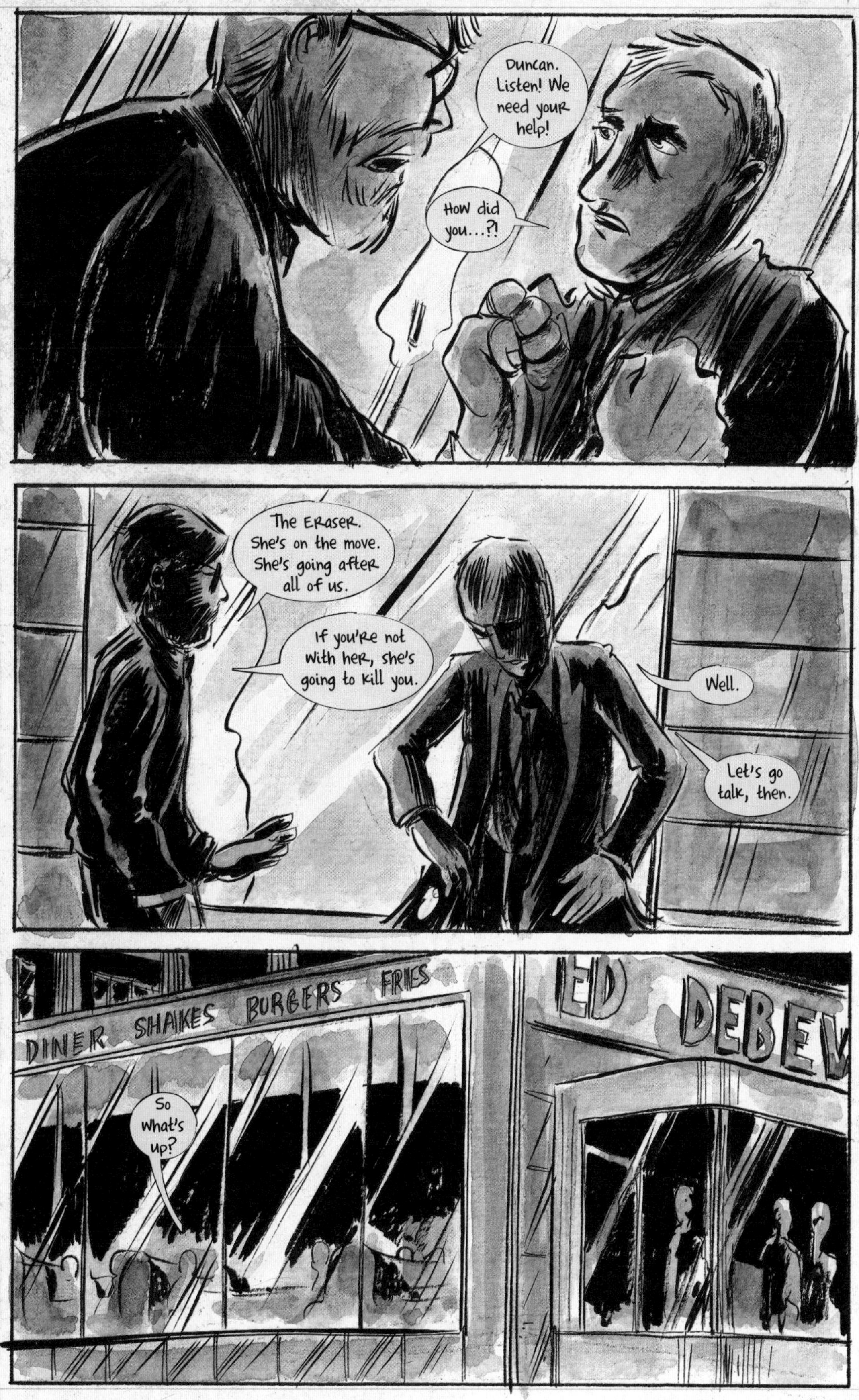
Duncan. Listen! We need your help!
How did you...?!
The Eraser. She's on the move. She's going after all of us.
If you're not with her, she's going to kill you.
Well.
Let's go talk, then.
DINER SHAKES BURGERS FRIES
ED DEBEV
So what's up?

This mysterious stranger grabbed her and muttered something in her ear. She wasn't sure she understood what he said, but it sounded something like, "Mug him again, rock."

WHEN FILING REPORT ALL ESSENTIAL DETAILS MUST FALL WITHIN THIS SOLID "LIVE AREA" BOX. THIS IS THE BORDER FOR A STANDARD, NON-BLEED FIELD REPORT

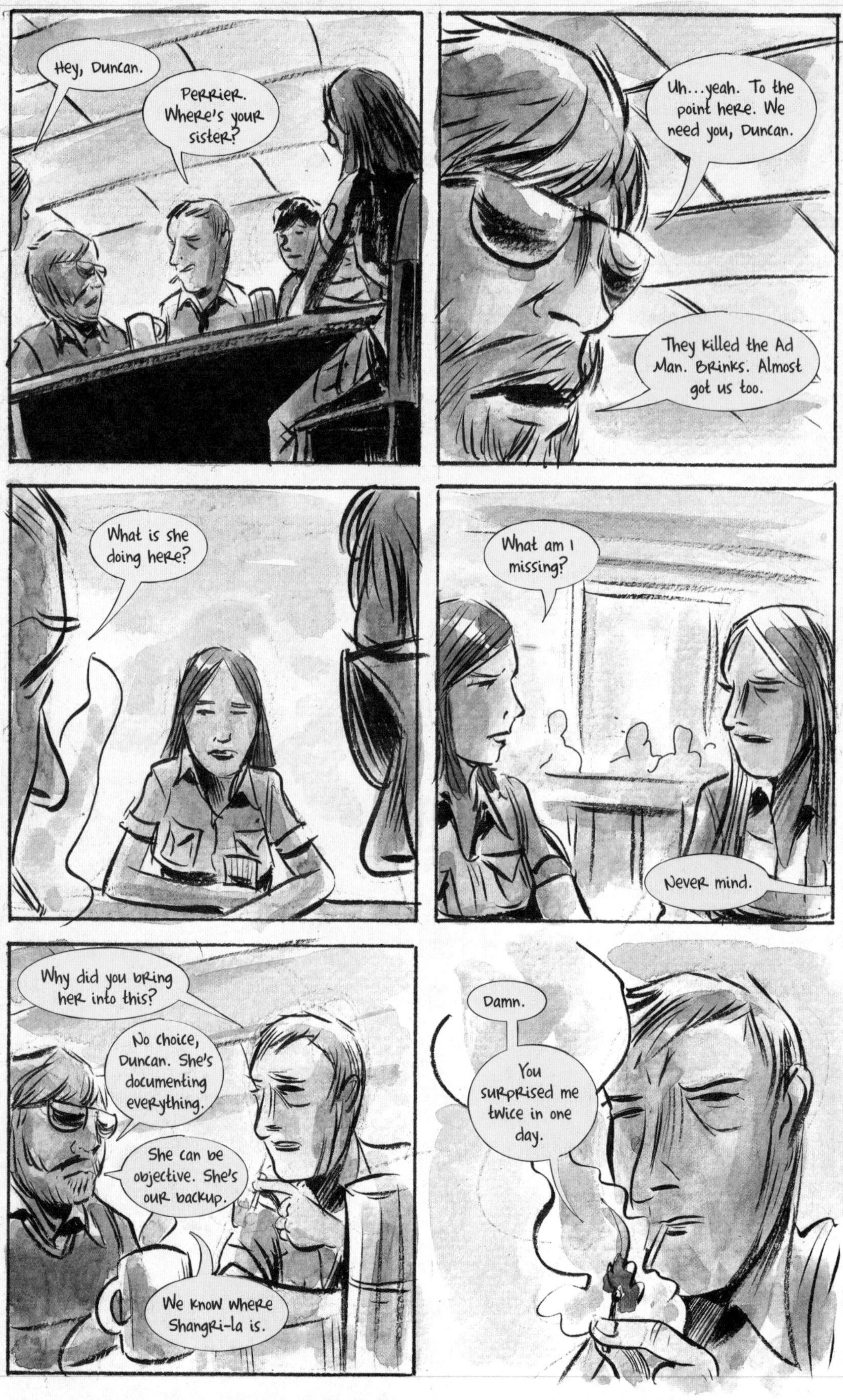
Hey, Duncan.
Perrier. Where's your sister?
Uh...yeah. To the point here. We need you, Duncan.
They killed the Ad Man. Brinks. Almost got us too.
What is she doing here?
What am I missing?
Never mind.
Why did you bring her into this?
No choice, Duncan. She's documenting everything.
She can be objective. She's our backup.
We know where Shangri-la is.
Damn.
You surprised me twice in one day.

Julianne's story about this mysterious stranger was completely discounted by the jury. However, I later found a man by the name of Jason Corridor who fit her description.

WHEN FILING REPORT ALL ESSENTIAL DETAILS MUST FALL WITHIN THIS SOLID "LIVE AREA" BOX. THIS IS THE BORDER FOR A STANDARD, NON-BLEED FIELD REPORT

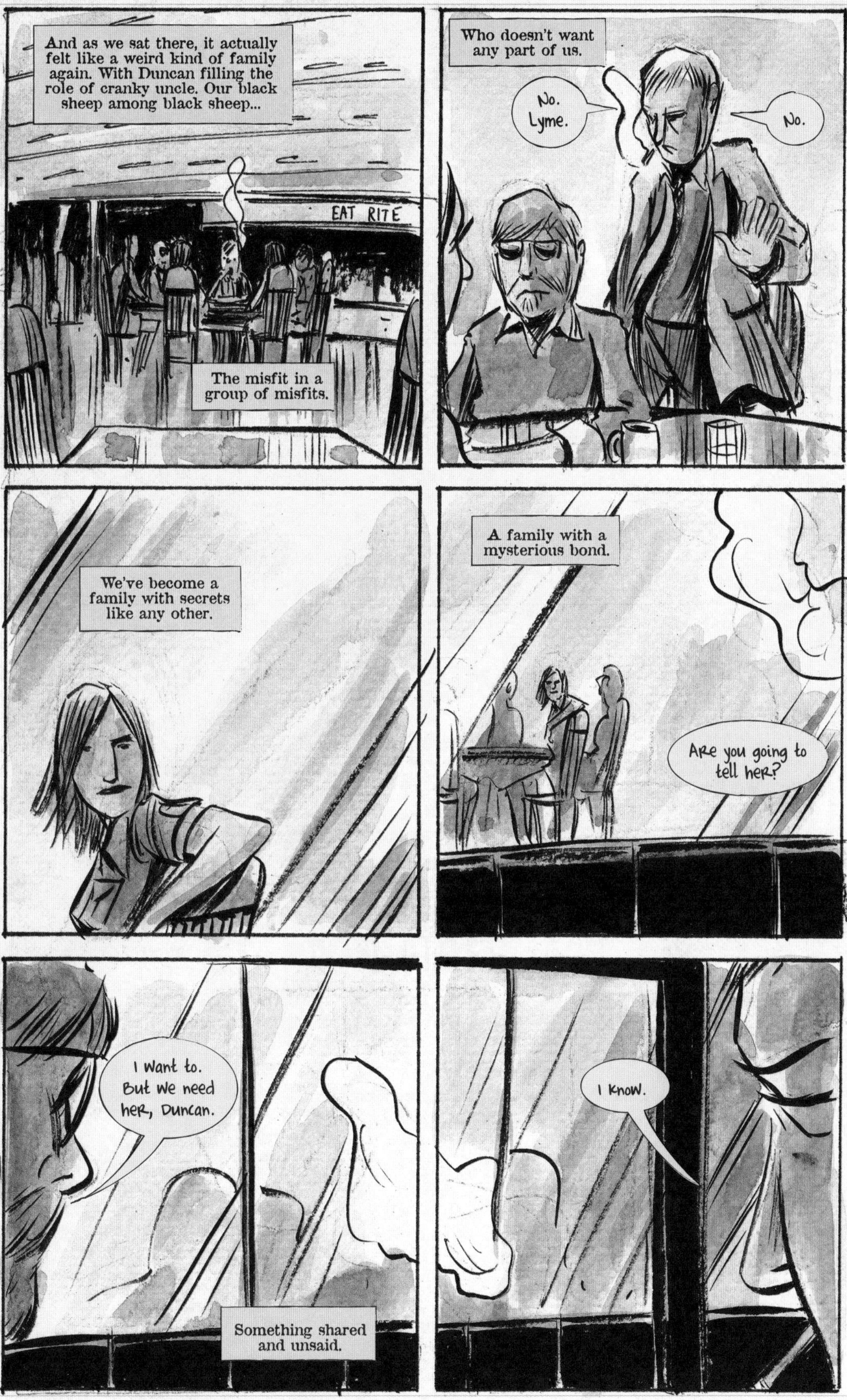

And as we sat there, it actually felt like a weird kind of family again. With Duncan filling the role of cranky uncle. Our black sheep among black sheep...
EAT RITE
The misfit in a group of misfits.
Who doesn't want any part of us.
No. Lyme.
No.
We've become a family with secrets like any other.
A family with a mysterious bond.
Are you going to tell her?
I want to. But we need her, Duncan.
Something shared and unsaid.
I know.

And it turned out that Julianne's murder convictions would ultimately lead me to an even bigger and more mysterious series of murders. She was simply the tip of the iceberg.

WHEN FILING REPORT ALL ESSENTIAL DETAILS MUST FALL WITHIN THIS SOLID "LIVE AREA" BOX. THIS IS THE BORDER FOR A STANDARD, NON-BLEED FIELD REPORT

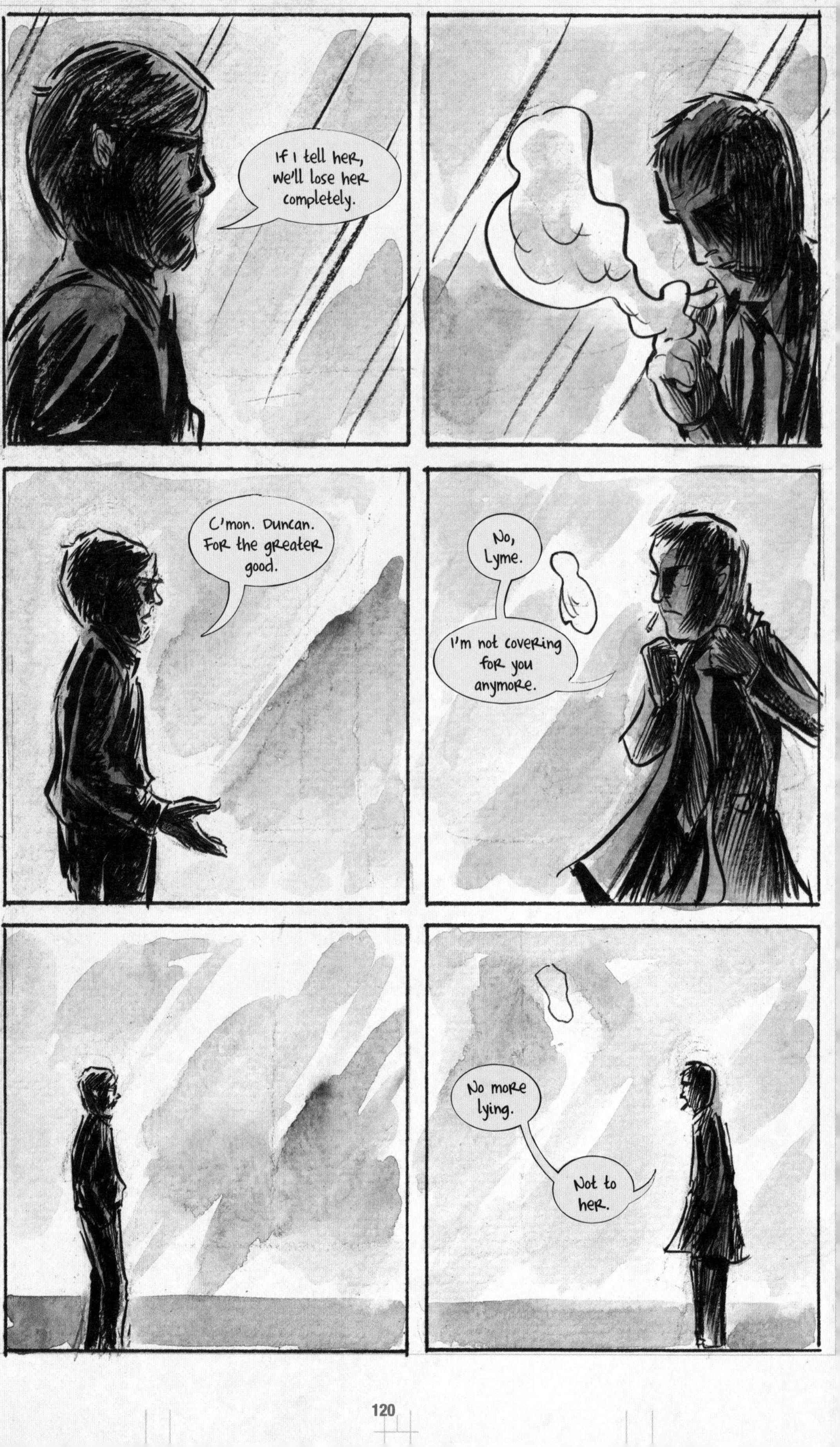

If I tell her, we'll lose her completely.
C'mon. Duncan. For the greater good.
No, Lyme.
I'm not covering for you anymore.
No more lying.
Not to her.

Julianne was more than willing to be interviewed in prison. She was racked with guilt and refused to appeal. She seemed sincere in her statements. She honestly didn't remember the murders but was willing to be executed for her crimes.

WHEN FILING REPORT ALL ESSENTIAL DETAILS MUST FALL WITHIN THIS SOLID "LIVE AREA" BOX. THIS IS THE BORDER FOR A STANDARD, NON-BLEED FIELD REPORT.

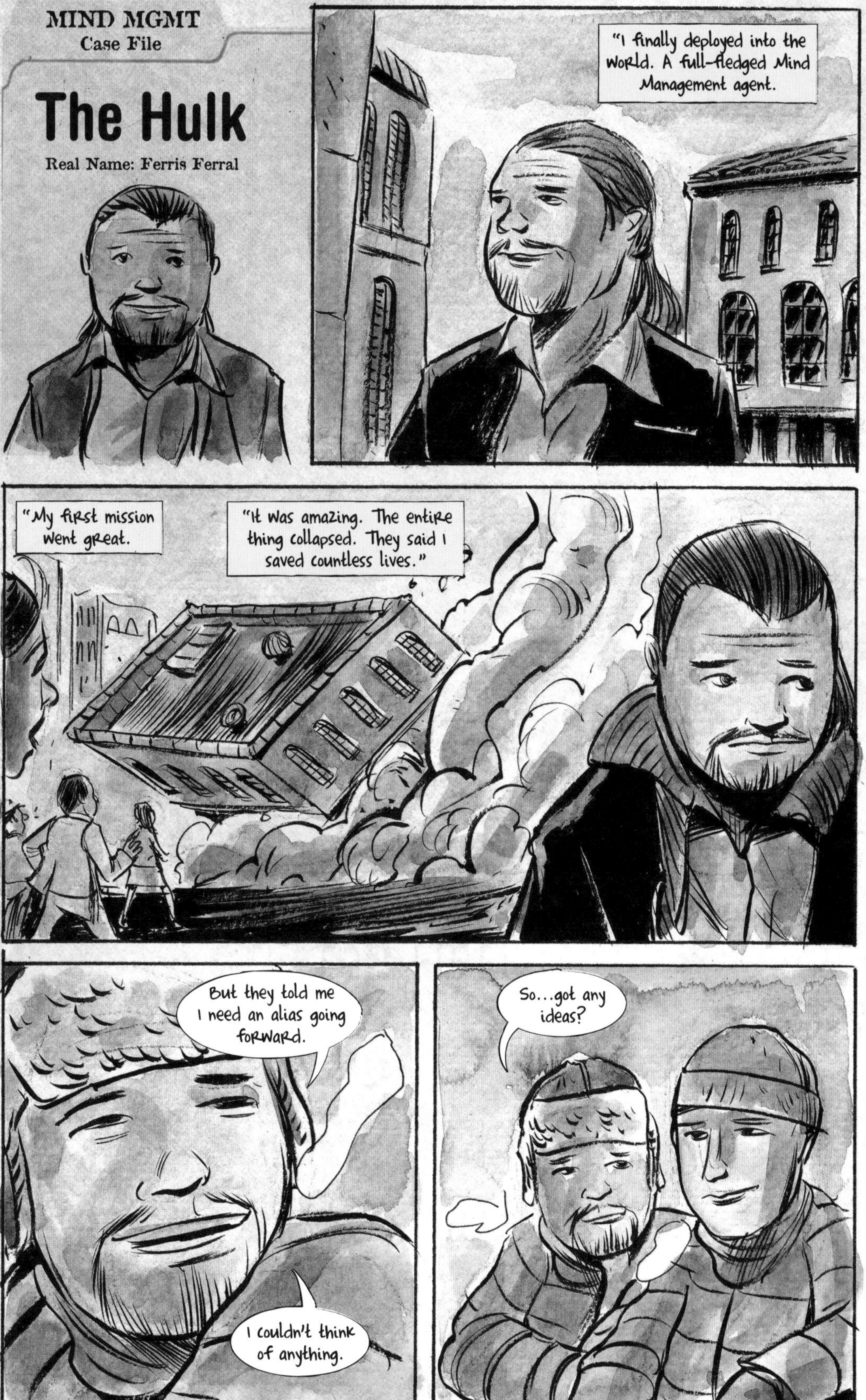

MIND MGMT
Case File
The Hulk
Real Name: Ferris Ferral
"I finally deployed into the world. A full-fledged Mind Management agent.
"My first mission went great.
"It was amazing. The entire thing collapsed. They said I saved countless lives."
But they told me I need an alias going forward.
I couldn't think of anything.
So...got any ideas?

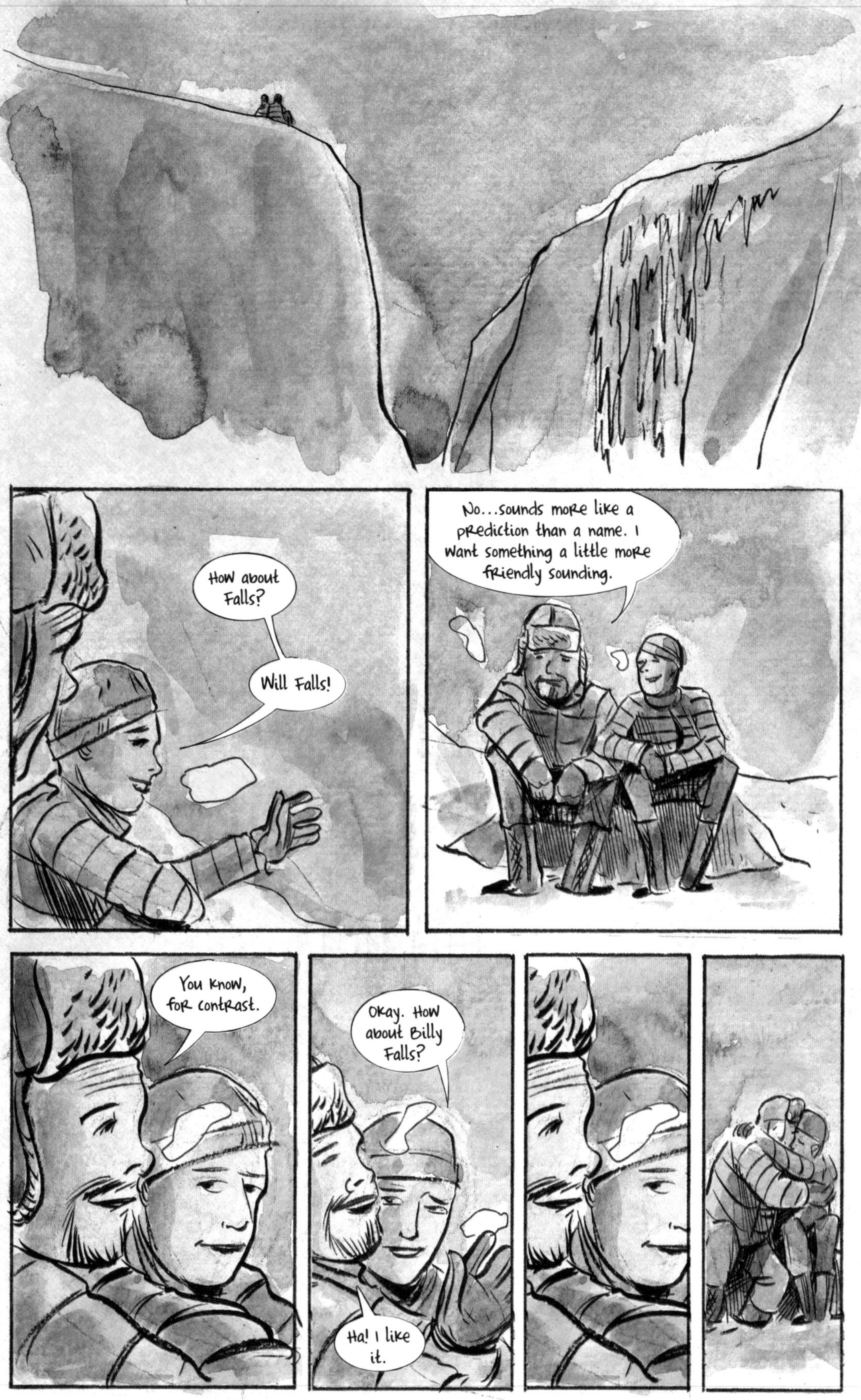
How about Falls?
Will Falls!
No...sounds more like a prediction than a name. I want something a little more friendly sounding.
You know, for contrast.
Okay. How about Billy Falls?
Ha! I like it.

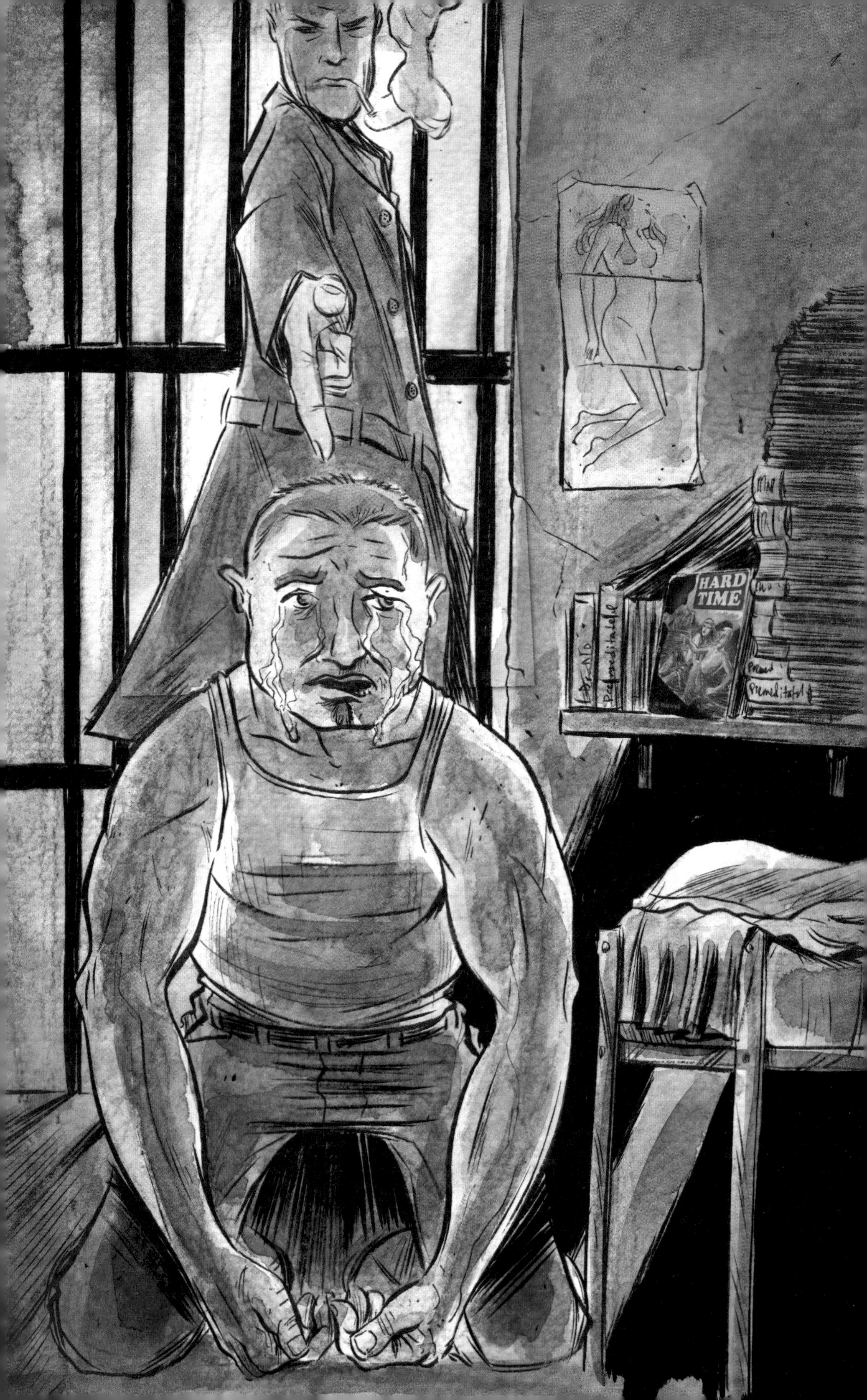
HARD TIME

11

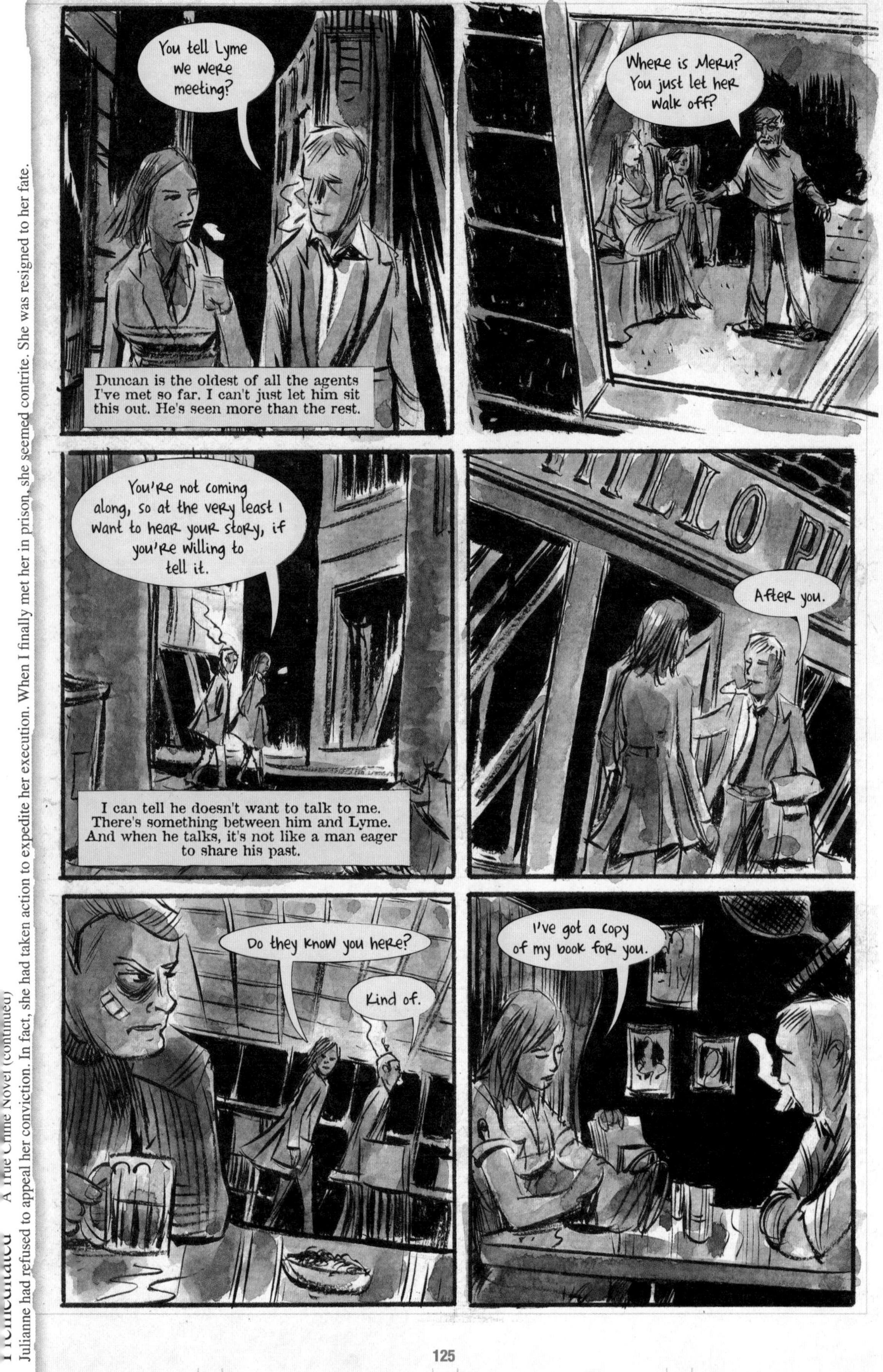
You tell Lyme we were meeting?
Duncan is the oldest of all the agents I've met so far. I can't just let him sit this out. He's seen more than the rest.
Where is Meru? You just let her walk off?
You're not coming along, so at the very least I want to hear your story, if you're willing to tell it.
I can tell he doesn't want to talk to me. There's something between him and Lyme. And when he talks, it's not like a man eager to share his past.
After you.
Do they know you here?
Kind of.
I've got a copy of my book for you.

Premeditated A True Crime Novel (continued)

Julianne had refused to appeal her conviction. In fact, she had taken action to expedite her execution. When I finally met her in prison, she seemed contrite. She was resigned to her fate.

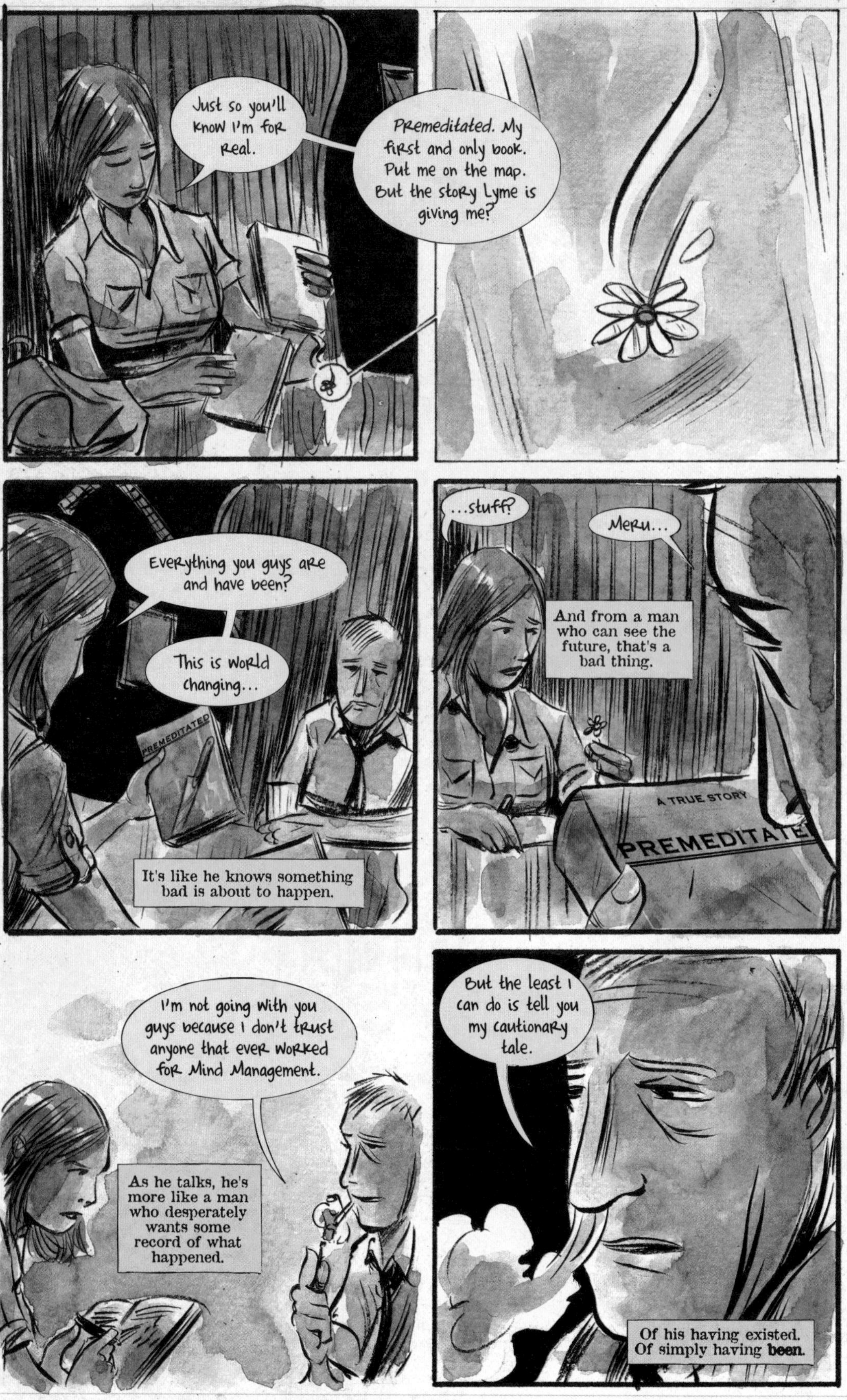
Just so you'll know I'm for real.
Premeditated. My first and only book. Put me on the map. But the story Lyme is giving me?
Everything you guys are and have been?
This is world changing...
PREMEDITATED
It's like he knows something bad is about to happen.
...stuff?
Meru...
And from a man who can see the future, that's a bad thing.
A TRUE STORY
PREMEDITATE
I'm not going with you guys because I don't trust anyone that ever worked for Mind Management.
As he talks, he's more like a man who desperately wants some record of what happened.
But the least I can do is tell you my cautionary tale.
Of his having existed. Of simply having **been**.

She spoke poetically of the loss of her family. Of her children as plucked flowers. But there was something odd about her speech.

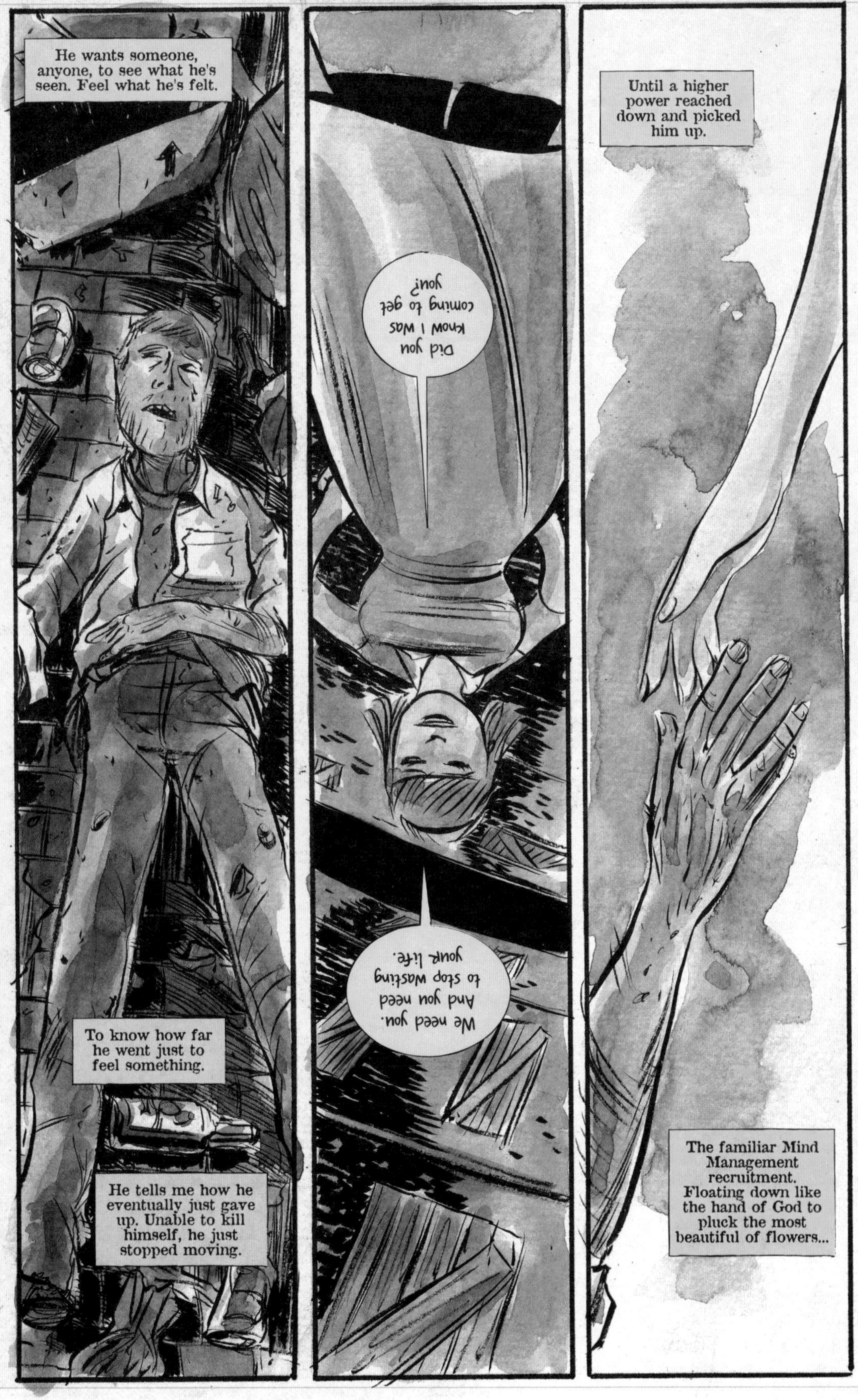
He wants someone, anyone, to see what he's seen. Feel what he's felt.
To know how far he went just to feel something.
He tells me how he eventually just gave up. Unable to kill himself, he just stopped moving.
Did you know I was coming to get you?
We need you. And you need to stop wasting your life.
Until a higher power reached down and picked him up.
The familiar Mind Management recruitment. Floating down like the hand of God to pluck the most beautiful of flowers...

It was as if she was reading from a script that was upside down. She spoke slowly. Deliberately. As if she was trying to retrieve the memories of her family from somewhere far away.

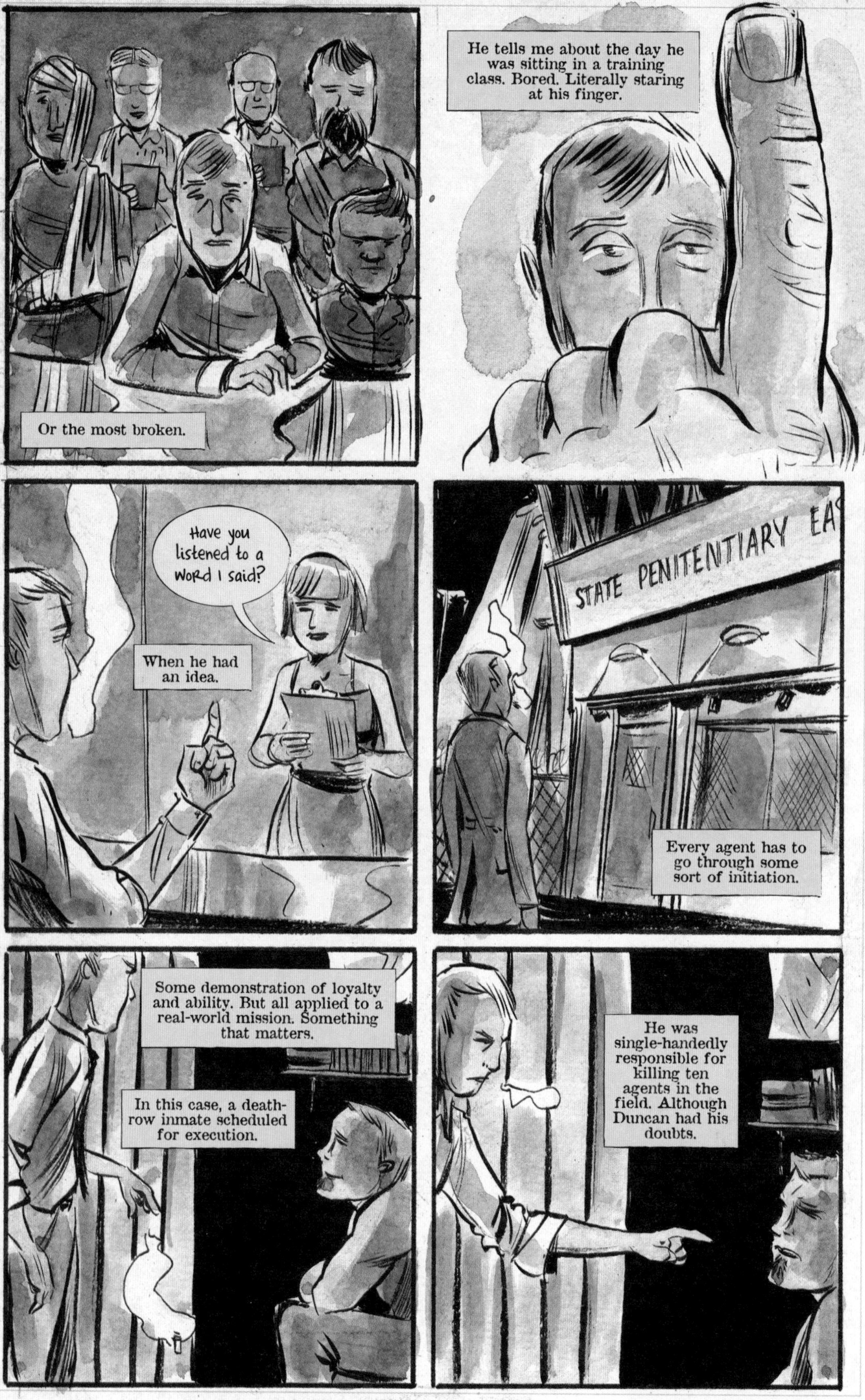
Or the most broken.
He tells me about the day he was sitting in a training class. Bored. Literally staring at his finger.
Have you listened to a word I said?
When he had an idea.
STATE PENITENTIARY EA
Every agent has to go through some sort of initiation.
Some demonstration of loyalty and ability. But all applied to a real-world mission. Something that matters.
In this case, a death-row inmate scheduled for execution.
He was single-handedly responsible for killing ten agents in the field. Although Duncan had his doubts.

Near the end of my interview, something strange happened. It was as if someone hit a reset button on her and she forgot who I was for a moment. She raised her eyes to me and asked for a moment...

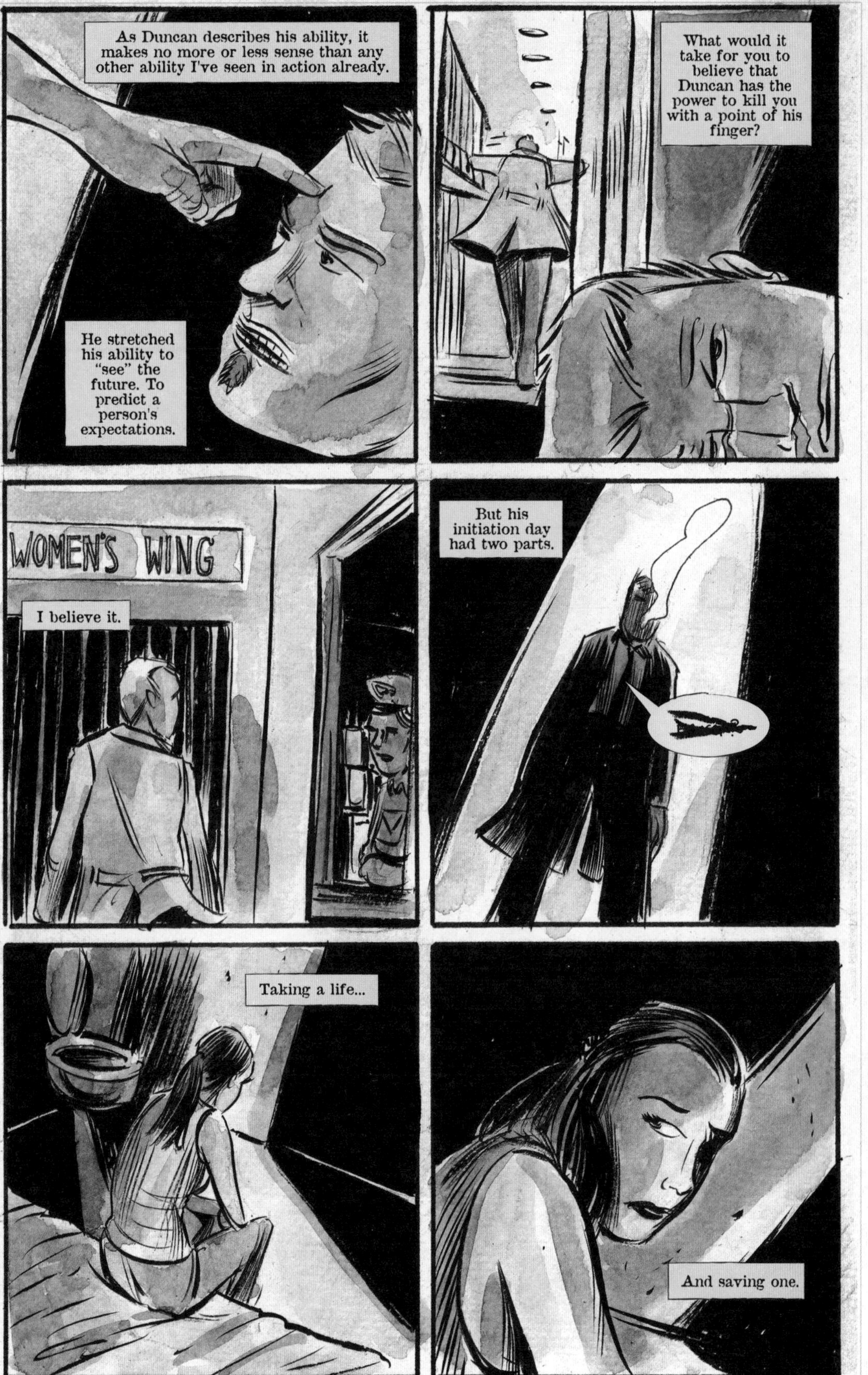
As Duncan describes his ability, it makes no more or less sense than any other ability I've seen in action already.
He stretched his ability to "see" the future. To predict a person's expectations.
What would it take for you to believe that Duncan has the power to kill you with a point of his finger?
WOMEN'S WING
I believe it.
But his initiation day had two parts.
Taking a life...
And saving one.

She turned away from me and when she turned back around to look at me it was as if I were looking at a different woman. Like she'd wiped some kind of internal mental slate. It's hard to put my finger on it.

WHEN FILING REPORT ALL ESSENTIAL DETAILS MUST FALL WITHIN THIS SOLID "LIVE AREA" BOX. THIS IS THE BORDER FOR A STANDARD, NON-BLEED FIELD REPORT

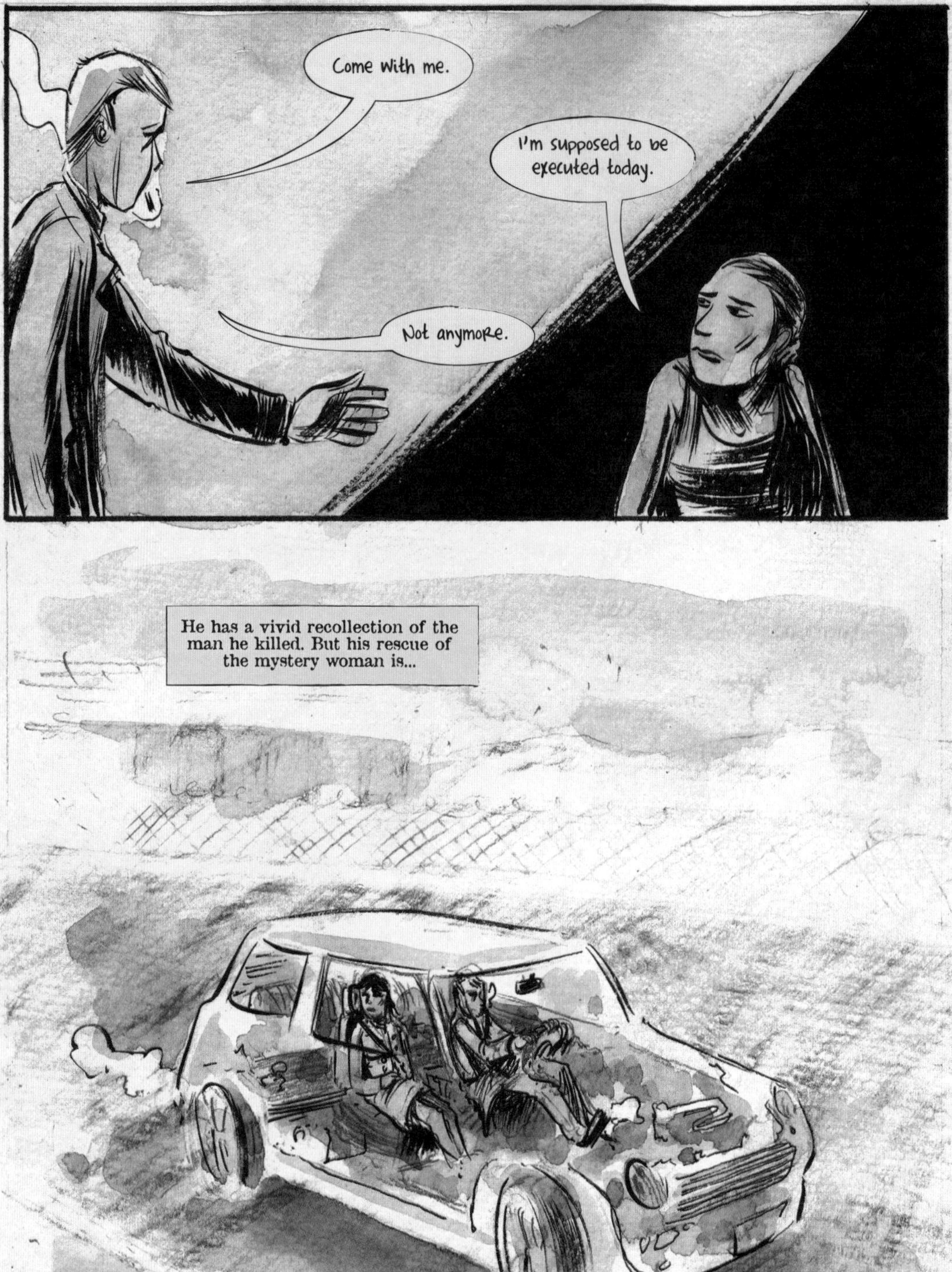
Come with me.
I'm supposed to be executed today.
Not anymore.
He has a vivid recollection of the man he killed. But his rescue of the mystery woman is...
Fuzzy.

And then she told me a completely different story. She told me of a man. Jason Corridor. The man she testified was in her house when she killed her family.

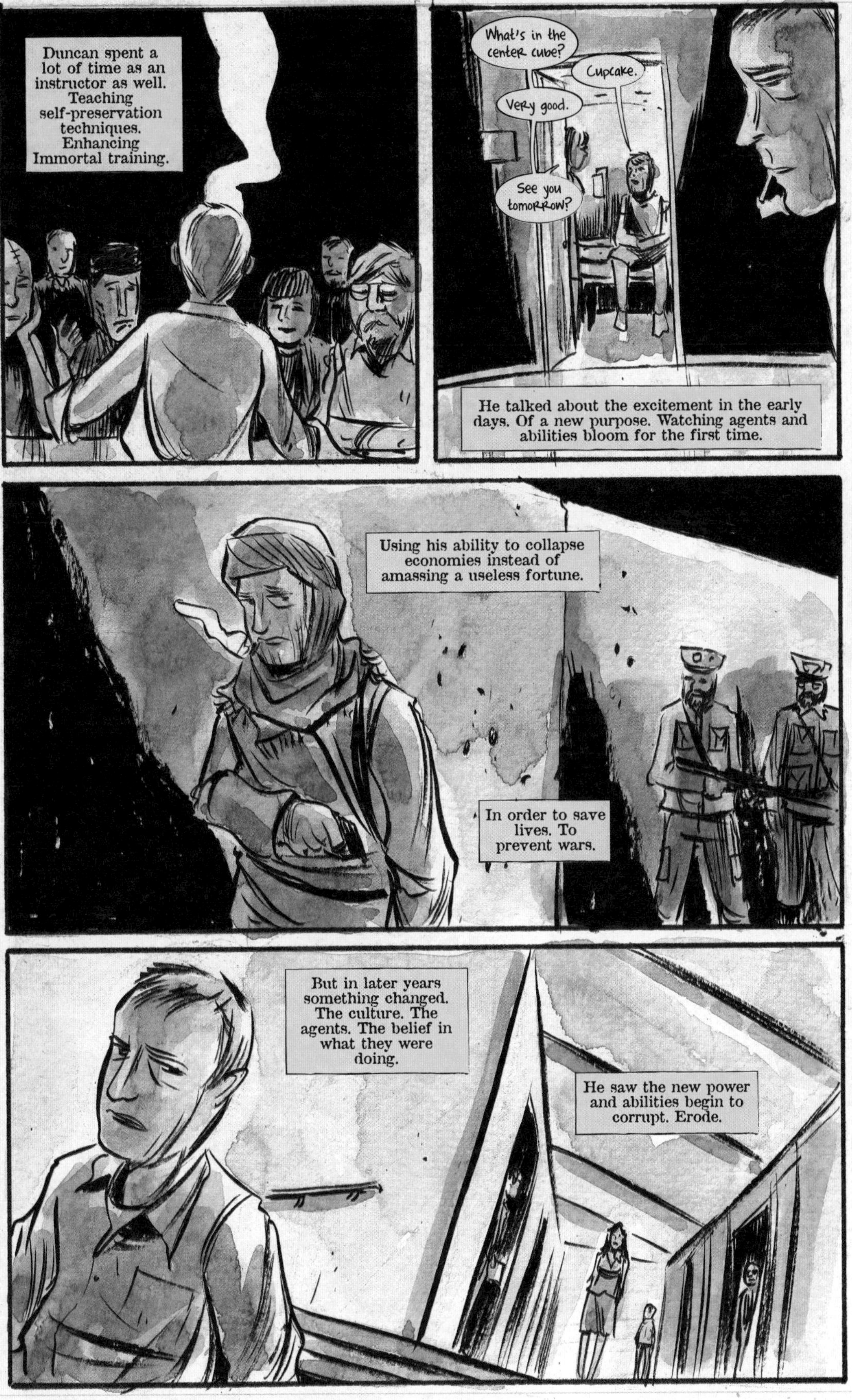
Duncan spent a lot of time as an instructor as well. Teaching self-preservation techniques. Enhancing Immortal training.
What's in the center cube?
Cupcake.
Very good.
See you tomorrow?
He talked about the excitement in the early days. Of a new purpose. Watching agents and abilities bloom for the first time.
Using his ability to collapse economies instead of amassing a useless fortune.
In order to save lives. To prevent wars.
But in later years something changed. The culture. The agents. The belief in what they were doing.
He saw the new power and abilities begin to corrupt. Erode.

She began describing him to me. And I couldn't help but think she was lying. She told me that she'd been followed. That her husband was a member of a secret organization that runs the entire world from behind the scenes. Truly crazy stories.

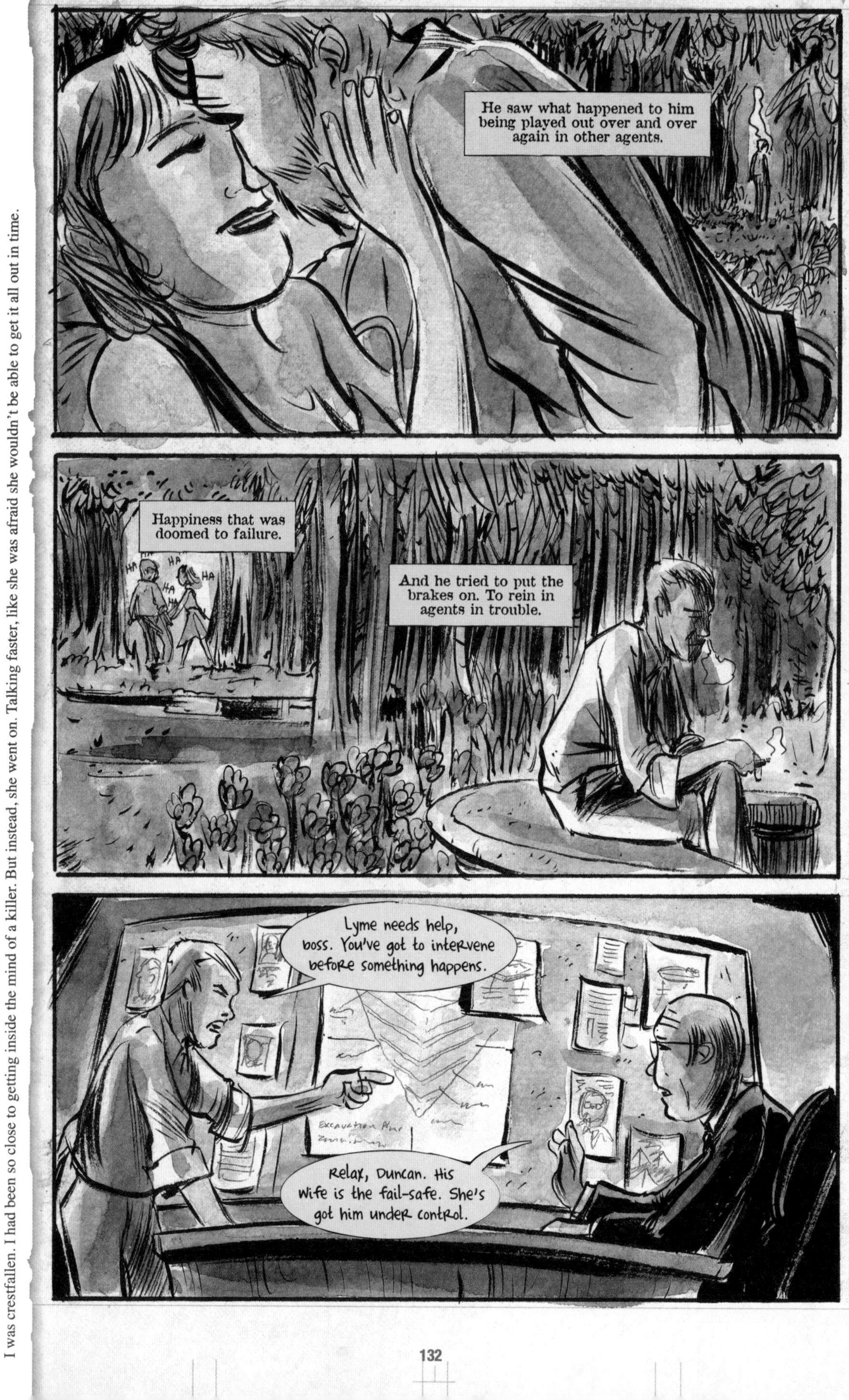
He saw what happened to him being played out over and over again in other agents.
Happiness that was doomed to failure.
HA HA HA HA
And he tried to put the brakes on. To rein in agents in trouble.
Lyme needs help, boss. You've got to intervene before something happens.
Relax, Duncan. His wife is the fail-safe. She's got him under control.

I was crestfallen. I had been so close to getting inside the mind of a killer. But instead, she went on. Talking faster, like she was afraid she wouldn't be able to get it all out in time.

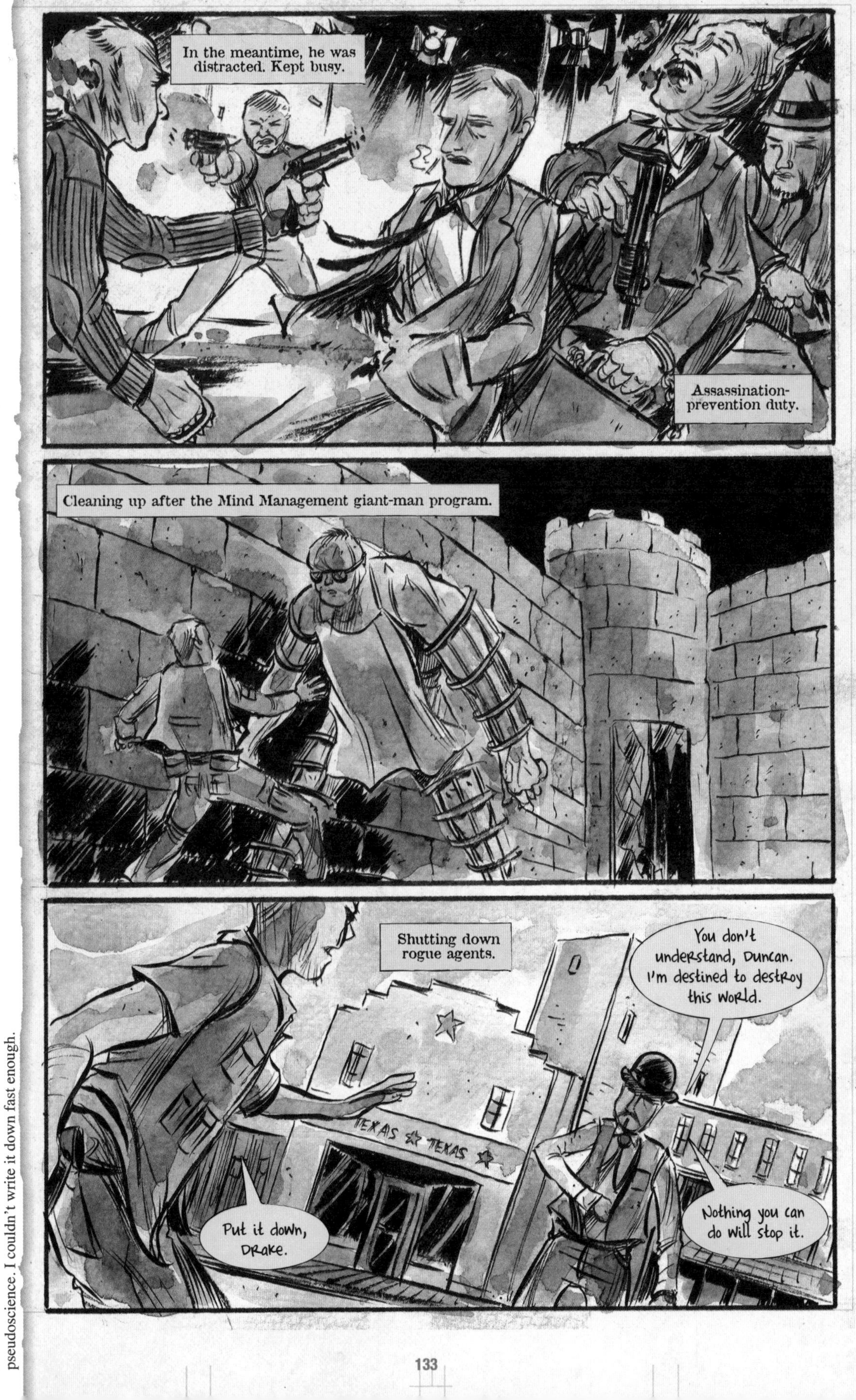
In the meantime, he was distracted. Kept busy.
Assassination-prevention duty.
Cleaning up after the Mind Management giant-man program.
Shutting down rogue agents.
You don't understand, Duncan. I'm destined to destroy this world.
TEXAS ☆ TEXAS
Put it down, Drake.
Nothing you can do will stop it.

She claimed that she found one of her husband's journals with details. Lists. Assassination plans. Contact information for other agents in his cell. Experimental drugs. Medical procedures based on pseudoscience. I couldn't write it down fast enough.

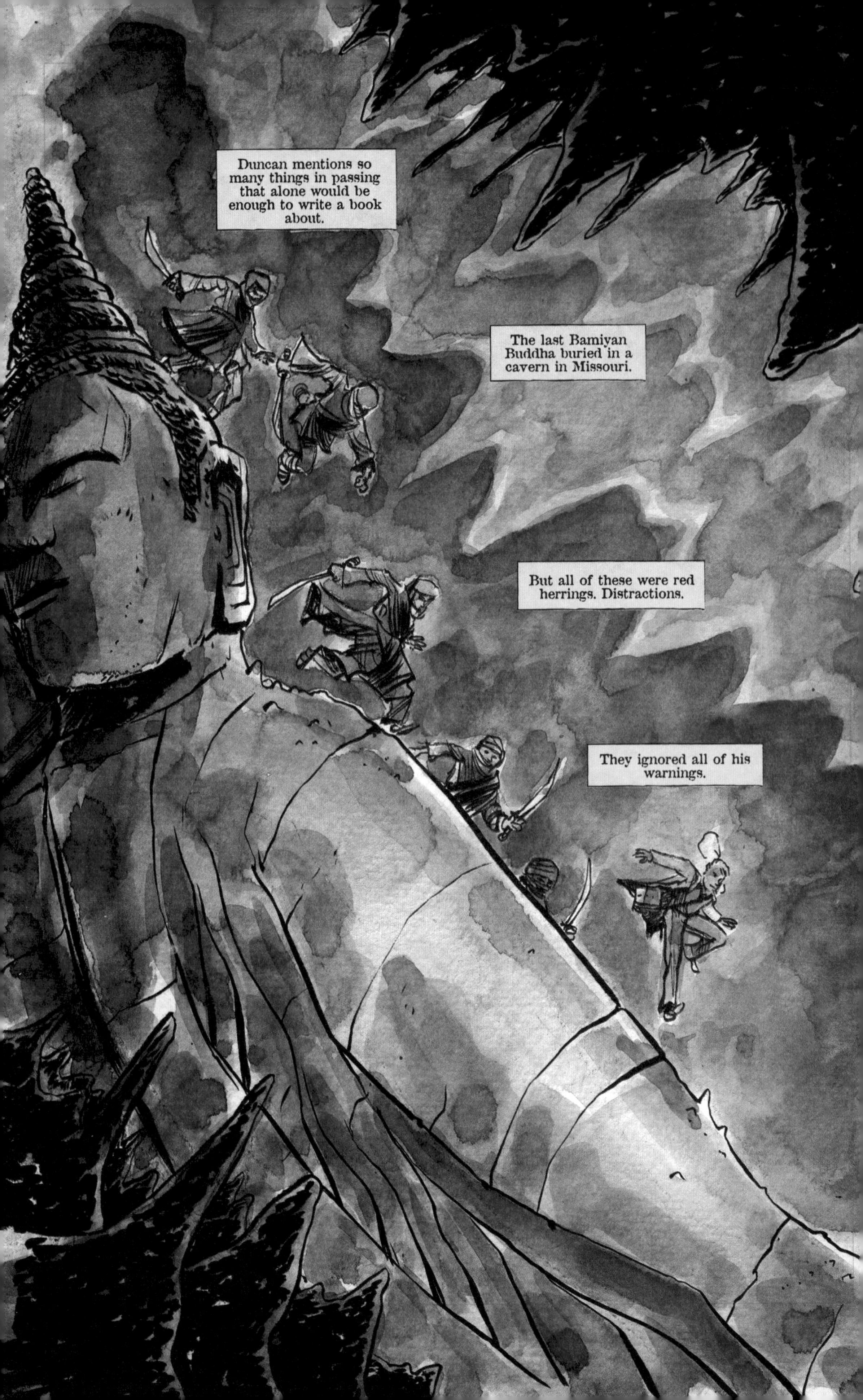
Duncan mentions so many things in passing that alone would be enough to write a book about.
The last Bamiyan Buddha buried in a cavern in Missouri.
But all of these were red herrings. Distractions.
They ignored all of his warnings.

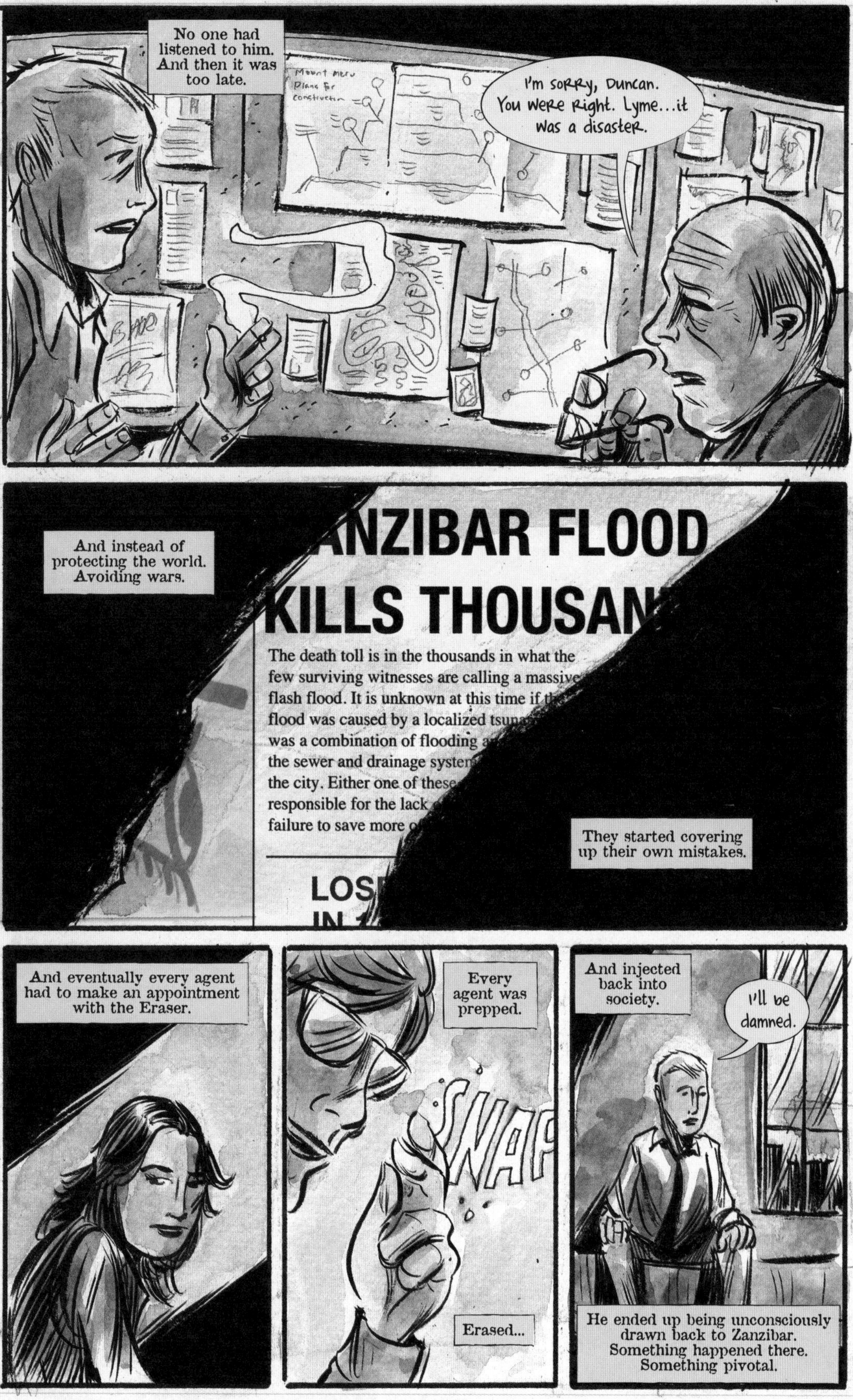
No one had listened to him. And then it was too late.
I'm sorry, Duncan. You were right. Lyme...it was a disaster.
And instead of protecting the world. Avoiding wars.
ANZIBAR FLOOD
KILLS THOUSAN
The death toll is in the thousands in what the few surviving witnesses are calling a massive flash flood. It is unknown at this time if the flood was caused by a localized tsuna was a combination of flooding a the sewer and drainage system the city. Either one of these responsible for the lack failure to save more o
LOS
IN 1
They started covering up their own mistakes.
And eventually every agent had to make an appointment with the Eraser.
Every agent was prepped.
SNAP
Erased...
And injected back into society.
I'll be damned.
He ended up being unconsciously drawn back to Zanzibar. Something happened there. Something pivotal.

I asked her to stop, to tell me more about herself. Her upbringing. Where she met her husband.

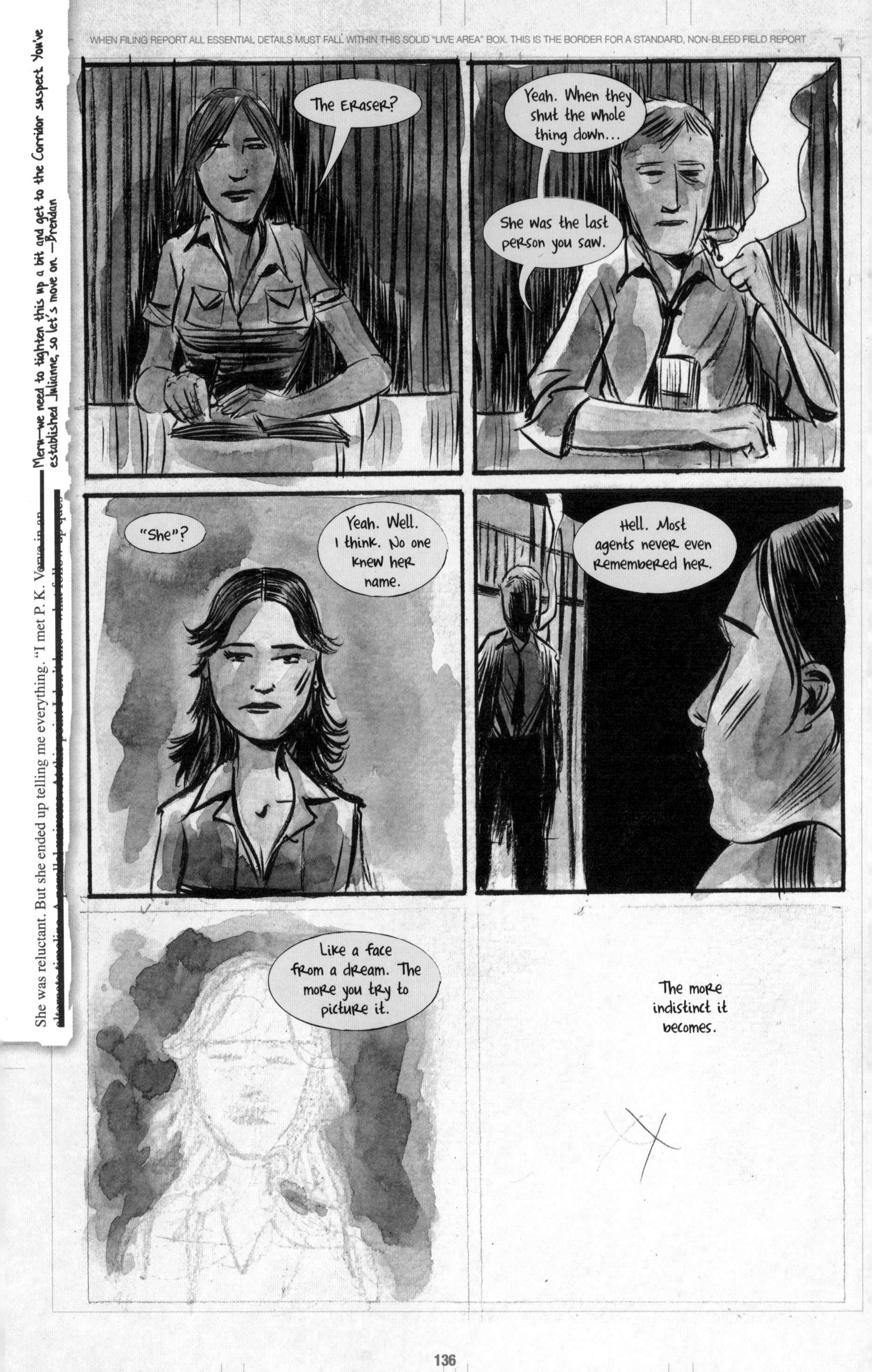
WHEN FILING REPORT ALL ESSENTIAL DETAILS MUST FALL WITHIN THIS SOLID "LIVE AREA" BOX. THIS IS THE BORDER FOR A STANDARD, NON-BLEED FIELD REPORT
She was reluctant. But she ended up telling me everything. "I met P. K. V
Meru—we need to tighten this up a bit and get to the Corridor suspect. You've established "Julianne," so let's move on. —Brendan
The ERASER?
Yeah. When they shut the whole thing down...
She was the last person you saw.
"She"?
Yeah. Well. I think. No one knew her name.
Hell. Most agents never even remembered her.
Like a face from a dream. The more you try to picture it.
The more indistinct it becomes.

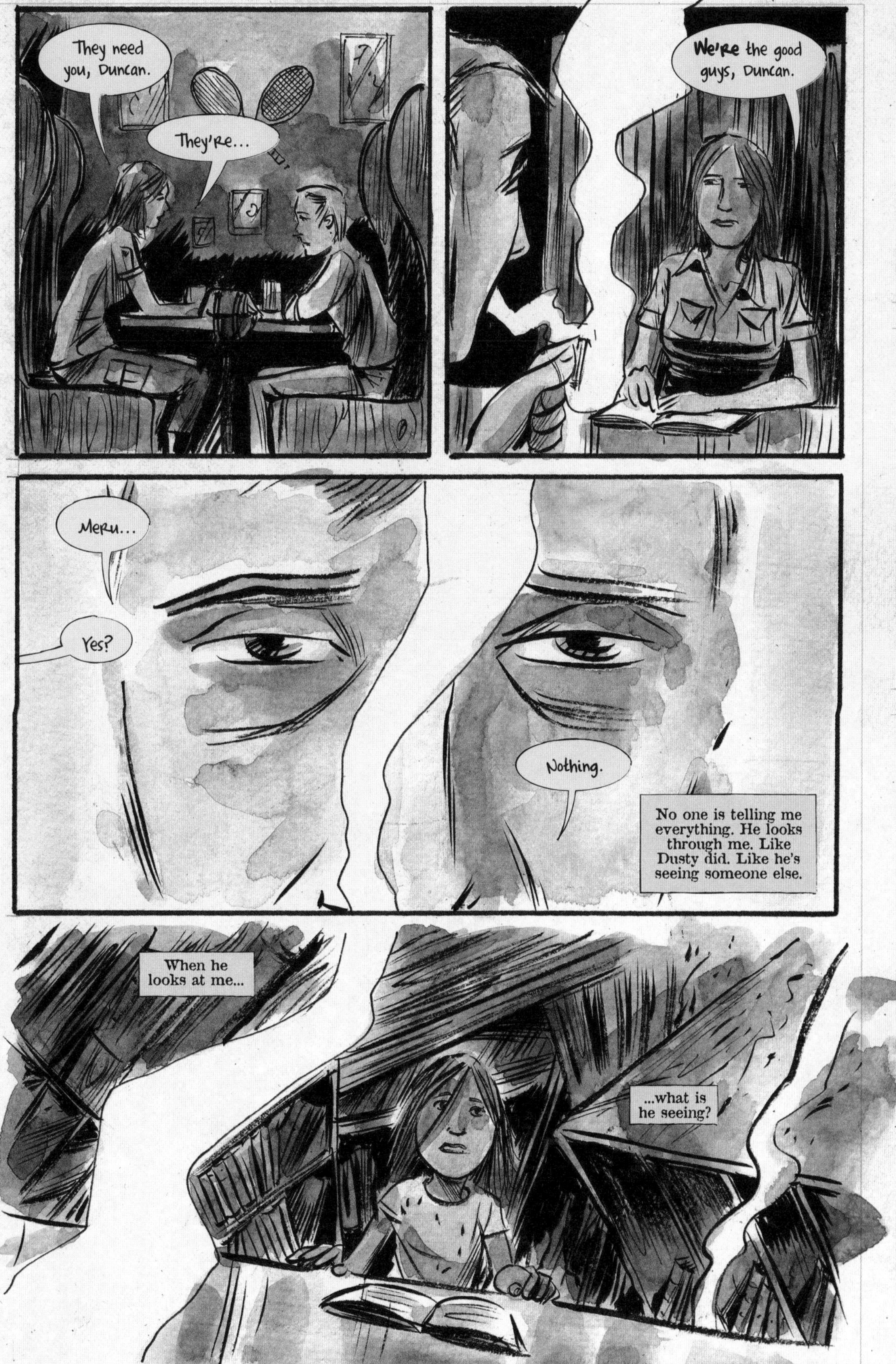
They need you, Duncan.
They're...
We're the good guys, Duncan.
Meru...
Yes?
Nothing.
No one is telling me everything. He looks through me. Like Dusty did. Like he's seeing someone else.
When he looks at me...
...what is he seeing?

MIND MGMT FIELD GUIDE. 11.13. When being questioned by a hostile agent, remember your seven layers of mental defense. Go through them all in the proper progression for maximum effect.

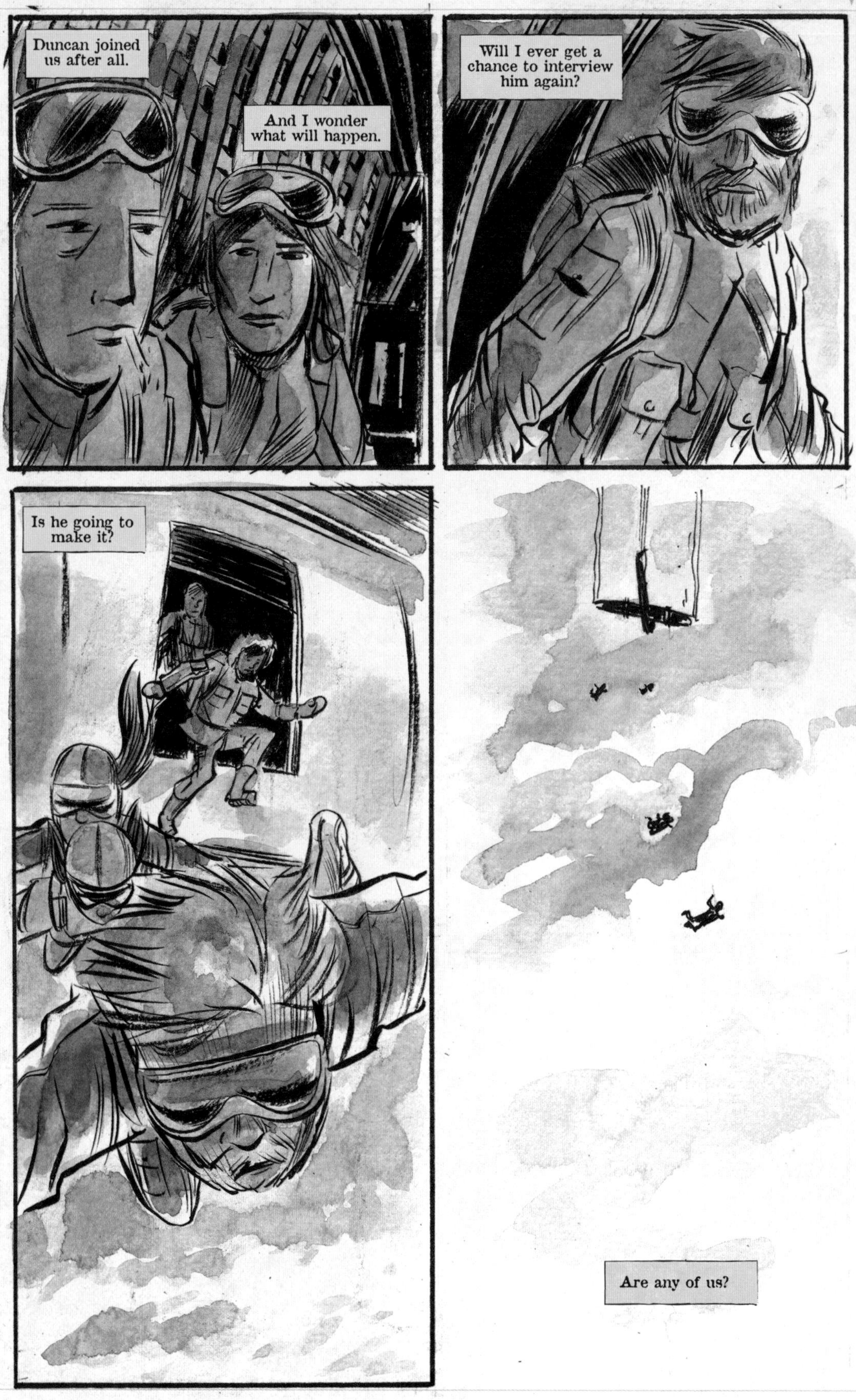
Duncan joined us after all.
And I wonder what will happen.
Will I ever get a chance to interview him again?
Is he going to make it?
Are any of us?

MIND MGMT FIELD GUIDE. 11.15. Trust your subconscious when returning home. Keep the location and mental image at the edges of your mind. With practice, it should become second nature.

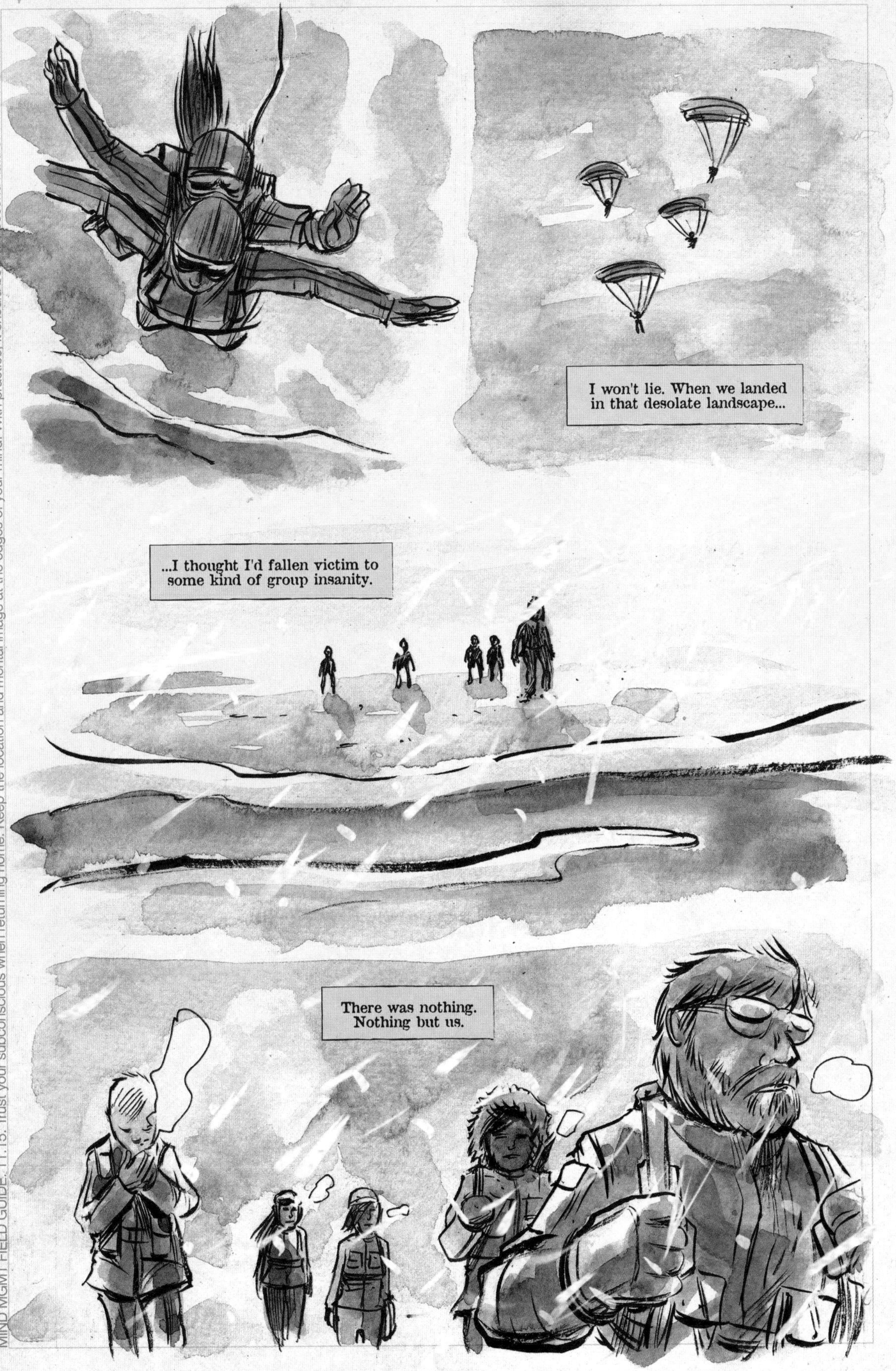
I won't lie. When we landed in that desolate landscape...
...I thought I'd fallen victim to some kind of group insanity.
There was nothing. Nothing but us.

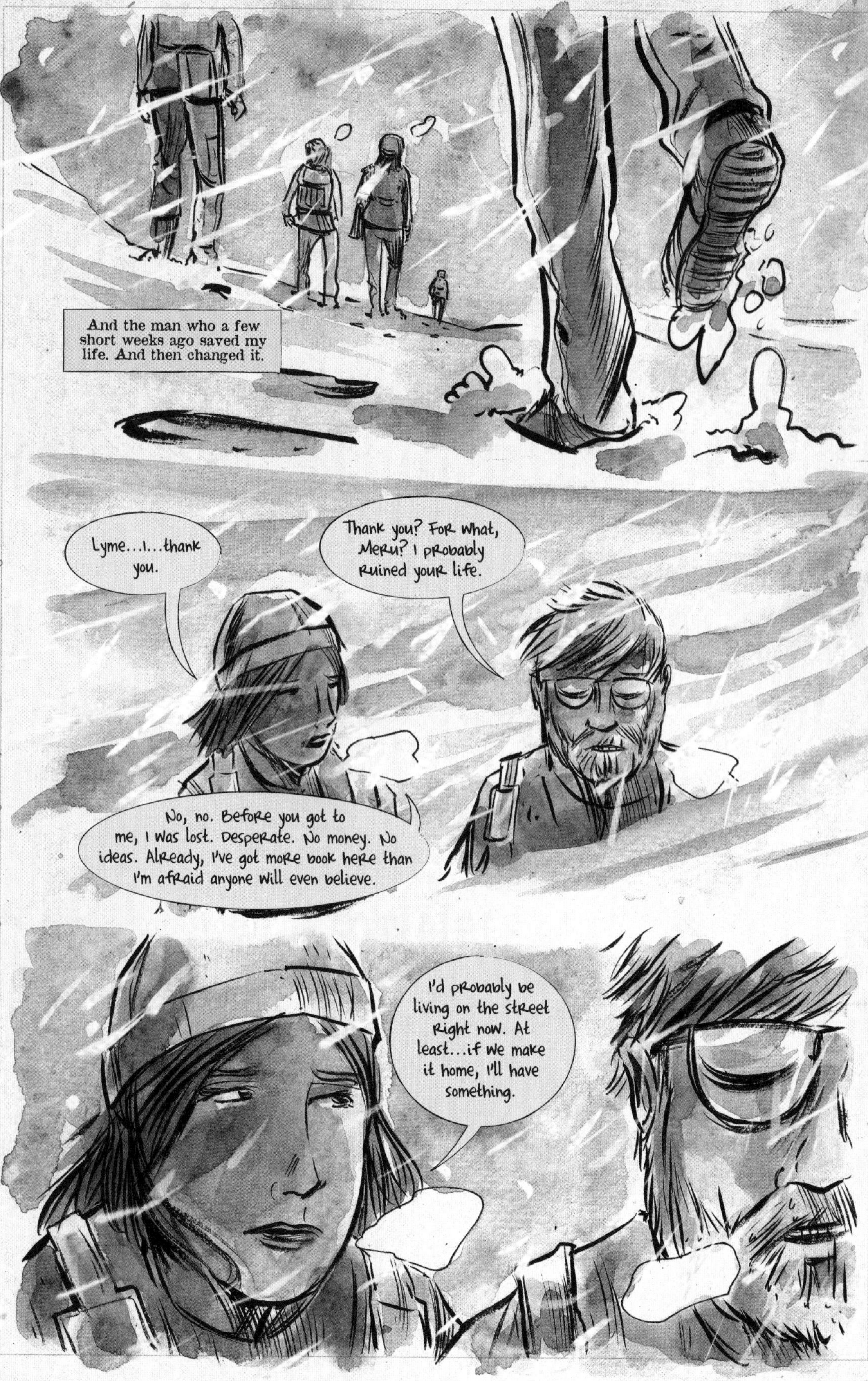
And the man who a few short weeks ago saved my life. And then changed it.
Lyme...I...thank you.
Thank you? For what, Meru? I probably ruined your life.
No, no. Before you got to me, I was lost. Desperate. No money. No ideas. Already, I've got more book here than I'm afraid anyone will even believe.
I'd probably be living on the street right now. At least...if we make it home, I'll have something.

MIND MGMT FIELD GUIDE.11.16. You won't remember your training. Your conditioning allows you to both find and see Shangri-la.

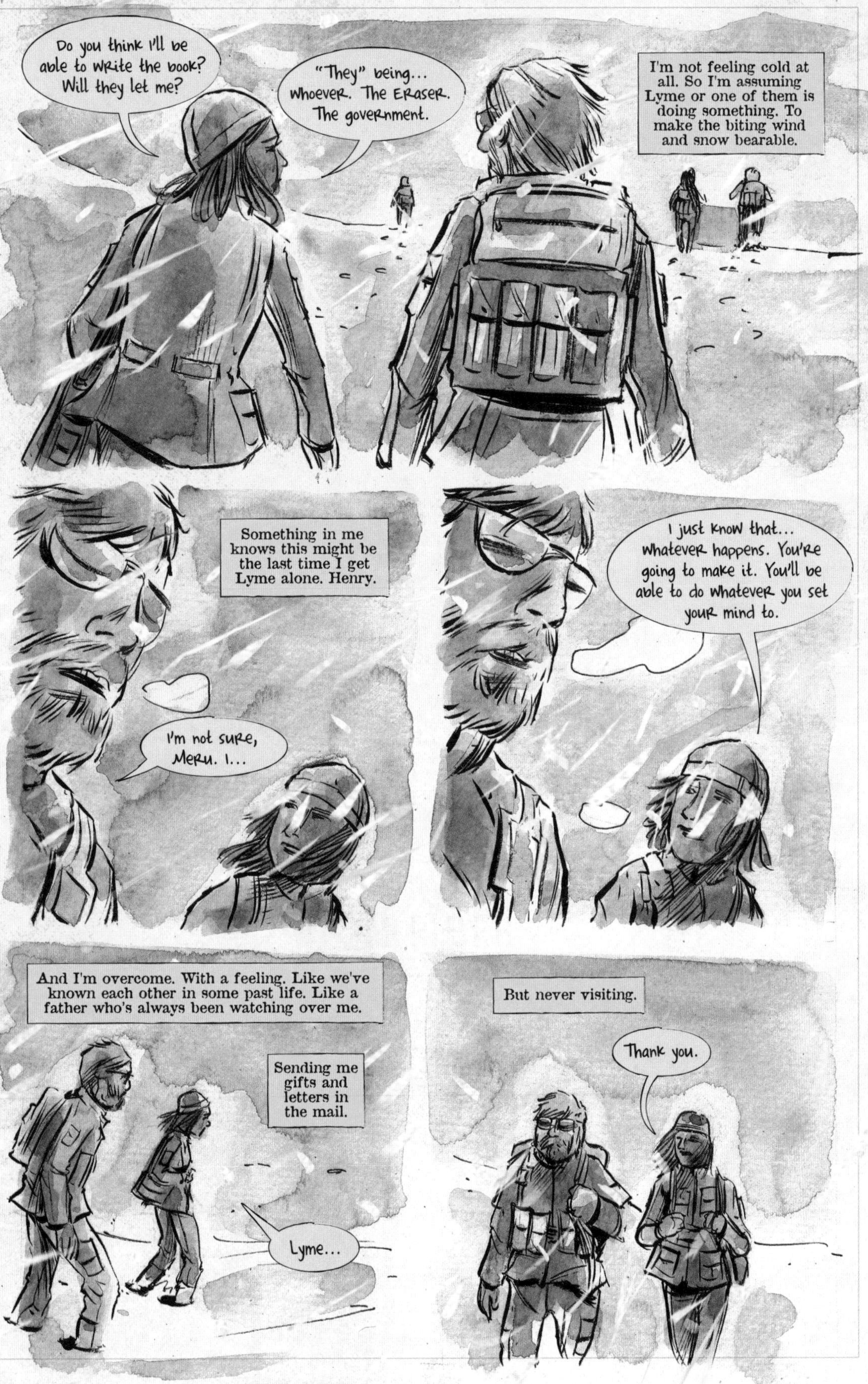
Do you think I'll be able to write the book? Will they let me?
"They" being... whoever. The Eraser. The government.
I'm not feeling cold at all. So I'm assuming Lyme or one of them is doing something. To make the biting wind and snow bearable.
Something in me knows this might be the last time I get Lyme alone. Henry.
I'm not sure, Meru. I...
I just know that... whatever happens. You're going to make it. You'll be able to do whatever you set your mind to.
And I'm overcome. With a feeling. Like we've known each other in some past life. Like a father who's always been watching over me.
Sending me gifts and letters in the mail.
Lyme...
But never visiting.
Thank you.

MIND MGMT FIELD GUIDE.11.17. Traveling in pairs or small groups is recommended. It is rare to recall an agent, but if you do receive a recall, never attempt the passage to Shangri-la alone.

MIND MGMT FIELD GUIDE. 1.18. When you arrive, be prepared for an intense feeling of déjà vu like you have never felt before, often accompanied by intense nausea and hallucinations. This is normal.

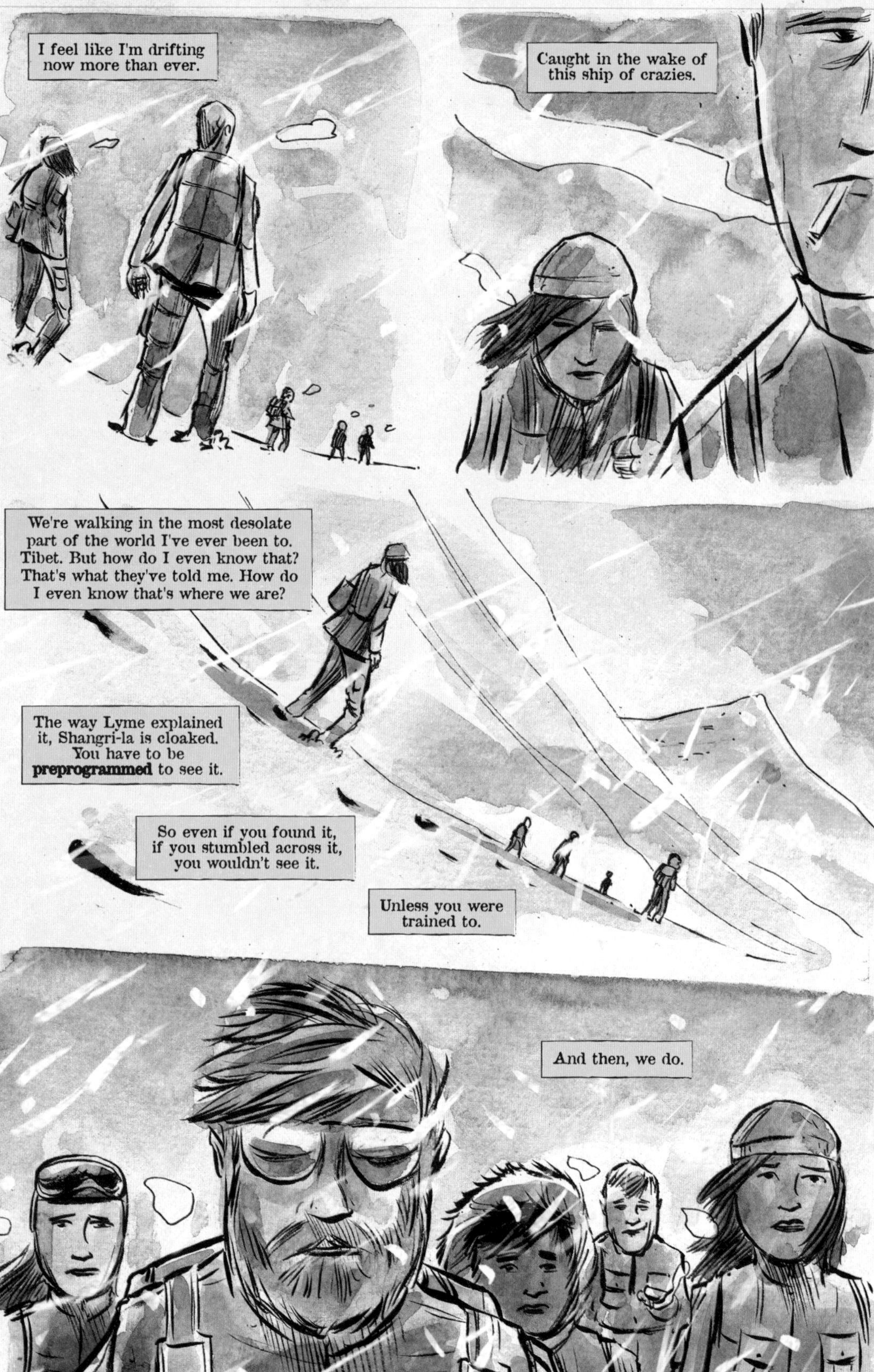
I feel like I'm drifting now more than ever.
Caught in the wake of this ship of crazies.
We're walking in the most desolate part of the world I've ever been to. Tibet. But how do I even know that? That's what they've told me. How do I even know that's where we are?
The way Lyme explained it, Shangri-la is cloaked. You have to be **preprogrammed** to see it.
So even if you found it, if you stumbled across it, you wouldn't see it.
Unless you were trained to.
And then, we do.

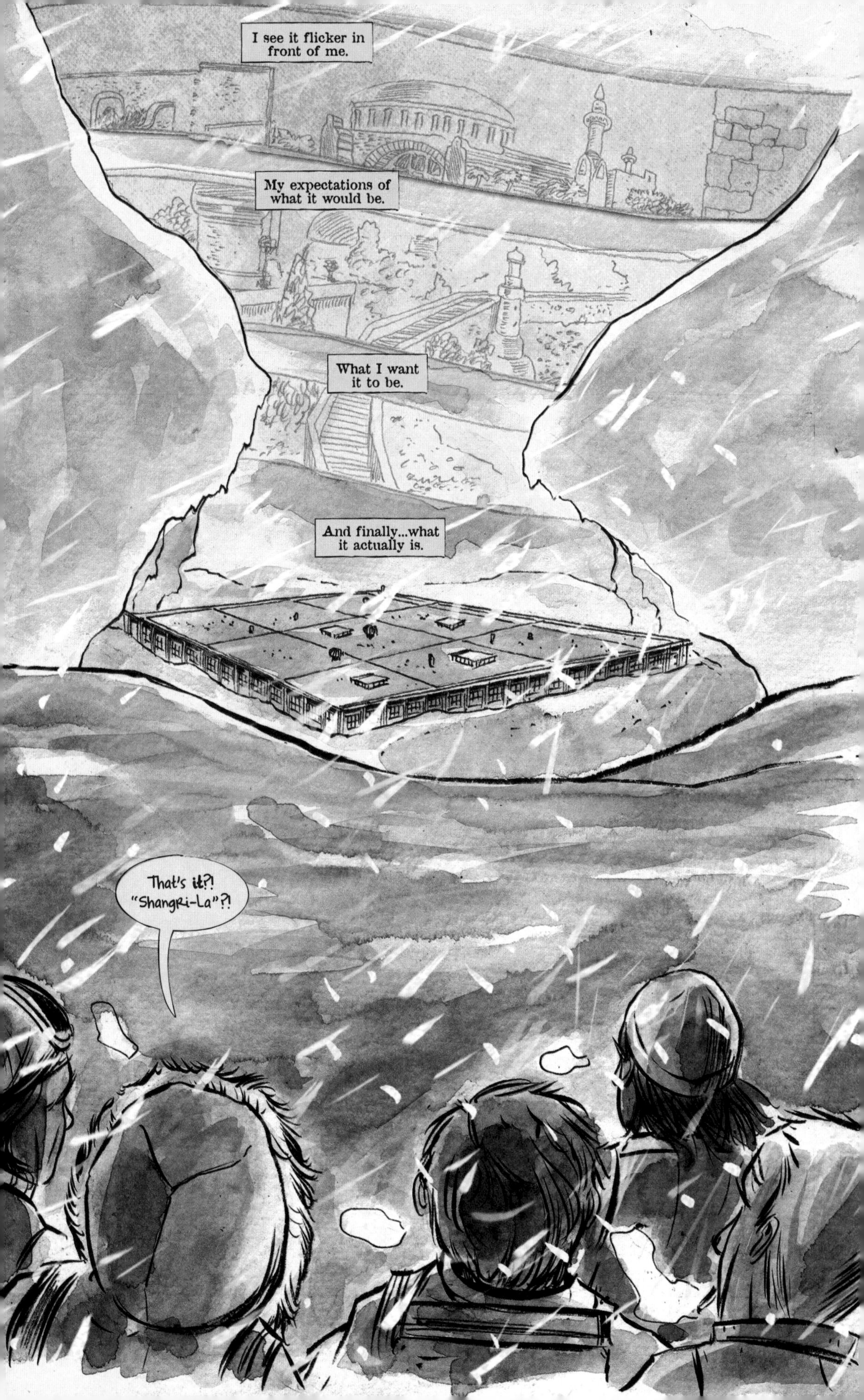
I see it flicker in front of me.
My expectations of what it would be.
What I want it to be.
And finally...what it actually is.
That's it?! "Shangri-La"?!

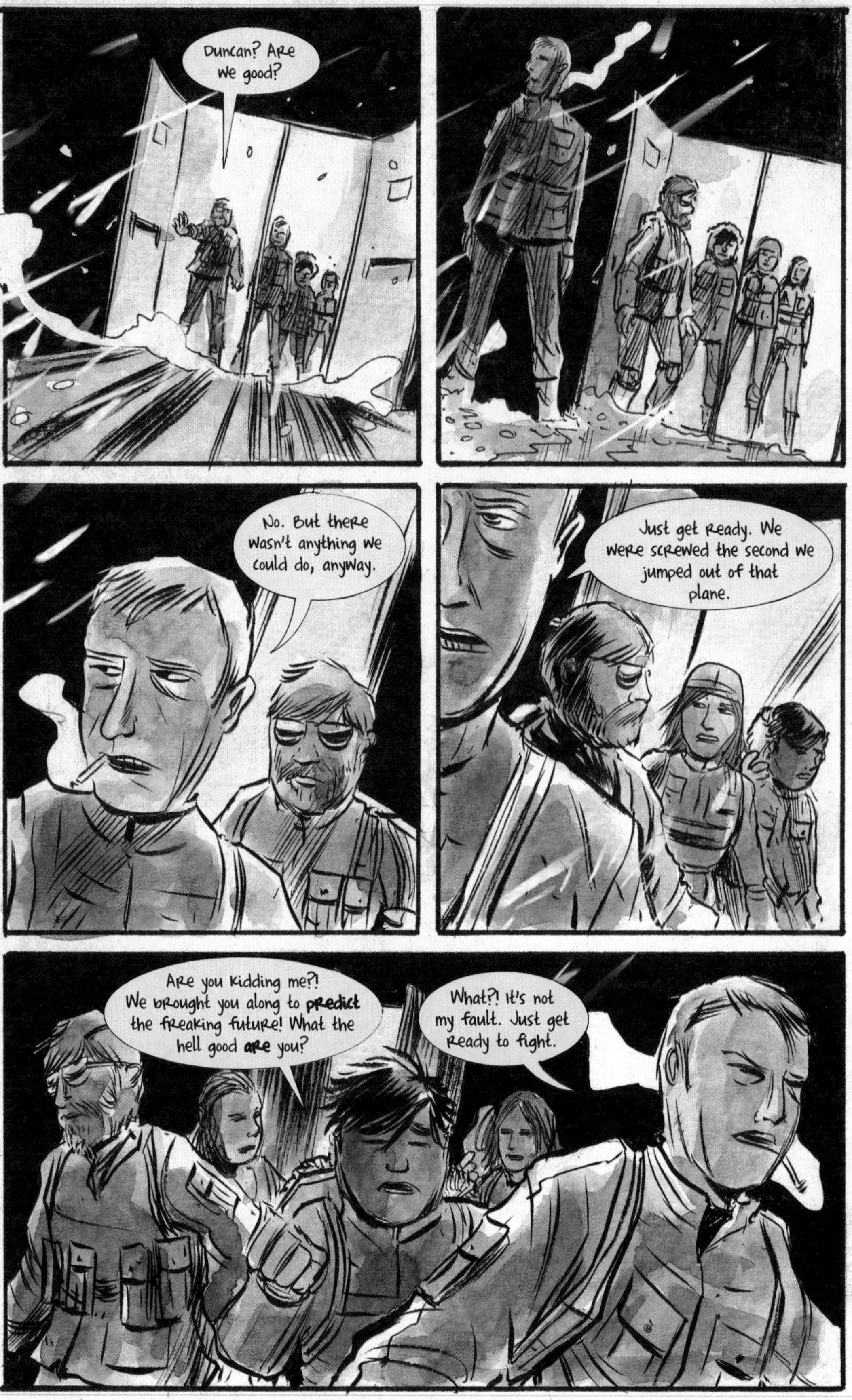
Duncan? Are we good?
No. But there wasn't anything we could do, anyway.
Just get ready. We were screwed the second we jumped out of that plane.
Are you kidding me?! We brought you along to **predict** the freaking future! What the hell good **are** you?
What?! It's not my fault. Just get ready to fight.

MIND MGMT FIELD GUIDE.11.20. There is no "front door." When you arrive, the correct entrance will present itself. You must check in with the central office, regardless of where you enter.

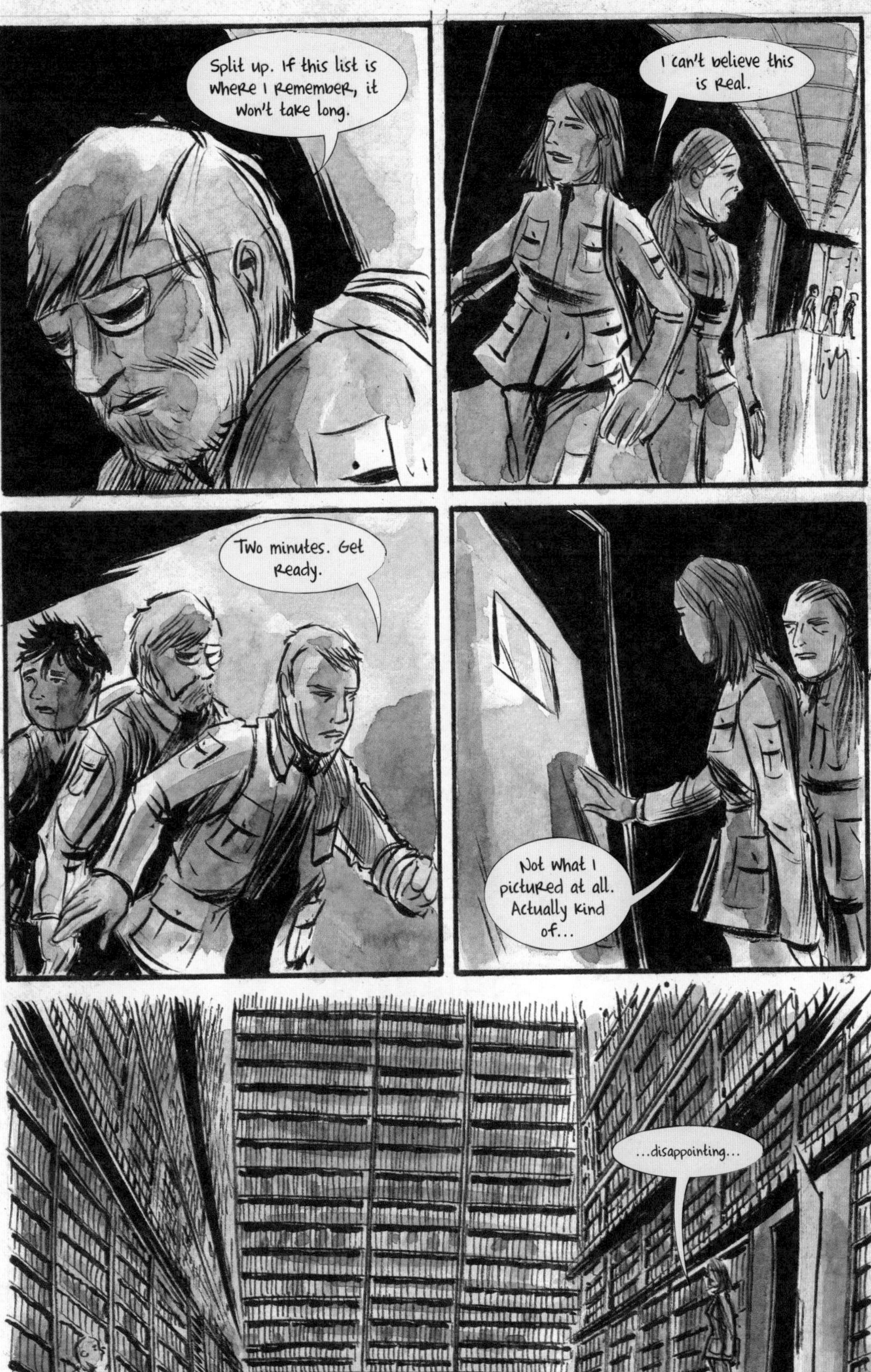
Split up. If this list is where I remember, it won't take long.
I can't believe this is real.
Two minutes. Get ready.
Not what I pictured at all. Actually kind of...
...disappointing...

MIND MGMT FIELD GUIDE. 11.21. At the central office, you will receive additional orders and be greeted by your Shangri-la handler. The preceding protocols must be followed in every case. Failure to observe procedure will result in termination.

WHEN FILING REPORT ALL ESSENTIAL DETAILS MUST FALL WITHIN THIS SOLID "LIVE AREA" BOX. THIS IS THE BORDER FOR A STANDARD, NON-BLEED FIELD REPORT

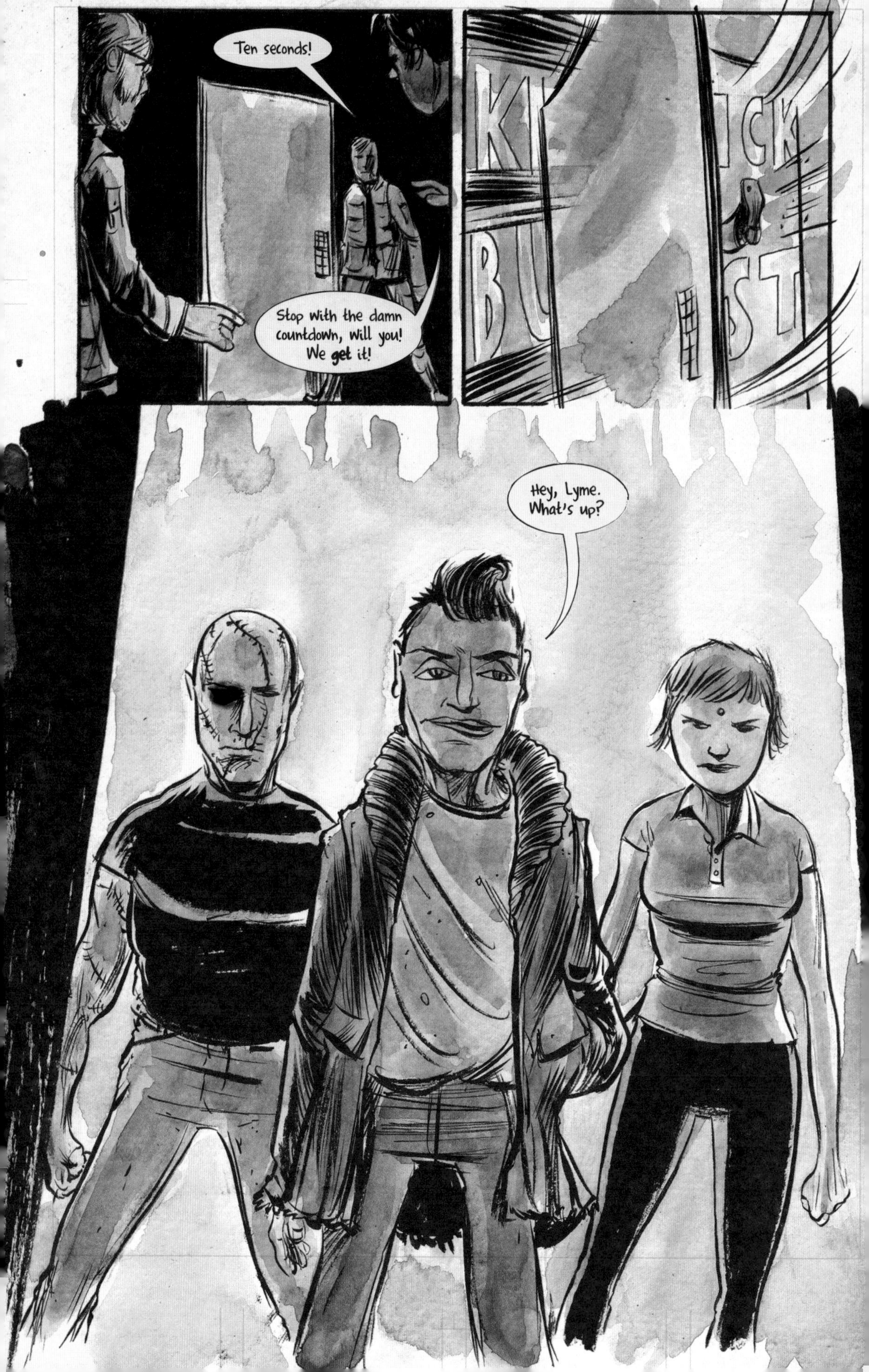
Ten seconds!
Stop with the damn countdown, will you! We get it!
Hey, Lyme. What's up?

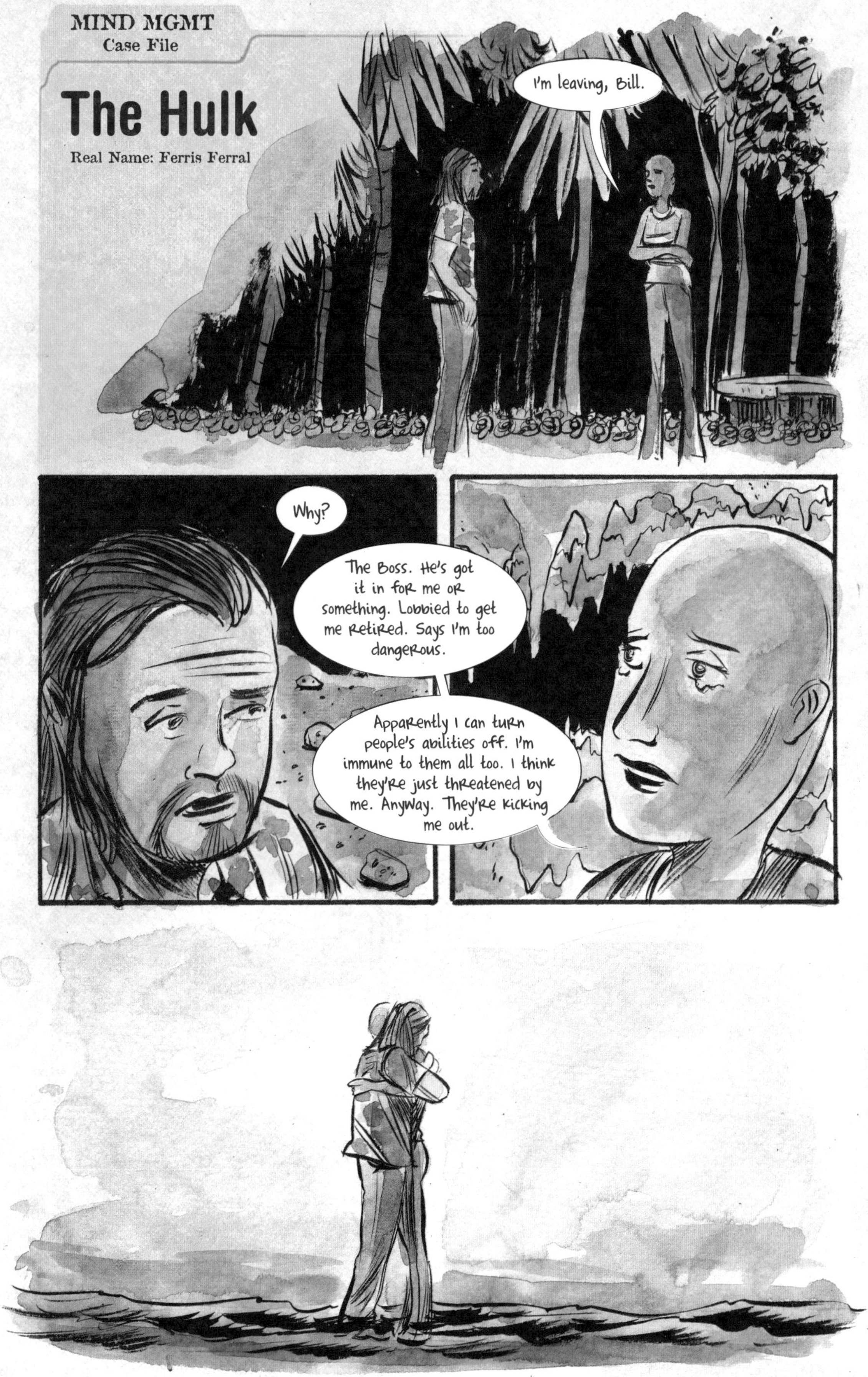
MIND MGMT
Case File
The Hulk
Real Name: Ferris Ferral
I'm leaving, Bill.
Why?
The Boss. He's got it in for me or something. Lobbied to get me retired. Says I'm too dangerous.
Apparently I can turn people's abilities off. I'm immune to them all too. I think they're just threatened by me. Anyway. They're kicking me out.

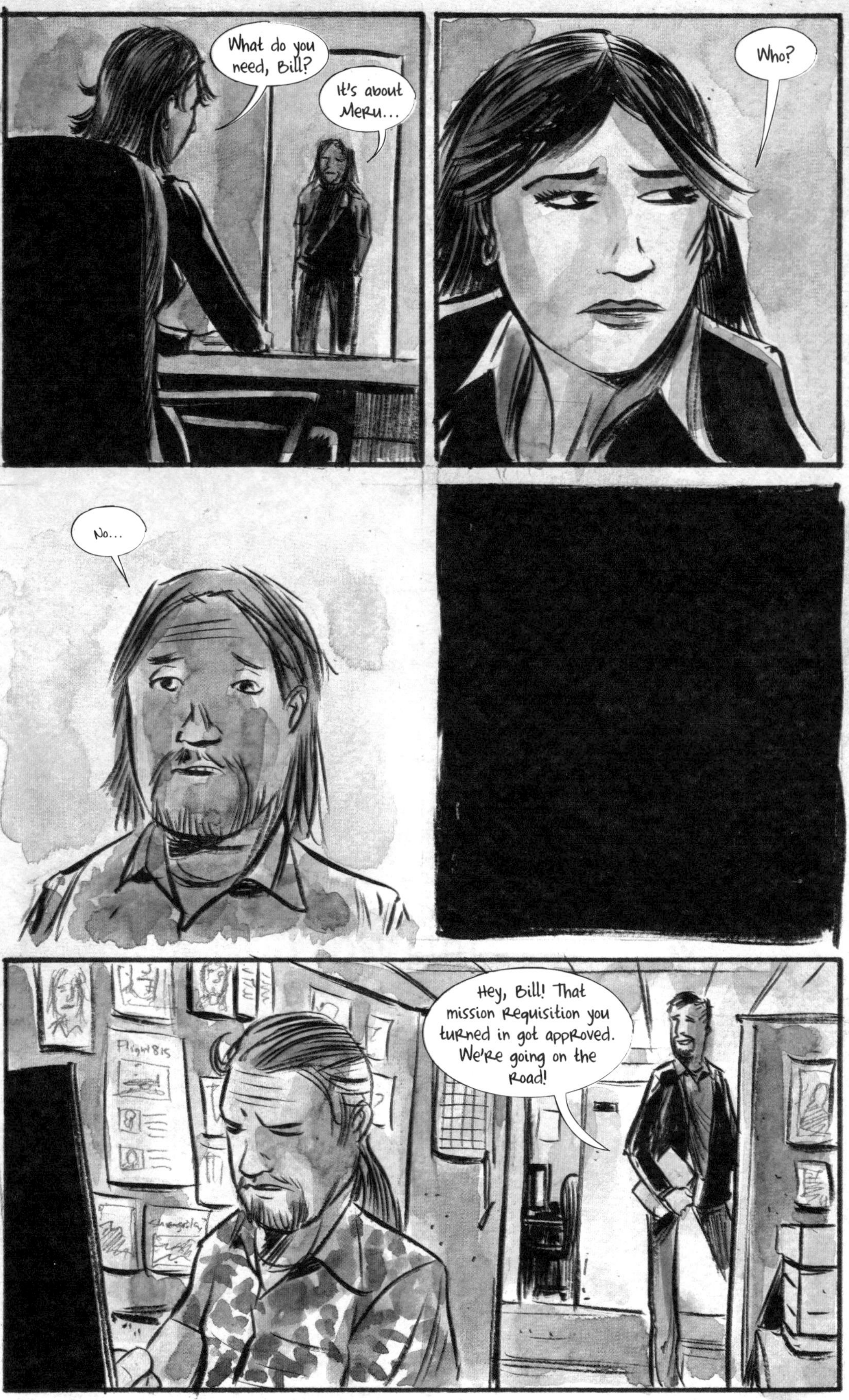
What do you need, Bill?
It's about Meru...
Who?
No...
Hey, Bill! That mission requisition you turned in got approved. We're going on the road!

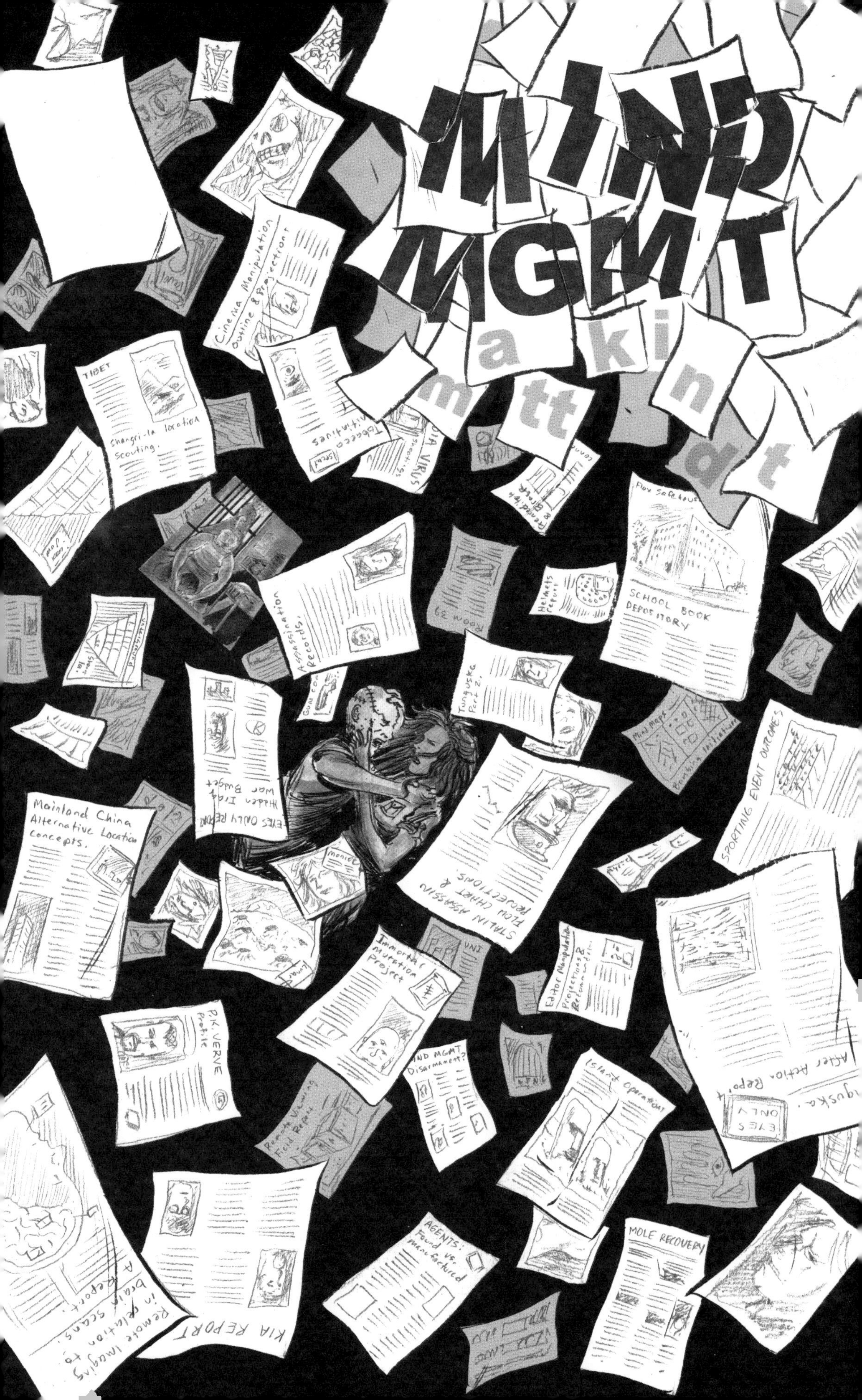
MIND MGMT
Cinema Manipulation Outline & Projections
TIBET
Shangri-la location Scouting.
Tobacco Initiatives
Assassination Records,
Room 39
Helmets Report
Flux Safehouse
SCHOOL BOOK DEPOSITORY
Tunguska Part 2.
Mind maps
SPORTING EVENT OUTCOMES
Mainland China Alternative Location concepts.
EYES ONLY REPORT
Hidden Iraq War Budget
STALIN ASSASSIN FLOW CHART & PROJECTIONS.
Immortal Mutation Project
Editor Manipulation Projections & Recommendations
P.K. VERVE Profile
MIND MGMT Disarmament?
Remote Viewing Field Report
Island Operation
After Action Report
EYES ONLY
AGENTS: Found vs. manufactured
MOLE RECOVERY
KIA REPORT
Remote Imaging in relation to brain scans. A Report

12

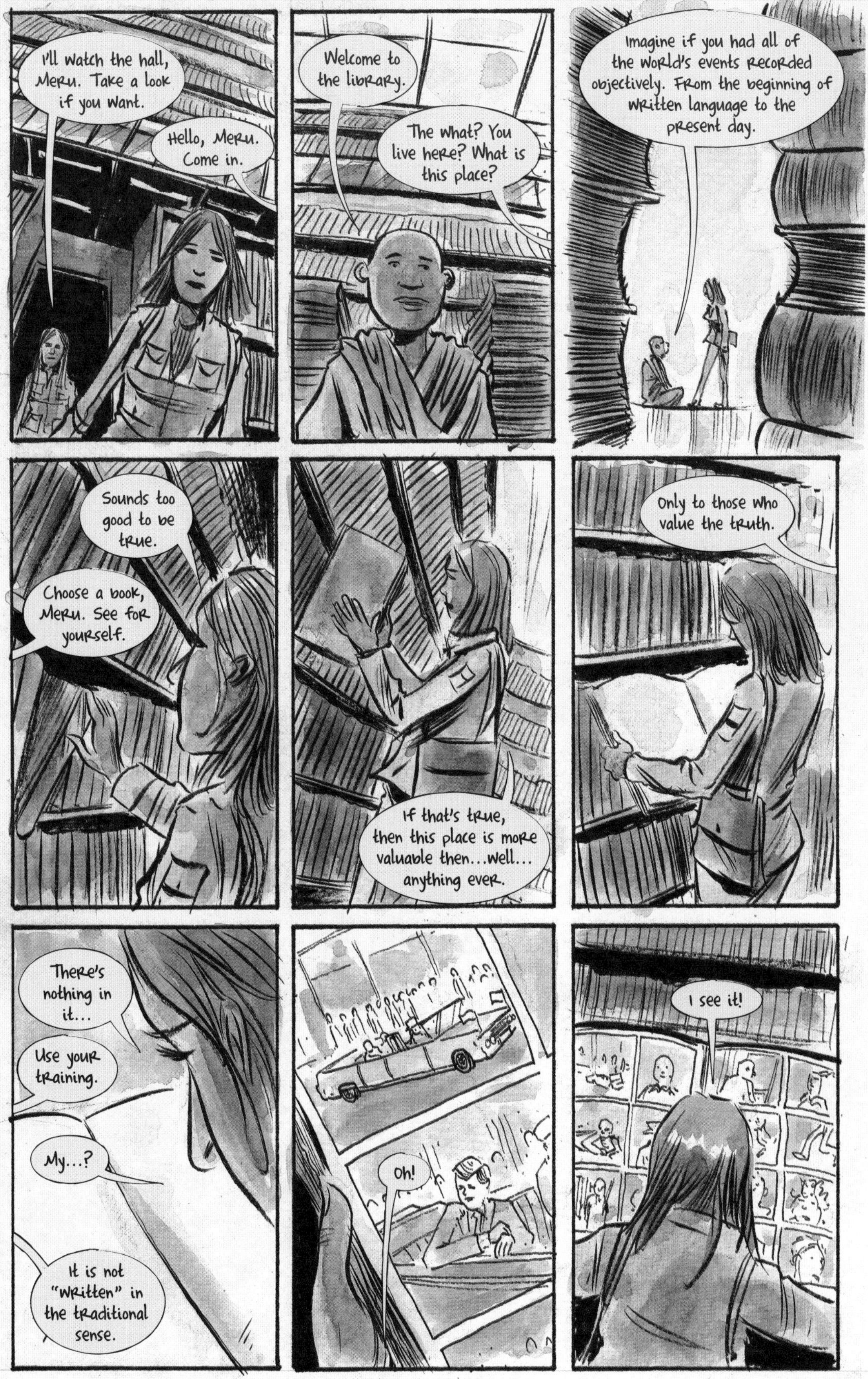
I'll watch the hall, Meru. Take a look if you want.
Hello, Meru. Come in.
Welcome to the library.
The what? You live here? What is this place?
Imagine if you had all of the world's events recorded objectively. From the beginning of written language to the present day.
Sounds too good to be true.
Choose a book, Meru. See for yourself.
If that's true, then this place is more valuable then...well... anything ever.
Only to those who value the truth.
There's nothing in it...
Use your training.
My...?
It is not "written" in the traditional sense.
Oh!
I see it!

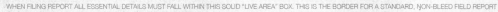

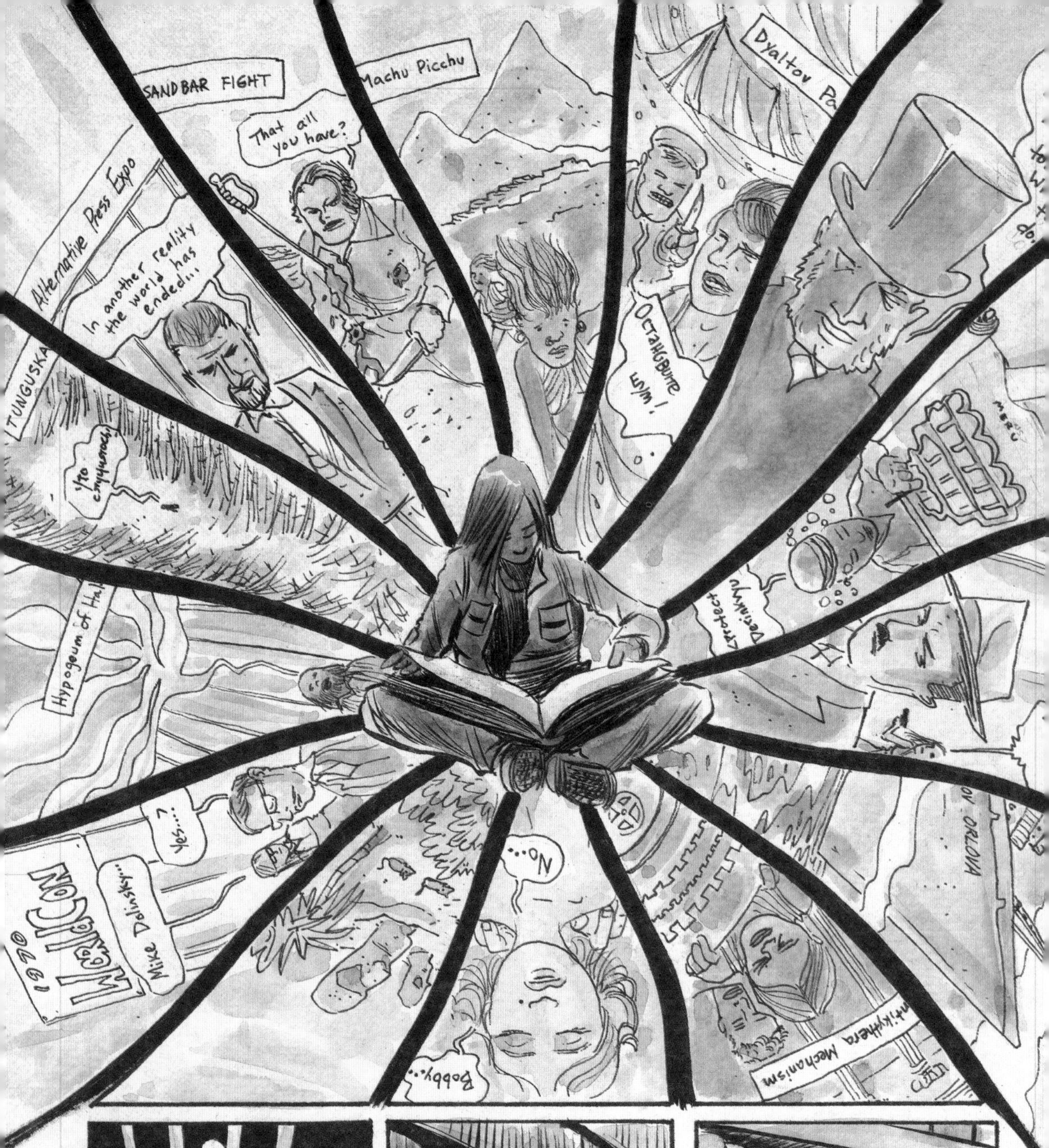
SANDBAR FIGHT
Machu Picchu
That all you have?
Alternative Press Expo
In another reality the world has ended...
TUNGUSKA
Hypogeum of Hal
1970 WorldCon
Mike Dolinsky...
Yes...?
...No...
Bobby...
Antikythera Mechanism

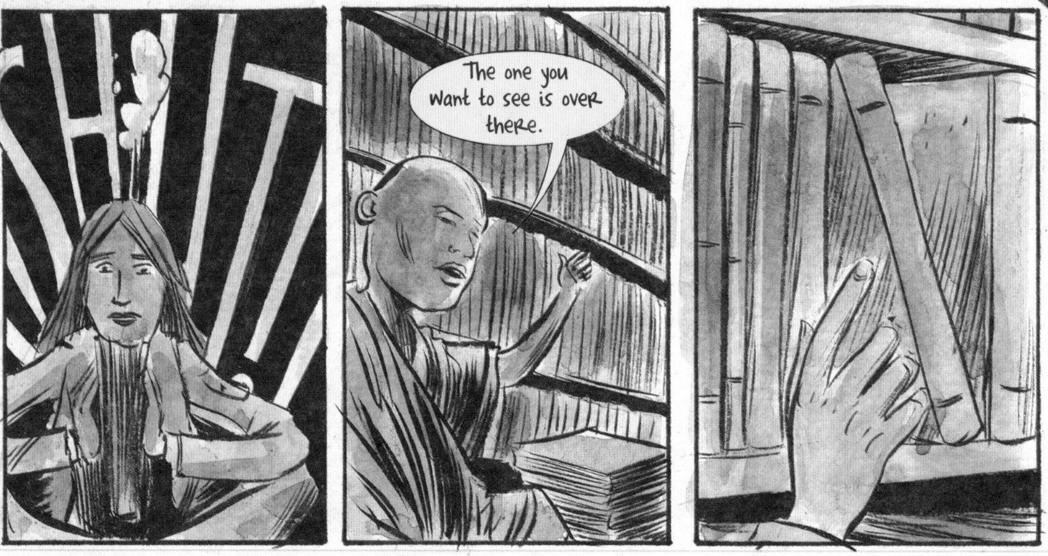
The one you want to see is over there.

MIND MGMT FIELD GUIDE. 12.2. Unsupervised reading is prohibited.

WHEN FILING REPORT ALL ESSENTIAL DETAILS MUST FALL WITHIN THIS SOLID "LIVE AREA" BOX. THIS IS THE BORDER FOR A STANDARD, NON-BLEED FIELD REPORT

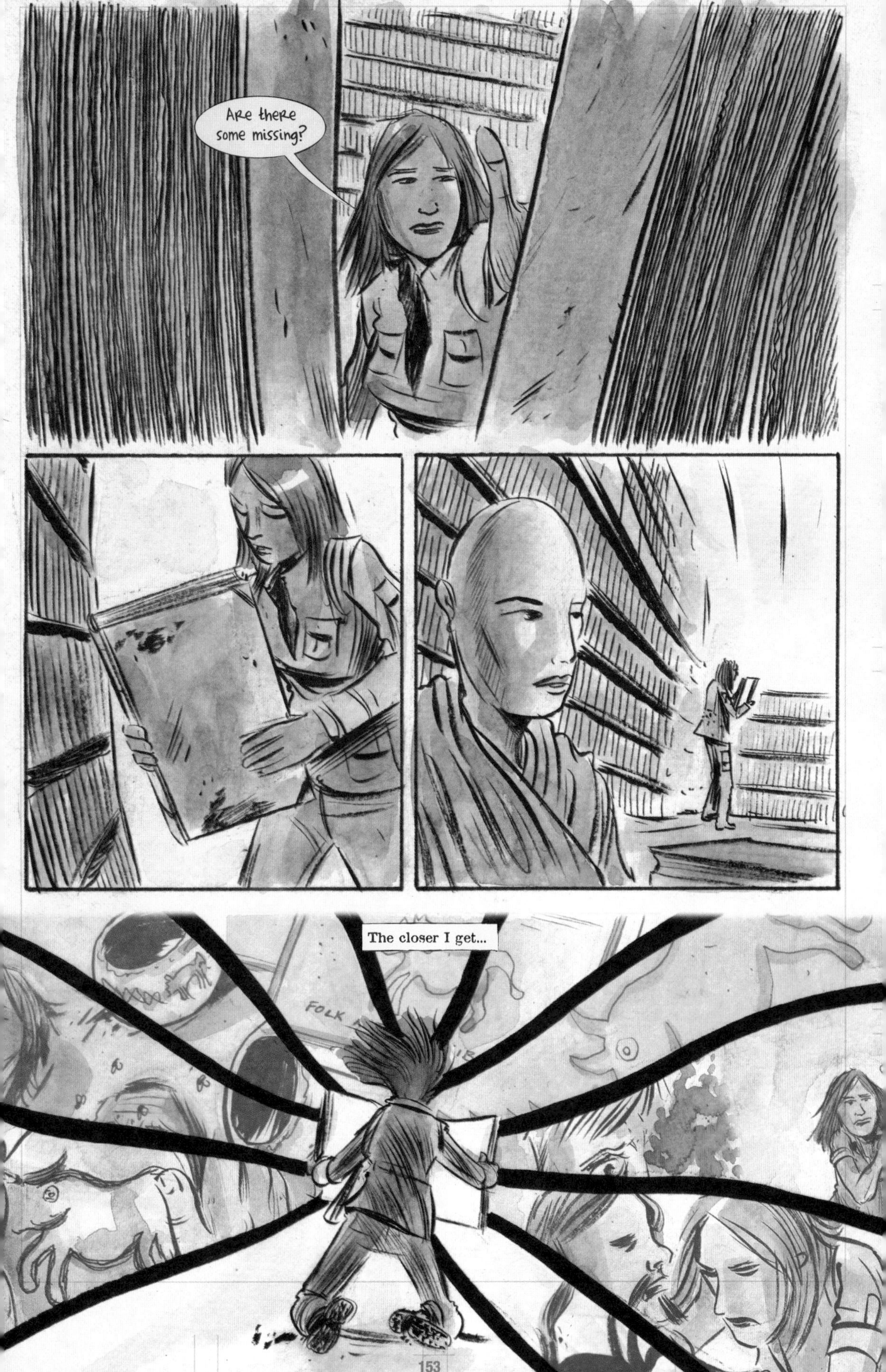
Are there some missing?
The closer I get...
FOLK

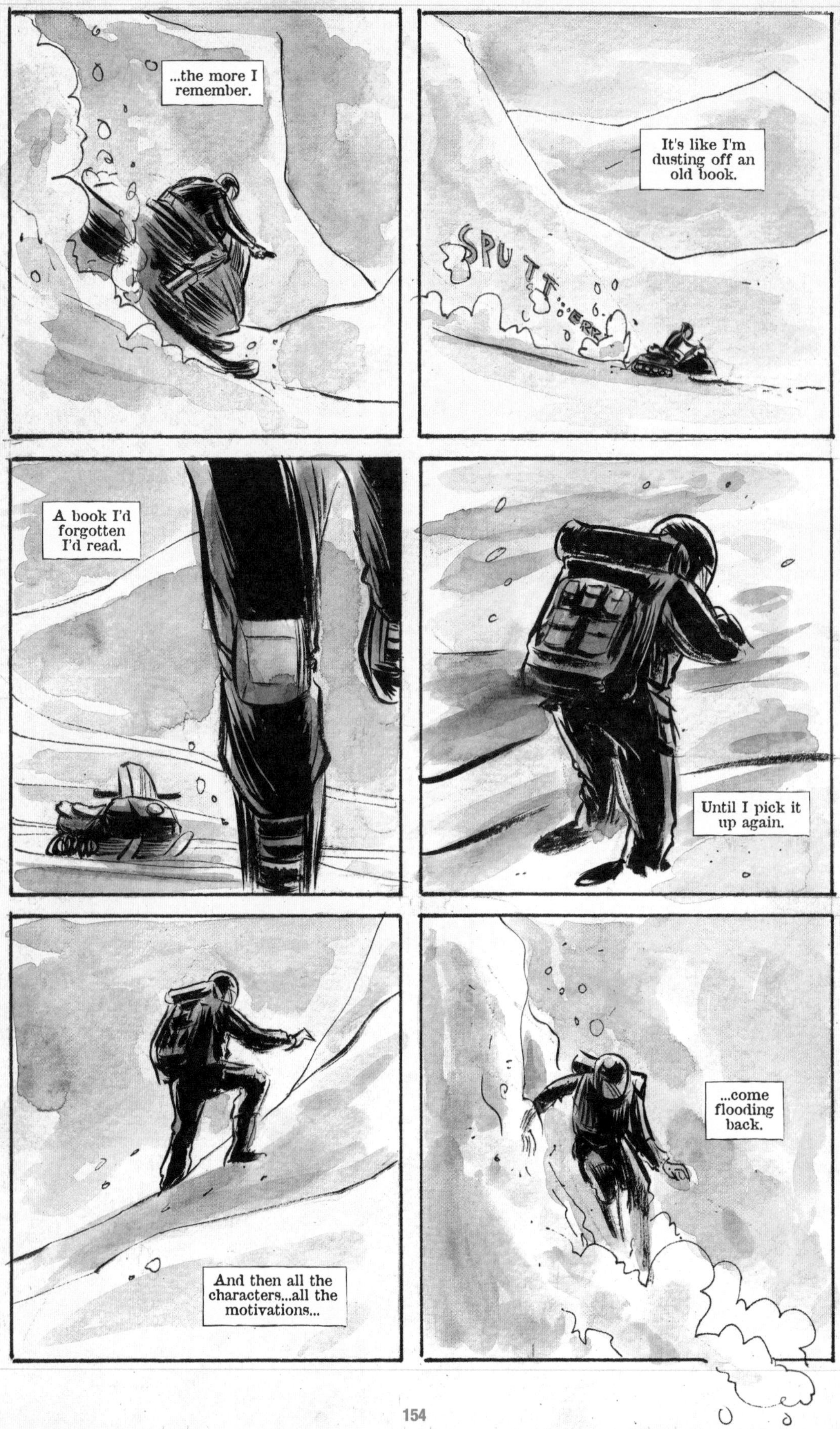
...the more I remember.
It's like I'm dusting off an old book.
SPUTT...ERR
A book I'd forgotten I'd read.
Until I pick it up again.
And then all the characters...all the motivations...
...come flooding back.

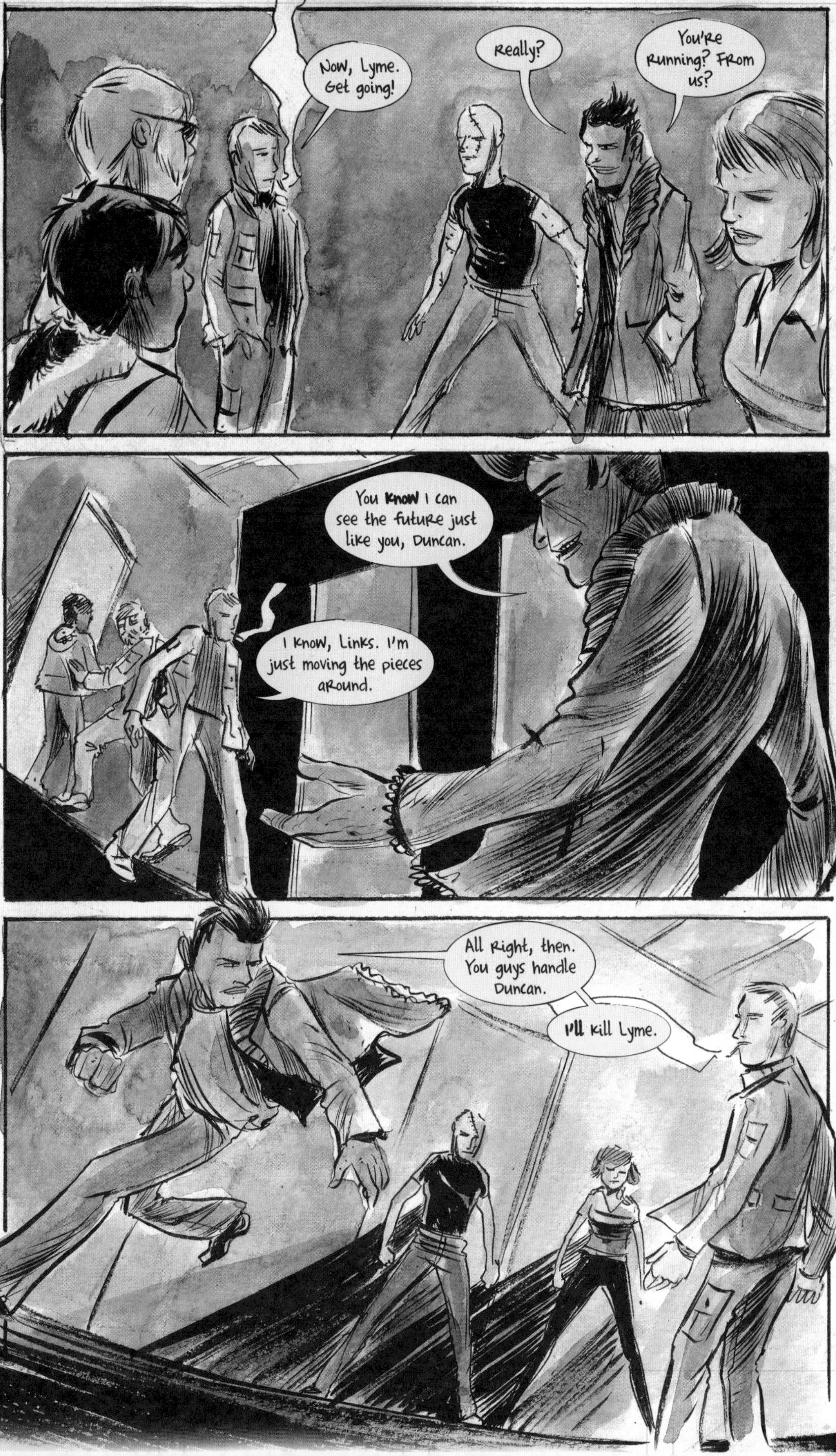
Now, Lyme. Get going!
Really?
You're Running? From us?
You KNOW I can see the future just like you, Duncan.
I know, Links. I'm just moving the pieces around.
All Right, then. You guys handle Duncan.
I'll kill Lyme.

MIND MGMT FIELD GUIDE. 12.5. Access to headquarters facilities is limited. Labyrinth technology is in full use, and entrance into prohibited areas may induce temporary dementia.

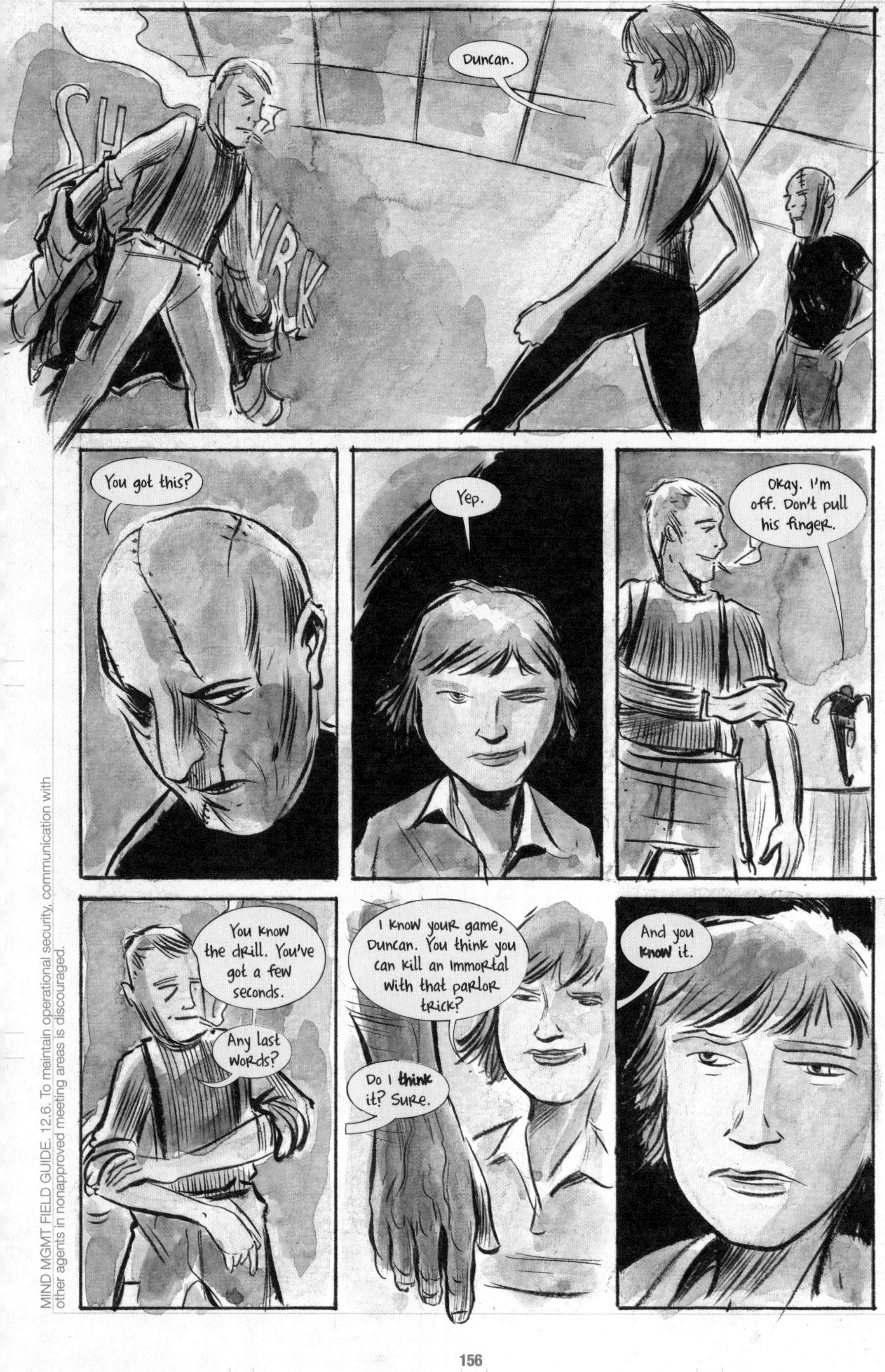
Duncan.
You got this?
Yep.
Okay. I'm off. Don't pull his finger.
You know the drill. You've got a few seconds.
Any last words?
I know your game, Duncan. You think you can kill an immortal with that parlor trick?
Do I **think** it? Sure.
And you **know** it.

MIND MGMT FIELD GUIDE. 12.6. To maintain operational security, communication with other agents in nonapproved meeting areas is discouraged.

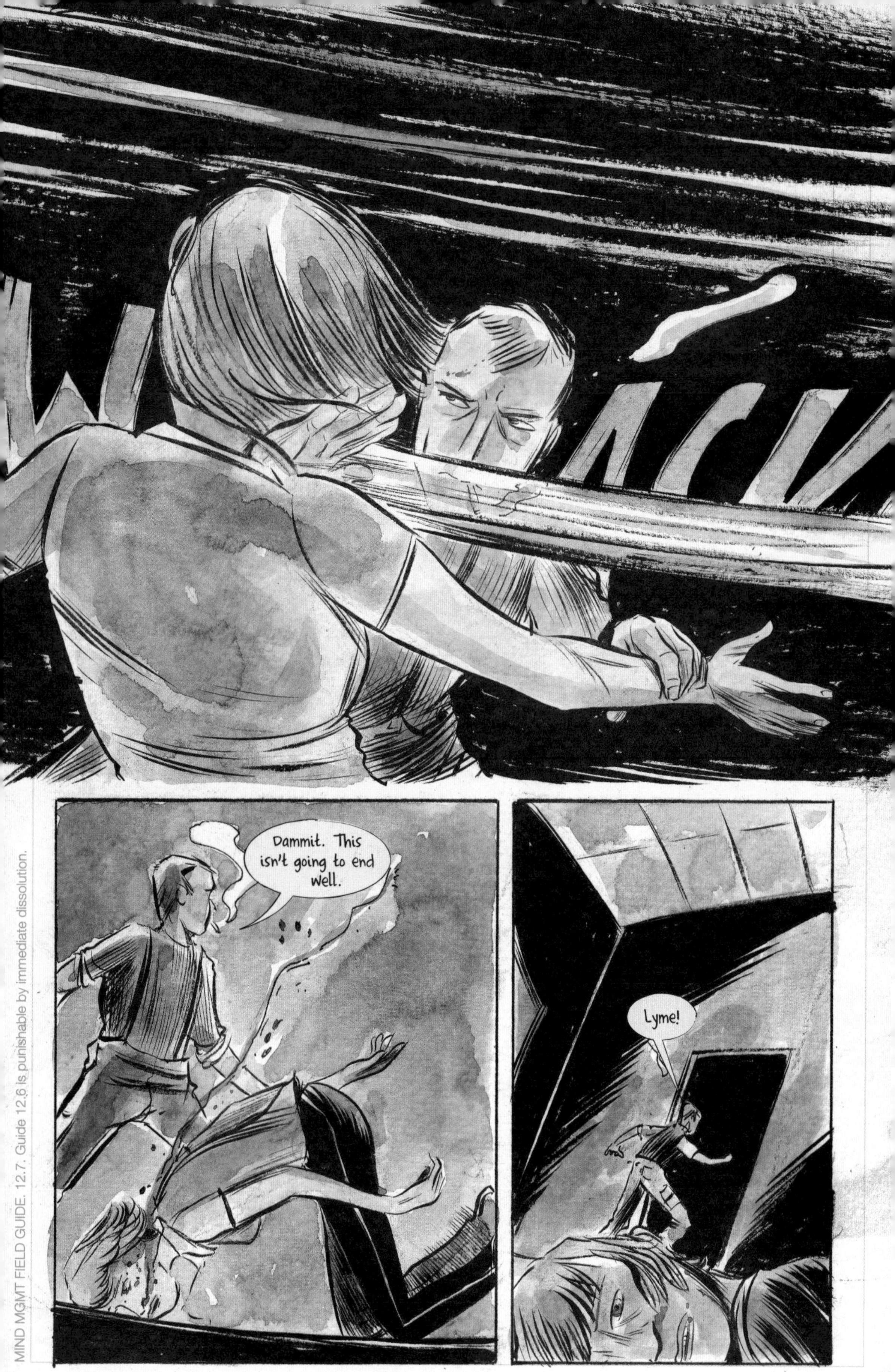
Dammit. This isn't going to end well.
Lyme!
MIND MGMT FIELD GUIDE. 12.7. Guide 12.6 is punishable by immediate dissolution.

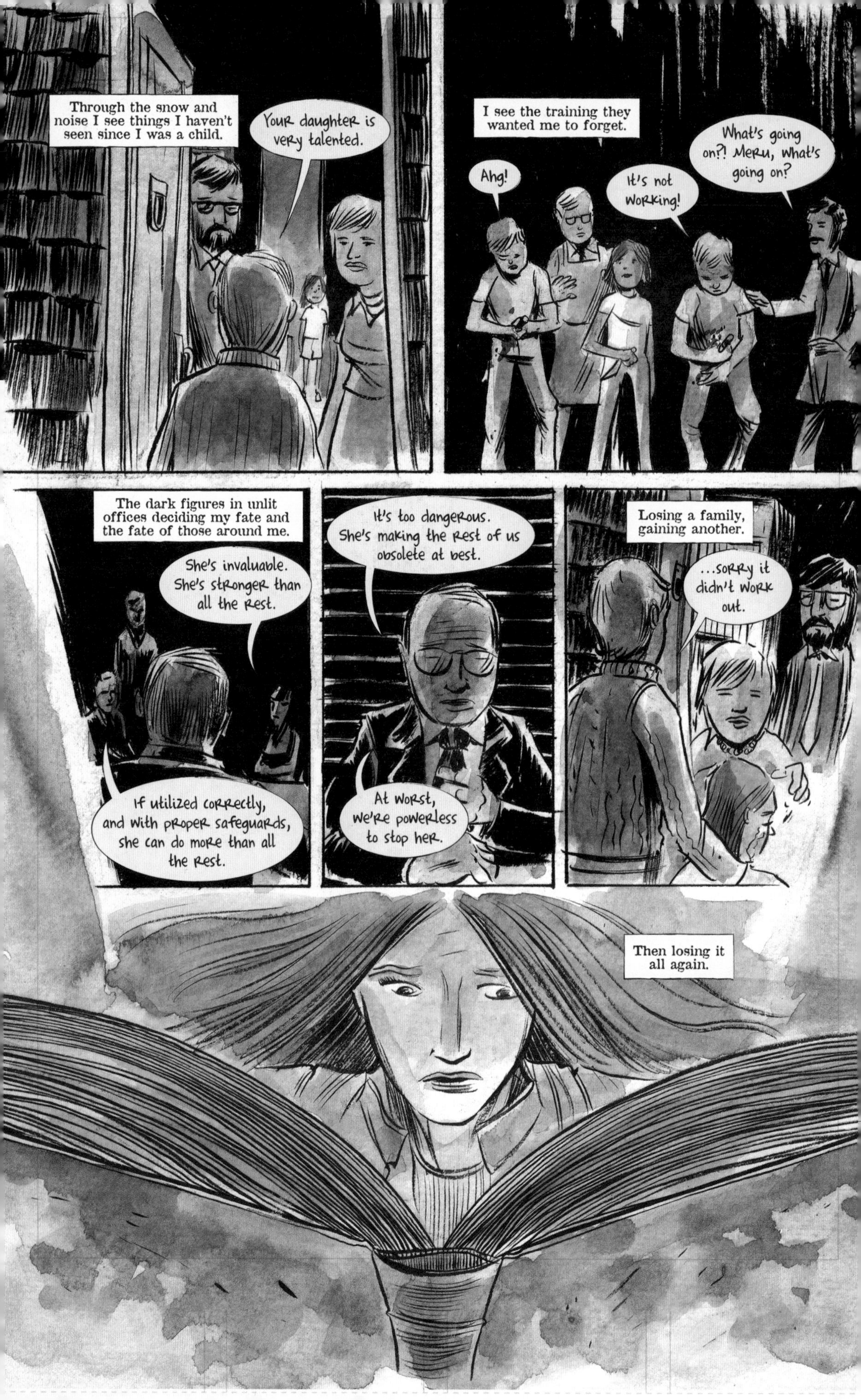
Through the snow and noise I see things I haven't seen since I was a child.
Your daughter is very talented.
I see the training they wanted me to forget.
Ahg!
It's not working!
What's going on?! Meru, what's going on?
The dark figures in unlit offices deciding my fate and the fate of those around me.
She's invaluable. She's stronger than all the rest.
If utilized correctly, and with proper safeguards, she can do more than all the rest.
It's too dangerous. She's making the rest of us obsolete at best.
At worst, we're powerless to stop her.
Losing a family, gaining another.
...sorry it didn't work out.
Then losing it all again.

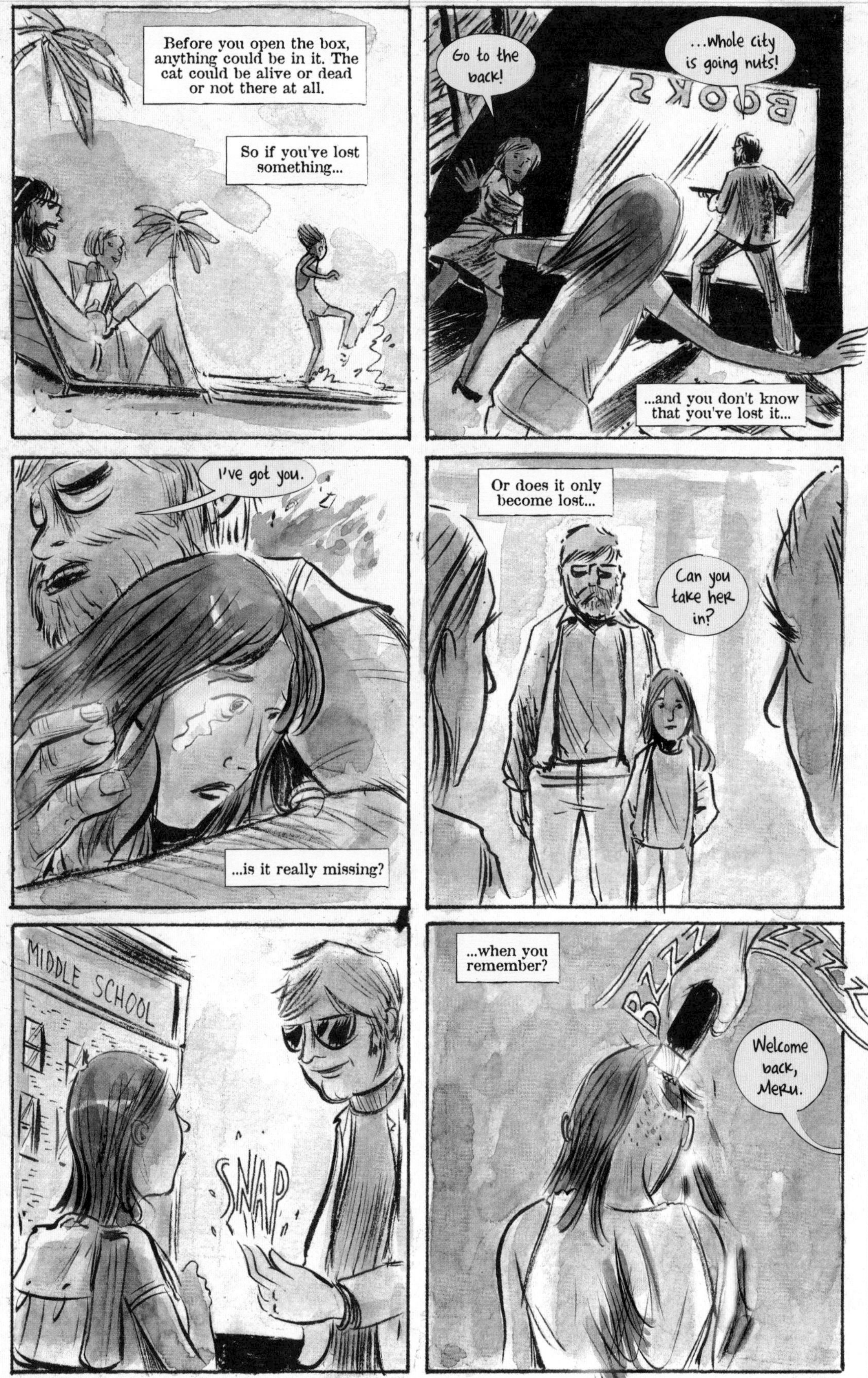
Before you open the box, anything could be in it. The cat could be alive or dead or not there at all.
So if you've lost something...
Go to the back!
...Whole city is going nuts!
BOOKS
...and you don't know that you've lost it...
I've got you.
...is it really missing?
Or does it only become lost...
Can you take her in?
MIDDLE SCHOOL
SNAP
...when you remember?
BZZZ
ZZZZ
Welcome back, Meru.

MIND MGMT FIELD GUIDE. 12.9. Erasure facilities are always open and available to agents in need of help coping with memories that could potentially interfere with fieldwork.

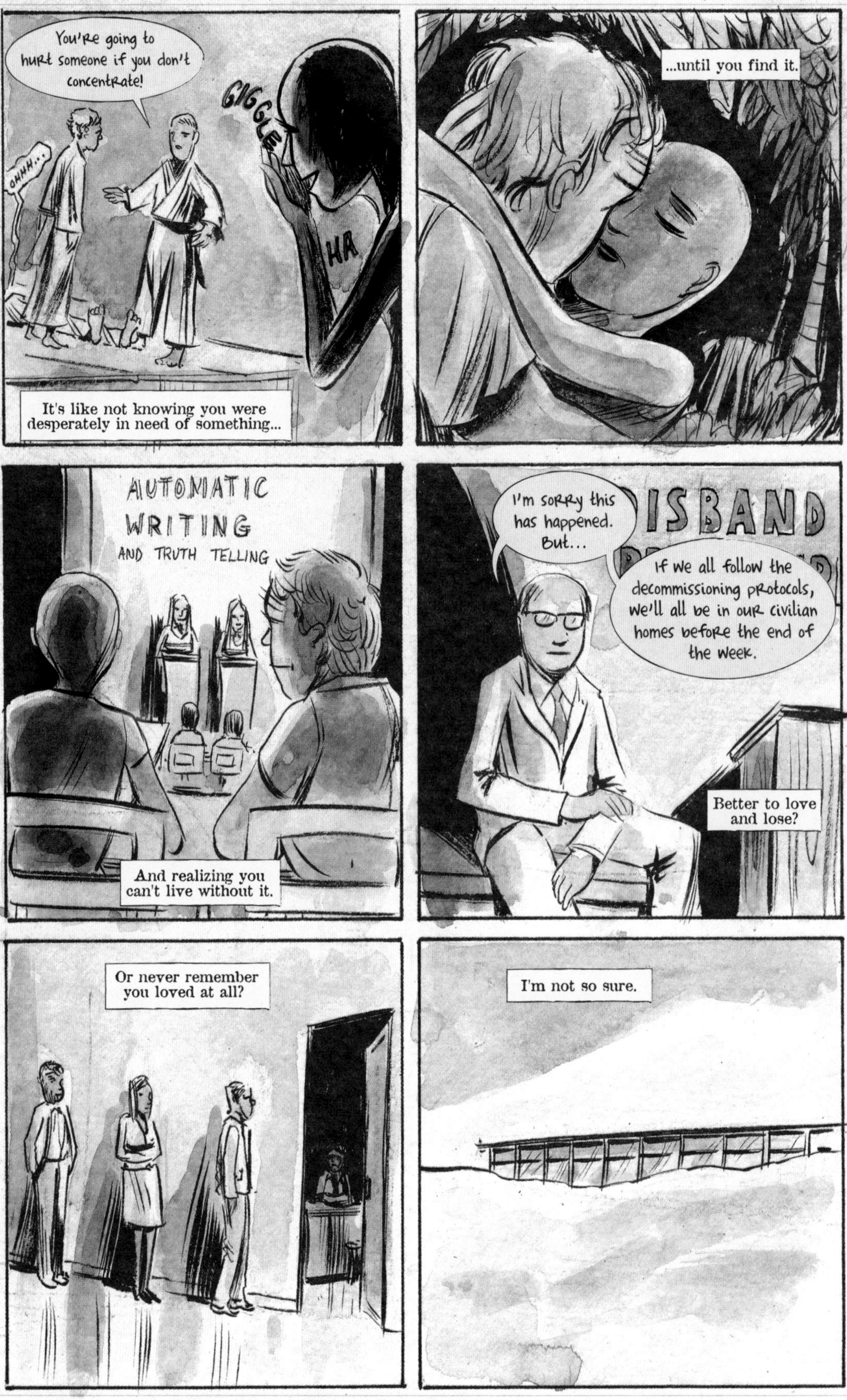
You're going to hurt someone if you don't concentrate!
OHHH...
GIGGLE
HA
It's like not knowing you were desperately in need of something...
...until you find it.
AUTOMATIC WRITING AND TRUTH TELLING
And realizing you can't live without it.
DISBAND
I'm sorry this has happened. But...
If we all follow the decommissioning protocols, we'll all be in our civilian homes before the end of the week.
Better to love and lose?
Or never remember you loved at all?
I'm not so sure.

MIND MGMT FIELD GUIDE. 12.10. Early training techniques should be***disbanding protocols begin with the exchange of all clothing and equipment that you have ever used in the line of duty.

Premeditated

Chapter One

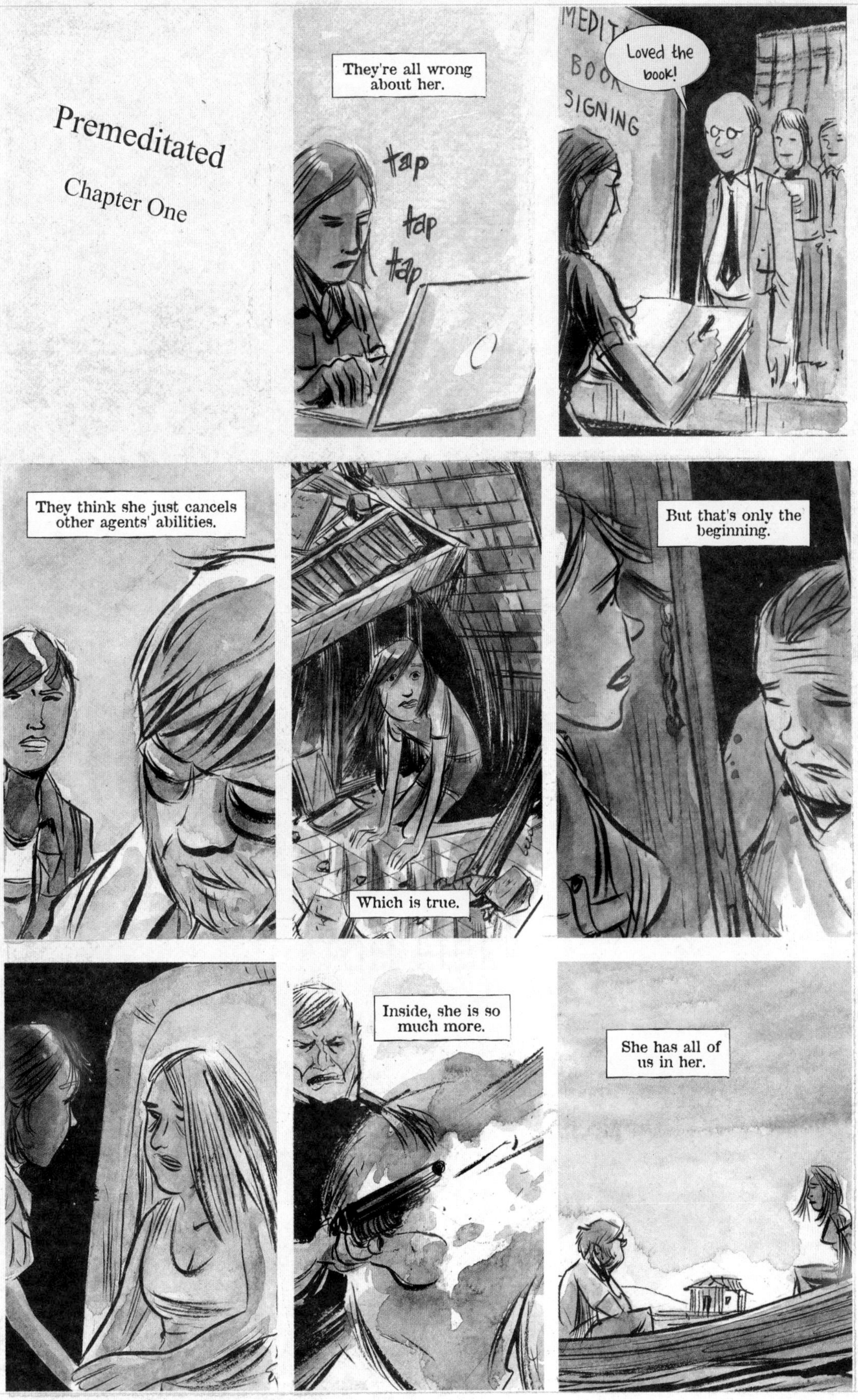
They're all wrong about her.
tap tap tap
MEDIT... BOOK SIGNING
Loved the book!
They think she just cancels other agents' abilities.
Which is true.
But that's only the beginning.
Inside, she is so much more.
She has all of us in her.

DISBANDING PROTOCOLS. 12.9. The Eraser offices will systematically reformat your programming and leave you much as you were when first recruited.

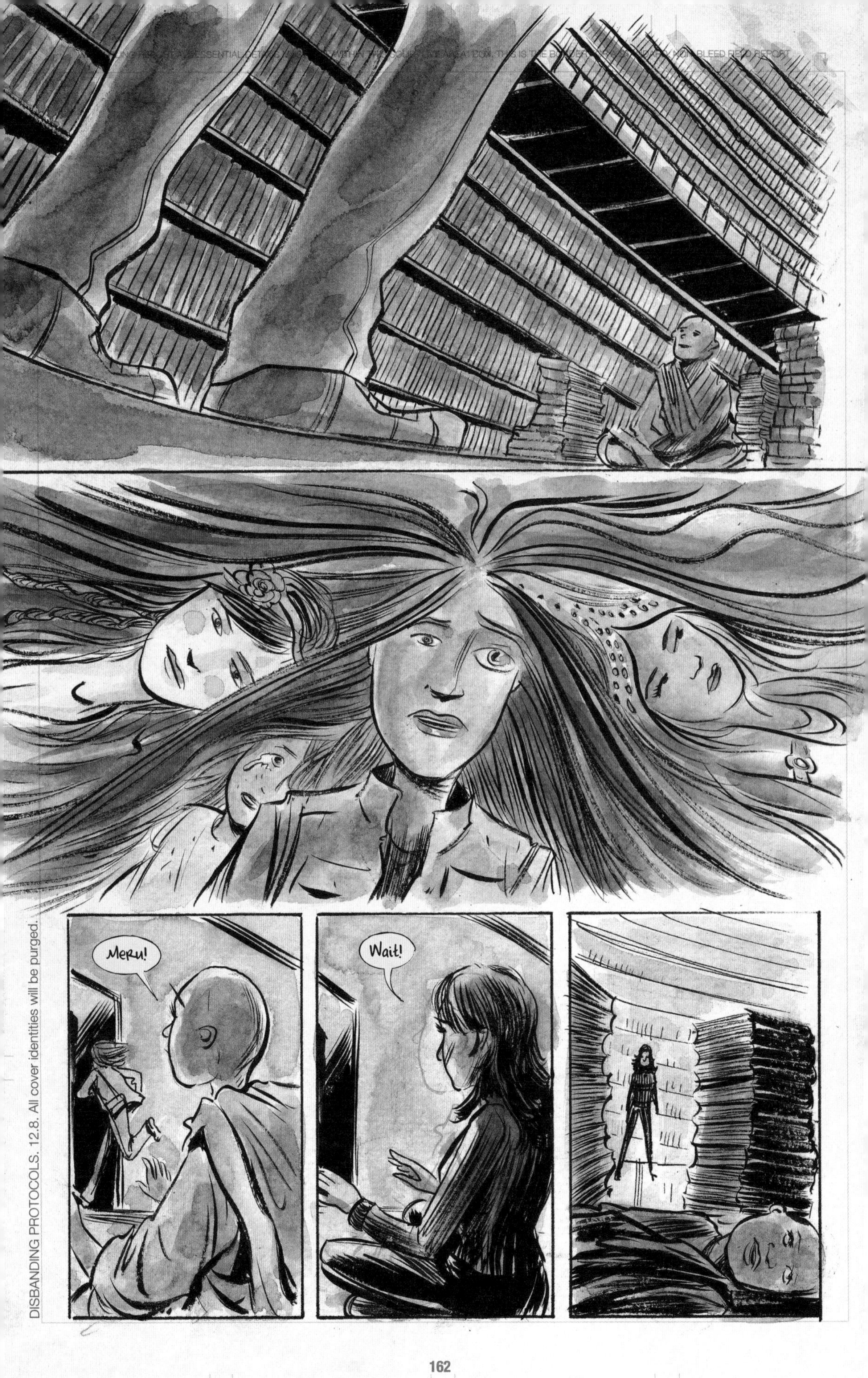
Meru!
Wait!

DISBANDING PROTOCOLS. 12.8. All cover identities will be purged.

WHEN FILING REPORT ALL ESSENTIAL DETAILS MUST FALL WITHIN THIS SOLID "LIVE AREA" BOX. THIS IS THE BORDER FOR A STANDARD, NON-BLEED FIELD REPORT

DISBANDING PROTOCOLS. 12.7. Existing paperwork will be destroyed and/or masked with OITO (Out In The Open) masking techniques.

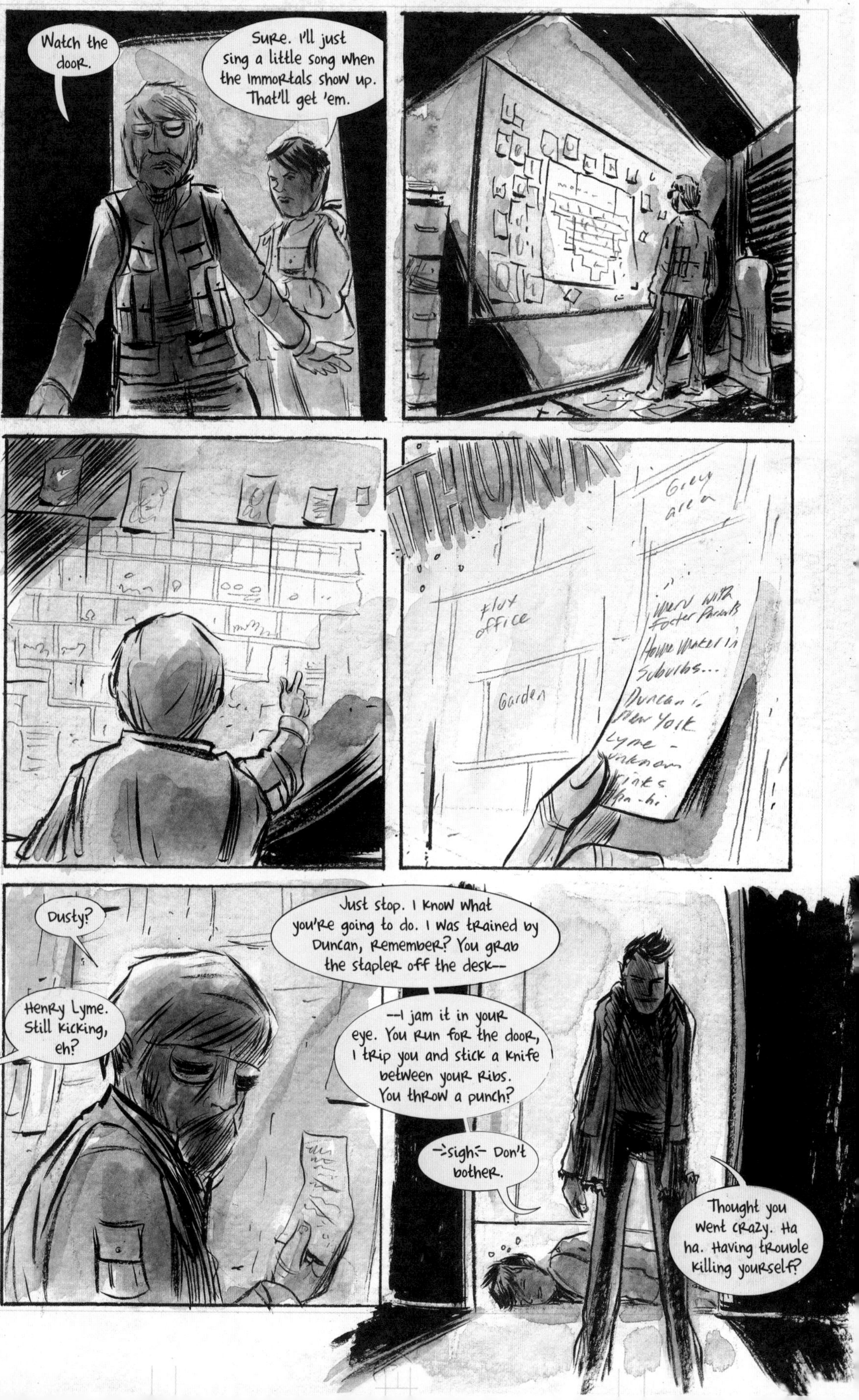

Watch the door.
Sure. I'll just sing a little song when the Immortals show up. That'll get 'em.
THUNK
Grey area
Flux office
Garden
Home Maker in Suburbs...
Duncan in New York
Lyme - unknown
Dusty?
Henry Lyme. Still kicking, eh?
Just stop. I know what you're going to do. I was trained by Duncan, remember? You grab the stapler off the desk--
--I jam it in your eye. You run for the door, I trip you and stick a knife between your ribs. You throw a punch?
-sigh- Don't bother.
Thought you went crazy. Ha ha. Having trouble killing yourself?

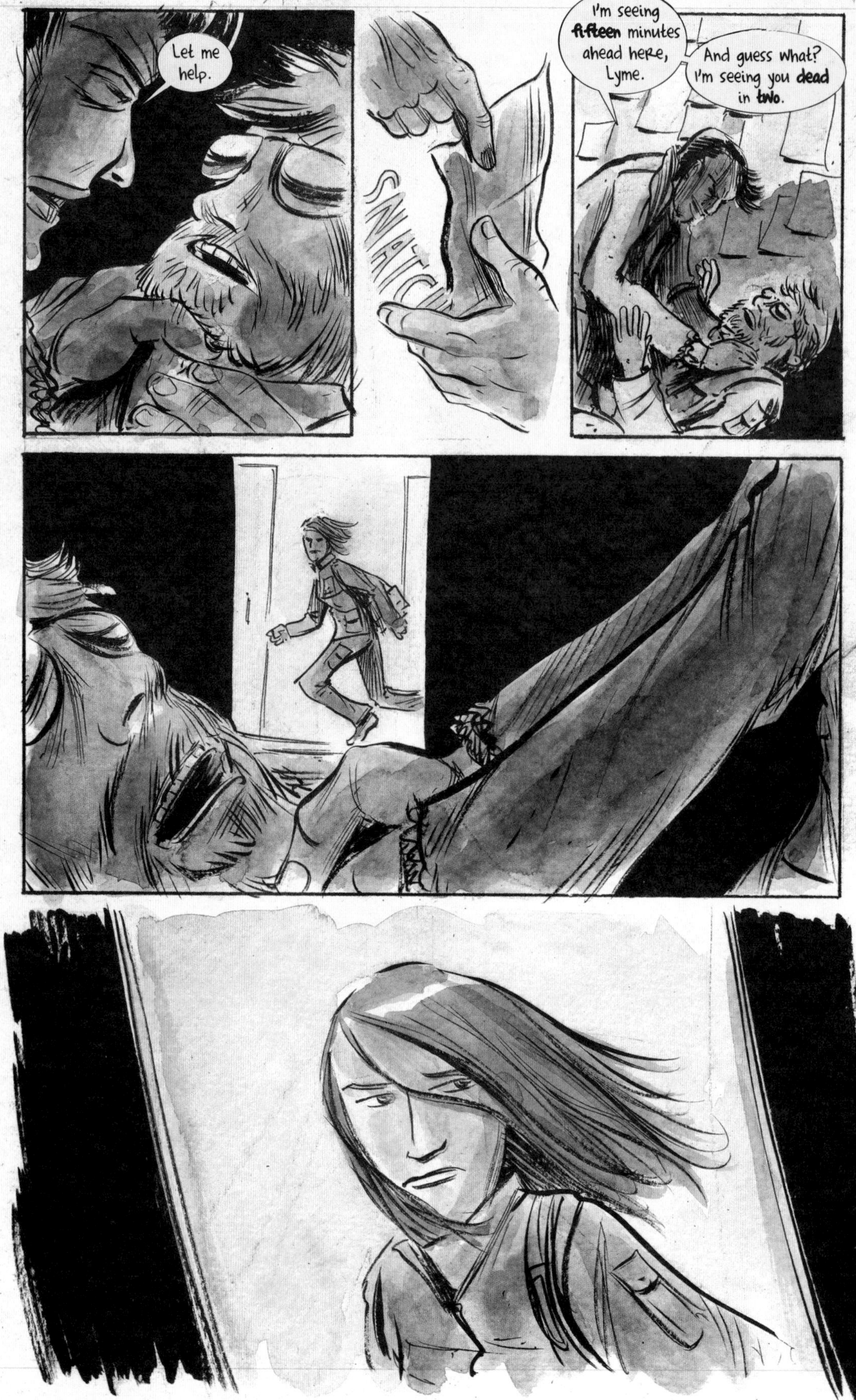
Let me help.
SNATCH
I'm seeing fifteen minutes ahead here, Lyme.
And guess what? I'm seeing you dead in two.

DISBANDING PROTOCOLS. 12.6. Protection of the identities of all former agents is the top priority. There will be no comprehensive list of agents once dissolution is complete.

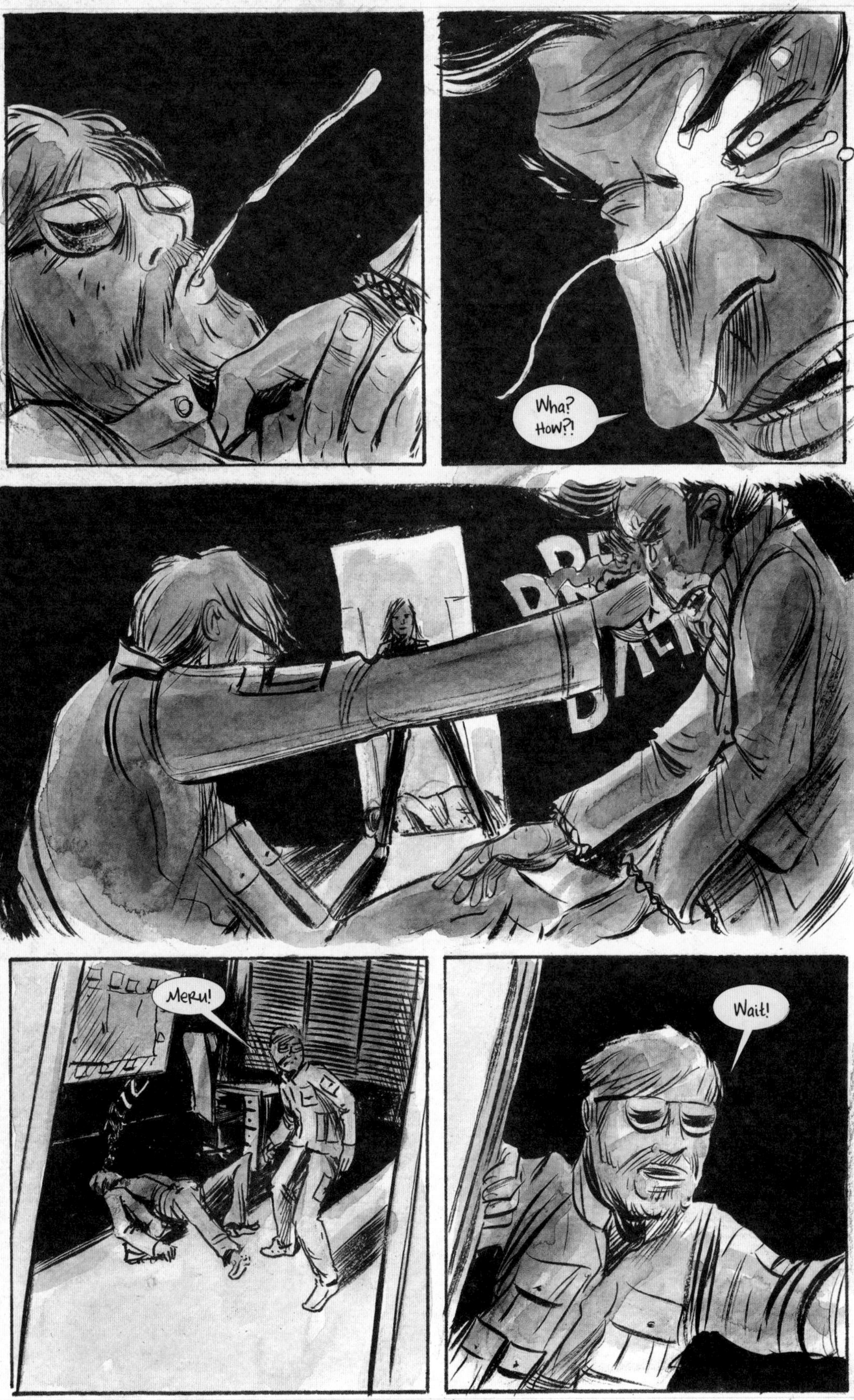
Wha? How?!
Meru!
Wait!

DISBANDING PROTOCOLS. 12.5. As a safety precaution, only a small contingent of agents will be left after disbanding. They will act as the final security, guarding vacant offices and archives.

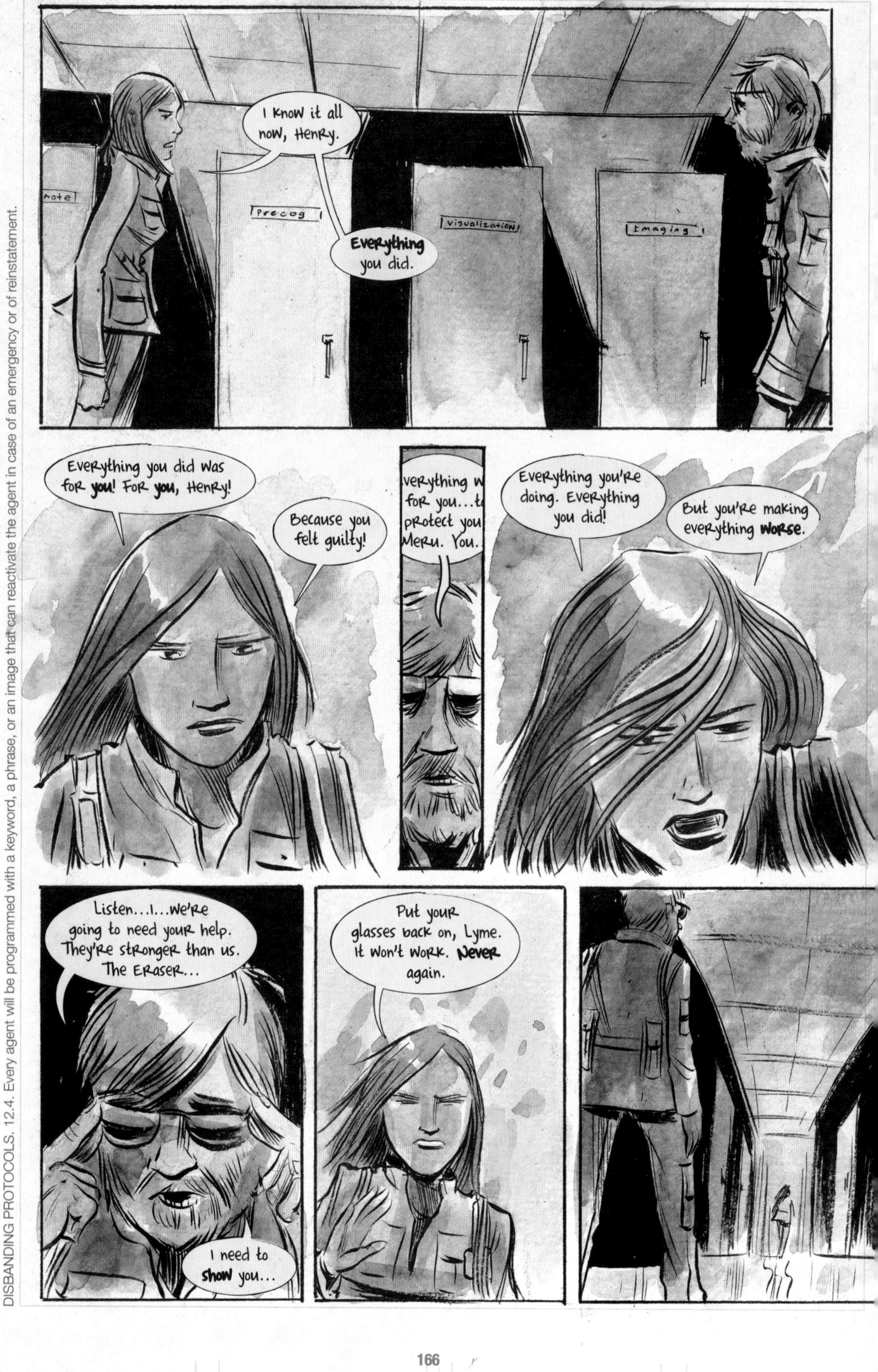
note
Precog
Visualization
Imaging
I know it all now, Henry.
Everything you did.
Everything you did was for you! For you, Henry!
Because you felt guilty!
verything w
for you...t
protect you
Meru. You.
Everything you're doing. Everything you did!
But you're making everything worse.
Listen...I...we're going to need your help. They're stronger than us. The Eraser...
I need to show you...
Put your glasses back on, Lyme. It won't work. Never again.

DISBANDING PROTOCOLS. 12.4. Every agent will be programmed with a keyword, a phrase, or an image that can reactivate the agent in case of an emergency or of reinstatement.

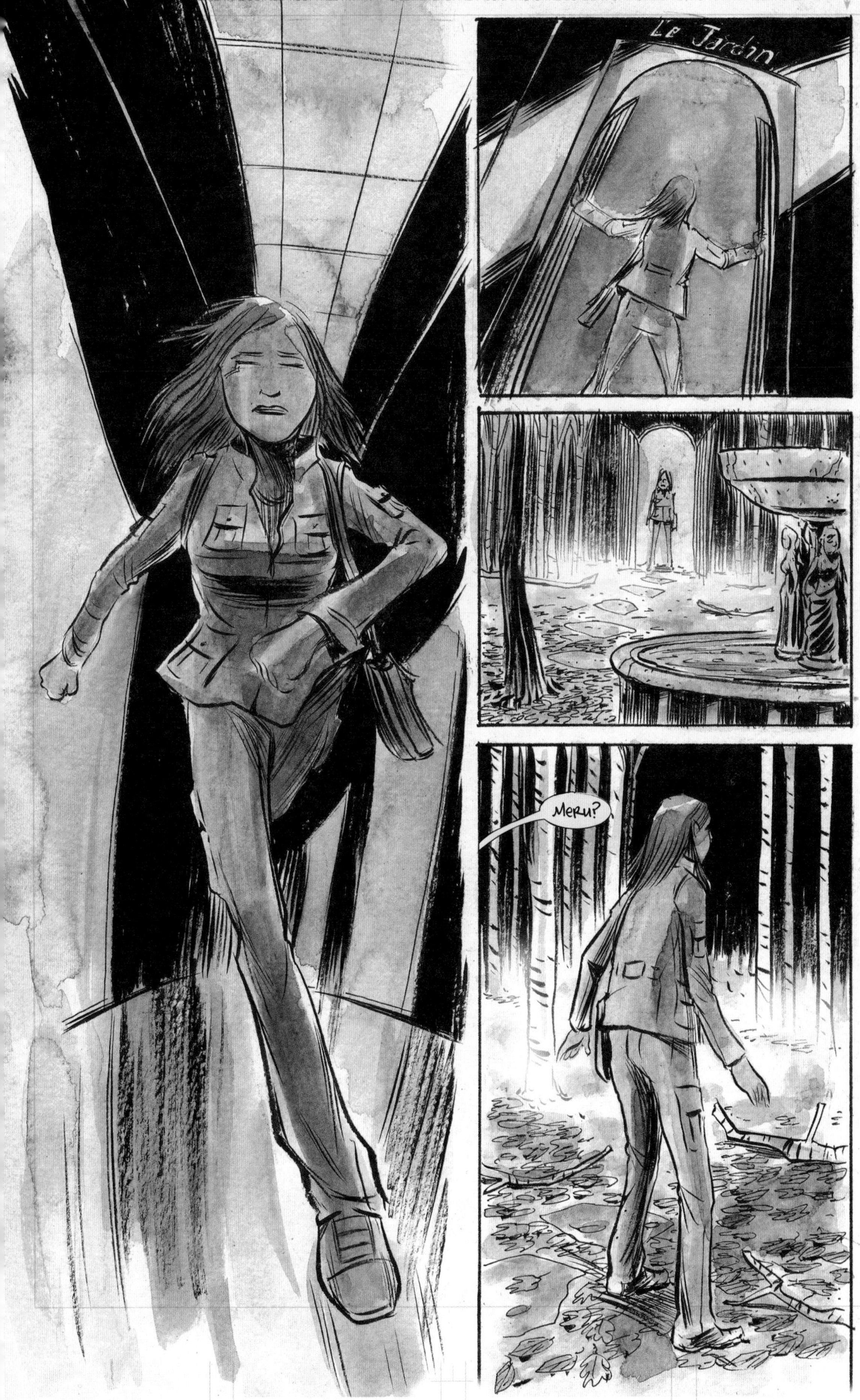
Le Jardin
Meru?

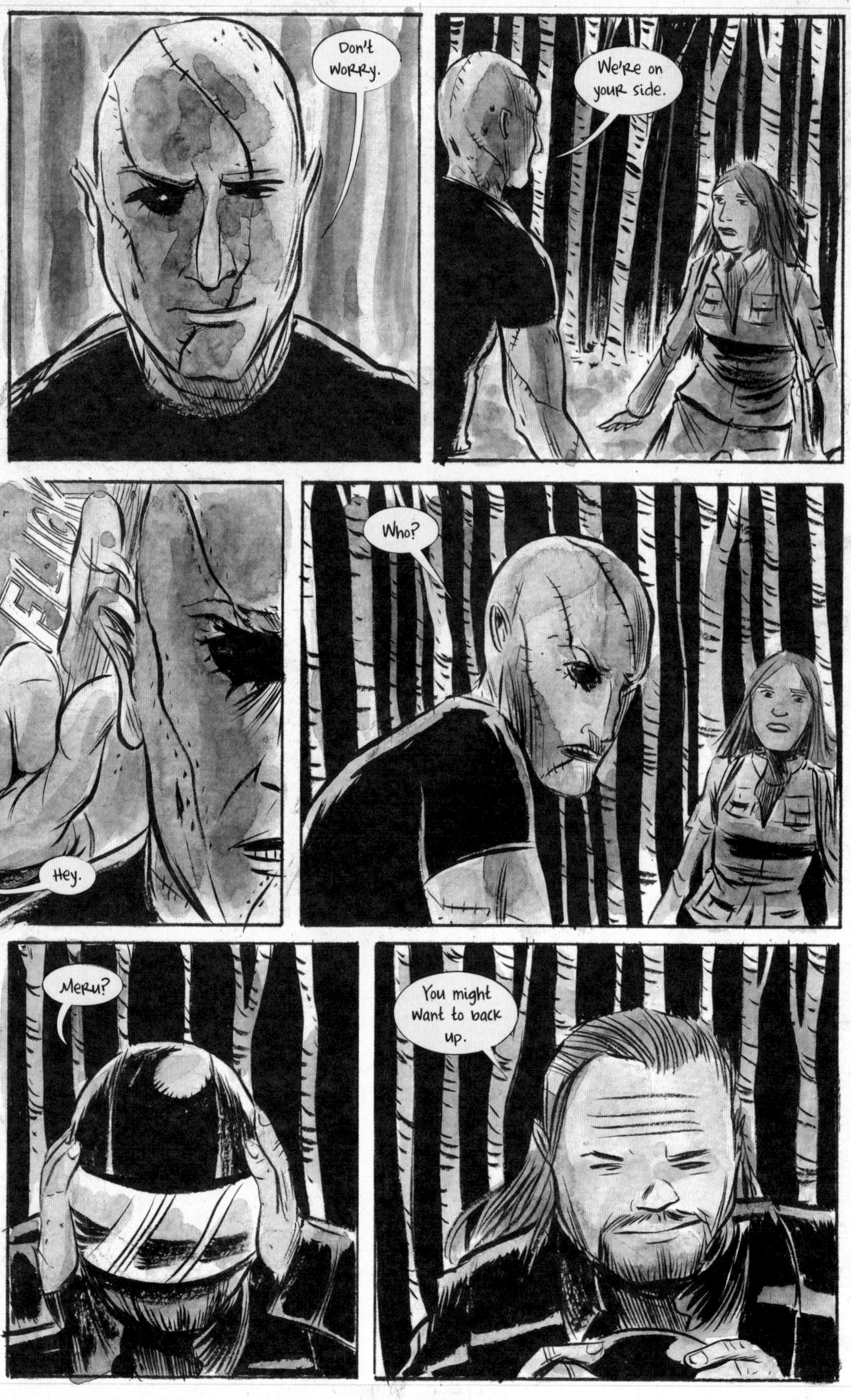
Don't worry.
We're on your side.
FLICK
Hey.
Who?
Meru?
You might want to back up.

DISBANDING PROTOCOLS. 12.2. The Black List holds the keywords and will be known only to the top remaining agents.

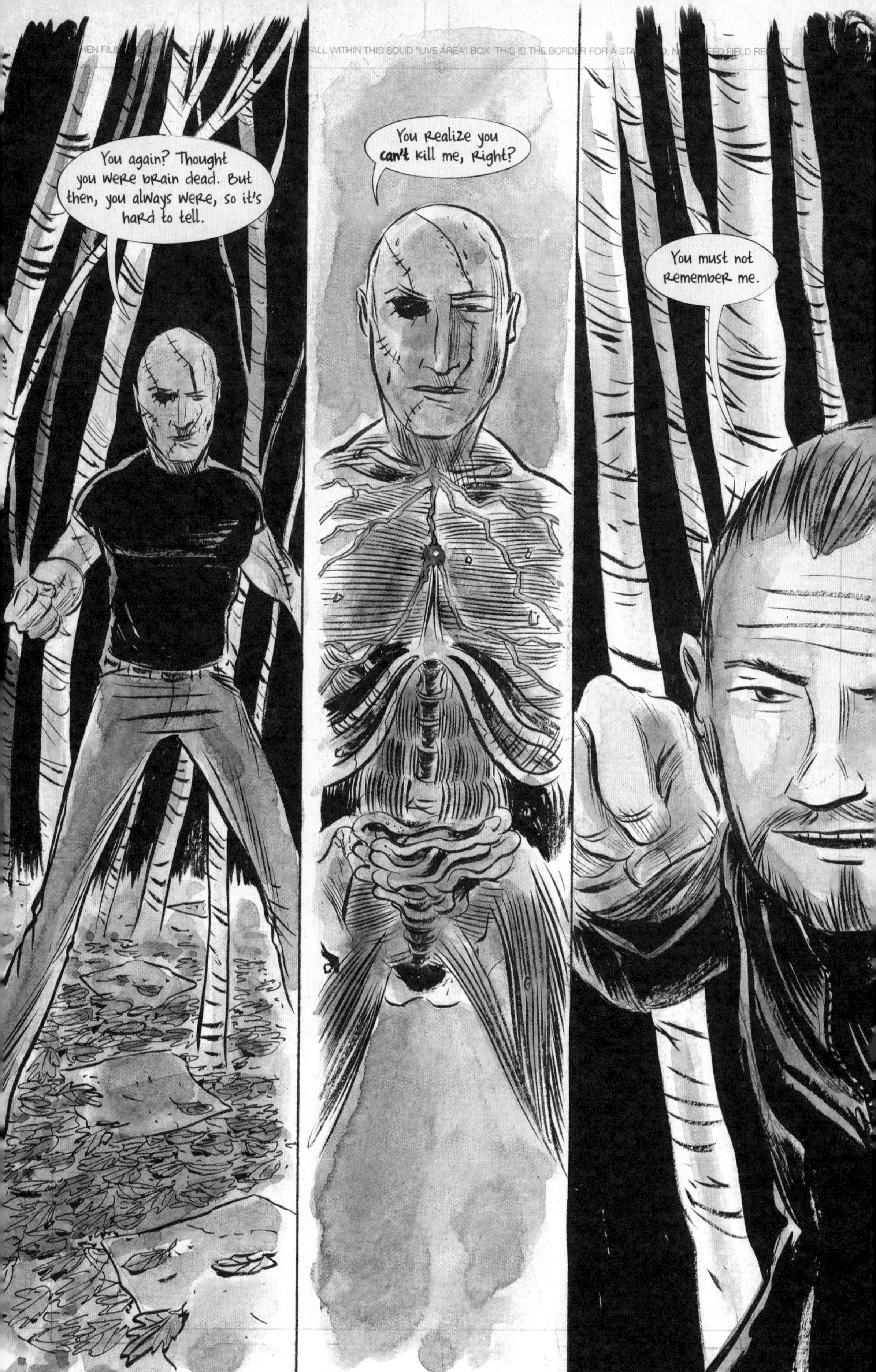
You again? Thought you were brain dead. But then, you always were, so it's hard to tell.
You realize you **can't** kill me, right?
You must not remember me.

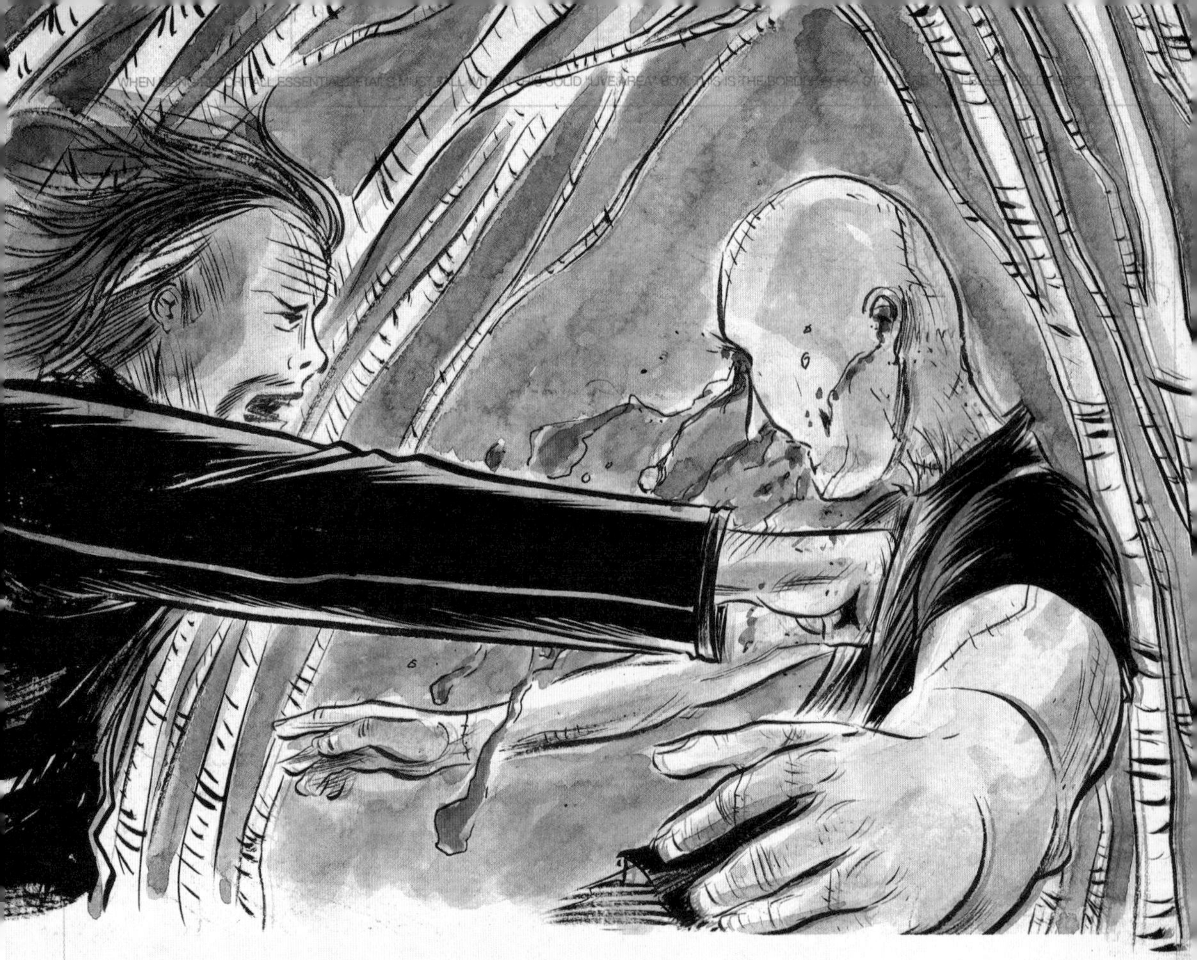

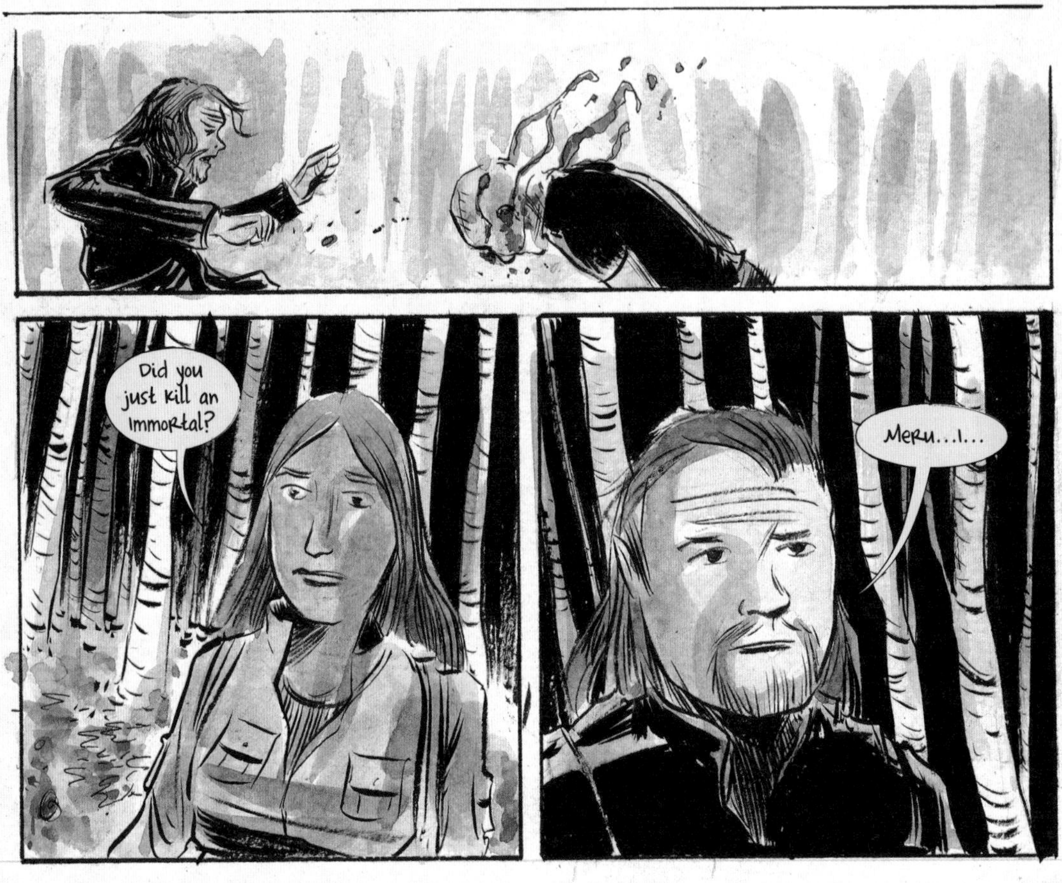
Did you just kill an Immortal?
Meru...I...

DISBANDING PROTOCOLS. 12.1. Until then, your life as an agent of Mind Management is over.

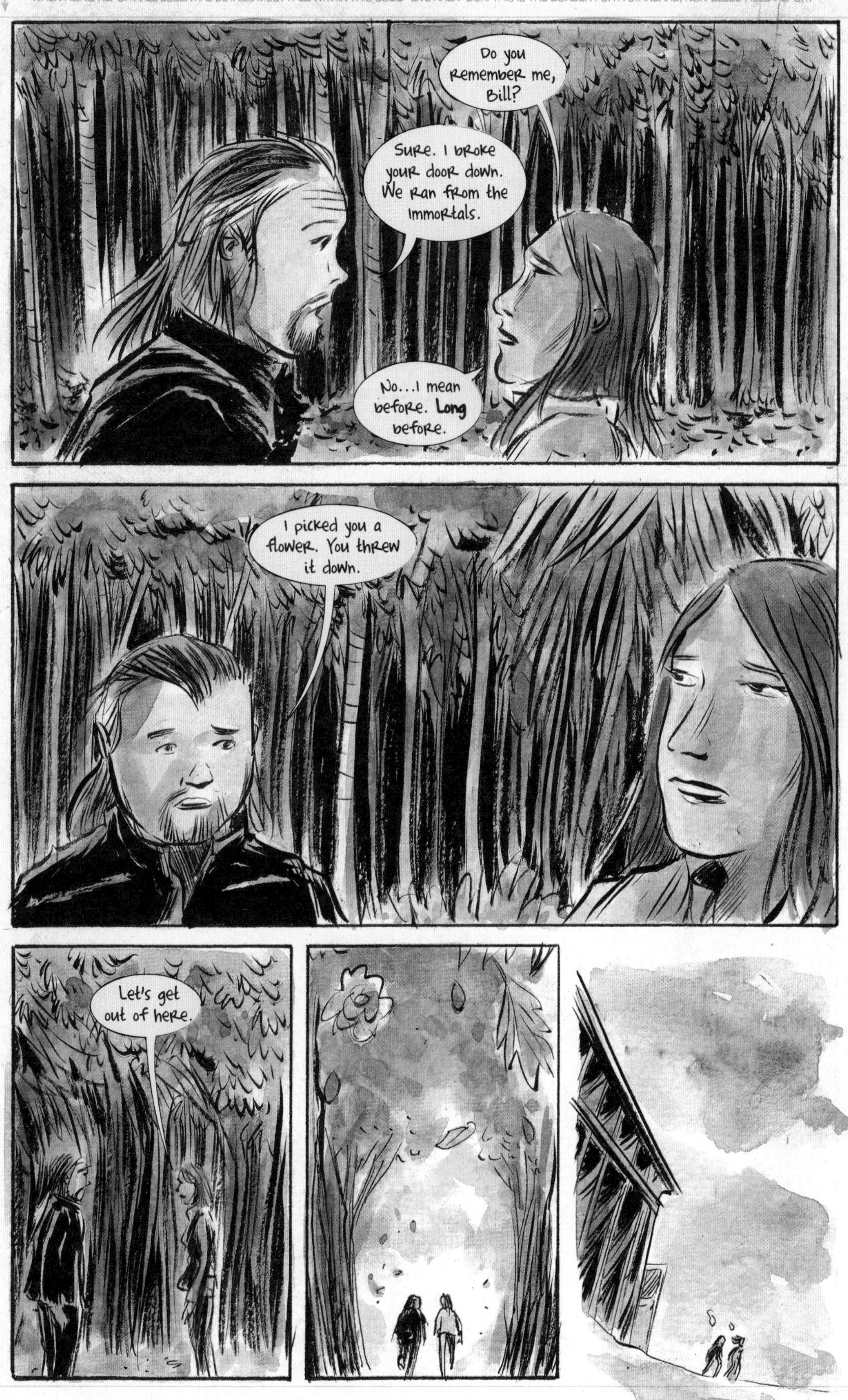
Do you remember me, Bill?
Sure. I broke your door down. We ran from the Immortals.
No...I mean before. **Long** before.
I picked you a flower. You threw it down.
Let's get out of here.

WHEN FILING REPORT ALL ESSENTIAL DETAILS MUST FALL WITHIN THIS SOLID "LIVE AREA" BOX. THIS IS THE BORDER FOR A STANDARD, NON-BLEED FIELD REPORT

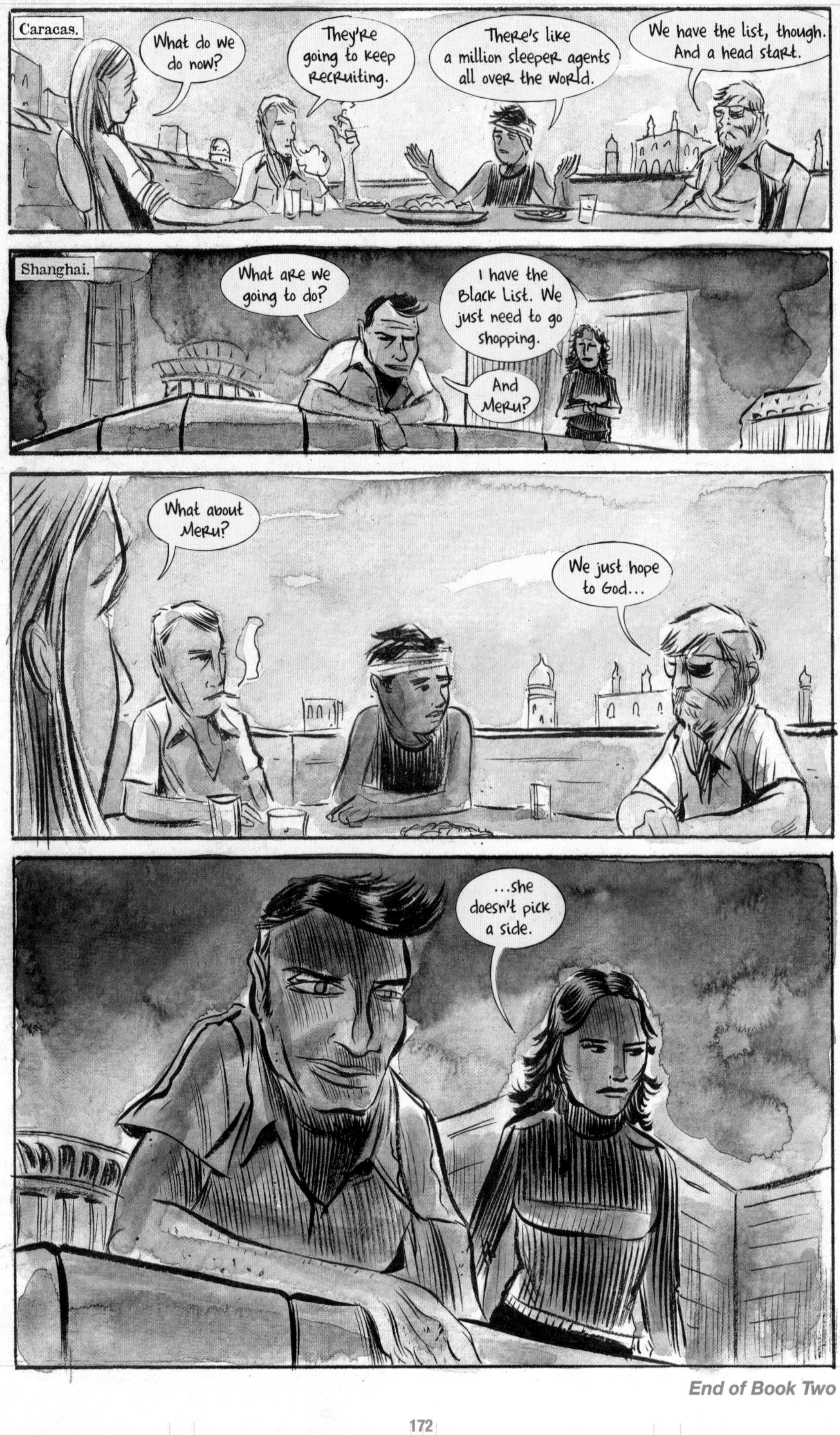

Caracas.
What do we do now?
They're going to keep recruiting.
There's like a million sleeper agents all over the world.
We have the list, though. And a head start.
Shanghai.
What are we going to do?
I have the Black List. We just need to go shopping.
And Meru?
What about Meru?
We just hope to God...
...she doesn't pick a side.

End of Book Two

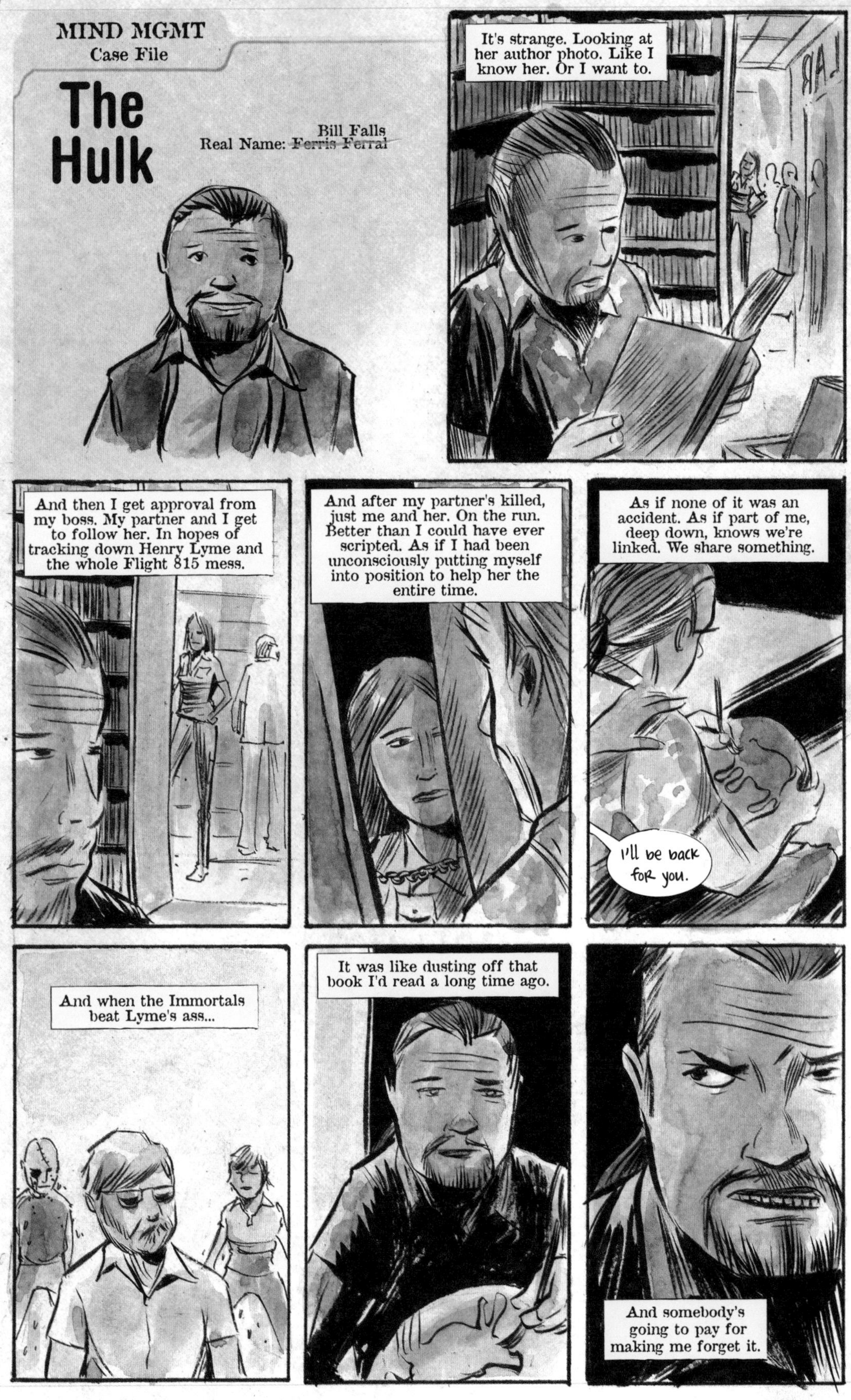
MIND MGMT
Case File
The Hulk
Real Name: ~~Ferris Ferral~~ Bill Falls
It's strange. Looking at her author photo. Like I know her. Or I want to.
And then I get approval from my boss. My partner and I get to follow her. In hopes of tracking down Henry Lyme and the whole Flight 815 mess.
And after my partner's killed, just me and her. On the run. Better than I could have ever scripted. As if I had been unconsciously putting myself into position to help her the entire time.
As if none of it was an accident. As if part of me, deep down, knows we're linked. We share something.
I'll be back for you.
And when the Immortals beat Lyme's ass...
It was like dusting off that book I'd read a long time ago.
And somebody's going to pay for making me forget it.

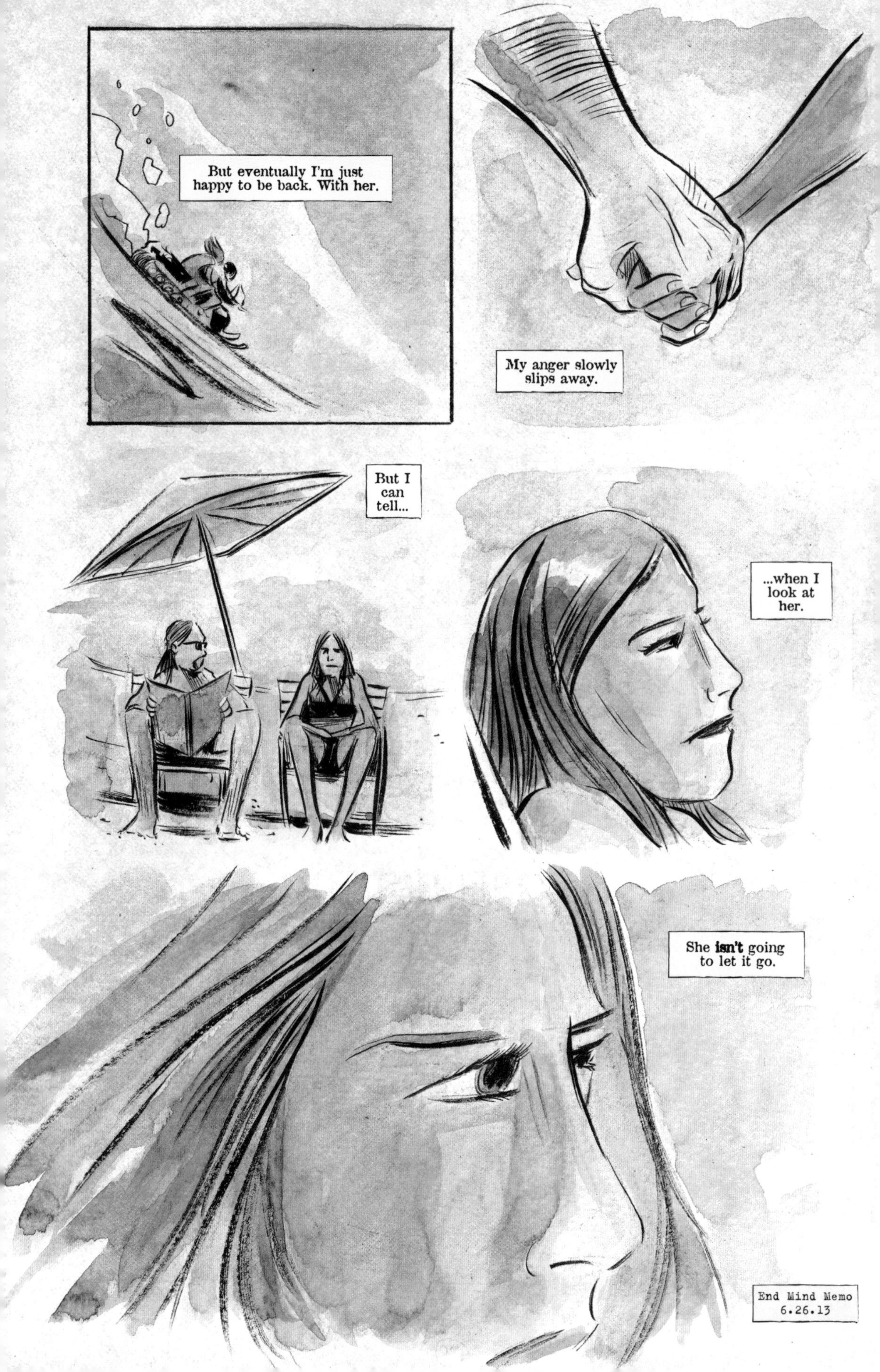
But eventually I'm just happy to be back. With her.
My anger slowly slips away.
But I can tell...
...when I look at her.
She **isn't** going to let it go.
End Mind Memo 6.26.13

MIND MGMT #1 second printing cover

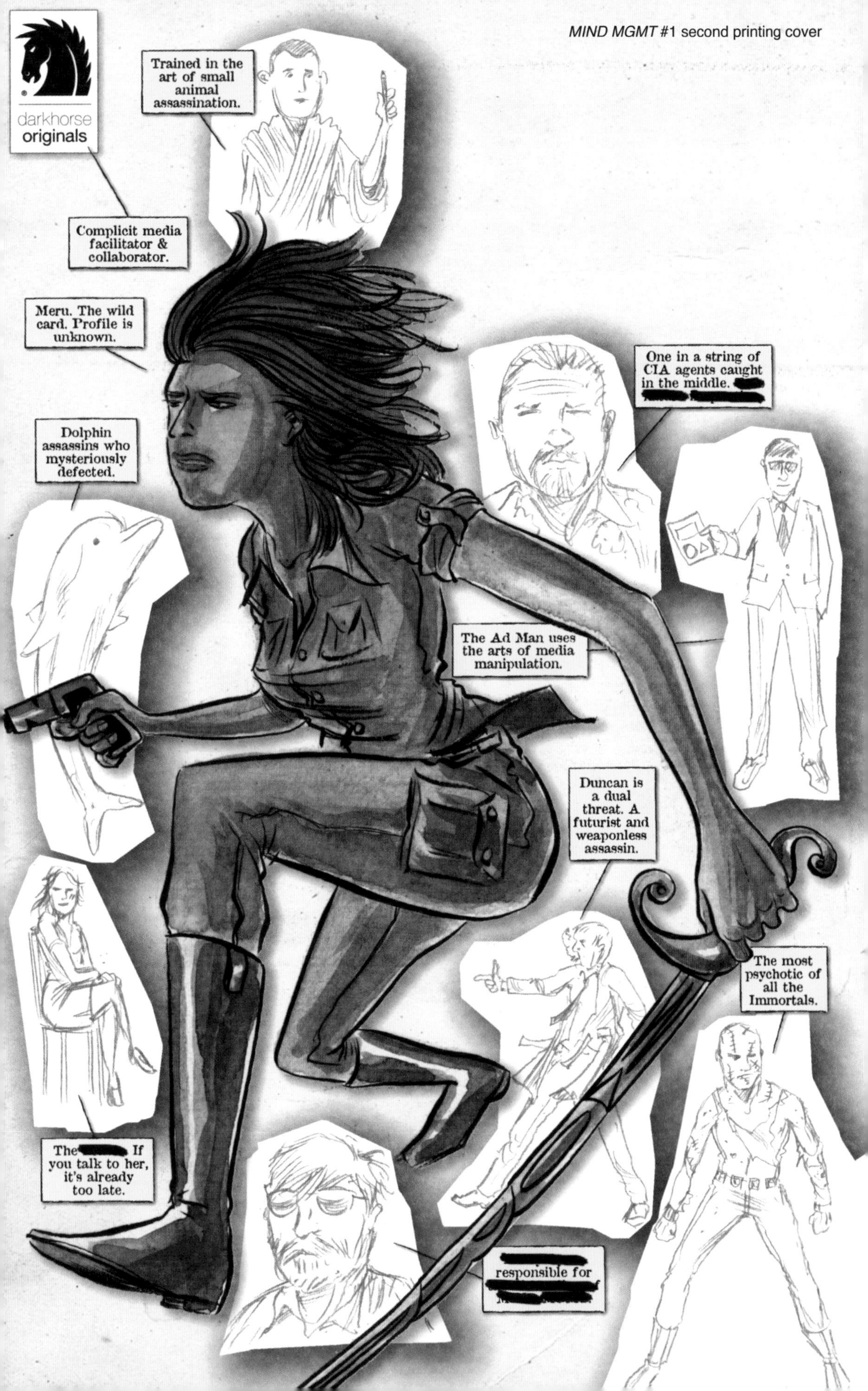
darkhorse
originals
Trained in the art of small animal assassination.
Complicit media facilitator & collaborator.
Meru. The wild card. Profile is unknown.
Dolphin assassins who mysteriously defected.
One in a string of CIA agents caught in the middle. [redacted]
The Ad Man uses the arts of media manipulation.
Duncan is a dual threat. A futurist and weaponless assassin.
The most psychotic of all the Immortals.
The [redacted] If you talk to her, it's already too late.
[redacted] responsible for [redacted]

SECRET FILES

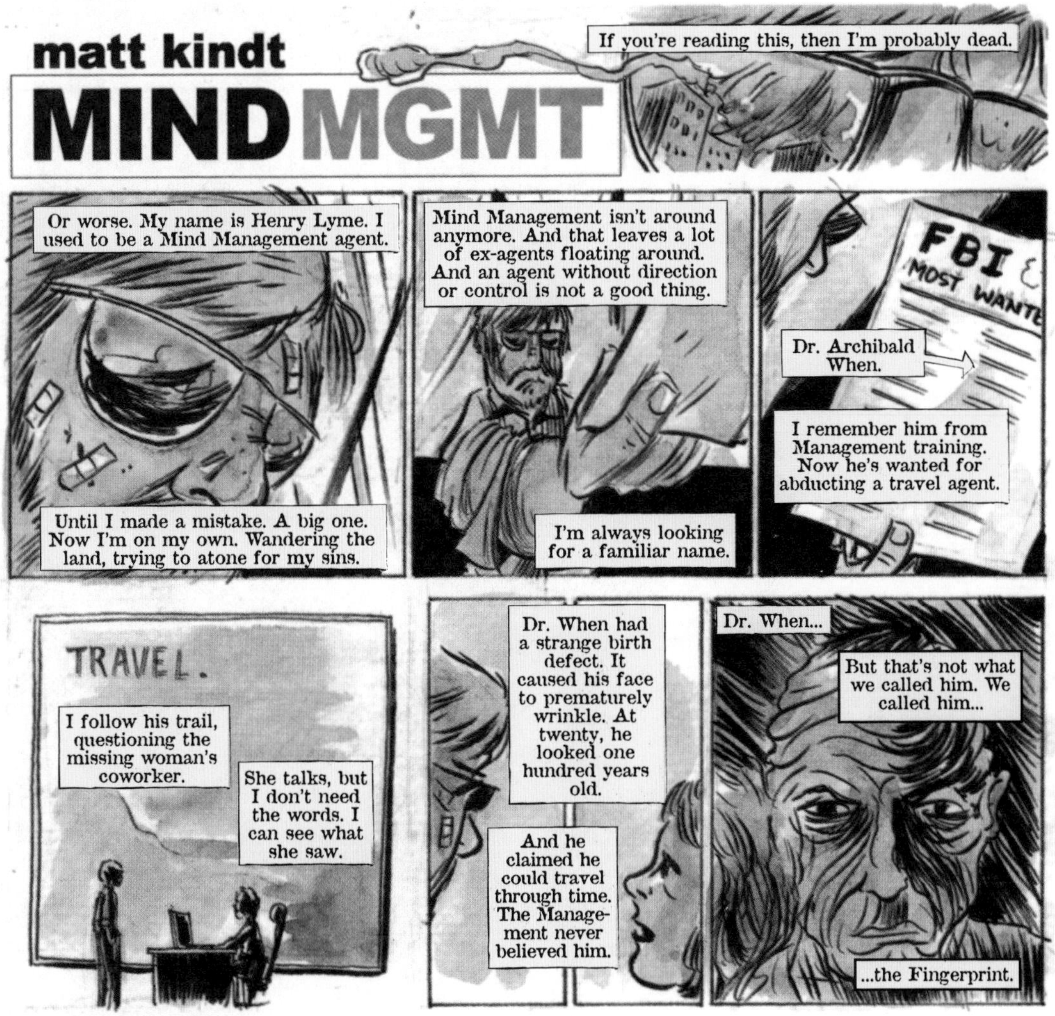
matt kindt
MIND MGMT
If you're reading this, then I'm probably dead.
Or worse. My name is Henry Lyme. I used to be a Mind Management agent.
Until I made a mistake. A big one. Now I'm on my own. Wandering the land, trying to atone for my sins.
Mind Management isn't around anymore. And that leaves a lot of ex-agents floating around. And an agent without direction or control is not a good thing.
I'm always looking for a familiar name.
FBI
MOST WANTE
Dr. Archibald When.
I remember him from Management training. Now he's wanted for abducting a travel agent.
TRAVEL.
I follow his trail, questioning the missing woman's coworker.
She talks, but I don't need the words. I can see what she saw.
Dr. When had a strange birth defect. It caused his face to prematurely wrinkle. At twenty, he looked one hundred years old.
And he claimed he could travel through time. The Management never believed him.
Dr. When...
But that's not what we called him. We called him...
...the Fingerprint.

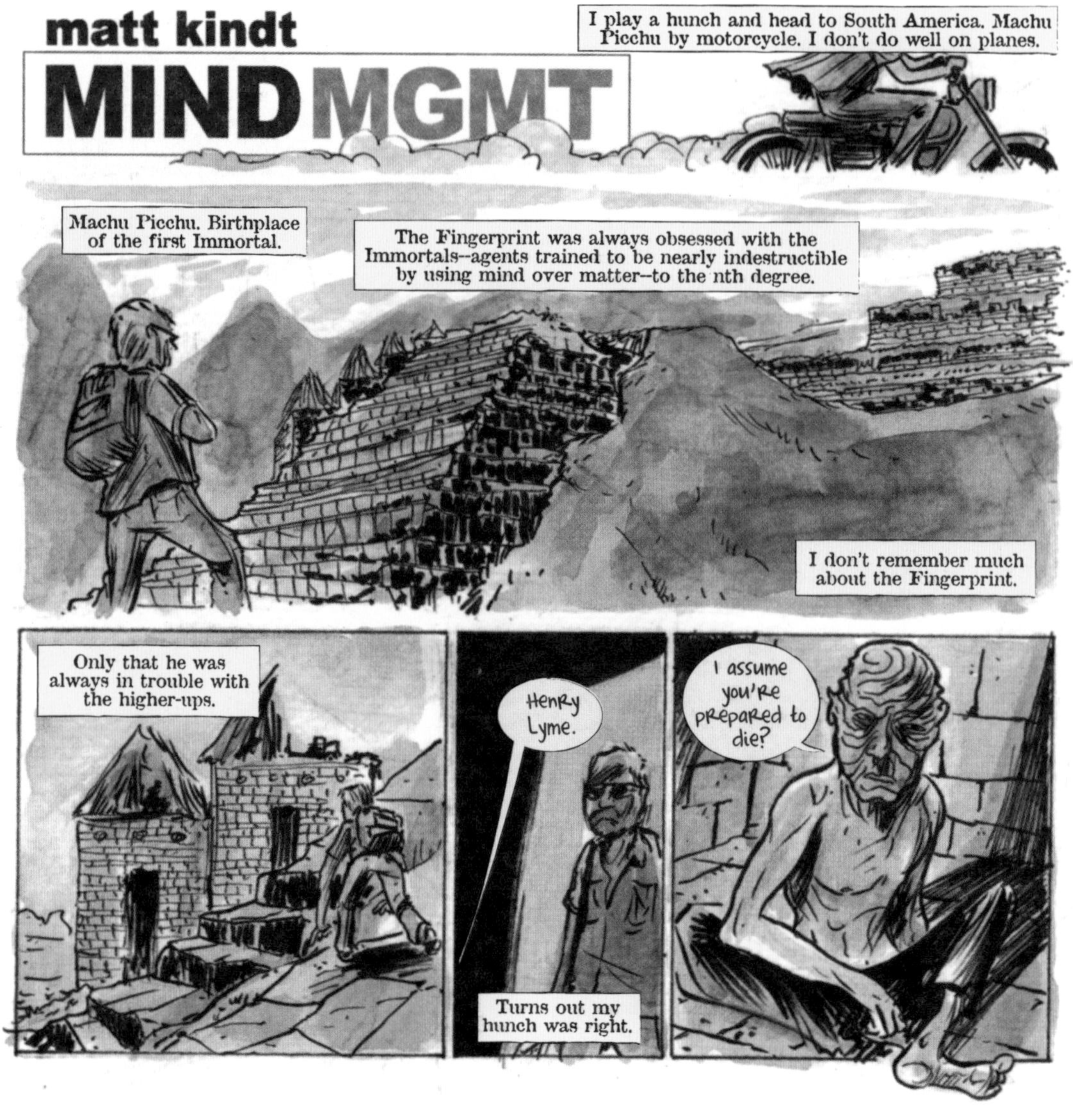
matt kindt
MIND MGMT
I play a hunch and head to South America. Machu Picchu by motorcycle. I don't do well on planes.
Machu Picchu. Birthplace of the first Immortal.
The Fingerprint was always obsessed with the Immortals--agents trained to be nearly indestructible by using mind over matter--to the nth degree.
I don't remember much about the Fingerprint.
Only that he was always in trouble with the higher-ups.
Henry Lyme.
Turns out my hunch was right.
I assume you're prepared to die?

matt kindt

MIND MGMT

I don't know what the Fingerprint has done to the travel agent, but I'm going to find out.

I just have to endure him telling his story.

The Fingerprint...Dr. When was always an interesting case. He could remember every second of his life. From conception through childbirth and every moment after.

He claimed he could time travel. The Management never believed him.

He also claimed that his immense and detailed memory of the past gave him memories of the future.

And visions of other people's pasts. Including the first Immortal...

...who nearly died on an expedition in the jungle near Machu Picchu back in the 1920s.

But instead of dying, he collapsed and fell into a hallucinatory state brought on by his heavy use of painkillers and another unknown substance.

He tells me he's trying to re-create the first Immortal's experience. But he needed a guinea pig. The travel agent.

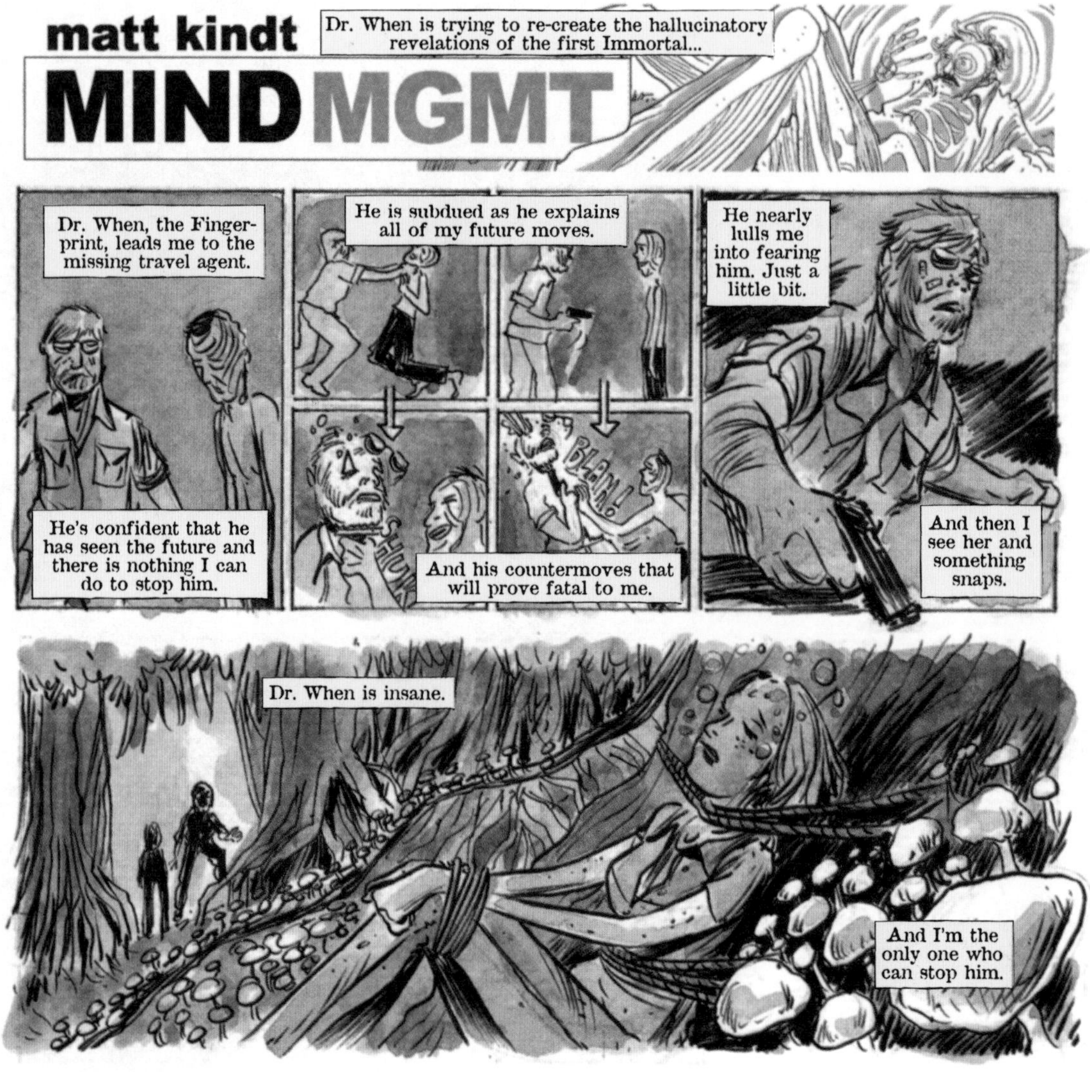
matt kindt
MIND MGMT
Dr. When is trying to re-create the hallucinatory revelations of the first Immortal...
Dr. When, the Fingerprint, leads me to the missing travel agent.
He's confident that he has seen the future and there is nothing I can do to stop him.
He is subdued as he explains all of my future moves.
BLAM!
And his countermoves that will prove fatal to me.
He nearly lulls me into fearing him. Just a little bit.
And then I see her and something snaps.
Dr. When is insane.
And I'm the only one who can stop him.

matt kindt

MIND MGMT

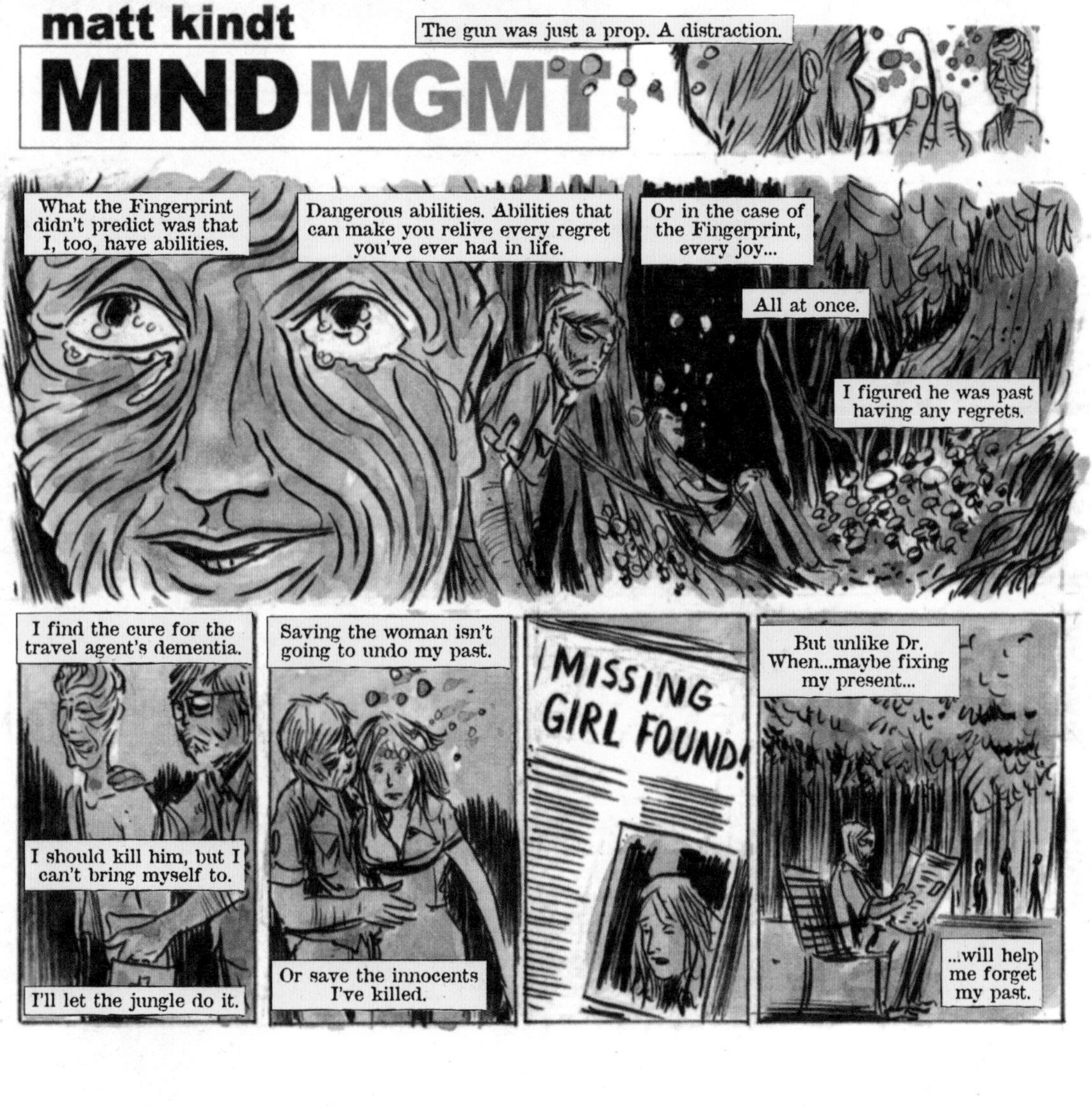
The gun was just a prop. A distraction.
What the Fingerprint didn't predict was that I, too, have abilities.
Dangerous abilities. Abilities that can make you relive every regret you've ever had in life.
Or in the case of the Fingerprint, every joy...
All at once.
I figured he was past having any regrets.
I find the cure for the travel agent's dementia.
I should kill him, but I can't bring myself to.
I'll let the jungle do it.
Saving the woman isn't going to undo my past.
Or save the innocents I've killed.
MISSING GIRL FOUND!
But unlike Dr. When...maybe fixing my present...
...will help me forget my past.

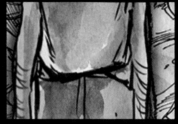This is not happening.

He is not killing you with his finger.

She is not a mole with mind control.

It is not magic.

He is not immortal.

This is not Matt Kindt's

MIND MGMT™

ALSO BY MATT KINDT

MIND MGMT
matt kindt
VOLUME ONE: THE MANAGER
FOREWORD BY DAMON LINDELOF

MIND MGMT VOLUME 1: THE MANAGER
978-1-59582-797-5
$19.99

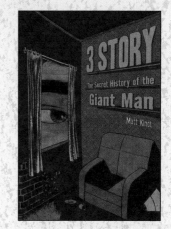

3 STORY
The Secret History of the
Giant Man
Matt Kindt

3 STORY: THE SECRET HISTORY OF THE GIANT MAN
978-1-59582-356-4
$19.99

RED HANDED
The Fine Art of
Strange Crimes
MATT KINDT

RED HANDED: THE FINE ART OF STRANGE CRIMES
978-1-59643-662-6
$26.99

Super
Spy
matt kindt

SUPER SPY
978-1-89183-096-9
$19.95

2 sisters
A SUPER-SPY GRAPHIC NOVEL
by Matt Kindt

2 SISTERS: A SUPER SPY GRAPHIC NOVEL
978-1-89183-058-7
$19.95

REVOLVER
MATT KINDT

REVOLVER
978-1-40122-242-0
$19.99

ONI PRESS
the Tooth
A New Beginning! The Tooth Unleashed!

THE TOOTH
(with Cullen Bunn and Shawn Lee)
978-1-93496-452-1
$24.99

PHOTO BY SHARLENE KINDT

4-09

ABOUT THE AUTHOR

Matt Kindt is the Harvey Award–winning author of the graphic novels *3 Story*, *Red Handed*, *Revolver*, *Super Spy*, and *2 Sisters*, and the artist and cocreator of the *Pistolwhip* series of graphic novels. He has been nominated for four Eisner Awards and three Harveys. Matt lives and works in St. Louis, Missouri, with his wife and daughter. For more information, visit MattKindt.com.